The
"SISSY BOY SYNDROME"
and the Development
of Homosexuality

The
"SISSY BOY SYNDROME"
and the Development
of Homosexuality

RICHARD GREEN, M.D.

YALE UNIVERSITY PRESS
New Haven and London

Designed by Susan P. Fillion and set in
Baskerville text and Optima display type by
Rainsford Type. Printed in the United States of
America by Vail-Ballou Press, Inc., Binghamton,
New York.

Library of Congress Cataloging-in-Publication Data

Green, Richard, 1936–
   The "sissy boy syndrome" and the
development of homosexuality.

   Bibliography: p.
   Includes index.
   1. Homosexuality. 2. Sex role in children—
Longitudinal studies. 3. Boys—Psychology—
Longitudinal studies. 4. Parent and child—
Longitudinal studies. 5. Children—Interviews.
6. Parents—Interviews. I. Title. [DNLM:
1. Homosexuality. 2. Psychosexual Development.
WM 615 G797s]
RC558.G74 1986   616.85′834   85–29489
ISBN 0–300–03696–5

*The paper in this book meets the guidelines for
permanence and durability of the Committee on
Production Guidelines for Book Longevity of the
Council on Library Resources.*

10   9   8   7   6   5   4   3   2   1

THIS BOOK IS DEDICATED TO

John Money, of Johns Hopkins,
    who prompted me;

Robert Stoller, of the University of California, Los Angeles,
    who sustained me;

Jack Wiener, of the National Institute of Mental Health,
    who supported me;

and to The Families,
    who trusted me.

WARNING

Artists lie to tell the truth, and scientists
    tell the truth to lie.

Robert J. Stoller
Sexual Excitement: The Dynamics of Erotic Life

Contents

Acknowledgments

No study, let alone one of this duration, is conducted by one person. All along the way, the effort is collaborative.

I would never have initiated this study without the instigation of John Money. From 1958 to 1962, he provided me with the encouragement to learn and the reward for effort that harnessed my compelling interest in psychosexual research. That was at a time when many medical career opportunities were being presented. Had it not been for the catalytic encouragement of Robert Stoller, beginning in 1962, I might not have continued my research in sexual identity. He provided me with the emotional support, professional guidance, and unfailing confidence that permanently set the course of my career.

Research of this type is not possible without funding. Over the years my peers on review committees of the National Institute of Mental Health (NIMH) have been very generous. Initially, they provided a five-year Research Scientist Development Award which freed me to conduct research, unfettered by the administrative and clinical chores that hamper, sometimes cripple, young academicians. Shortly thereafter, the project received a big boost from the Foundations' Fund for Research in Psychiatry with a three-year grant to pay research assistants, typists, and subjects. During the last ten years the NIMH provided the major funding for project completion (Grant MH26598). If one person at the NIMH epitomizes the unfailing support given me, spiritual and fiscal, it is Jack Wiener. He was always my friend in court.

At two critical times, Burton Joseph, as president of the Playboy Foundation, came to the rescue. A cranky NIMH project reviewer briefly disrupted the flow of this fifteen-year study, jeopardizing a considerable investment of money and personnel. While we maneuvered past this obstacle, a small grant from the Foundation kept research assistants and secretaries on the job. Later, when it became apparent that many of the families we needed to see in long-term follow-up had scattered about the United States, the Foundation underwrote the travel expenses necessary to conduct those final interviews.

Another boost was the invitation to be a fellow at the Center for Advanced Study in the Behavioral Sciences at Stanford. There, I organized fifteen years of interview transcripts, dutifully typed by Anna Tower and her associates. During my last week as a fellow, I learned that thanatologist Edwin Shneidman, a previous fellow at the Center, had nominated me for fellowship. Thus, he joins those to whom I am grateful.

Data collection during the early UCLA project phase was the toil of Marielle Fuller. Administration and typing at UCLA were accomplishments of Thelma Guffan.

Full-time project supervision during the Stony Brook phase has been the burden of Katherine Williams. A mountain of interview transcripts was conquered by Marilyn Goodman. Expert administration and secretarial skills, plus transcript and manuscript typing, flowed from the exceptional professional dedication and personal commitment of Virginia Bentley and Carol Sancimo.

The statistical transformation of trees into forests derived from the mathematical skills of Stephen Finch, Carl Roberts, Anthony Mixon, and Paul Donato. The metamorphosis of forests into people was effected by Howard Rebach's coupling of statistical wisdom and clinical sensitivity.

An earlier version of this book was read by Joe Hyams (journalist and author), Robert Stoller (psychoanalyst), and Richard Whalen (psychobiologist). Credit is due them for enhancing clarity and condensing text.

Most importantly, without the enduring collaboration of the families described in this study, all this support would have been in vain. More than anyone or anything else, the families (as they say on Academy Award night) "made this moment possible."

A final credit goes to the silicon chip. It pared years off data analysis and manuscript preparation. It made this project long-term instead of lifelong.

The
"SISSY BOY SYNDROME"
and the Development
of Homosexuality

Children and Parents Enter Our Study

EXAMPLE A

Mother (speaking of a nine-year-old son)

MOTHER: His kindergarten teacher noticed that something was wrong because he got in the girls' line instead of the boys' line at the drinking fountain.

R. G.: What else?

MOTHER: He started cross-dressing when he was about three.

R. G.: How did you react to that?

MOTHER: He got nothing but static from me.

R. G.: Did it continue?

MOTHER: Yes. Then a neighbor woman and her daughter moved in with dolls and all that shit. I didn't remember being horrified right at the outset. But it seemed I was very uptight about it.

R. G.: How about the neighbor woman?

MOTHER: She wasn't. She said "Let it flow, if he's having a fantasy let him flow with it. You know it's not going to hurt him." He was three when he first started doing that stuff. It always bothered me. I remember a contest of wills going on. "You will *not* do that. You will be a *boy* and will be boyish." I can remember from age five and six him saying, "I want to be a *girl*." Then, my saying, "*No*, you can't." Then, him saying, "*Yes*, I can."

EXAMPLE B

Parents (speaking of a nine-year-old son)

FATHER: At an early age you don't pay too much attention to those things. One thing was that he liked to put on female clothing, especially his mother's clothing, and at first we thought it was just like playing with dolls as a child. Later on we thought it should have diminished, and it didn't, and it was brought to our attention that this could be a problem, even at that age.

R. G. (to mother): What's your feeling about this?

MOTHER: Very similar. He was playing with dolls, playing dress-up, playing school in nursery school at the age of three. By the time he was four it didn't diminish. The interest in dolls seemed to grow, and he has an older sister who had these little Barbie dolls, and he used to take them and dress them up. As he got into his fourth year we started to take those things away from him. I think he has sort of gone underground with the female—I think he's sort of changed his tactics.

FATHER: That could be. For example, I've seen him when he's playing school, and now he's playing the part of the male teacher rather than the female teacher.

R. G.: Looking back, what is the earliest thing?

MOTHER: I would say, probably at nursery school he would dress up— age three.

FATHER: Probably right at his third birthday.

EXAMPLE C

Mother (speaking of an eight-year-old son)

MOTHER: He acts like a sissy. He has expressed the wish to be a girl. He doesn't play with boys. He's afraid of boys, because he's afraid to play boys' games. He used to like to dress in girls' clothing. He would still like to, only we have absolutely put our foot down. And he talks like a girl, sometimes walks like a girl, acts like a girl.

R. G.: How long have you had these concerns?

MOTHER: For about three years.

R. G.: What was the very earliest thing that you noticed?

MOTHER: Wanting to put on a blouse of mine, a pink and white blouse which if he'd put it on it would fit him like a dress. And he was very excited about the whole thing, and leaped around and danced around the room. I didn't like it and I just told him to take it off and I put it away. He kept asking for it. He wanted to wear that blouse again. And I said, "No, I'm sorry that belongs to me, not to you. You wear your clothes and I wear mine." But he asked many times for it.

R. G.: You mentioned that he's expressed the wish to be a girl.

MOTHER: I remember distinctly his making this remark. And it's such a dramatic remark that you don't forget it. He'd make it many times.

R. G.:   What does he say, exactly?

MOTHER: "I would like to be a girl. I don't like to be a boy. Boys are too rough. When I play boys' games the ball hurts my legs. I don't want to go to school today because I'll have to play baseball." So he goes and plays gently with the girls.

R. G.:   Has he ever said, "I am a girl"?

MOTHER: Playing in front of the mirror, he'll undress for bed, and he's standing in front of the mirror and he took his penis and he folded it under, and he said, "Look, Mommy, I'm a girl."

EXAMPLE D

Mother (speaking of a seven-year-old son)

MOTHER: The first thing I noticed, one day at a friend's house—she has four little girls, he likes to go back in their room and play with their dolls. He went back there and grabbed a doll and wanted to make a dress. He took Kleenex and paper towels and tore them and folded them and poked holes in them and really made a very attractive dress for these dolls. And my friend commented on it and said, "Gee, I think he's going to be a dress designer."

R. G.:   How old was he?

MOTHER: He was four, four-and-a-half. You know, I don't know what I'm afraid of—if it's homosexuality. I even hate the word.

R. G.:   What else?

MOTHER: I think a lot of it is that he likes the sight of feminine things. He would tie aprons around himself. I got so that I never kept aprons in the house anymore, because he'd get my aprons and tie them around him—here up at his shoulder or under his arms—to make a nice long skirt, and would go around the house in aprons. He'd have to have an apron tied around up here with a nice full skirt and then one tied around his head to make a nice flowing hood. It got so that if there was nobody in the house I would let him do it. It got so that we were taking aprons and just sticking them places and hiding them. Even today I go around and find aprons wadded clear back on the closet shelves where we had tried to hide them, just in a fit of panic.

R. G.:   Are there other things which concern you?

MOTHER: He won't play with boys. They tease him. He has said he wants to be a girl. I don't know if it should worry me or not. That's why I'm here. Maybe it's something that he can grow out of. Maybe it's something that he's going to need some help to grow out of.

1

(Some) Boys Will Be Boys: A Long-term Study of Two Diverse Patterns of Sexual Identity

This is a fifteen-year study of two behaviorally different groups of young boys growing up to be two behaviorally different groups of young men. I call one group "feminine boys." Other children called them "sissy." Although tagged with that unhappy label, these boys differed from many other boys also called "sissy." Our boys would have preferred being girls. They liked to dress in girls' or women's clothes. They preferred Barbie dolls to trucks. Their playmates were girls. When they played "mommy-daddy" games, they were mommy. And they avoided rough-and-tumble play and sports, the usual reasons for the epithet "sissy." By contrast, our second group of boys was conventionally masculine. They were content being boys, dressed in boys' clothes, preferred truck play, played with boys, role-played as daddy, and enjoyed rough-and-tumble play and sports.

Both groups were studied in the time-honored strategy of unearthing the roots of a complex system by researching its contrasting forms. In behavioral science, when we hope to understand interpersonal relationships, we learn more about aggressivity when we also study passivity. In medical science, when we hope to understand cell functioning, we learn more about tumor cell division when we also study normal cell growth. When contrasting forms are compared, each may be understood better by what it is not; distinctions may illuminate what is shared. Contrasting conventionally masculine boys with pervasively feminine boys as they mature into adolescence and young adulthood provides fertile soil in which to observe the roots of the complex, fundamental human feature, sexual identity.

We study the development of sexual identity because our self-concept as male or female, the behaviors by which we convey this conviction, and the direction of our erotic passion permeate our existence. Understanding sexual identity is basic to understanding human behavior.

SEXUAL IDENTITY

A book using the term *sexual identity* as often as any other pair of words ought to define the term early on, particularly when there are far more meanings to sexual identity than there are sexes. Not only are the terms *sexual identity* and *gender identity* used interchangeably by some authors, but others speak of "sex role orientation," "sex role preference," and "sex role identification" (for example, Biller, 1981).

Ronald LaTorre offered what he believed to be "the most concise and complete set of conceptions" regarding sexual identity. It began: "Sexual identity, in its broadest sense, has been compared to a symphony" (1979, 7), continued for another eight pages, and included a table and a figure.

I make claim to neither brevity nor clarity, but will define what I mean by sexual identity. There are three components, as I use the term.

(1) Core-morphologic identity. This is a cumbersome term suggested to me by a mentor, John Money, more than a decade ago. In retrospect, *anatomic identity* would have been less tedious. Simply, this component is a person's identity as either male or female. In its earliest form, it might be only a gross self-categorization into one of two classes (like mommy or like daddy).

(2) Gender-role behavior, or sex-typed behavior, or masculinity and femininity. These are the culturally fixed signals that discriminate males from females. Depending on the person's age, the signals may be whether one picks up a Barbie doll or a toy truck, or how one positions one's feet under a chair or table when reading *Cosmopolitan* or *Road and Track.*

(3) Sexual orientation, or sexual partner preference, or sexual object choice. This is the anatomical category of persons one finds erotically exciting. Most sensible people without graduate degrees in behavioral science call this heterosexuality, bisexuality, and homosexuality.

An advantage of this three-part definition is that it permits a clear behavioral separation of three types of persons with an atypical sexual identity: the homosexual, the transsexual, and the transvestite (table 1.1).

The most comprehensively atypical person is the transsexual, who is atypical on all three components. If anatomically male, his sense of core-morphologic or anatomic identity is female. His gender-role behavior with regard to dressing preference (women's clothes) and social role preference (living as a woman) is atypical. His sexual partner preference is also atypical (directed to males). By contrast, the transvestite has a typical anatomic identity (not wanting sex-change surgery), but periodically needs to cross-

TABLE 1.1. Distinguishing Features of Homosexual, Transvestite, and Transsexual Persons

	Homosexual	Transsexual	Transvestite
Component One:			
Core-morphologic identity		Atypical	
Component Two:			
Gender-role behavior		Atypical	Atypical
Component Three:			
Sexual partner preference	Atypical	Atypical	

dress, experiences sexual arousal from cross-dressing, and, when cross-dressed, may behave socially as a woman (atypical component 2). However, his sexual partner preference is typical (heterosexual). By contrast, the homosexual male is content being male, is usually unremarkably masculine, but does have an atypical sexual partner preference.

PLANNING A LONG-TERM STUDY OF SEXUAL IDENTITY DEVELOPMENT

With definitions out of the way, I will summarize the evolution of this marathon study. It was a flirtation in 1958 when I interviewed my first "feminine boy" family with John Money (Green and Money, 1960, 1961). It became a serious affair in the mid-1960s when I interviewed about a hundred persons requesting sex-change surgery. These interviews were conducted in New York with patients of Harry Benjamin and at the UCLA Gender Identity Research and Treatment Clinic with Robert Stoller. Invariably, the patients recalled a lifelong cross-sex identity, replete with extensive cross-gender behaviors and an unswerving commitment to changing their sex (Green and Money, 1969). While I could be sure that such a profound commitment did not evolve during the few weeks prior to interview, I was unsure as to precisely when and, more importantly, *how* this cross-sex identity emerged.

PROBLEMS WITH PATIENTS' RECALL: THE RATIONALE FOR A PROSPECTIVE STUDY

Accurately tracing a transsexual's life history is highly problematic. Transsexuals come for psychiatric evaluation to utilize the psychiatrist as gatekeeper to the surgical suite. Surgeons are reluctant to operate on a patient requesting sex-change without a "green" light from at least one psychiatrist with whom to share blame if something goes wrong. Knowing this, few preoperative patients report any ambivalence to psychiatrists about their "proper" gender or about any of their conventional sex-typed behaviors beginning with childhood. Nor do they report events from their life history that do not fit the well-publicized autobiographies of "successful" transsexuals. In the circular universe of transsexual auto-biographies and clinical evaluations, patients convince physicians of their transsexual nature by repeating the published developmental histories of transsexuals who preceded them. History has a habit of repeating itself.

Aside from this overriding motivation of the sex-change candidate to convince the psychiatrist that here is a "true transsexual," to what extent should I have faith in the reported psychosexual history of anyone? How accurately can any of us recall preschool behaviors? Or preschool rela-tionships with parents? Or how our parents related either in our presence or in our absence? And how accurately do parents recall behaviors of their children?

Other researchers have systematically assessed the extent to which peo-ple recall significant life events. While these studies do not specifically address the recall of gender-typed behaviors, they provide a sobering view of all retrospective research.

The reliability of the mother's recall of the early period of her child's life is pivotal in studies of child development. To assess such reliability, Ernest Haggard and his coworkers interviewed nineteen women during their pregnancy, one year later, and six to eight years later (Haggard et al., 1960).

As the parental wish for a boy or a girl during pregnancy is a key question in our study, the consistency of such reports is critical. In the Haggard study, only 64 percent of mothers remembered accurately six months after delivery which sex they had wanted during pregnancy. Fur-ther, the strength of the mother's wish for the sex of the child correlated only 25 percent between the time of pregnancy and six months after delivery, and after eight years the correlation had plummeted to 5 percent.

Parental anxiety over the welfare of a child is also an important concern in our study. In the Haggard study, this element of child care when recalled at six years correlated only 24 percent with what had been de-scribed in the newborn period. A conclusion of the study warns retro-spective researchers: "It appears that the anamnestic [historical] material did not reflect the mother's earlier experiences and attitudes so much as their current picture of the past. . . . In coming to a guidance clinic, . . . the informant usually is anxious and unable to cope with some kind of prob-lem. . . . In situations of this sort . . . it is an ironic possibility that . . . where accurate information is most needed, it may be most distorted" (317).

The accuracy of mothers' recall was measured in another study by having a nurse visit the family to record information about the child's development every three months during the child's first year, and then interviewing the mothers when the child was twenty-one months old. One item studied was illness during the child's first year.

Recall of the child's medical history was terrible. A five-point rating scale was devised to appraise the degree of a child's illness. A rating of 4 was given to children who suffered illnesses or physical handicap "of frequency, severity, and duration to justify the assumption that development was definitely modified." The two children rated 4 had experienced asthma and several colds, whooping cough and eczema. At twenty-one months, however, their mothers failed to report *any* illness during the first year. The mothers of twenty-eight children rated 3—a rating given if the illness would slightly modify development—also failed to report any illness (Pyles et al., 1935). While it is understandable that parents may not want to recall unpleasant events, these data should be alarming to child development researchers who use retrospective recall.

While early life recollections may be robust in a therapeutic context, for the developmental researcher they are fragile. Recording data is far more accurate if we are there, seeing and hearing the unfolding behaviors of the child and the relationships of the family members.

DEFINING A GROUP FOR STUDY: DRAWING A COMPOSITE PICTURE OF BOYS EVOLVING AN ATYPICAL SEXUAL IDENTITY

Transsexual "Boyhoods"

Invariably, transsexuals report that their childhood was distinctive from that of other children of the same sex on those behaviors that distinguish boys from girls. Harry Benjamin's *Transsexual Phenomenon* (1966) was the first scholarly book describing persons seeking medical and surgical treatment to "change sex." The case histories he collected, numbering in the hundreds by the mid-1960s, were remarkably consistent. Males seeking transsexual surgery recalled feeling like members of the "opposite" sex since early childhood. They recalled wanting to dress in girls' or women's clothes, wanting to play with girls' toys, relating more comfortably to girls, and avoiding conventional boyhood activities.

My interviews of thirty males requesting medical and surgical sex reassignment at UCLA confirmed Benjamin's report. Figure 1.1 summarizes some of their recalled behaviors.

Here are excerpts from two life histories:

1.

My problem to begin with is of very long standing, in fact, all my conscious life, I have been aware that I was of the wrong sex. There was a place way up in the branches of a tree where I grew up that branched out close

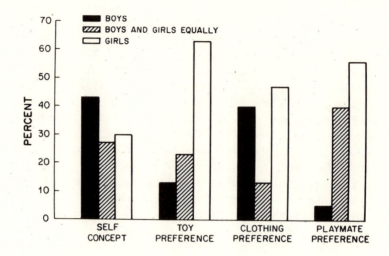

FIGURE 1.1 **Recalled childhood features of thirty males requesting sex-change surgery.**

enough I could lie in it like a hammock. I would lie there and look up through the leaves to the sky and pray. I would promise, and I would offer anything if God would do a miracle for me and make me a girl some day. Any day.

2.

I remember that as a little girl [sic] I used to lie in bed at night with my penis between my legs and my ankles crossed real tight and play a silly game and say if I did this, in the morning when I'd wake up, it would be gone. And I was so disappointed because every morning I'd reach down there and there it was.... I used to like to play with girls. I never did like to play with boys.... I wanted to play the girl games. My sister and I used to dress up in our mother's clothes.... Sometimes when we'd play doctor and nurse I'd get a piece of a curtain or something and put it over my head like it was a scarf. I always played the nurse. Or if we played husband and wife, I'd always be the wife.

Homosexual Boyhoods

It is not only the male-to-female transsexual who recalls childhood cross-gender behavior. Behaviors recalled by homosexual men add to the association between "feminine" behaviors in a boy's childhood and atypical sexuality in a man's adulthood. Histories from ninety homosexual men, gathered by Marcel Saghir and Eli Robins, revealed that two-thirds recalled "having been girl-like during childhood." Only 3 percent of the heterosexual men recalled such a childhood. For the homosexuals, 77 percent reported "having no male buddies, having avoided boy's games and [having] played predominantly with girls. All of them were called sissy.... Among the homosexual males a high proportion reported a repetitive desire to become a girl or a woman before the adult years, specifically 27 percent of the homosexual males and 3 percent of the heterosexual controls" (Saghir and Robins, 1973, 18-21).

Of fifteen hundred homosexual men described by Joseph Harry, 46 percent recalled playing primarily with girls, 36 percent recalled cross-dressing, 22 percent recalled wanting to be girls, and 42 percent were called "sissy." By comparison, for two hundred heterosexual men, this was true for only 12, 5, 5, and 11 percent, respectively (Harry, 1982).

In a study of early boyhood sex-typed play activities of two hundred male heterosexuals and two hundred homosexuals, Edward Grellert and his colleagues found that five recreational activities clearly discriminated the groups: playing baseball and football (more for the heterosexuals) and playing house, school, and with dolls (more for the homosexuals) (Grellert, et al., 1982).

"Childhood gender nonconformity" was more strongly related to adult homosexuality than any other variable in an exhaustive interview study of six hundred homosexual men and three hundred heterosexual men by Alan Bell and his coworkers. Far fewer homosexual men recalled having enjoyed boys' activities (such as baseball and football) "very much" (11 versus 70 percent). More homosexual men recalled enjoying stereotypical girls' activities (playing house, hopscotch, and jacks) "somewhat" or "very much" (46 versus 11 percent). More homosexual men recalled dressing in girls' clothes and pretending to be female on occasions other than Halloween (37 versus 10 percent). And only 18 percent of the homosexual men recalled having been "very" masculine, compared to 67 percent of the heterosexual men (Bell et al., 1981).

These studies were conducted in the United States. "Culturally invariable" properties of homosexual behaviors also exist, according to Frederick Whitam, an anthropologist who has trekked to Guatemala, Brazil, the Philippines, Hawaii, and Fire Island, New York, for field work. Homosexual groups in all four societies manifest similar patterns of early childhood cross-gender behavior: "playing with toys of the opposite sex, cross-dressing, being regarded as sissies, preference for female playmates, and preference for the company of older relatives. There can be little doubt that this behavior is linked to adult sexual orientation" (Whitam, 1983, 222).

Even if these retrospective accounts are not entirely valid, they provide a starting point for a prospective study. The consensus of features from these reports helps sketch the portrait of a boy with greater than average probability of evolving with an atypical sexual identity.

As we inspect the chronology of the papers linking cross-gender behavior in childhood and atypical sexuality in adulthood, the evidence associating the two emerged first for transsexuals, then for homosexuals. Consequently, when we began to generate our group of boys, we thought we were studying pretranssexuals. Ultimately, it appeared that the pattern was probably prehomosexuality (if we were seeing children evolving toward atypical sexuality). The reason is simple: the behaviors recalled by these atypical adults show considerable overlap, and there are far more homosexual than transsexual males.

This change in perspective did not modify the research design. Nor did it modify its goals. Our purposes were still to understand why some boys show extensive cross-gender behaviors while others do not and to identify the relationship between these boyhood behaviors and adult sexuality.

OBTAINING A GROUP FOR STUDY

Boys rather than girls were selected for study because we wanted to maximize the probability that, after starting with a sample of atypical children, we would have a reasonable number of atypical adults. While cross-gender behaviors are more common in girls—for example, cross-dressing—and while many girls express a wish to be boys because of the apparent cultural benefits, it is the rare boy who regularly cross-dresses and expresses the wish to be a girl. On the other hand, there are far more sexually atypical adult males. The ratio of males to females requesting sex-change surgery is about three to one (Benjamin, 1966). Predominant or exclusive homosexuality is about twice as common among males (Kinsey et al., 1948, 1953). Thus, if we hypothesize a developmental chain formed by an atypical behavior in childhood (link 1) and an atypical behavior in adulthood (link 2), with link 1 being more rare but link 2 more common in males, we have a greater chance of completing the chain if we start with atypical boys. In other words, more "feminine" boys ("sissies") should evolve as homosexuals or transsexuals than should "masculine" girls ("tomboys").

The fact that "sissiness" causes social problems for boys while "tomboyism" does not cause problems for girls provided the final impetus for beginning the study with boys. The researcher located in a medical school department of psychiatry has access to children and families experiencing psychological distress.

But since "feminine" boys do not parade in with their parents on a daily basis to a medical center, it was necessary to advertise to the larger community. Letters announcing a research program for prepubertal boys showing an unusual degree of cross-gender behavior were sent to psychiatrists, clinical psychologists, and some family physicians in Los Angeles. A few behavioral features of such boys were outlined: frequent dressing in girls' or women's clothing, a preference for traditional girls' activities, and statements of wanting to be a girl. The boys were to be

TABLE 1.2. Ages of "Feminine" Boys at Initial Evaluation

Years	n
4–5	7
5–6	12
6–7	9
7–8	8
8–9	16
9–12	14
Total	66

prepubertal so that we could better study the association between early gender-role behaviors and later patterns of erotic preference. Additionally, some "feminine boy" families were self-referred. They telephoned UCLA after hearing me describe the clinical project on a local television talk show or reading about it in a Los Angeles newspaper.

A group of sixty-six boys was obtained. Their age distribution is shown in table 1.2.

Prior to our scheduling an initial interview, each parent completed a behavioral checklist. Parents noted whether cross-dressing, playing with dolls, use of cosmetics, female role-playing, feminine gestures, or assertions of wanting to be a girl occurred frequently, occasionally, or not at all. If cross-gender behavior was frequently present across most parameters, the family was scheduled for interview.

Not all families who were interviewed were included in the long-term study. In about 10 percent of the cases we concluded that the boy did not have a substantial degree of sexual identity conflict. In retrospect, these were boys who would not be diagnosed today as having the "gender identity disorder of childhood" (APA, 1980). Usually they had an aversion for rough-and-tumble play and sports, but did not show an extensive degree of cross-gender interests and were content being boys.

The "feminine" boys had few behavioral problems other than sexual identity conflict. A handful were not achieving well in school, one had a minor speech defect, and a couple were enuretic, or bedwetters. One had been evaluated a few years earlier for childhood autism but was never considered severely autistic and by the time of our evaluation showed no autistic behavior. These problems were dealt with by other clinical centers. None of the boys had an extra X chromosome as found in Klinefelter's syndrome (Harrison, 1958), an intersexed state that may be associated with a higher rate of atypical sexuality (Bancroft, 1983).

OBTAINING A COMPARISON GROUP

About three years after we began evaluating "feminine boy" families, we began to recruit a comparison group of boys and their families. Matching "feminine boy" families was initially simple. An advertisement in local

TABLE 1.3. Sibling Sequence

	"Feminine" Boys (66) (%)	"Masculine" Boys (56) (%)
Only child	15	23
Older brother(s)	40	37
Younger brother(s)	37	41
Older sister(s)	23	22
Younger sister(s)	36	37

newspapers offering fifty dollars for participation in a psychological study for families with a boy between the fourth and twelfth birthdays brought a large volume of responses. From this pool, it was easy to match families with common demographic configurations. Matching was on parameters that should relate to patterns of parenting and the socialization experiences of the child. These included age of the boy; number, age, and gender of siblings; marital status of the mother; and race, religion, and educational level of the parents. After these common family patterns were matched, the remaining matchings became progressively more challenging. Ultimately, individual family constellations were advertised for, in both English- and Spanish-language newspapers, to match the most exotic of the "feminine boy" families. Fifty-six of the families were matched.

None of the boys in the potential comparison group was excluded on the basis of sex-typed behaviors. The comparison boys were not selected because of the extent of their "masculinity." As long as his family configuration matched that of a "feminine boy" family, a boy was included.

TWO GROUPS OF CHILDREN

The "feminine" boys' sibling sequence is shown in table 1.3. No distinct pattern of younger or older brothers or sisters was found in association with being a "feminine boy."

Ethnicity of the families was about 80 percent white, 10 percent black, and 10 percent Hispanic. Religious affiliation was about 28 percent Protestant, 25 percent Catholic, 20 percent Jewish, 20 percent none, and 8 percent other. The distribution is representative of the Greater Los Angeles area from which the groups were drawn. Frequency of attending religious service was at least weekly for 28 percent, more than twice a month but less than weekly for 14 percent, on special occasions only for 35 percent, and never for 22 percent. Educational level of the mothers was high school education or graduation for 43 percent, some college or college graduation for 51 percent, and postcollege education for 5 percent. Fathers' educational levels were somewhat higher, with 30 percent having postcollege education, 41 percent some college or college graduation, and only 28 percent not progressing beyond high school. The

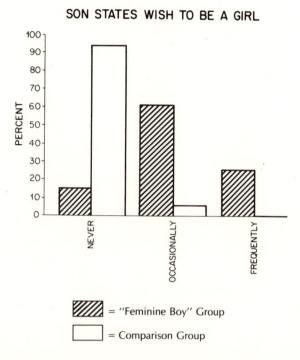

SON STATES WISH TO BE A GIRL

/////// = "Feminine Boy" Group

☐ = Comparison Group

FIGURE 1.2   Frequency of son's stating the wish to be a girl or woman: parent report.

mother's marital status at the time of initial evaluation was 75 percent married and living with husband, 4 percent separated, 19 percent divorced, 1 percent widowed, and 1 percent never married (Green, 1976).

Contrasting the sex-typed behaviors of the two groups of boys is best illustrated graphically. The descriptions of these behaviors were given by parents at the initial evaluation.

Figure 1.2 is a report of the frequency with which the boys stated their wish to be girls. Only 15 percent of the "feminine boy" group, by parents' report, had not stated a wish to be female. This minority might therefore not be diagnosed today as having the "gender identity disorder of childhood," a diagnosis that had not been formalized by the American Psychiatric Association when the group was generated.

Dressing in girls' or women's clothes clearly discriminated the two groups (figure 1.3). Age of onset of cross-dressing was early (figure 1.4). Interest in female-type dress-up doll play (usually Barbie doll) was far more extensive in one group (figure 1.5). When playing house or other "make-believe" games, such as imitating characters from television, the gender of the persons imitated was clearly different for the groups (figure 1.6). The gender of the boys' best friends differed greatly (figure 1.7). Social

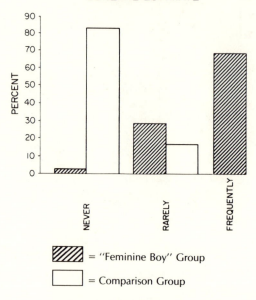

BOYS
FREQUENCY OF CROSS DRESSING:
GENERAL ESTIMATE

= "Feminine Boy" Group

= Comparison Group

FIGURE 1.3   Frequency of son's cross-dressing: parent report.

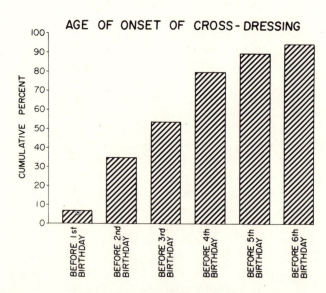

AGE OF ONSET OF CROSS-DRESSING

FIGURE 1.4   Age of onset of son's cross-dressing: parent report.

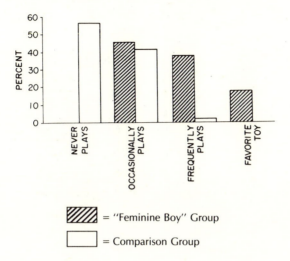

BOY'S FEMALE-TYPE DOLL PLAY: INTEREST

= "Feminine Boy" Group

= Comparison Group

FIGURE 1.5   Extent of son's interest in female-type dolls (Barbie): parent report.

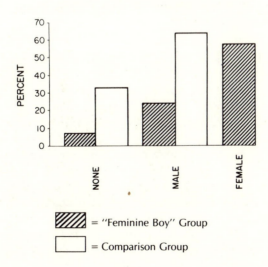

BOY'S ROLE IN PLAYING HOUSE

= "Feminine Boy" Group

= Comparison Group

FIGURE 1.6   Son's role when playing house or mother-father games: parent report.

BOY RELATES BEST TO

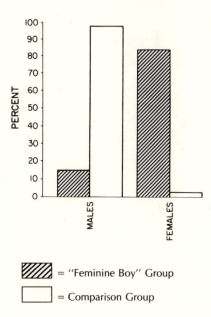

= "Feminine Boy" Group

= Comparison Group

FIGURE 1.7   Gender of son's peer group: parent report.

status among male peers discriminated against one group (figure 1.8). Extent of interest in rough-and-tumble play (figure 1.9) and sports (figure 1.10) was widely divergent.

REPRESENTATIVENESS OF THE "FEMININE BOY" GROUP

How might our "feminine" boys differ from comparably behaving boys not referred to a clinical program? In order to find their way into our study, most families lived in or close to Los Angeles. Generally, the parents (or at least one parent) had concern about the boy's behavior and/or the boy was being teased by other children about his behavior. A boy behaving in a comparably cross-gendered fashion, in a geographic area with no professional focus on such behavior, would probably not be evaluated. And parents unconcerned about the boy's behavior, irrespective of geographic location, are less likely to bring him for study. However, non-evaluated boys' behaviors might be equally atypical. In the final chapter, I speculate about the adult sexual identity of "feminine" boys whose parents do not bring their sons for consultation because of the absence of parental concern.

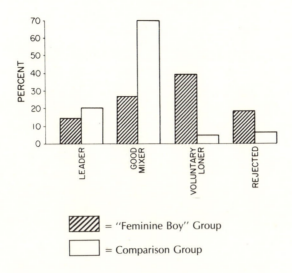

FIGURE 1.8   Son's peer group status: parent report.

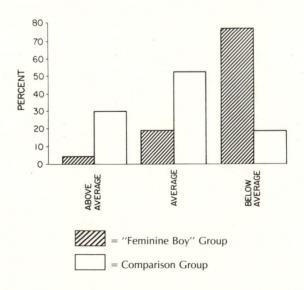

FIGURE 1.9   Son's interest in rough-and-tumble play: parent report.

BOY'S INTEREST IN SPORTS

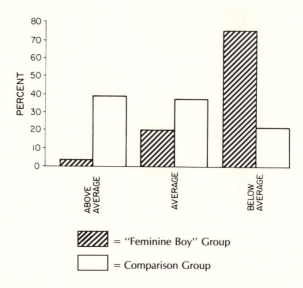

= "Feminine Boy" Group

= Comparison Group

FIGURE 1.10   Son's interest in sports participation: parent report.

Are our cross-gendered boys representative of such boys in general, and of boys with the gender identity disorder of childhood in particular? Evidence supporting the representativeness of such a sample of clinically referred boys derives from data obtained with a sex-typed game inventory (Bates and Bentler, 1973). "Gender disturbed" boys were found to have similar game preferences as "normal" girls, and "normal" boys did not differ from boys referred for general psychiatric problems. The study conclusion was that "psychiatric status *per se* does not appear to account for the differences between gender disturbed boys and normal boys" (Doering, 1981, 54).

BASE RATES OF BOYHOOD CROSS-GENDER BEHAVIORS

Our comparison group of boys, not selected on the basis of their traditional sex-typed interests, provides some indication of the extent to which boys in the general population show individual cross-gender behaviors. Other researchers have also studied "normal" samples of boys in this age range to determine the rates of such behaviors.

In an assessment of "normal" second-grade boys and boys referred for psychiatric consultation (for a problem other than sexual identity), parents reported these percentages for "cross-gender" behaviors: feminine dress-ing, 13 percent; use of cosmetics, 6 percent; preference for female play-mates, 3 percent; desire to be a female, 7 percent; doll play, 3 percent; and an aversion to boys' games, 2 percent. Only one cross-gender or "feminine" behavior was usually reported for a given boy (Zuger and Taylor, 1969).

In another survey, here with two- to five-year-old boys, cross-gender behaviors were rated on a 1–5 or 1–8 scale, with 1 designating the lowest frequency. Approximate ratings for specific items were: acts like a little girl, 1.2; is called a "sissy," 1.3; likes to play the role of mother in fantasy games, 1.3; says he would like to be a girl, 1.1; says he will grow up to be a mommy, 1.1; likes to wear his mother's shoes, 2.8; likes to wear makeup, 2.4; likes to wear his mother's clothes, 1.3; likes to wear things like wigs, towels, and shirts on his head, 2.1; and dresses in female clothing, 1.2 (Zucker et al., 1980). A survey with five- to ten-year-old boys also revealed low cross-gender rates: wears a shirt or towel around his waist as a skirt, 1.3; imitates females, 1.2; dresses in female clothing, 1.0; plays with dolls, 1.3; wears things like wigs, towels, and shirts on his head, 1.4; plays with girls at school, 3.5; and plays with girls at home, 4.5 (Bates et al., 1973).

Finally, a large survey used a behavioral checklist with thirteen hundred children being evaluated in twenty-eight mental health settings and an-other thirteen hundred nonpatient children being evaluated in a home survey. The item "behaves like opposite sex" or "wishes to be of the opposite sex," was noted by 10 percent of the mothers of the clinically referred boys during ages four to eleven. For the nonpatient boys, this item was noted for about 5 percent (Achenbach and Edelbrock, 1981).

EVALUATING THE BOYS

Playroom Toy Preferences

A playroom was stocked with traditionally sex-typed toys: a dress-up doll, an embroidery set, a carriage, a handbag, a tea set, a truck, a gun, a rocket, a wagon, a ball, and a punching dummy. The child was left alone in the room and his toy selections were observed through a one-way mirror.

The extent of play with two toys differed significantly for the "femi-nine" and "masculine" boys. "Feminine" boys played about four times as much with the doll, and about a third as much with the truck, as "mas-culine" boys did. The "feminine" boys' selections were like those of girls of the same age (Green et al., 1972).

Doll-play Fantasy

Children were permitted access to a set of "family dolls": grandmother, grandfather, mother, father, boy, girl, and baby. They were told to make up a story using any of the dolls and to hold onto the doll while that family member was doing something in the story. The time spent holding each doll was recorded.

"Feminine" boys spent nearly twice as much time holding the mother doll and the grandmother doll as "masculine" boys did. They tended to hold the father doll less, the boy doll less, and the girl doll more. They held the infant doll more than twice as long as "masculine" boys did (Green and Fuller, 1973).

Physical Behavior

One group of parents reported that their sons were teased for physically "acting like a girl." Peer group teasing was directed at the manner in which the boys walked, ran, used their hands, and (if pressed into the athletic arena) threw a ball. The boys, too, complained that they were being made fun of for these actions, actions that were usually outside their awareness.

We sought to assess objectively the extent to which this peer group labeling was an accurate reflection of sex differences in the way boys and girls walked, ran, gestured, or threw a ball, and whether these boys "acted like girls." A subsample of "feminine" boys (age four to ten) was compared on the four physical activities with boys of the same age from the "masculine" contrast group and with girls of the same age who were not selected for the extent to which they played sports. The children were dressed to conceal gender: a bathing cap obscured hair style, a jumpsuit was gender-neutral, and each child wore sneakers.

The children were videotaped performing four behavioral sequences: 1) running toward and away from the camera; 2) walking toward, away from, and across the field of the camera; 3) throwing a ball overhand toward the camera and at right angles to the camera; and 4) narrating a story about something interesting that had happened to them that day (with no sound recorded, only the posturing of the child).

The videotape segments were put into triplets, with one "feminine" boy, one "masculine" boy, and one girl, all of the same age, performing the same task. Two adult males and two adult females viewed the tapes in an order that was random in terms of age of the child, the task, and the sequence with which children from the three groups were placed within each triplet. Raters were told only that they would be seeing boys and girls (not two subgroups of boys) and were asked to judge whether the child was definitely a boy, probably a boy, maybe a boy, maybe a girl, probably a girl, or definitely a girl.

The results not only provide support for the peer group comments about the boys "acting like girls," they also document that these sex-typed differences emerge at an early age. "Masculine" boys were clearly distinguished from girls. However, the raters were unable to label decisively the "feminine" boys as boys or girls. This was true for all four behaviors, and it was true *as young as four years of age* (Green et al., 1983).

Psychological Tests

Two psychological tests were given, both of which discriminate typical boys and girls. One was the It-Scale for Children (Brown, 1956), the other the Draw-A-Person test (Machover, 1953). These tests and the results are described in chapter 6.

Interviews

We discussed the boy's understanding of why he was seeing me, his preferences for doing the things that boys or girls usually do, and his reasons for these preferences. Chapter 5 contains transcript segments from these interviews.

EVALUATING THE PARENTS

Questionnaires

Parents completed questionnaires describing demographic features of the family, sex-typed behaviors of their son, the age of onset and frequency of his cross-gender behaviors, their attitudes toward his behaviors, reactions of other relatives to the behaviors, and the son's peer relations. They also described their relationship to their son, their marital relationship, and their own psychosexual background.

Interviews

An interview was developed for use with parents, together and singly. The conjoint interview began with a reporting by parents of each aspect of gender-role behavior of the child, including patterns of dressing; toy, game, and peer group preferences; roles taken in fantasy games; and statements of wanting to be a girl. The parents were asked when each of these behaviors was first noted, what they had initially thought the behaviors signified, and how they had responded. Subsequent changes in their attitude, if any, were recorded.

The interview progressed to the parents' earliest impressions of the child with respect to physical appearance and temperamental and personality features. This was considered relevant because Stoller (1968) had found that cross-gender-identified boys were often described by their mothers as having been "beautiful" babies (see chapter 3). Questions during solo interviews focused on the amount of time the mother recalled holding the child during its first two years. Stoller had hypothesized that extensive mother-son contact "feminized" a boy by preventing psychological separation from his mother (see chapter 3). Comparisons were made with her other children, if any. Since parental availability to a child is seen as critical in most social learning theories of sexual identity development (see chapter 2), the amount of time the mother spent with the child during each of the first five years was investigated and, again, comparisons were made with the amount she spent with her other children. Similar questions were asked of the father.

Because Sears et al. (1965) had found that parental (especially fathers') restrictive attitudes toward a child's sexuality (such as household nudity and sex play) had a "feminizing" influence on children, these areas were covered, along with attitudes about sex education. Stoller suggested that parental attitudes and relationships with a child were influenced by parents' relationships with *their* parents. He found that mothers of "feminine" boys had had distant relationships with their mothers (see chapter 3). He also found that these mothers had been more "tomboyish" during childhood. Thus, parents were interviewed about their relationships with their parents and about their childhood play interests. Finally, since common sense suggests that the relationship between the parents, in terms of emotional closeness and family responsibilities, should have an influence on the child's psychosexual development, these areas, too, were explored.

Rating Interviews

All interviews were tape-recorded, transcribed, and retyped to eliminate personally identifying data and extraneous remarks. They were then cut into sections which included responses to specific areas of inquiry, with the sections assigned a code number. Sections were rated by two raters unaware of the subject group from which the interviews had originated.

Six-point rating scales were developed to judge the interview segments. Anchor points were constructed from a random sampling of transcribed responses from parents that tapped the range of typical responses. Following this, another sampling of interview segments was utilized to pilot test the utility of the rating scales.

Two raters who had not conducted the interviews then received code-numbered interview sections for rating. When the two raters did not differ by more than one point, the average was taken for tabulation. When raters differed by more than one point, a third rater, also unaware of the group from which the interview segment emanated, judged the section and the average was taken.

To list all interview questions and anchor points from the dozens of interview sections would take too much space. One interview that distinguished "feminine boy" families from "masculine boy" families concerned perceived infant "beauty." Here are the questions and anchor points for the rating scale for the responses to that section:

QUESTIONS

What was he like as an infant?

What sort of personality did he have?

How would you describe his face?

How did he compare to your other children (or other children you've seen)?

ANCHOR POINTS (SUMMARIZED)

(Not Beautiful)
1. Very aggressive. Very masculine, big, husky, tough. Ordinary eyes. Never mistaken for a girl.

2. Moderately aggressive. Looks like most boys. Ordinary eyes. Never mistaken for a girl.

3. Somewhat aggressive. Attractive. Large eyes. Perhaps occasionally mistaken for a girl.

4. Less aggressive than most boys. Somewhat pretty. Attractive eyes, perhaps with long lashes. Occasionally mistaken for a girl.

5. Sweet, pretty. Big, girl-like eyes. Frequently mistaken for a girl.

6. Beautiful. Big eyes, long lashes, "just like a girl." "Everyone says the child should have been a girl."
(Beautiful)

FOLLOW-UP EVALUATIONS

Interviews, questionnaires and psychological tests also constituted the follow-up assessment. Follow-up interviews with parents became less structured and those with children more structured. Parents described changes, if any, in their son's behavior, their relationship with the boy, and their relationship with each other. They completed two questionnaires, one describing their son's current rates of gender-role behaviors and the extent of change, if any, during the past one and two years, the other describing their reactions to the boy's gender-role behaviors and their impression of the reactions of their spouse.

Interviews with the boys were tape-recorded. A precoded response sheet was used for noting the best-fitting response on a range of possible answers to a question. Topics included the boy's friendship network, recreational interests, media preferences, idols, and vocational aspirations. There was a specific focus on romantic feelings, erotic attractions, and fantasies during masturbation and nocturnal erotic dreams (wet dreams), genital responsivity to visual erotica (pornography), and interpersonal genital experiences. Psychological tests at follow-up included the age-appropriate version of the Cattell Personality Factor Instruments, the Bem

Sex Role Inventory, the Adjective Check List, and the Tennessee Self-Concept Scale. These are described in chapter 6.

The frequency of follow-up evaluations varied from family to family. Some families elected not to be seen for years after the initial evaluation and were not reevaluated until the son was in mid-adolescence or young adulthood. Others were seen about every eighteen to twenty-four months. Some were lost to follow-up after the initial evaluation or an early follow-up. For the "feminine boy" group, 57 were reevaluated once, 37 twice, 28 three times, 24 four times, and 24 five or more times. Twenty-two had no follow-up after their thirteenth birthday. For the comparison group, 35 were reevaluated once, 33 twice, 30 three times, 18 four times, and 9 five or more times. Twenty-one have not been reevaluated after their thirteenth birthday.

CHARACTERIZING THE GROUP

Consideration was given to whether these atypical boys should be considered "feminine." Some critics of this label claim that a more appropriate term is *androgynous*. The popularity of androgyny, with its pronouncement of an overarching capacity for mental health, makes the criticism more than a semantic quibble.

Had our boys played with dolls and trucks they would be androgynous. Had they engaged in sports and rough-and-tumble play as well as cross-dressing, they would be androgynous. But *androgynous* hardly seems appropriate, considering the behavioral descriptions presented here and in chapter 5.

An additional argument against calling our boys androgynous derives from a study where children identified by their peer group as "sissies" were rated by their peers on behavioral attributes thought to contribute to androgyny.

[The] results showed that many of the positive flexible attributes of adults labeled "androgynous" were not present in the younger elementary school children labeled by peers as sissies. . . . Some of the qualities considered androgynous in males such as nurturance, supportiveness, friendliness, affectivity, sensitivity, and relationship orientation (traditionally feminine and expressive) were not evident with [these] males. (Hemmer and Kleiber, 1981, 1210-11)

The boys are referred to as "feminine," not as feminine. Quotes signify that this term is imprecise shorthand for a constellation of behaviors. The sex-typed behaviors of these boys are more commonly seen with female children. However, not all girls show these behaviors; some have interests more commonly shared with male children. Such girls are often called "tomboys" when they display such "masculine" behaviors. *Tomboy* is not a pejorative term, *sissy* is. Therefore, while other children call one of our groups "sissy," I do not use that term except to convey quickly the picture of a cluster of behaviors that distinguishes these boys, as in the book's title. Since "masculine behaviors" and "feminine behaviors" are relative, and not all girls behave similarly to one of our groups of boys, the quotation marks should remind readers of the imprecision. Occasionally, the boys are also referred to as *cross-gendered*, but this term is not used generally because it is imprecise for the same reason as *feminine* and is also more cumbersome. In describing the two groups of boys, it is both simpler and more descriptive to refer to them as "feminine" and "masculine" than as cross-gendered and same-gendered.

PITFALLS OF A PROSPECTIVE STUDY

In addition to requiring body and soul with a commitment to longevity, there are other obstacles to initiating a long-term study. An investigator's interest in finding out how families evolve over many years does not necessarily mean that families are equally interested in reporting their progress. Some families who might have been interested move away, leaving no trace for bill collectors or warring ex-spouses. Some introduce new husbands, new family names, and hide in plain sight.

An equally formidable hurdle is that federal research grants do not initially provide funds to carry a long-term study through to completion. Rather, projects are funded for only three to five years at a time, and the reviewers who approve project initiation are not the same reviewers who decide on renewal. If the later reviewers do not share the enthusiasm of the earlier ones, the project dies of starvation in late childhood or adolescence. Similar threats to survival continue throughout the project's life span.

However, as Michael Rutter, England's preeminent professor of child psychiatry, has observed: "[While] prospective or longitudinal studies are time consuming and expensive to undertake, are subject to a variety of sampling hazards and the data obtained are difficult to analyze... for certain types of research questions longitudinal data are essential" (Rutter, 1977, 223).

2

Chickens and Eggs: The Emergence of Sex Differences in Children

Do boy and girl infants behave differently? Do mothers and fathers treat boy and girl infants differently? To what exent does the infant condition the parent and the parent the infant? Which comes first?

When I wrote *Sexual Identity Conflict in Children and Adults* in 1974, my retrieval of research papers on the emergence of sex differences was far less comprehensive than in 1984. In 1974, the citations in one article led me to others, which in turn led along a chain of further referrals. The process was terribly time consuming and terribly incomplete. Today, computerized retrieval systems rapidly flush out an exhaustive series of citations from the depths of a university library. Inevitably, at some point one's mind and one's secretary both say, "Stop! Enough!" I hope that point came only after our original research findings could be viewed in proper perspective.

This chapter describes behavioral differences between males and females that appear early in life and that may not reflect differences in parental behavior with infant boys and girls. It also summarizes differences in the ways parents relate to boys and girls that may not reflect early sex differences of children. A variety of other forces that direct boys and girls to different developmental tracks are also described.

EARLY BEHAVIORAL DIFFERENCES BETWEEN MALES AND FEMALES: "LIKE ME"/"NOT LIKE ME"

Infants may discriminate male and female age-mates as early as the first year. When boys and girls aged ten to eighteen months were shown pictures of infants of the same and the other sex (faces only), males looked at faces of males longer, and females looked at faces of females longer (Lewis and Weinraub, 1974). This early awareness of "like me"/"not like me" was also apparent from placing two male and two female one-year-olds at the four corners of a room and permitting one at a time to crawl to any other child. Although the odds of crawling to an opposite sex child are two to one, the infants more often crawled to the child of the same sex (Michalson et al., 1974).

Even more startling is the finding that in the second year children appear to be able to discriminate the pattern of body movements of other boys and girls without actually seeing the children. Twelve small light bulbs were attached to the limbs and torsos of children, and then the childrens' actions were filmed in a darkened room. When the moving light patterns were shown to other children, they paid more attention to those made by same-sex infants (Bower, 1982).

If these findings are valid, they suggest a very early, perhaps innate, self-classification as male or female, the first component of sexual identity.

PLAY PATTERNS

In play styles and toy preferences, boys and girls also differ early. In their first year, boys seem more rambunctious. When twelve-month-olds were observed with their fathers in a waiting room, boys were more likely to handle "forbidden" objects, such as trays and vases (Maccoby and Jacklin, 1980). They were also more likely to play with wall plugs or sockets, pull on curtains, and climb on office furniture. With more standard toys, one-year-olds' preferences also differed. Girls preferred soft toys and dolls; boys preferred transportation toys (Fagot, 1974) and robots (Jacklin et al., 1973).

By age two to four, boys and girls seem to prefer different parents as playmates. Preferences were determined by asking children with which parent (in the adjoining room) they would prefer to play a game ("London Bridge"), build something from blocks, or make a sketch. By age two to three, both boys and girls preferred father. At four, girls shifted to mother, but boys stayed with father (Lynn and Cross, 1974).

Another early sex difference may be play with newborns. Nonhuman primate females, nine months old and still nursing, show considerable interest in picking up and holding babies. Male monkeys at any age rarely show comparable behavior (Lancaster, 1971). This sex difference does not appear to result from modeling after adults: it is apparent in young monkeys raised without ever seeing their mother or any adult female (Chamove et al., 1967).

LATER TOY PREFERENCES

Since the early 1970s, toy selection has been a target of those who want to disrupt patterns of rigid sex-typing in children. In the past decade much has been written about "unisex" toys. A logical study a decade later asks, "*Have* changes occurred in children's toy preferences?"

In 1980, when children between four-and-a-half and six years were offered a baby doll, plastic high-heeled shoes, a purse, a set of miniature dishes, a fire engine, a plastic tool set, a racing car, and an airplane, their selections were highly consistent with those made by children in the 1950s and 1960s. No boys selected the doll, shoes, or purse. Even when another child or an adult stated that all the toys were appropriate for both boys and girls, three-fourths of the children did not change their choices (Frasher et al., 1980).

Who better to ask whether children's preferences for sex-typed toys have changed than Santa Claus? In 1983, seven-year-old boys and girls were asked to write letters to Santa requesting any toy they wanted. Boys were equally likely to request traditionally "masculine" and neutral toys, but they rarely requested "feminine" toys. Girls requested neutral toys the most, then "feminine" toys, and rarely "masculine" toys (Douns, 1983).

The optimal setting for modifying these rigid sex-typed toy preferences would appear to be preschool and day-care centers, where young children have the opportunity of selecting from a spectrum of toys as they begin to evolve activity preferences. Thus, many "nonsexist" centers have sprouted. But do the children in these schools deviate in toy preferences from the stereotypical selections of their predecessors?

In one Canadian day-care center, parents "routinely discussed and explored issues of sexism." In another, run by the YMCA/YWCA, there was no emphasis on "nonsexist" child-rearing. The children averaged five years in age and had been attending their day-care center for an average of four years. Yet when children from both centers were permitted free access to a variety of conventionally masculine and feminine toys in a playroom, those attending the "nonsexist" center were as stereotyped as those at the more traditional center. One explanation for this lack of distinction comes from observations in the children's homes. When the investigators counted the number of traditionally sex-typed toys at home, there was no appreciable difference between the children in the two types of center. Mothers' actions may speak louder than their words (Cole et al., 1982).

EARLY PEER RELATIONS

Play patterns with other children are another early sex difference. Two-and-a-half-year-olds were observed with "stranger" children in boy-boy, boy-girl, and girl-girl pairs, in the presence of their mothers (Jacklin and Maccoby, 1978). Both boys and girls were more likely to cry and remain close to their mothers when paired with a boy. Girls showed more "passive" behavior when paired with a boy—they stood or sat quietly watching their partners play.

The preference for same-sex playmates also emerges early. Three-and-a-half- to four-and-a-half-year-olds saw pairs of photographs of boys and girls and were asked to select those with whom they would like to play. Boys preferred boys; girls, girls (Strayer, 1977).

AGGRESSION AND ROUGH-AND-TUMBLE PLAY

Young boys are more aggressive than young girls and roughhouse more. When two- to three-year-olds were observed in an indoor free-play setting, boys were more aggressive toward their peers (Pedersen and Bell, 1970). They also showed more rough-and-tumble play (Smith and Connolly, 1972). Observations in such diverse cultures as the Philippines, India, Okinawa, Mexico, and Kenya generally confirm these findings. Except in Kenya, boys from age three on were observed more often assaulting other children and more often engaging in "horseplay" (Whiting and Whiting, 1975, 146-47).

Are these differences innate or learned? The comprehensive review of the development of sex differences by Eleanor Maccoby and Carol Jacklin (1974) discarded nearly all nonanatomical sex differences and saw sex-role socialization as the overarching principle. However, the researchers also concluded that greater aggression and rough-and-tumble play among young males has "a biological foundation." In an update of the Maccoby and Jacklin review, Maccoby summarizes her view on the origin of three sex-typed behaviors: "The higher incidence of boys' aggression, rough-and-tumble play, and attempts to dominate is closely paralleled by similar behavior among monkeys and apes. And we can certainly assume that the subhuman primate infants are not being deliberately trained by their parents in accordance with sex-role concepts" (1980, 244).

EARLY KNOWLEDGE OF SEX STEREOTYPES

Boys and girls become aware of sex-typed attributes such as "I'm strong" and "I like to play ball" surprisingly early. This is shown by first having children hear a sex-typed statement and then having them select a male or a female paper doll that they would expect to make that statement.

Two-year-olds believe that boys like to play with cars and help father. Three-year-olds believe that boys like to build things and that only boys like to play with trains. They believe that girls like to play with dolls, help mother, and cook dinner. They also believe that girls talk a lot, never hit, and say "I need help" (Kuhn et al., 1978).

By three-and-a-half years, when children are shown child or parent dolls and asked who is smartest, who jumps rope, who rakes leaves, who sets the table, who works in an office, and who cooks, these designations, too, are sex-typed (Flerx et al., 1976). Other sex differences present at this age (in the eyes of children) include who cries a lot, who is cruel, who is quiet, who is afraid, and who is strong (Reis and Wright, 1981).

At four, five, and six years, the list of stereotypes grows. Children selected a boy or a girl doll that would be expected to engage in a described behavior. "Male behaviors" now include independence, aggression, strength, fearlessness, and leadership. "Female behaviors" include dependence, passivity, nurturance, obedience, and concern with physical appearance. For those who decry such sex-stereotyping, the good news is that the four-year-old boys associated the male doll with nurturance, expressiveness, concern with physical appearance, and passivity, and did not accept "negative aggression" (acting rough and hitting) as characteristic of the male doll (Albert and Porter, 1983).

Thus, children categorize males and females on personality dimensions, not just on clothing preferences or vocational and recreational activities. If this categorization occurs at the same time as the emergence of the self-concept of belonging to one of the two sexes (component one of sexual identity), this complex organization may shape the behaviors we call gender role (component two). Of course, selections may not be consonant with a child's awareness of being male or female. A boy may *know* he is a boy, *wish* he were a girl, and select "feminine" items. Indeed, much of this book is about such boys.

PARENTS' BEHAVIOR TOWARD MALE AND FEMALE CHILDREN

Mothers and Infants

Mother-infant contact plays a central role in theories of sexual identity development. Differences in the extent of contact in relation to the gender of the infant are apparent very early. At three weeks and at three months, mothers of sons appear to hold, stimulate, and look at their children more than mothers of daughters. These differences are largely accounted for by the fact that males exhibit more fussing or cranky and whiny behaviors. However, mothers stimulate and arouse male children more, even discounting the influence of males' greater fussing. Furthermore, at three months, mothers respond to males' fussing by close physical contact more than they do to daughters' fussing. Males appear to be more difficult to calm.

Mothers may train children to make physical contact. Male and female infants were observed with their mothers at six months, and the mothers were rated for how they handled their infants. The same pairs were observed again at thirteen months. At six months, mothers touched boys less. At thirteen months, boys touched mothers less. The more a mother touched her son at six months, the more the son touched his mother at thirteen months (Goldberg and Lewis, 1969).

Growing up with Father

Differences in the ways fathers interact with young sons and daughters also emerge early. When the children were aged twelve months, fathers were found to withdraw from daughters and, during the second year, to become more than twice as active with sons. During the same period, mothers remained equally involved with sons and daughters (Snow et al., 1983).

At twelve months, fathers and children were observed in a staged "waiting room" which contained sex-typed toys out of the children's reach. The toys the father presented to sons or daughters differed. Fathers were less likely to give their sons dolls and more likely to give them trucks. Daughters were given trucks and dolls equally. Among those children (boys or girls) who were given dolls, boys played with them less (Snow et al., 1983). This could reflect either the child's earlier parent-trained experience with dolls or a higher innate disposition for doll play in girls, perhaps sex-hormone dependent. The latter interpretation is suggested by studies of play preferences in girls exposed to high levels of male hormones before birth, described later in this chapter (Ehrhardt and Baker, 1974).

Mothers, Fathers, and Infants

In an observational study of parents and eighteen-month-olds, parents talked to same-sex infants more and got down on the floor to play with them more (Weinraub and Frankel, 1977). Parents may also respond differently to specific behaviors of boys and girls in the second year. Girls appear to get more positive responses when they ask for help or try to help an adult. Boys get more positive responses when playing with blocks and are also allowed to explore objects with less criticism. Parents generally give positive responses to girls for play with dolls and negative responses to boys. Fathers more than mothers give negative responses to boys playing with dolls (Fagot, 1978). These findings document the *obvious:* parents can tell whether they have a boy or girl. But at what age do children correctly distinguish "mommy" from "daddy," at least by using those labels?

Children aged nine to twenty-four months were shown slides of their mothers and fathers as well as of other adults. Infants from fifteen months on more often correctly used the label *daddy* than *mommy*. Although early, this laboratory finding appears to be *later* than that found in a naturalistic setting. The children's mothers reported that at home, 25 percent of nine-month-olds, 58 percent of twelve-month-olds, and all fifteen- to twenty-four-month-olds used the terms *mommy* and *daddy* correctly (Brooks-Gunn and Lewis, 1979).

Baby "X"

Tricking adults into believing an infant is a male or a female has become a favored pastime of developmental psychologists. In one study, mothers of five- to ten-month-old infants were observed with six-month-old "actor babies," two males and two females. Two of the infants were cross-dressed and given cross-sex names.

The findings were poignant. The actual biological sex of the infant had no significant effect on the mothers, but the *perceived* sex of the infant did influence them. They verbally encouraged "boys" to physical action and gave them more "whole-body stimulation" in response to the infants' movements. Only "girls" were initially offered a doll, while "boys" were offered a hammer or an hourglass rattle (Smith and Lloyd, 1978).

Another study also disguised the gender of a six-month-old infant and presented it to sets of parents who had both male and female children. Half the parents saw the infant dressed in blue overalls and were told the infant's name was Adam. The other half saw the infant dressed in a pink dress and were told its name was Beth. Three toys were within reach of the infant: a duck, a doll, and a train.

"Beth" was more often given the doll by the female parent. Paradoxically, when interviewed, three-fourths of these parents stated that there should be no difference in the behavior of male and female six-month-olds, and four-fifths reported that it was important for boy and girl infants to play with all types of toys (Culp et al., 1983).

Another study of this genre observed women pregnant with their first child interacting with an infant labeled as either a boy or a girl. The infants were a six-month-old male and a nine-month-old female, neither of whose sex was readily determinable. The infants randomly became Paul and Paula and were dressed gender-neutrally. Then adult-infant interactions were studied. The designated gender of the infant had no major impact on any of the adult behaviors. The researchers concluded: "Adult perceptions and reactions are determined to a large extent by the child's behavior" (Bell and Carver, 1980, 927).

Contradicting this impression, however, is the finding from a related study where parents heard tape recordings of children identified as boys or girls and then reported their reactions to the children's voices. Mothers were more permissive of the statements allegedly made by a boy, while fathers were more permissive of those allegedly made by a girl (Rothbart and Maccoby, 1966).

Then there is the "two-part series," "Baby X." The original "episode" starred one three-month-old female staged to perplex adults. (The infant was introduced as a boy, a girl, or without any gender information.) Sex-typed toys were available to parents for play with the infant (Seavey et al., 1975). Adults interacted differently, depending on whether they thought the child was male or female. A doll was given more often to an infant believed to be female, primarily by the men.

The replication study of "Baby X" cast two males and one female, aged six-and-a-half months, again similarly clothed. As before, toy choice by adults was related to perceived gender of the child. "Male" infants were presented with footballs, "female" infants with dolls. Teething rings and dolls were more often selected for gender-neutral infants.

Strong, bald babies were seen as male; soft, fragile ones were seen as female. Sex differences in the eye of the beholder did not correlate with the child's actual gender. One child was believed to be female because "she is friendly, and female infants smile more" (a male describing a *male*). Another was believed to be female because "girls are more satisfied and accepting" (a female describing a *male*) (Sidorowicz and Lunney, 1980, 71).

Not only have adults been misled into thinking an infant was male or female and then asked to describe it, but children have also been duped. Boys and girls, three-and-a-half and five-and-a-half years old, watched videotapes of twelve-month-old male and female infants dressed alike and playing with the same toys. The children were randomly told which child was Bobby and which was Lisa. Then they were asked to ascribe "sex-typed" attributes (such as big/little, quiet/loud, smart/stupid, strong/weak) to the two infants. As early as three-and-a-half years, adjectives were responded to in a sex-stereotyped way (Haugh et al., 1980).

PEERS AND SIBLINGS

Too little attention has been paid to the influence of the peer group on psychosexual development (except as a source of sexual *mis*information). Chapter 1 reported that the peer group of "feminine" boys is composed primarily of girls and that "feminine" boys are low on the totem pole of social status. It is therefore important to know the circumstances under which the peer group rewards or punishes sex-"appropriate" and sex-"inappropriate" behavior, as well as the effect of the peer group's reactions on the child's behavior.

Four-year-olds were observed and the usual sex-typed behavioral differences found; that is, girls played with dolls more than boys did, boys were more involved with chasing and climbing, and boys more often role-played as male characters. Then the reactions of other children to these behaviors were noted. Boys more often received positive responses for "male" activities than girls did for "female" activities. Boys seemed more responsive to peer pressure: they terminated "female" activities more rapidly than girls did "male" activities following negative responses from either girls or boys.

The consequence of a "moderate" degree of cross-gender behavior in three- and four-year-old boys was recorded in a preschool setting. Boys were defined as showing cross-gender behavior if they behaved in a way similar to 15 percent of boys and 85 percent of girls, or did not show behaviors exhibited by 85 percent of boys. The behaviors that discriminated boys from girls were art activities, playing in the kitchen, playing dress-up, and playing with dolls (higher for girls), and using building blocks, carpentry tools, or transportation toys, and playing in the sandbox or with mud (higher for boys).

From teachers, boys received more criticism when they engaged in dress-up behaviors, and girls received more criticism when they played in the sandbox. Boys received more approval from teachers when playing with blocks and engaged in art activities. From peers, boys received more criticism when they engaged in doll play or dress-up, and less approval than girls received when they played in the kitchen, played with dolls, or played dress-up. Teachers did not react differently to cross-gender boys compared to other boys. Peers, however, were more punitive toward these boys: cross-gender boys played alone three times as much as other children (Fagot, 1977).

Fagot wondered why the boys maintained their cross-gender preferences in the face of so much negative reaction from their preschool environment. She cited Green (1974) to explain: "Feminine choices in boys are often multiply determined and subtly reinforced by their home environment" (Fagot, 1977, 906).

A unique two-phase study looked at the reactions of mothers, fathers, and peers to the sex-typed behaviors of three- and five-year-olds in a laboratory setting. In phase one, mothers were videotaped and told to respond to the child's play activities with peers as they would respond at home. Here, boys were censured by both mothers and peers for playing with girls' toys and rewarded by other boys for playing with boys' toys. However, the boys also received some reward from mothers for play with girls' toys.

Fathers and children were observed in phase two of the study. Here, boys consistently received more punishment from the parent when playing with girls' toys. The researchers concluded that "the father's role in the socialization of traditionally sex-typed behaviors appears to be important, perhaps more so than that of the mother" (Langlois and Downs, 1980, 1246).

Siblings may serve as social (not just anatomical) models of maleness and femaleness. The classic study of the influence of sibling's gender on the sexual identity of a child was done by Helen Koch (1956). Five- and six-year-old-boys and girls with siblings were assessed by teachers for masculinity and femininity. Boys with sisters a couple of years older were considered more "sissyish," but not those boys with sisters substantially older. The availability of sisters' playmates was considered responsible for the finding.

Over a decade later, Koch's finding was not confirmed. Classmates and teachers rated children from preschool through eighth grade on how closely each child fit their expectations of what a boy or girl should be like. The most masculine and least masculine boys and the most feminine and least feminine girls were compared for sibling sequence. This time, no relationship was found (Vroegh, 1971).

GENDER CONSTANCY AND STABILITY

Many of the "feminine" boys in our study had wanted to be girls (see chapters 1 and 5). Some, when very young, would say they *were* girls. It is therefore important to know at what age children label themselves as boys or girls, what cues they use, and how permanent their classification is. Can children "change sex"? Several studies focus on "gender constancy"; that is, if a male, do you stay a male, no matter what (short of transsexual surgery)?

At two years, about 80 percent of children were correct in their answers to the question, "Are you a boy or girl?" At three, about 80 percent were correct for the question, "Are you like this doll [boy] or this doll [girl]?" Also at three about 80 percent correctly answered the question, "Are you going to be a mommy or a daddy?" (more correctly put, "*Could* you be ...?").

When hair or dress was the cue, nearly all five-year-olds discriminated the sexes. Genital appearance was a less important cue. Only half of the seven-year-olds discriminated males from females on this basis (Levin et al., 1972). However, in an earlier study, genital cues were used by younger children. Then, nearly three-fourths of six-year-olds determined sex on the basis of genitals (Katcher, 1955).

Early gender awareness (twenty-eight to seventy-four months) is also evident from a study where children were asked "Are you a boy or a girl?", "When you were a little baby were you a little boy or a little girl?" and "When you grow up, will you be a mommy or a daddy?" (These questions measure gender *stability*—the knowledge that boys become men and girls become women.) Children were also asked, "If you played with [something played with by the other sex], what would you be?" and "If you wore [other sex] clothes, what would you be?" (This is a measure of gender *constancy*—the knowledge that changing one's activity does not change one's sex.) The final question was, "If you *really* wanted to be [the other sex], *could* you be?"

Over 95 percent of the children labeled themselves correctly. Nearly

90 percent showed gender stability, and about two-thirds understood that they could not change sex (Eaton and Von Bargen, 1981).

Children have also been presented with nude dolls with anomalous sex characteristics, such as male genitals and female breasts, and either long or short hair. The children were age five and selected clothes and a name for the doll and stated whether the doll would grow up to be a mommy or a daddy. The doll's hair was the primary cue used by the children, followed by body type and *then* genital configuration. Only 24 of 144 children mentioned genitals as the basis on which they decided the doll's sex (Thompson and Bentler, 1971).

Children have also been asked if they could change genitals: "Could you sometime stop having *that* [pointing to a depiction of genitals on a child of the same sex] and get *that* instead?" *Gender* permanence preceded *genital* permanence. When younger children said that a boy can't become a girl, they did not base the belief on genital appearance (McConaghy, 1979).

Gender constancy may be relevant to whether a child models itself after other males or females. Thus, the extent to which a child has achieved gender constancy has been studied in relation to the extent to which he or she pays attention to a filmed depiction of an adult male or female. The adults were shown concurrently and were engaged in "absorbing" activities such as popping corn, drinking, or building a fire. Boys with high gender constancy spent more time watching the male. In fact, gender constancy was a better predictor than the age of the child for same-sex watching (Slaby and Frey, 1975).

A last note. Children show more gender constancy with respect to themselves than to other children (Marcus and Overton, 1978). Thus, the age at which full gender constancy is reported in these laboratory studies may be later than that which is clinically relevant. The age at which a boy knows he is a boy, will remain male, and why, becomes more than an academic exercise, as seen in chapters 1 and 5.

THEORIES OF PSYCHOSEXUAL DEVELOPMENT

Henry Biller has aptly condensed several theories of masculine sex-role development:

Freudian theory stresses that identification occurs because the father is perceived as punitive and threatening (Fenichel, 1945). Status-envy theory emphasizes that the father needs to be perceived as the primary consumer of resources (Burton and Whiting, 1961). Learning theory underscores the importance of the father being affectionate and rewarding (Sears, 1957). Role theory stresses that the father should be a primary dispenser of both rewards and punishments (Parsons, 1955). Social power theories suggest that the model most likely to be imitated is the person who controls valued resources (Mussen and Distler, 1959). (Biller, 1981, 320)

Two types of learning pervade these theories—imitative and vicarious. In imitative learning, behaviors are adopted that simulate those of another person (the model) (Mowrer, 1950). In vicarious learning, something happens to a model, and the viewer's behavior is subsequently modified to resemble the model's (Kagan, 1958).

Why should the child modify its behaviors? Theory holds that the child perceives the model as possessing attributes or being able to obtain goals the child wants. The wish to obtain these goals makes the child want to be like the model because the child believes that similarity to the model will help it obtain the goals.*

Maccoby and Jacklin's comprehensive review of social learning theory as applied to sex differences (1974) found no strong evidence for the role of imitation in the learning of sex-"appropriate" behaviors. But in an effort to retrieve this theory from the ashes, two other researchers (Perry and Bussey, 1979) conducted studies that supported same-sex imitation as a mechanism of sex-role development. They argued that most research in the 1974 review studied the extent to which children imitate the behaviors of a same- or other-sex adult, usually a stranger, who performed a behavior once. This, they assert, is not the real world in which the child develops. What really happens is that children observe many adult males and females and note the frequency with which they perform certain behaviors.

To test this, two studies were carried out with eight- to nine-year-olds. Male and female adult models made selections that were not traditionally masculine or feminine. From some choices all the male models made one selection, from some choices a majority of males made that selection, and from other choices men and women selected equally. Children then made their selections. The striking finding was that the choices made by the children were in direct relation to the extent to which adults of the same gender made these choices.

In the second study children had the opportunity to make new selections after seeing selections made by the "minority" male or female model (that is, the only model of a given sex to make a selection preferred by three models of the other sex). Girls were more likely to imitate the minority male who had made a choice like females, but boys were not more likely to imitate the minority female who behaved like a male. "Boys may ignore rather than imitate females who behave masculinely" (1707).

A clinically relevant study looked at parental imitation by three- to five-

---

*I vividly recall being asked, as a boy, whenever I was reluctant to eat my bland breakfast cereal, "Don't you want to grow up to be tall like your cousin Bobby?" (who was well over six feet). Consequently, I ate all my cereal and grew to be five feet nine inches.

year-olds who came from mother-dominant or father-dominant homes. Children were also grouped by whether the parents were high or low on warmth and marital conflict. Criteria for these parental qualities were based on reading hypothetical problem situations involving children to parents and then asking them to resolve differences in child management. A typical problem situation: "A neighbor calls up and complains that your son/daughter has been throwing rocks at her child. What do you do?" Parental dominance was determined by noting who speaks first, last, or passively accepts a spouse's solution, and the degree to which a parent moves from his or her initial position. Measures of parental conflict included disagreements, interruptions, and failures to agree. Ratings of warmth versus hostility were determined by the extent of nurturant and affectionate responses a parent made about the child.

Children were then given a parent imitation task. They watched each parent alternately perform a series of activities, such as golf putting and shooting rubber darts at a target. Behavioral patterns that might be imitated included squatting and lining up the golf shots and shooting with two hands in the dart game. The dominant parent was imitated more. Parental warmth was also associated with more imitation (Hetherington and Frankie, 1967). Hetherington and Duer later warned: "If inversions of the parental power relationship occur in such a manner that the mother exerts more control in decision making and disciplinary functions, considerable disruption in sex typing occurs" (1971, 235).

The cognitive developmental theory of Lawrence Kohlberg (1966) is an alternative view of the development of sexual identity. Of critical distinction here is which is chicken and which is egg. While social learning theorists see children as developing sex-typed behaviors because parents reward them for these behaviors and punish cross-sex behaviors (for example, Mischel, 1966), Kohlberg argues that the child first labels itself male or female, then finds the behaviors associated with that label to be rewarding.

The social-interactionist perspective is an attempt to merge social learning and cognitive developmental models. Biological sex differences are seen not as directly influencing sex-role development but rather as operating indirectly, as a result of typical social reactions to such differences. Here, "gender development is not explicable solely in terms of patterns of reinforcement...the unfolding of an innate cognitive program...or a biographic drama resulting from universalist reactions to anatomical characteristics" (Cahill, 1983, 9-10).

The potential significance of the child's appearance and the impression of others that a boy is a girl is underscored in this last perspective. "Research attention [should] be focused on others' sex labeling of children, especially during the first two years of life. Observation of others' use of sex-designating terms to refer to children in naturally occurring interactions would be particularly useful" (12). Our research finding that "feminine" boys were seen as more "beautiful" infants confirms this thesis (see chapter 3).

STUDIES OF HERMAPHRODITIC CHILDREN

Hermaphroditic infants are born with characteristics that are not consistently male or female. For example, their genitalia may appear ambiguous or intersexed; or their genitalia may appear normally male or female, but their internal sex structures are like that of the other sex. As "experiments of nature," these children are of particular interest for the study of sexual identity development. They permit an examination of the relative influences of sex hormones, male or female gonads, genital appearance, and sex-role socialization.

An early study of the sexual psychology of hermaphrodites was conducted in 1945 by Albert Ellis. His article summarized findings on over eighty hermaphrodites (or "pseudohermaphrodites," as they were known), published as early as 1767. Only postpubertal cases were reported, so that sexual partner preference could be assessed.

In the great majority of cases, the individual adopted the gender-role in which it had been socialized (its "masculine or feminine upbringing") and not the role consistent "with his or her internal and external somatic characteristics." In most cases these hermaphrodites were erotically attracted to persons of the sex "opposite" that in which they were reared (in other words, they behaved heterosexually). Ellis concluded: "Physiological factors are not decisive in determining the masculinity or femininity of pseudohermaphrodites."

Seven years later, John Money reviewed the literature describing over 250 cases of hermaphroditism (Money, 1952), and three years after that copublished with John and Joan Hampson the studies of over a hundred hermaphrodites at The Johns Hopkins Hospital (Money, Hampson, and Hampson, 1955). The findings of these investigators were similar to the conclusions of Ellis: "Thus, it appears legitimate once again, to conclude that there is a very close relationship between the sex of assignment and rearing and the establishment of a masculine or feminine gender role and psychosexual orientation" (Hampson and Hampson, 1961, 1413).

In the Johns Hopkins studies, the hermaphroditic person's gonads, sex chromosomes, sex hormones, internal sex organs, and external genitalia were considered, in turn, in relation to the sex in which the child was reared. "In only seven of the cases . . . was there any inconsistency between the sex of rearing and [the] gender role [developed], despite other incongruities between these and other [somatic] variables of sex" (1413).

These studies suggested a critical early period in sexual identity development, during which the person's basic concept as male or female (component one of sexual identity) was established. This thesis derived from the study of twelve patients whose sex designation was changed from the original one given at birth. The degree to which these persons were able to adjust psychologically to the new sex role was related to their age at sex reassignment. Of the five children who were one year or younger at reassignment, four were later judged to have made a "healthy adjustment" and the other a "mildly non-healthy adjustment." Of the four children who were one to four years old at reassignment, only one was later judged to have made a "healthy adjustment," while three were "mildly unhealthy." Finally, three reassigned after age four were "moderately non-healthy."

Based on these studies, the medical wisdom became that nurture could overrule nature in the sexual identity development of intersexed infants and that a clear designation of the infant as male or female should be made in the first two years, since efforts to reassign sex after that were hazardous.

The chorus supporting this dictum was not entirely harmonious, however. Critics offered alternate interpretations of some clinical cases (Zuger, 1970), and some cases were reported in which reassignment succeeded during adolescence (Norris and Keetel, 1962). On the other hand, some writers who held to the early critical period dictum argued that these cases of successful reassignment later in life were persons who had not been reared unambiguously as male or female and so had developed a hermaphroditic identity, permitting the later change (Stoller, 1968). However, there was also the case of an apparent triumph of nature over nurture where a child appeared to be a normal female at birth, was reared as a girl, developed a masculine identity during childhood, and then physically masculinized at puberty. The previously cryptic intersexed condition had emerged, with the later anatomy confirming the earlier identity (reported by Stoller, 1968).

A fundamental criticism of the research on hermaphrodites challenged the hermaphrodite model itself as unrepresentative of the process of sexual identity development in normal children (Diamond, 1965). Diamond argued that by the very nature of their intersexed state, these persons are more malleable and can therefore develop masculine or feminine identity on the basis of their pattern of socialization. This flexibility, it was argued, is not present in normal children.

The type of clinical case that could adequately weigh the influences of nurture and nature would be a person who had a normal prenatal development (and therefore was not born intersexed) but who was then reared as an opposite-sex child. The "ideal test case" emerged from a tragic situation when one of a pair of genetically identical (monozygotic) male twins lost his penis through a circumcision accident at seven months. Because of the difficulty in reconstructing a penis, this twin was reassigned as a girl at seventeen months. Since the noninjured male twin is genetically comparable, the critical distinction here is nurture, the sex-role socialization of the twin reared as a girl.

When the reassigned twin was four-and-a-half, the mother described her in this way: "One thing that really amazes me is that she is so feminine. I've never seen a little girl so neat and tidy.... She is very proud of herself, when she puts on a new dress, or I set her hair." (Money and Ehrhardt, 1972, 119-20).

For years, this case, without additional follow-up, was hailed as the ultimate demonstration of the triumph of nurture over nature in the development of sexual identity. However, a documentary broadcast in Great Britain by the BBC cast serious doubt on the success of this sex reassignment. According to the BBC (Williams and Smith, 1980), "psychiatrists familiar with the case" in 1979, when the twins were young adolescents, claimed that "the [reassigned] child . . . has a very masculine gait, . . . looks quite masculine and is being teased. . . . They . . . call her cavewoman. . . . At the present time she does display certain features which make me suspicious that she will ever make the adjustment as a woman" (reported by Diamond, 1982, 183-84).

On the other hand, a compelling argument for the overriding influence of nurture over nature derives from cases of matched pairs of hermaphrodites (Money and Ehrhardt, 1972). Here, two children with a comparable degree of ambiguous intersex are assigned different sexes. For example, two persons are born with the female sex chromosome pattern and ovaries, but, owing to excessive prenatal androgen (male hormone) exposure, have ambiguous external genitalia. One is designated male, the other female. Years later, the infant assigned as female has adopted a female sexual identity (which is not surprising, since she has most of the physiological attributes of normal females). However, the comparably female twin, raised as a male, has adopted a male identity.

Returning once more to the "other hand," arguing now for an innate predisposition overriding socialization, we have the report of the rare "penis-at-twelve" people who live in the Dominican Republic. Such children are born looking essentially like females, are reared as girls, and experience extensive body masculinization at puberty, including the growth of a penis. Over a period of a few years they also metamorphose their sexual identity to male, masculine, and heterosexual (being erotically attracted to normal females). The reason for their anatomical "femaleness" at birth and the subsequent change to "maleness" is that, although they have testes (within the abdomen at birth), they have a deficiency in the production of one male hormone. This missing hormone is needed to masculinize before birth, but not at puberty. The investigators who reported these cases argue that these persons, reared as girls, show a male sexual identity in adolescence because the male pattern was "organized" in the brain by male hormones present before birth, an "organization" that was then "activated" by those male hormones during adolescence (Imperato-McGinley et al., 1979).

This argument is strongest for the first generations in which this condition occurred. Since then, children who will undergo masculinization at puberty are recognized by a subtle genital distinction at birth and are labeled "penis-at-twelve." Thus, later generations are hardly being reared as normal girls. Additionally, a socialization explanation can account for the apparent alteration in sexual identity in *all* the generations. Here we invoke the concept of "cognitive dissonance" (Festinger, 1957), or "making the best of a bad thing." In a society where males are considered superior and homosexuality is condemned, a "young woman" whose body takes on the appearance of a "young man" may find it far easier to adapt to social conditions by living as a man and marrying a woman rather than insisting that, in spite of a male appearance, she is actually a woman and "her" romantic affiliation with a male, although appearing to be between two males, is really heterosexual.

Since this hermaphroditic puzzle from the Dominican Republic was reported, another hormonal defect has been found, this time among Arabs in Israel, where children reared as girls also "transform" to men during adolescence (Rosler and Kohn, 1983). The chemical defect in these cases is similar to the case reported by Stoller, described earlier.

But this series, too, is open to alternate interpretations. The affected persons are from an inbred family going back eight generations, and while the young children appear to be girls, their genitalia are not entirely normal but rather show "moderate degrees of ambiguity." Thus here too there may be some clue that these are children for whom puberty brings masculinization. And again, social mores may exert their force: "In the Arab society the preferred sex is male, and an inadequately functioning and/or sterile male is indeed preferable to a functional but sterile female" (Rosler and Kohn, 1983, 668). Finally, in spite of all these influences toward adapting to life as a male, about one-third of the individuals "continued in their female gender role."

In 1981, through the courtesy of Dr. Michael Besser in London, I interviewed three persons with the hormonal defect reported from the Dominican Republic, but who were born in southern Europe. They were reared as girls and stated that there was no knowledge in their communities that they were to experience anything unusual at puberty. However, the three reported feeling that they were boys "as far back" as they could remember. At puberty, the body of each masculinized. Subsequently, they came to England and commenced living as men.

How best to explain these three cases? Their statements about childhood sexual identity are reminiscent of those given by transsexuals (see chapter 1), and their hormonal defect could be coincidental. There is no reason to believe that persons with a hormonal defect should be immune to transsexualism developing from a purely psychosocial factor. Moreover,

I do not know whether their reports of early cross-sex identity are valid or are merely reconstructions of the past to fit the present. However, taken together with the previously described series, these interviews impressed me with the extent to which a critical mass of data is gathering that suggests a strong hormonal force influencing (at least these persons') sexual identity.

A last note about the anatomically intersexed. The studies summarized above have looked at a gross measure of sexual identity (the self-concept of being a male or female, component one of sexual identity). Subtle influences of prenatal levels of sex hormone on gender-role behaviors ("masculinity" and "femininity" [component two]) have also been shown, notably in females with excessive male hormone production before birth. These are girls with the virilizing adrenogenital syndrome (Bongiovanni and Root, 1963), who provide an excellent opportunity for study because they can be compared behaviorally with their sisters (Ehrhardt and Baker, 1974), who usually did not have excessive male hormone exposure (the illness generally afflicts one child per family).

During childhood, the girls exposed to male hormones, compared to their sisters, show considerably more interest in rough-and-tumble play and much less interest in infant care and its surrogate, doll play. Thus, while the exposed girls' behaviors remain within the range of a normal female sexual identity, some features of their gender-role behavior differ notably from that of their sisters.

Gender-role behaviors also discriminate the two groups of boys in our study. One of our groups was also less engaged in rough-and-tumble play and more engaged in doll play. This suggests the possibility of an innate contribution to some early sex-typed behaviors in our groups, behaviors that may influence the larger picture of sexual identity.

CROSS-CULTURAL EVIDENCE

Here the measures of sexual identity are cultural customs, such as pubertal initiation rites or the practice of couvade. Pubertal initiation rites may include genital mutilation or other sex-linked rituals and are seen as ensuring transition to masculine status when there has been early sex-role conflict. In couvade, husbands whose wives are undergoing childbirth take to bed during the wife's labor and experience severe abdominal pains. This is seen as reflecting a pervasive, but less conflicted, female identity.

Extensive early mother-son contact, in the absence of father-son contact, with the young child living in a female-dominant home, should lead to "unconflicted femininity." A less consistent "feminine" pattern of socialization should lead to a conflicted identity.

If the interpretation of the two tribal customs is valid, the theory is confirmed. When sons slept with their mothers for the first two years and lived in the residence of the mother's family (a pattern seen as consistently promoting "feminization"), they practiced couvade as adults. However, when male infants slept with their mother for the first two years but lived in the house of the father's family (a pattern seen as initially feminizing and later masculinizing) they later resolved that conflict with a pubertal initiation rite. Exclusive mother-son co-sleeping during the first two years appeared sufficient to establish a primary feminine identification in the male (Whiting et al., 1958).

While provocative, these cross-cultural studies would be more relevant to our research if the person's sexual identity was individually assessed rather than universally assumed by cultural practice, where one style suits all.

CONCLUSION

Sex differences in children's identity, behaviors, and attitudes emerge early. So do the different ways in which mothers, fathers, and peers interact with boys and girls. For the question of which comes first, these studies, if they do not provide the answer, can at least furnish the backdrop against which to evaluate two strikingly divergent patterns of boys' sexual identity development.

3

Parents and Sons

THE WORK OF OTHERS

Mothers and Sons

Mothers bear a paradoxical burden. They must be "good enough" (Winnicott, 1958; Shields, 1964), but not "too good." Like fathers, they should not be remote. But unlike fathers, their involvement and investment with sons must be only temperate. It must be finely tuned to provide the son with security and emotional warmth. There must be just enough of mother to round off the hard edges carved by father; she must not smother, stifle, or feminize.

Boys bear a distinct burden from their mothers. As a boy's first "love," the first person with whom he "identifies," the mother must be snipped away at just the right time so that he can "dis-identify" from her (Greenson, 1968).

Psychoanalytic Theories

Psychoanalytic theories of sexual identity development derive from the writings of Sigmund Freud. Freud's training in biology and his knowledge that before birth all mammals have primordial male and female anatomic structures led him to postulate a similar psychic bisexuality. Whether the male or female psychologic components would assume ascendancy depended on the child's drives and ensuing experiences with parents.

Freud saw male and female children developing similarly for the first three years, through oral and then anal stages of development and up to the onset of the phallic stage (the names for these stages corresponding to the body zone to which the child primarily directs attention). By the end of the third year, significant differences in male-female development were considered to be unfolding. Crucial to this phase is the child's awareness of anatomic genital differences between males and females. For the male child, awareness of the existence of persons without a penis evokes "castration fear," the fear that something destructive can happen to a part of his body from which he derives considerable pleasure. For the female, awareness that males have something where she apparently has nothing arouses "penis envy."

Children of both sexes were believed to enter into a relationship of love and jealousy with their parents. For the boy, love for his mother is accompanied by the wish to replace his father. Fear that his father, who is also admired, will retaliate against this wish was seen as arousing anxiety that the punishment would be loss of the boy's penis. During this phase, which lasts from about age three-and-a-half to about age six, the boy ultimately reaches a compromise. He will behave as a male (like father) and will later seek out another female (perhaps like mother). On the other hand, the girl, blaming her mother for her lack of a penis, turns to her father as an object of love. Realizing the impossibility of her aspiration to replace her mother, she then identifies with her and will later seek out another more suitable male. These were believed to be the normal phases of psychosexual development.

Freud wrote:

The erotogenic zones are not all equally generous in yielding pleasure; it is therefore an important experience when the infant . . . discovers, in the course of feeling around, the specially excitable region afforded by his genitals and so finds his way from sucking to masturbation. . . .

If . . . a boy makes the discovery of the vagina from seeing his little sister or a girl playmate, he tries to begin with to disavow the evidence of his senses, for he cannot imagine a human creature like himself who is without his precious portion. . . . He comes under the sway of the castration complex. . . .

We call the mother the first *love*-object. . . . With this choice of the mother as love-object is connected . . . "the Oedipus complex." You all know the Greek legend of King Oedipus, who was destined by fate to kill his father and take his mother to wife. (1963, 314, 317, 330)

More contemporary psychoanalysts have underscored the period before the classic oedipal phase as crucial for distinguishing males and females. Herman Roiphe and Eleanor Galenson (1981) have observed one- and two-year-olds with their mothers and argue that the castration reaction is prior to the oedipal phase and is managed differently by boys and girls. Whereas boys attempt to deny the anatomical difference between the sexes, girls acknowledge it and become angry. These reactions occur during the second half of the second year. At that time, "the infant begins to take on a discernible sense of sexual identity" (Roiphe and Galenson, 1981, 2).

In an imaginative departure from the traditional concept of castration fear stressed by most psychoanalysts, Anita Bell asserts that one of the most significant anxiety-provoking experiences in a boy's first six years is his awareness of the quick, uncontrollable retractions of his testes. This experience evokes feelings of helplessness and passivity and moves him back toward an identification with the powerful mother. Blending social conditioning with this dynamic insight, Bell sees fathers who play ball games with their sons, whereby the boys learn to handle and control balls, as responding intuitively to their sons' need (Bell, in Clower, 1970).*

A few theories of the special role of the mother in disrupting the typical masculine maturational process of the son are noteworthy. In a chapter graphically titled "The Transsexual Boy: Mother's Feminized Phallus," Stoller found in the mother of a transsexual boy

an ecstatic acceptance [of her son] because this is her treasured phallus, an excessively close, blissful, and prolonged symbiosis, and a resultant profound disturbance in the infant's body ego, in that he feels himself to be somehow female despite knowing that he is male. These mothers do not do their part in getting their sons to separate from their bodies and do not encourage the boy's first moves toward masculine behavior (Stoller, 1976, 53).

Stoller's psychoanalytic study of the mother of a very feminine boy provided the thesis that "his marked femininity was caused primarily by his mother's wishes." A specific contribution

was her creating a merging of their identities so that each identified extensively with the other. There had been excessive sharing of each other's anatomy by identification, made possible by continuous skin contact all through the day. He had sat or lain enfolded in her body for much of the first year of his life. . . .

Another prime factor is a disturbance in gender identity, her bi-sexuality (here meaning a heavy proportion of sensed and observable thought, feelings, and behavior reflecting both masculine and feminine identification). . . . On the one hand, the boy was [the phallus] of her flesh; on the other, he was clearly a male and no longer of her flesh. *He was his mother's feminized phallus.* (1968, 110–12, 120)

To Stoller, the pretranssexual infant serves as a "transitional object" (Winnicott, 1953) for its mother, like the security blanket of Linus and a

---

*I recall remarking at the conference at which this insight was offered that castration in the nonpsychoanalytic world typically refers to removal of the testes, not the penis. However, my attempt to promote conceptual order went unrecorded in the published proceedings of that conference.

multitude of children. Her "continuous skin-to-skin contact" and her re-
fusal to "abandon him to frustration enhanced in him an overidentification
with his mother, a smudging of ego boundaries, and therefore of gender
identity" (1968, 124–25).

Psychoanalyst Charles Socarides, the inveterate treater of troubled
homosexuals (1968, 1978), writes:

> To the homosexual, the mother has, in infancy, been, on the one hand,
> dangerous and frightening, forcing separation, threatening the infant
> with loss of love and care; on the other hand, the mother's conscious
> and unconscious tendencies were felt in working against separation. . . .
>
> The homosexual not only loves his partner as he himself wished to
> be loved by the mother, but reacts to him with sadistic aggression as
> once experienced toward the hostile mother in forcing separation. . . .
> Homosexuality, therefore, can be seen as a resolution of the separation
> from the mother by running away from all women. (1968, 50)

Some of these theories are testable. Indeed, Stoller's theses regarding
the mother-son relationship and the mother's psychosexual background
have been put to the test throughout our long-term study. The findings
of some other writers are testable to a lesser extent and, when possible,
encompassed within our research design. By contrast, the next theory
defies scientific verification, if our definition of science includes objective
observation of data and prediction with testable hypotheses. However,
the theory, in part synthesized by Alan Beitel (1985), soothes those who
need to have a conceptual framework within which to "explain" the development of the diversities of human behavior, sexual or otherwise. Beitel
has undertaken the formidable task of applying the object relations theories of Otto Kernberg, Heinz Kohut, and others to cross-gender-role
development in males. The nonpsychoanalytic reader may have to reread
the next section a few times before the logic of the theory leaps from the
printed page.

First, consider Kernberg's division of the process of internalizing object
relations into four phases. Stage one occurs in the first to third months
of life. The infant lays down memory traces regarding its mother. Pleasurable traces are linked with one instinct, libido, unpleasurable ones with
the other instinct, aggression. In the second stage (two to five months),
good representations gather at one pole and bad ones at the other. However, there is still no separation between these experiences of the infant
and mother. In stage three (six to eight months), there is some differentiation between the infant and his mother, but the process of "splitting"
keeps separate the good and bad representations of the child, on the one
hand, and the good and bad representations of the mother, on the other.
In the fourth stage (beginning at twelve to eighteen months) there is a
joining of good and bad images, of either the child or the mother.

To Kernberg, if the child is endowed with excessive aggression or has experienced excessive frustration, good and bad images of the self and others are not integrated but, instead, remain split. Previously, Freud (1961) had discussed "splitting of the ego," the part of the mental apparatus that mediates between primitive drives and societal demands, in his writings on fetishism. To Freud, a male with considerable castration fear due to unresolved anxiety induced by his discovery of a person without a penis (his mother) would on the one hand (in one part of his ego) construct a woman with a penis, and on the other hand (in the other part of his ego) retain his unresolved anxiety. This mechanism is the basis of Otto Fenichel's later explanation of transvestism (1945), whereby the male, while cross-dressed, becomes the "phallic woman," thereby denying the existence of "castrated" persons. As the "phallic woman," he is relieved of castration anxiety and experiences erection.

To Kohut, these contradictory personality organizations may exist side by side through *disavowal*, a vertical splitting of the ego, rather than by the Freudian concept of repression (1971).

The next conceptual hurdle is extending these formulations to gender pathology.

> The split-off portion of the ego represents that portion of the ego where there exists a disturbance in core gender identity. The good self (child) and good object (mother) representations may be somewhat fused when the male has a substantial component of female identity. Although the central disturbance is one of self-esteem regulation, it becomes gender focused presumably because the perceived lack of expected acceptance and confirmation from the mother is identified by the boy as being the result of his maleness. . . . The child perceives that his mother wanted him to have been a girl. . . . The splitting that then occurs is the result of an attempt by the child to defend against the perceived rejection this awareness entails, through the development . . . of the illusion in the split-off ego that he is a girl. (Beitel, 1985)

In an alternative formulation, transsexuals and transvestites experience "unconscious merger fantasies with the mother" (Person and Ovesey, 1984). Here there is identification with the lost mother of infancy. By contrast, cross-dressing homosexuals are seen as seeking to become the mother, to take her place. In this theory the young male who will become a cross-dressing homosexual wants the mother's *power* rather than (like most boys) wanting *her*. However, he fears engulfment by her and so transfers his dependency and sexual needs to a male.

Mothers and Homosexual Sons

The theory that a too-close early mother-son relationship, coupled with a distant father-son relationship, yields a homosexual man is not recent. In 1910, Freud proclaimed in his creative reconstruction of the life of

Leonardo da Vinci: "His illegitimate birth deprived him of his father's influence until perhaps his fifth year, and left him open to the tender seductions of a mother whose only solace he was" (Freud, 1957, 131). Even though the validity of Freud's psychobiography of Leonardo has been challenged (Wohl and Trosman, 1955), the notion of the unbalanced triad endures.

In the Bieber group's study of homosexual versus heterosexual men in psychoanalytic therapy, two-thirds of the mothers of the homosexual men were described as "close-binding-intimate." The outstanding characteristic of these mothers was an "extraordinary intimacy" with the son. In many cases, the mother "exerted a binding influence on her son through preferential treatment and seductiveness on the one hand and inhibiting, over-controlling attitudes on the other. In many instances, the son was the most significant individual in her life" (Bieber et al., 1962, 47). Over four-fifths of these mothers reportedly favored their homosexual son over his siblings. Three-quarters reportedly "drew the son into an alliance against the fathers [and] openly preferred the son to the husband" (50).

The Saghir and Robins study (1973) (see chapter 1) found mothers of male homosexuals to be "possessive" and "overbearing." The mother of the homosexual was usually the closest to him in childhood, "physically and emotionally." She "discouraged his spontaneous 'boyish' activities and encouraged him instead to stay around the house and help with domestic work" (148).

On the basis of his clinical experience treating homosexual males, Lawrence Hatterer (1970) listed fifteen factors in the mother-son relationship that lead to homosexuality. Factors not generally cited by others include the son's repressed hostility toward or fear of his mother's "hypercritical, hostile, aggressive, emasculating demanding attitudes and behaviors"; transference of the mother's "passivity, anxiety, and fear of men, and/or hatred and distrust of other women to her son"; and the mother's "unconscious wish to act out her own homosexual tendencies through her son." Other factors include the mother's absence, lesbianism, bisexuality, or asexuality (35).

In the comparison of several hundred mainly nonpatient homosexual men with heterosexual men by Bell and his colleagues (see chapter 1), twice as many homosexuals reported having been "close" to their mothers while growing up. Twice as many homosexual men also felt their mothers had been "somewhat over-protective." There were no differences in reports of how hostile, rejecting, controlling, or detached their mothers had been. In the researchers' analysis of the data identifying childhood events that led to heterosexuality or homosexuality, all mother-son variables "washed out" early. One, "closeness to mother," survived but was the weakest of fifteen variables in the developmental model (Bell et al., 1981).

Finally, while male homosexuals more often recalled negative relationships with their fathers than did heterosexuals in a study of 167 British men, they did not more often recall affectionate relations with their mothers. In fact, more homosexual men recalled hostile feelings coming from their mothers (Bene, 1965).

Fathers and Sons

Even though Freud wrote in 1910 that "the presence of a strong father would ensure that the son made the correct decision in his choice of object, namely someone of the opposite sex" (1957, 99), mothers occupied, indeed preoccupied, the clinical quest of psychoanalysts. The reluctance to study fathers directly in the psychosexual development of children was revealed with remarkable candor in a 1969 study by Pedersen and Robson: "It causes me [sic] great embarrassment to report that the actual data on father participation were secured by interviewing the mothers. Perhaps we did not have the courage of our convictions to do a proper observational study or reorient our work schedules to coincide with the availability of fathers" (467–68).

But fathers are making a big comeback. Two book-length reviews, edited by Michael Lamb in 1976 and revised in 1981, bear witness to major research energies being devoted to understanding the father-son relationship. And the title of a text by Henry Biller, *Paternal Deprivation*, adapted a term traditionally applied to the deficient mother-son relationship. Husbands are being brought from the bedroom into the living room, where they become fathers. It is increasingly clear that they have considerable impact on the sexual identity development of both sons and daughters.

Psychoanalytic Theories

Dorothy Burlingham, Anna Freud's long-term friend and professional colleague, observed: "In psychoanalytic writings, the preoedipal father is accorded a minor role. . . . Nevertheless, long before the child has reached the Oedipal stage, much has gone on between fathers and their infants" (1973, 24–25).

Sigmund Freud wrote in 1921 of the role of the preoedipal father: "A little boy will exhibit a special interest in his father, he would like to grow like him and be like him, and take his place everywhere. We may say simply that he takes his father as his ideal. . . . It fits very well with the Oedipus complex, for which it helps prepare the way" (Freud, 1955, 105).

Observations of fatherless children by Anna Freud and Dorothy Burlingham in 1943 and 1944 revealed intense attachments to a fantasied father whom children constructed from meager or nonexistent relationships (Freud and Burlingham, 1944).

It is the second year that looms as critical for the father-son relationship in the observational studies of Roiphe and Galenson:

The importance of paternal availability and support for the boy's growing sense of his male sexual identity during the second part of his second year of life cannot be too strongly stressed. We believe it is a crucial factor in providing the boy with confirmation of his own phallic body image and allows him to eventually acknowledge the absence of a penis in his mother.... The father's interest in the boy's urinary progress and technique (the standing posture) [is] an important aspect of their mutual involvement. (1981, 273–74)

In psychoanalytic oedipal theory, the father must be a dominant force within the home if the young boy (about eighteen months old) is to identify with him. Otherwise, the mother's dominance will prevent the father from actively loving and possessing her (Abelin, 1978). Without a powerful "rival," the boy will not identify with the father in his wish for the mother.

Stoller described the father's atypical role in families with "very feminine" boys: "The Oedipal situation in the families of these boys is unusual. Father absents himself from home, avoids emotional involvement with his wife or the patient, and does not present himself as a rival for mother's affection or as a model for masculine identification" (1976, 95).

The Sexual Identity Development of Sons

Like father, like son. Why? There is no consensus regarding the mechanism(s) whereby sons utilize fathers as they evolve masculine behaviors. As summarized in chapter 2, social learning theorists or the punish-and-reward school believe that sons imitate fathers because they are rewarded for doing so (Mischel, 1970). Alternatively, modeling may occur through vicarious learning, in the absence of direct reward to the son for identifying with or imitating the father (Bandura, 1962). The model's qualities are deemed critical in determining whether imitation or identification (a less conscious adoption of another's qualities than imitation) will occur. Among other attributes, models who are "nurturant" or who resemble the modeler are more likely to be modeled (Kagan, 1958).

If these theories are valid, boys with a strong masculine identification and those who are less masculine should see their fathers in a different light. A test of these theories by Parsons and Bayles (1955) asked whether fathers are seen by highly masculine boys as nurturant and rewarding (consistent with the developmental identification hypothesis [Mussen and Distler 1959]), as punitive and threatening (the defensive identification hypothesis [Freud, 1963]), or as a powerful agent of both reward and punishment (the role-theory hypothesis).

The It-Scale for Children (see chapter 6) was given to five-year-old boys as a measure of "masculinity," and the boys completed stories about parent-child relations by utilizing dolls. The most masculine appearing boys perceived their fathers as both rewarding and nurturant. They also rated their fathers as more powerful. Thus, the prevailing hypothesis here was role theory.

But studies like this do not tap the essence of the father-son relationship in the context of daily life. Moment-to-moment details of the father-son experience are often overlooked. As one example, the manner in which children respond to fathers' return from work may be representative of the father-son and mother-father relationships. First, how is anticipation of the father's return typically shaped during the day? Is it, "Wait until Daddy gets home, you'll get yours!" or "Here I am working my fingers to the bone in a hot kitchen while your father sits in an air-conditioned office" or "Won't it be nice when Daddy comes home so you can both go out and play a while before dinner?" Second, what happens when Daddy does return? How is he greeted? Does mother interrupt her activity to meet him at the door and impart some physical gesture of welcome? Do the children interrupt their play or television viewing? What is the correlation between the mother's response and the children's? Consider this excerpt from our group of "feminine" boys (R.G. represents the author):

MOTHER: He will come home. He's tired. I'm pissed off because I've had the three kids all day, and for him the day starts very early and he gets home and he's tired. He walks in and he'll look at me and he'll say, "I don't want to hear it. I know what kind of day you had." I'll say, "But you listen to everybody else. You won't listen to me. Can't I tell you how rotten the day was?" No one ever says hello to my husband when he comes home. This bugs him. He'll say, "Hey, I'm home!"

FATHER: I read in books all these magnificent articles how the wife is supposed to act with the children—here comes Daddy—slippers and pipe, you know—warmth.

R. G.:   What happens when you come home?

FATHER: Nothing.

MOTHER: I yell and the kids just sit there. They don't know he's alive, so he says, "Did you clean your room?" They say, "No." He yells, "Get in there and clean it now." They yell, "I hate you."

Clearly, both the quality and the quantity of the father-son experience must be appraised. While it is true that most mothers spend more time with their children than do fathers, children also respond to novelty. This we know from the "Sunday father/Santa Claus" experience where divorced fathers with visitation rights one day a week shower children with affection and privileges. The parent with minimal time packs in high-quality experiences that are far more positive than forced "nutritional" feeding, curbed television watching, or the overseeing of homework assignments. But at what point is the novelty of time spent with "good-time daddy" reduced by his minimal contact so much that he no longer has impact on modeling and identification?

Father Absence

Early father absence is often associated with less traditionally masculine behavior in sons. In one assessment, two groups of boys aged nine to twelve were compared, one-half of whom did not live with their father. For 50 percent of this group, the father had left before the boy's fifth birthday. There were no father substitutes and few male siblings (Hetherington, 1966).

The boys were rated for dependency, aggression, and physical contact with adults. Their recreational activities in the following categories were scored: those involving physical skill and contact (boxing, football), physical activities without contact (bowling, table tennis), nonphysical competitive games (Monopoly, cards), and nonphysical, noncompetitive activities (TV, reading). They were also given the It-Scale for Children as a psychological test of masculinity.

Boys separated from their fathers were more dependent on peers. Those separated before the fifth birthday were less aggressive, played in fewer physical games involving contact and in more nonphysical, noncompetitive activities, and scored as more "feminine" on the It-Scale than those separated later or not at all. These findings are consistent with our long-term study, where separation from the biological father during these years was significantly more common in the "feminine" boy group, a group with substantially lower rates of contact sports participation (see chapter 1) and significantly more "feminine" scores on the It-Scale (see chapter 6).

More support for the early influence of the father comes from the study of boys who entered an orphanage in their first six months and who were then raised entirely by women. These boys were compared with boys who went to live in a cottage with a married couple after five years in this setting. The boys were aged six to fourteen when evaluated. On testing with a doll-play procedure (a measure of aggression), and the Draw-A-Person test (see chapter 6), those who lived later with the couple scored as more masculine than those who had been brought up entirely by women. However, they scored as more feminine than boys raised by male-female couples from birth (Nash, 1965).

"Father-absent" boys are also "mother-present." Five-year-old boys, half of whom were father-absent for at least one year, were studied for sex-role development, with the focus on their mothers' attitudes toward sex-role behaviors. Mothers completed questionnaires regarding their encouragement of behaviors such as wrestling with another boy, playing in the mud, climbing a tree, and responding to being pushed by another boy. They also reported on the extent of availability of the boy's father.

To assess the boy's masculinity, the It-Scale was used, as was a game-preference task (baseball, basketball, etc. versus hop-scotch, jump rope, etc.) and a behavior rating (is active and energetic, leads other children, etc.). Father-present boys had more masculine It-Scale scores and game preferences. Boys separated two or more years from their fathers prior to age four had more feminine scores. For father-absent boys, maternal encouragement of masculine behaviors was positively related to masculine game preferences, but for father-present boys, there was no relationship between maternal attitude and the boys' scores. Thus, the mother-son relationship appears to be more salient to masculine development in one-parent families, and separation from the father before age four appears to depress traditionally masculine development (Biller, 1969).

Father absence during a specific developmental period, the extent of maternal encouragement of masculine behavior as perceived by the boy, and a boy's masculine self-concept have also been studied in a group of boys with an average age of fourteen. Sex-typed adjectives were checked off by the boys to indicate whether they thought the adjectives described their behaviors (adventuresome, gentle, independent, sensitive, etc.). Boys also rated their mothers' encouragement of aggressive behaviors (for example, "my mother tried to keep me from fighting") and independence (for example, "my mother always made sure she knew where I was"). Early father absence was defined as the father having left the home prior to the son's fifth birthday. For early-father-absent boys, perception of the mother as encouraging aggression was associated with a high masculine self-concept. However, there was no relationship between self-concept and maternal attitude for late-father-absent or father-present boys (Biller and Bahn, 1971).

The classic study of aggression, as measured by doll play, was conducted over thirty years ago by Pauline Sears (1951) with father-present and father-absent three- to five-year-olds. In the doll-play format there was a father, a mother, a boy, a girl, and a baby doll in a dollhouse. In a fantasy play situation, the extent and content of aggression were recorded. Boys attributed more aggression to each of the dolls than girls did. Boys directed more aggression to the father doll than to the mother doll, while girls directed the least aggression to the father doll. Styles of aggression also differed. Boys' aggression involved bodily injury, violence, and impulsivity. Girls' aggression was more often verbal disparagement or nonphysical punishment. Sex differences were appearing at age three, were more pronounced at age four, and were still greater at age five. Father-absent three-year-old boys were equal in aggression to girls, and father-absent four-year-old boys showed slightly more aggression than girls. Finally, at age five, father-absent boys were significantly more aggressive than girls. Father-absent boys did not show the girls' *patterns* of aggression, only a *delay in the appearance* of the "masculine" patterns.

With the father absent, a sibling's or surrogate father's influence on a child's sexual identity development should be greater. Four- to six-year-old boys whose biological fathers were absent, and who had older brothers but no sisters, were found to be more masculine on a doll-play measure and in an interview than father-absent boys with older sisters and no brothers. The presence of a father substitute living in the home had no effect on the extent of masculinity (Santrock, 1970).

Finally, Norwegian children aged eight to nine whose fathers were away at sea nine or more months a year were studied for their sex-role development. The boys showed compensatory masculinity—that is, they sometimes displayed an exaggerated masculinity and at other times behaved in a feminine manner (Lynn and Sawrey, 1959).

Fathers and Homosexual Sons

The strained relationship between fathers and homosexual sons has been reported by clinicians and researchers alike. In the widely cited psychoanalytic study coordinated by Irving Bieber, homosexual men in therapy described having detached or hostile fathers more often than did heterosexual men. Fewer of the homosexual men considered themselves to have been their father's favorite child (Bieber et al., 1962). In another comparison study, homosexual men less often reported feeling accepted by their father, more often reported spending little time with him, hating him, and less often accepted or respected him (Thompson et al., 1977).

While the Bieber group stressed the importance of the close-binding, intimate mother and the detached, hostile father as the parental configuration of the prehomosexual male, this combination was found for only 28 percent of the homosexual patients and was also found for 11 percent of the heterosexual patients (Bieber et al., 1962, 143). While this overlap weakens the significance of the finding, it must be added that two-thirds of the heterosexuals with this family pattern also had "homosexual problems."

An attempt to extend the Bieber group's findings to a different sample assessed men being separated from military service because of homosexual behavior. A questionnaire covered the items highlighted in the Bieber study, but here they were reported directly by the patient, not by the therapist as with the Bieber report. One control group consisted of heterosexual military men and a second was composed of heterosexual male college students (Snortum et al., 1969).

The greatest differences between the homosexual and control groups were on the following items: I never got along very well with my father, I was much closer to my mother than to my father, and when my parents fought I usually felt my mother was right (checked true by more homosexuals); my dad and I spent a lot of time together, my mother and dad were interested in the same things, and my mother and dad were happily married (checked false by more homosexuals).

Two other questionnaire studies were also adapted from the Bieber clinical study. In the first, with subjects of unstated psychiatric status, more homosexual men than heterosexual men recalled spending little time with their father, not being accepted by him, hating him, and having been afraid that they would be physically harmed by him (Evans, 1969). In the second study, young male homosexual activists were evaluated. In contrast to the Bieber sample, where 64 percent would have preferred being heterosexual, only 21 percent of this sample were discontent being homosexual. Whereas 40 percent of the Bieber sample had wanted to be female, this was true for only 10 percent here. Other findings were not as dissimilar to those of Bieber. More homosexuals than heterosexuals reported that their father had been absent, had not encouraged masculine behavior, and had been less dominant than their mother. Homosexuals reported more often than heterosexuals that their mother had encouraged "feminine" behaviors (Stephan, 1973).

The recalled father-son relationship also differed for homosexual and heterosexual men in the study of Saghir and Robins (1973). Over four-fifths of the homosexuals, but less than one-fifth of the heterosexuals, reported that their fathers were indifferent to them or uninvolved with them. In the Bell group's study of six hundred homosexual and three hundred heterosexual men, twice the percentage of heterosexual men gave positive descriptions of their fathers. About twice as many hetero-sexual as homosexual men thought they had been their fathers' favorite son. Furthermore, boys with a negative relationship with their fathers were more likely to have been "feminine" boys, and "feminine" boys were somewhat more likely to emerge as homosexual men (Bell et al., 1981).

A gnawing question in these studies is what percent of heterosexuals answer all items in the "homosexual direction" and what percent of ho-mosexuals answer all items in the "heterosexual direction." If *any* such subjects exist, we need to explain the development of people whose early life events lead to a "contradictory" sexual outcome.

OUR DATA

Extent of Boys' "Femininity"

Since a major research goal was correlating sons' "feminine" and "mas-culine" development with features of the parents, we needed a composite measure of boyhood "femininity." The extent of an individual boy's "fem-ininity" was assessed in two ways. The first method was to rate the tran-script of the initial family evaluation interview in which parents described their son's sex-typed behaviors. This rating will be referred to as a clinical global measure of the extent of "femininity."

The second method was with a discriminant function analysis. Here we isolated those characteristics of the "masculine" and "feminine" boy groups that best discriminated one from the other.* Our data for the discriminant analysis describing the boys derive from the two question-naires administered to each parent at the initial evaluation and from tape-recorded and transcribed interviews with the parents. There are sixteen variables related to cross-gender behavior, but ten are closely related to each other in that they overlap at least 10 percent in defining the groups. Thus, although the two groups differ significantly on all sixteen indicators, ten are so interrelated that they may be eliminated without sacrificing appreciable precision in defining the two groups.

Comparing the groups of boys, their greatest difference is in the amount of cross-dressing. Next is the "feminine" boys' disinclination to participate in rough-and-tumble play. Then are their statements of wishing to be girls, their disinclination to grow up to be like their fathers, their greater interest in the style and texture of women's clothes, and their preference for playing with dolls. On the basis of these six variables, all boys were correctly classified as members of the "feminine" or "masculine" group (table 3.1).

This rating of "feminine" versus "masculine" boys is made on the basis of a combination of the six variables. Their composite scores for the six behaviors reflect the degree of "feminine" behavior displayed by boys within each group. It weights more heavily those behaviors that more strongly differentiate the two groups of boys (Roberts et al., in preparation).

The correlation between these two methods of rating the extent of "femininity" of each boy was high ($r = .92, p = .001$).[†] These "femininity"

---

*Simply stated, in such an analysis one could begin (hypothetically) with one behavior (say, cross-dressing) and the frequency with which all the boys in both groups exhibit that behavior. We might find a frequency that correctly discrim-inates 80 percent of one group of boys from the other—that is, 80 percent of the "feminine boy" group cross-dresses once a week or more, and 80 percent of the "masculine boy" group cross-dresses less than once a week. Next, we could consider the extent to which all the boys play with dolls, in addition to the extent to which they cross-dress. With these two criteria, we might now correctly categorize 90 percent of all the boys into one or the other group. If we then consider the extent of each boy's female role-playing, along with cross-dressing and doll play, we may correctly discriminate 95 percent of all the boys. We would continue adding specific behaviors until our accuracy in classifying boys as "feminine" or "masculine" is no longer increased by the addition of another behavior, or until we achieve 100 percent correct classification.

[†]Before proceeding to the results, a note about p levels ($p = .001$) and r levels ($r = .92$). Nonstatisticians should know that p is statistical shorthand for the probability that a reported finding may have occurred by chance. The lower the p level, the less likely that the finding is a chance occurrence. Assume (hypothet-ically) that our interviews reveal that the "feminine" boys spent more hours per week watching television with their mothers than "masculine" boys did ($p = .01$). This p level indicates that with the method used for analyzing our data, the

TABLE 3.1. Discriminating Behavioral Variables: "Feminine" Boys versus "Masculine" Boys

Behavior	Standardized Coefficient
Cross-dressing	.59
Rough-and-tumble play	−.48
Wish to be a girl	.40
Desire to be like father	−.34
Attention to mother's fashion	.26
Female-type doll-play	.25

Note: All boys correctly classified by this discriminant analysis.

scores were then compared with various features of the parent-son relationship.

Mothers

Early Mother-Son Physical Contact and Mother-Son Shared Time

Interview items regarding the mother-son relationship in the son's first years tapped dimensions of mother-son physical contact and mother-son

---

probability that the finding is due to chance is .01, or 1 percent.

There are conventions for accepting certain probability levels as signifying a "real" or "statistically significant" finding. Generally, when p is .05 or less, a finding is considered statistically significant. When p is between .05 and .1 (that is, when the probability that the finding would have occurred by chance is between one in twenty and one in ten), it is customary to refer to such a relation as a *trend* (weaker than a finding). Behavioral scientists generally disregard possible differences when the p level is greater than .1. However, as patterns appear among the data, it is occasionally informative to look at larger p levels, as long as we appreciate the limitations involved. Such "weak trends" are rarely reported in this book. When they are, it is because I believe that they help to fill in small but informative parts of a statistical picture drawn primarily from stronger findings.

The correlation coefficient r is a measure of association between two variables. The range of r is between -1 and $+1$. When $r = +1$, knowing the value of one variable predicts the value of the other with complete accuracy. When $r = 0$, knowing the value of one variable tells nothing about the value of the other. When $r = -1$, there is a perfect negative association between the two. The value of r multiplied by itself reveals the extent to which the proportion of the variation of one variable can be explained by the other variable. Thus, when $r = .4$, 16 percent of the variation in variable 2 is accounted for by variable 1.

time. The transcribed responses of parents were rated as described in chapter 1.* Examples of interview questions and anchor points for rating interview segments follow.

MOTHER-SON PHYSICAL CONTACT—Year One

QUESTIONS

Was he breast-fed?

What would stop his crying?

What was his reaction to being held? Was he cuddly?

If he'd been crying and you picked him up, what would happen?

Could you estimate the number of hours a day you would hold him?

Would you rock him to sleep?

Would you carry him from room to room with you when you went about the house?

Would you sleep alongside him? How often? Beginning when? Through the end of the first year?

ANCHOR POINTS

Least Contact

1. Child was bottle-fed from birth because mother had an aversion to breast-feeding. Was usually not held when fed because bottle was propped. Child cried very little and would cease to cry when needs were met, that is, when fed and dry. The child didn't like being held and would push away; not at all cuddly. Was held only when fed or taken places and was not taken with the mother when she went about the house. The child was usually left in the crib or playpen. The child never slept alongside mother and was seldom rocked to sleep.

2. Child was bottle-fed after the mother unsuccessfully tried to breast-feed. The child was usually not held during bottle-feeding. The child cried very little and usually didn't like being held. The mother would hold the child to feed it or take it places but wouldn't take the child with her around the house very much. The child never slept alongside mother and was rocked to sleep only occasionally.

3. Child was breast-fed for the first couple of months and then switched to the bottle. The child would do an average amount of crying, sometimes not stopping unless held. The mother would hold the child to feed it and take it places. She would take the child with her about the house if she were going to be in one place for any length of time. The child might have slept alongside her once or twice a week. Cuddliness is rated about average.

*The average interrater reliability on the interview segments was $r = .7$.

4. Child was breast-fed for the first three or four months and then switched to bottle. The child was held during bottle-feeding and for other feeding. The child cried quite a bit, sometimes not stopping unless held. The mother would hold it frequently and take it about the house with her if she were going to be in one place for any length of time. The child was somewhat above average in cuddliness. The child would sleep alongside her occasionally and she would rock the child to sleep almost every night.

5. Child was breast-fed for the first six months and then switched to bottle for most feedings. The child was always held during bottle-feeding. It cried frequently and wouldn't stop unless held. The mother would hold the child much of the time and would almost always take it about the house with her. The child was very cuddly. It would sleep alongside her a few nights a week and she would rock it to sleep for most naps and every night.

Most
Contact

6. Child was exclusively breast-fed from birth to beyond six months, the mother feeling that this was the best, most natural approach. The child cried constantly and needed to be walked and held. It would start crying again if put down. It was a very cuddly baby, much more so than other children she had held. She took it everywhere. The child was held several hours every day and rocked to sleep for naps and at bedtime. The child frequently would sleep alongside the mother.

MOTHER-SON TIME AVAILABLE—Year One

QUESTIONS

How would you rate the amount of time you had available for him during his first year compared to your other children?

Was there any difference? If so, why?

What sort of things would you do together?

ANCHOR POINTS

Least
Time

1. Mother had very little time available for the child because she worked full-time or was absent from the home completely. The only things they had time for together were the necessary care and feeding when she was home.

2. Child spent part of every weekday with a baby-sitter and in addition was left with a sitter one or two nights a week when mother went out. However, the mother did have part of the day to spend with the child.

3. Child spent part of the day two or three times a week with a sitter while mother was out. The child also was left with a sitter two or three times a month in the evening when mother went out.

4. Most of the mother's time was spent with the child, but the child occasionally spent part of one or two days a week as well as occasional evenings with a sitter.

5. With the exception of going out in the evenings occasionally, the mother spent all of her time with her child. The child would go places with her during the day and would be present during her daily chores.

Most
Time

6. All of the mother's time was available for the child. Besides bathing, feeding, etc., she would spend much time holding, talking to, playing with, and going all places during her day with the child. She would not be away evenings or weekends.

Within the symphony of theories that too much mothering feminizes sons, our data strike a discordant note. In year one, there was no difference in reported time spent holding the infant. However, mothers of "feminine" boys reported having spent less time with their sons. Within the "feminine boy" families, there was no reported difference between the time spent holding the "feminine" boy and his "masculine" brother. While there was also no reported group difference for such mother-son physical contact in year two, mothers in the "feminine boy" group again reported spending less time with these sons than was reported by the mothers of "masculine" boys. When time spent with the "feminine" son was compared with time spent with "masculine" brothers, there was again no difference. However, for years three to five, mothers of "feminine" boys once again reported spending less time with "feminine" sons (table 3.2).

Reaction to Cross-gender Behaviors

The theories and studies in chapter 2 suggest that the manner in which parents initially respond to a male child's experimentation with traditionally female-type activities will influence the extent to which those activities are given value by the child. That value should influence the extent to which the behavior is repeated.

In our study, parental reactions to the emergence of "feminine" behaviors were assessed by rating transcribed tape-recorded replies to questions regarding parents' attitudes toward each cross-gender behavior. Parents were asked what they felt the behavior had initially meant and how they had reacted to it.

Some parents recalled first thinking that the behavior was "cute" or "funny," a reaction that was evident to the child. Such reactions were rated toward the positive end of the parent-response continuum. Other parents reported having ignored and not having interrupted the behavior. They considered it to be a "normal, passing phase." These reactions were rated "neutral." When such reactions persisted over the years, still without

TABLE 3.2. Mother-Son Shared Time: "Feminine Boy" versus "Masculine Boy" Families

Variable	"Feminine Boy" Families	t^*	df	p
Mother-Son Time, Year 1	Less	−2.26	104	.03
Mother-Son Time, Year 2	Less	−2.88	97	<.05
Mother-Son Time, Years 3–5	Less	−1.97	102	<.05

parental sanctions, the reaction was rated as mildly positive. The rationale here was that a child manifesting atypical behaviors over an extended period of time without parental interruption would tend to consider the parental response as somewhat accepting. When parents' initial reactions to cross-gender behaviors were attempts to divert the child's attention to another activity, or to tell the child directly not to perform the activity, they were rated toward the negative end of the continuum.

EXAMPLE OF POSITIVE, NEUTRAL, AND NEGATIVE MOTHER RESPONSES

POSITIVE

MOTHER: About two years ago I got his sister a complete Barbie set for Christmas, the dollhouse and the carrying case and everything, and this is the only time I had a real problem with him doing anything I considered socially unacceptable. He actually swiped Barbie clothes from the dime store for that doll. Boy, I really went into such a fit over that. I marched him into the store, and I embarrassed him in front of the manager and made him replace all of the items, and that was the only time that I have ever forbidden him from playing with dolls. It irked me so bad to think he would go to the extent of stealing. I said he would have to save his money and then he could buy clothes for the dolls!

NEUTRAL

MOTHER: Well, for a long time I just ignored—I mean, if he wanted to wear something, fine, it really didn't bother me, and then people—I

*The t-test is a statistical measure used here to determine the significance of the difference between two independent sample means. The abbreviation *df* (degrees of freedom) refers to the number of values, such as the number of observations, that are free to vary after certain restrictions are placed on the data. For example, if there is a fixed number of cases and two categories, df = 1, because knowing the number of cases in one category reveals the number in the other category.

didn't mind the stockings and I didn't want to stop him plus he was a little smaller then, but now he's grown taller and he really looks stupid to me when he puts on the slip and the dress, it really annoys me, and one time he was gonna put on the slip in front of some boys, it was like he really wanted to put it on then; these boys were eight or so, and I told him not to put it on, I said, "It isn't a good thing to do, especially when people come over."

NEGATIVE

R. G.:   Initially, how did you feel about the behavior?
MOTHER: Very upset.
R. G.:   Even at the beginning?
MOTHER: Even at the beginning. It was transitory upset at first, and then when it continued on a steady basis it began to be much more of a long-term fear that set in.
R. G.:   Did you convey at first your concern about the dressing up to him?
MOTHER: Yes. I reacted, overreacted is more the word, with sharp words mainly.

Parental responses in interviews were also rated for the extent to which they encouraged or discouraged traditionally "boyish" activities, such as sports, chasing, or playing tag, cops and robbers, etc. From these responses, along with responses to initial cross-gender behaviors, a rating scale was constructed utilizing responses to both sets of questions. Thus a parent supportive of "feminine" behavior and discouraging of "masculine" behavior would be at one end of the scale, a parent supportive of "feminine" behavior and neutral to "masculine" behavior would be next, etc.

Strong support was found for the thesis that parental reactions to a son's early gender-role behaviors are associated with the extent to which these behaviors are subsequently shown. The degree to which mothers in both groups were rated as supportive of the boy's early cross-gender behavior rather than his "masculine" behavior was highly correlated with the ratings of the extent of the boy's "femininity" ($r = .60$, $p < .001$).

The extent to which the mothers in both groups were rated as supportive of cross-gender behavior rather than same-gender behavior was also highly correlated with individual cross-gender behaviors. This was true for doll play, cross-dressing, female role-playing, interest in the mother's clothes and fashion, and drawing pictures with female rather than male subjects. By contrast, for the mother's support of "feminine" behaviors and the extent of the boy's interest in conventionally masculine behaviors, the correlation was negative (table 3.3).

The data may be analyzed in yet another way. Here we examine parental reports to the initial "feminine" behaviors only, within the "feminine boy" group. The argument for this approach is that there is too little

TABLE 3.3. Correlation between Mother's Support of Cross-gender Behavior and Specific Behaviors (All Families)

Behaviors	r	p
Doll-play	.37	<.001
Cross-dressing	.54	<.001
Female role-playing	.50	<.001
Interest in mother's fashion	.37	<.001
Females drawn	.48	<.001
Interest in conventionally masculine behavior	−.53	<.001

cross-gender behavior in the "masculine boy" group to combine the groups for a rating on the same dimension. When we inspect only the mothers of "feminine" boys for their initial reaction to their son's cross-gender behaviors in relation to the statistically derived measure of the son's "femininity," the correlation, while smaller, is still significant ($r = .26$, $p = .04$).

The different patterns by which parents socialize boys and girls were described in chapter 2. The mother's wish for a girl as the next child and therefore treating her son as though he were a girl is a venerable factor in theories of the development of homosexuality (for example, Hatterer, 1970, 35). Treating sons "as though they were daughters" usually entails dressing the boys in girls' clothes, keeing their hair long beyond the age of the traditional first haircut, and perhaps calling them by girls' names.

Comparing the full group of "feminine boy" parents and "masculine boy" parents, we find no difference in reports of wanting a son versus wanting a daughter, although examples of this cross-gender wish occurred, such as the mother of Reuben (see chapter 5), who said, "I used to dress him like a little girl. I wanted a girl so bad."

A mother's desire for a girl during pregnancy with a son was also not related to either rating of the extent of the son's "femininity." Nor was it related to several parameters of cross-gender behavior, including cross-dressing, female role-playing, or the gender of persons drawn in pictures. It was, however, related to the extent of his interest in her clothes and fashion ($r = .17$, $p = .05$) and to the extent of his play with dolls ($r = .25$, $p = .05$). There was no relation between her desire for a daughter and the extent of his participation in rough-and-tumble play.

Mothers' Psychosexual Development

Stoller's psychodynamic formulation of the development of boyhood "femininity" drew first on a remote relationship between the mother of the "feminine" boy and her own mother ("hated and unloving") (Stoller, 1969, 155). This early developmental deficit resulted in the mother's "incomplete femininity." That incompleteness could be partly compensated for by a son, as long as he was "feminine" and became her (phallic) "extension" (Stoller, 1968).

When the mothers of the boys in our study were interviewed about their childhood relationships with their mothers, this aspect of Stoller's thesis was supported. Mothers of "feminine" boys reported more distant relationships than did mothers of "masculine" boys ($t = 1.99$, $df\ 96$, $p = .05$). No differences were reported in the mothers' relationships to fathers.

Mothers of very "feminine" boys were also described by Stoller as having a unique "bisexuality" (more commonly termed *psychological androgyny*). In childhood, these women had a need to "compete as equals with males" and "to dress in males' clothes" (Stoller, 1969, 155). In our study, the mothers of the "feminine" boys did not report early girlhood sex-typed behaviors that were statistically different from those reported by the mothers of the "masculine" boys.

Another factor contributing to the development of boyhood "femininity" reported by Stoller was the mother's lack of enthusiasm for dating relationships and interpersonal sexual experience prior to marriage (Stoller, 1968, 1969). In our larger study there was some support for this earlier finding. There was a trend for the "feminine boy" mothers with a more distant relationship with their own mother to have less premarital dating and sexual experience ($r = .21$, $p < .1$). Mothers with less premarital dating and sexual experience also tended to have sons with higher ratings of "femininity" ($r = .17$, $p = .07$), when all the families were considered. (Within the "feminine boy" families only, the correlation was significant [$r = .33$, $p = .04$], whereas there was no relationship within the "masculine boy" families.) There was also a trend for mothers with less dating and premarital sexual experience to react more favorably to a son's early cross-gender behavior ($r = .18$, $p < .08$).

Fathers

Early Father-Son Shared Time

Interview items regarding the father-son relationship in the first years focused on the extent of time spent together. Questions and anchor points for rating interview segments follow.

FATHER-SON TIME—Year One or Year Two

QUESTIONS

To what extent were you able to spend time with your son during his first year?

What working hours did you have?

What time would you leave in the morning?

Return in the evening?

Was your son awake before you left in the morning?

Was he awake when you returned in the evening?

What working hours did you have on Saturday? On Sunday?

Did you go out of town overnight? How often?

Did you have a hobby? When would you devote time to it?

What sort of things would you and your son do together?

Compared to most fathers, how would you rate the amount of time you and your son were able to spend together?

INTERVIEW RATING ANCHOR POINTS

Most
Time

1. Father spent all his spare time with his child. He worked a regular nine-to-five day and saw his child in the mornings before leaving and in the evenings. He never had to work on the weekends or go out of town overnight. Whatever hobbies he had would not take him away from home. He spent a lot of time holding the child, feeding and bathing it, and taking it for walks. Compared to most fathers, he spent much more time with his child.

2. Father spent most of his spare time with his child. He worked regular hours and would see his child either before he left in the morning or in the evening when he came home. He might have had to work an occasional weekend. He might also spend a few hours a month in recreational activities away from home. He and the child would play together or go places together and he would often hold the child. He spent more time with his child than most fathers.

3. Father worked regular hours although he might have to work overtime and/or on weekends every two or three months. He very seldom had to be away overnight. The child was usually up when the father was home, although they were not necessarily doing things together. He had a few recreational activities that would take him away from home on weekends but spent a fair amount of time holding and talking to his child, perhaps feeding the child once in a while. He feels he spent about the same amount of time with his child as most fathers do.

4. Father usually worked regular hours but had to put in overtime and work on weekends once a month or so. He might have to be away overnight three or four times a year. Although the child was awake when he was around, the father didn't usually pay too much attention to it because he was more interested in other things. He would, however, occasionally enjoy holding the child, talking to it, and taking care of it. He spent a little less time with his child than most fathers.

5. Father worked long hours, having to work weekends and go out of town two or three times a month. He occasionally saw his child in the morning or evening. What free time he had was usually spent in recreational activities but he would sometimes talk to and play with his child or take the child for a walk. He spent moderately less time with his child than most fathers.

Least   6. Father was either absent from the home entirely or had long
Time   and unusual working hours so that he was seldom home when
                 the child was awake. He left in the morning before the child was
                 up and returned when the child was asleep. He was frequently
                 absent on weekends and overnight. For all practical purposes, he
                 had very little contact with his child. He spent much less time with
                 his child than most fathers.

A very weak trend emerged for fathers of "feminine" boys to report
having spent less time with their sons in the first year compared to fathers
of "masculine" boys. There was a significant difference in reported father-
son shared time in the second year, and the difference became greater in
years three to five. A difference is also found in comparing time spent
by the father with his "prefeminine" son in the son's second year and with
this son's "premasculine" brother in the brother's second year. Fathers
spent less time with the "prefeminine" son (table 3.4).

Less father-son shared time in the son's first year was associated with
more "femininity" in the son ($r = .20$, $p = .02$). This was also true for
the second year ($r = .21$, $p = .02$) and for years three to five ($r = .25$, $p
= .01$).

Less father-son contact in the early years in the "feminine boy" group
could reflect more separation of fathers of "feminine" boys from their
families, and not that fathers in intact families were spending less time.
However, less father-"feminine son" time was not merely a function of a
disrupted family. With families where the father left the home before the
boy's second birthday, there was a trend for the fathers of "feminine"
boys to have spent less time with these sons during year two. Then, for
the son's third to fifth years, there was substantially less time shared by
"absent" fathers and "feminine" sons compared with "absent" fathers and
"masculine" sons. Looking only at fathers still living in the boy's household, there was also less father-"feminine son" contact reported for years
three to five.

Specific "feminine" behaviors were also associated with less father-son
shared time. For all the families, less father-son time in year two was
associated with more female role-playing ($r = .35$, $p = .001$) and more
doll play ($r = .23$, $p = .01$). Within the "feminine boy" group only, the
association was also significant for doll play ($r = .23$, $p = .05$), but not
for female role-playing.

In families in which the father had moved away from the home prior
to the son's fifth birthday, the son was significantly more "feminine" ($\chi^2
= 7.0$, $p < .01$).* Comparing the extent of "femininity" for boys separated
from their father by age two with those separated during the third to
fifth years reveals no difference. Therefore, the significant component of
the association is whether the separation occurred before the fifth birthday, with no discrimination as to whether that separation occurred before
or after age two.

Adult male absence per se cannot be indicted here in the development

TABLE 3.4. Father-Son Shared Time: "Feminine Boy" versus "Masculine Boy" Families

Variable	"Feminine Boy" Families	t	df	p
Father-Son Time, Year 1	"Less"	1.25	107	.21
Father-Son Time, Year 2	Less	2.02	108	<.05
Father-Son Time, Years 3–5	Less	2.97	105	<.01
Father-Son Time, Current	"Less"	1.89	107	.06
Father-"Feminine Son" Time, Year 1, Compared to Time with "Masculine" Male Sibling, Year 1	"Less"	1.56	47	.12
Father-"Feminine Son" Time, Year 2, Compared to Time with "Masculine" Male Sibling, Year 2	Less	2.67	44	.01

of extensive cross-gender behavior. There was no difference in the percentage of boys in both groups with an adult male (eighteen or over) living in the household during the boy's first eleven years. Thus, the presence of the biological father appears especially significant.

The amount of time fathers reported having spent with their sons in the sons' first years is correlated with the extent to which the father reported having wanted a boy or a girl during the pregnancy. The more the father wanted a girl, the less time he spent with his young son (table 3.5).

Because fathers of "feminine" boys spent less time with their sons, and because the wish for a girl is associated with time spent with a son, it is not surprising that the father's desire for a girl was also somewhat asso-

*Chi-square (χ^2) is a test of statistical significance. It is used in determining whether a systematic relationship exists between two variables. The χ^2 compares the frequency with which the subjects (or phenomena) are distributed between the various categories of the two variables to the expected distributions if no relation existed between the variables. Therefore, if the discrepancy between the actual and the expected frequencies is small the value of χ^2 will be low and, conversely, if the discrepancy is great the value of χ^2 will be large. Probabilistically, we can then determine if the value of χ^2 is larger than we would expect to find based on chance.

TABLE 3.5. Correlation between Father-Son Shared Time and Father Wanting a Girl during the Pregnancy

	All Families		"Feminine Boy" Families	
	r	p	r	p
Year 1	−.19	.05	−.29	.05
Year 2	−.23	.02	−.32	.03
Years 3–5	−.13	.13	−.26	.07

TABLE 3.6. Correlation between Father's Desire for a Girl During the Pregnancy and Son's Gender-Role Behaviors

Behaviors	r	p
Female role-playing	.26	<.05
Females drawn	.35	<.05
Rough-and-tumble play and sports	−.22	<.05

ciated with the extent of the boy's "femininity" ($r = .25, p = .07$). However, when we compared the relative influence of the father's desire for a girl and of the time shared with his son in year two on the extent of the son's "femininity," using a multiple regression technique, the influence of time shared appeared to be greater. (The time variable remained significantly associated with the extent of "femininity," while the variable for the father's desire for a girl did not.)

Father's desire for a girl was also related to specific cross-gender behaviors. This is true for the son's female role-playing, and for the extent to which the son drew females rather than males in his pictures. Conversely, the father's wish for a girl is negatively associated with the son's participation in rough-and-tumble play and sports (table 3.6).

As with mothers, fathers' initial reactions to a son's gender-role behaviors were rated for approval or disapproval. Here is an example of a father's reaction that was rated positive:

R. G.: What have been the things that you have been most concerned about?

FATHER: My difference with my wife would be that I don't think he has a problem. On the other hand, I am away working most of the day and some of the things that my wife has picked up, I obviously haven't. On your previous questionnaire we were in disagreement on several points, but on the other hand, I do notice that his activities do center on preferring to play with girls, but there are just more girls to play with in our neighborhood too. Also, he uses cosmetics.

MOTHER: There are also a lot of boys too, dear. There are as many boys as girls, but he prefers girls.

TABLE 3.7. Correlation between Father's Support of Cross-gender Behavior and Specific Behaviors (All Families)

Behaviors	r	p
Female role-playing	.20	.03
Interest in mother's fashion	.21	<.02
Doll-play	.21	<.06
Females drawn	.34	<.01
Rough-and-tumble play	−.31	<.001

R. G.:   What's been your approach to the cosmetic use?

FATHER: Just so you don't make a mess in the bathroom. In the other house it wasn't particularly reachable because of the location of the cosmetics, and in this house the counters are lower and of course he can climb up on them and get into it. I offer no discouragement at all except don't spread it around the bathroom and make more of a mess.

The father's reaction to the son's early gender-role behaviors ("feminine" and "masculine") was also significantly correlated with the son's clinically derived global rating of "femininity." Fathers' more accepting attitude of cross-gender behaviors, as opposed to same-gender behaviors, was associated with a more "feminine" score ($r = .32$, $p < .001$). The correlation with the statistically derived extent of femininity variable was also significant ($r = .29$, $p < .01$). For the fathers of the "feminine" boys only, the correlation was not significant.*

Fathers' early reactions to cross-gender behaviors in general were also associated with specific cross-gender behaviors. This was true for female role-playing, for interest in mothers' clothes and fashions, for doll-play, and for the sex of persons drawn in pictures. The father's support of cross-gender behavior was negatively correlated with the extent of the son's participation in rough-and-tumble play (table 3.7).

Fathers' Psychosexual Development

Fathers who were less conventionally "masculine" during boyhood (less interested in rough-and-tumble play and sports) had a more positive reaction to sons' early expressions of "feminine" behavior compared to their reactions to sons' early "masculine" behavior ($r = .23$, $p = .03$).

*As noted regarding mothers' reactions to sons' behaviors, the responses of fathers in the contrast group to sons' cross-gender behaviors may be less relevant, since the "masculine" boys had fewer cross-gender behaviors. This argues for analyzing the groups separately. On the other hand, with a very restricted range of "feminine" behaviors in the "feminine boy" group (high for all boys) the correlation coefficient, requiring a range of the two variables being compared, may be an insensitive measure.

Mother-Father Relationship

The mother-father relationship is typically recalled as far less than idyllic by homosexual men. It has been characterized as frigid or cold rather than as warm, the characterization usually given by heterosexual men (Thompson et al., 1977) or more frequently as combatitive (Saghir and Robins, 1973).

Stoller described the marriages of his sample of very "feminine" boys as "unhappy ... with bouts of explosive rage, (and) marked sexual dissatisfactions" (1969, 164). In our study, the marital relationship in general, rated as positive or negative from interview descriptions of the good and bad things in the marriage, was not significantly different for the two groups of parents. (They had been matched for marital status at the time of evaluation.) Regarding the marital sexual adjustment, rated from interview descriptions of the frequency of and satisfaction with sexual relations, mothers of "feminine" boys tended to report a poorer adjustment than did mothers in the contrast group ($t = 1.78$, df 88, $p = .08$). Fathers reported no difference.

Traditional theories of how parents influence sons' sexuality, summarized in chapter 2, emphasize the importance of parental power for a child's identification (for example, Parsons, 1955). Our strategy was to compare husbands' and wives' methods of resolving conflicts, adapting a procedure described in chapter 2, to see if there was a difference in mother or father dominance in the "feminine boy" versus "masculine boy" families.

Parents were required to select independently, from a list of ten alternatives, their top three and bottom three choices on several hypothetical issues, such as what kind of restaurant to visit next, a new magazine subscription, which country to visit on holiday, etc. The mother and father were then brought together to reach a consensus on their top three and bottom three choices. The degree of shift made by each parent was recorded. After dozens of hours listening to parents quibble over these hypothetical momentous life decisions, a quick tabulation of the relative movement of mothers and fathers in both groups showed virtually no difference. A dead end on this developmental path.

According to Jerome Kagan's formulation of identification (1958), the parent who dominates as household decision maker should be the parent with "mastery" or control over the environment for things the child thinks are important, thereby promoting identification by the child with that parent. Thus, researchers comparing the family backgrounds of homosexual and heterosexual men have looked at mother-father role division. In one study, 60 percent of the fathers of homosexual men were described as having left decision making to their wives, compared with less than 40 percent of the fathers of heterosexual men (Saghir and Robins, 1973).

In our study of family role division, less than overwhelming support was found for the dominant mother/submissive father pair leading to

TABLE 3.8. "Feminine" versus "Masculine" Boys

Boyhood Variable	"Feminine" Boys	t	df	p
Seen as a "beautiful" infant	More	4.12	97	<.001
Other people comment: "He would make a beautiful girl."	More	1.76	105	.08
Weight	Lighter	1.83	108	.07
Age at first hospitalization	Younger	2.53	108	.01
Duration of hospitalization	Longer	2.55	110	.01

boyhood "femininity." For financial planning, there was no group difference. For child disciplining, there was no group difference. For planning family activities, "masculine boy" fathers more often took the initiative, as reported by fathers ($t = 2.26$, df 86, $p = .03$). For who generally wins arguments, there was no difference. Finally, for a global assessment of overall family "boss," while mothers reported no difference, fathers of "masculine" boys more often reported that they were boss ($t = 2.08$, df 86, $p = .04$).

Sons

The next variables, though primarily features of the son, would also be expected to influence strongly the behaviors of parents.

Beauty

Infants on their way to extensive boyhood "femininity" were reported by Stoller (1968) to be "beautiful" babies, at least as described by their parents. We therefore asked the parents in our study to describe the face of their infant son. The descriptions were tape-recorded, and then rated by persons who did not know whether the description they were reading emanated from parents of a "masculine" or "feminine" boy (as described in chapter 1). True to prediction, parents of "feminine" boys described their infant sons in terms rated significantly more "beautiful" and "feminine" (table 3.8).

With the family groups combined, the association between parental perception of the infant son's beauty and the son's later extent of "femininity" was significant ($r = .36$, $p < .001$). Within the "feminine boy" families only, the correlation, though tending in that direction, was not significant. Within the comparison group of families, the association was significant ($r = .36$, $p < .001$). (Again, the ceiling effect for the global "femininity" rating and the relative lack of variation in the "feminine boy" families may have seriously attenuated the correlation coefficient. Boys had higher "feminine" ratings in families where parents described sons as more "beautiful.")

When sons were described as more "beautiful," mothers were rated as reacting more positively to sons' early "feminine" behaviors as opposed to "masculine" behaviors ($r = .36, p < .001$). For fathers, the association, though weaker, was also significant ($r = .17, p < .05$).

The manner by which people outside the family react to the boy's appearance should also influence the boy's self-concept, and perhaps his parents' perception of him. Stoller described one reaction: "Since his infancy, strangers had stopped her on the street to comment on how remarkably pretty he was. In his first months of life, she was already thinking how beautiful he might be as a girl. . . . Observers of the research team who have seen the boy all agree that he is indeed a lovely-looking child, though no one shared his mother's feeling that he was like a beautiful girl" (1968, 177).

In our study, the statement, "He would make a beautiful girl" tended to be recalled more often as a reaction by adults other than the parents to the appearance of the behaviorally "feminine" boys (table 3.8). For example:

R. G.: How would you describe his face as a baby?

MOTHER: He had a beautiful face.

R. G.: Beautiful?

MOTHER: Yes, and curly hair, and people would say, "What a cute little girl you have."

R. G.: How about when he got older?

MOTHER: Now they do because of the hair.

R. G.: What do they say?

MOTHER: "What a pretty little girl you are." And he laughs.

Cuddliness

A son's reaction to being held should influence a parent's enthusiasm for holding. "Cuddly" versus "squirmy" infants should differentially reinforce parental holding. As a group, our "prefeminine boy" infants were not more often recalled as having been cuddly babies, relative to siblings or other children. However, individual examples did occur:

MOTHER: I would say that this son was held more by other people and myself. Because at that particular time it seems like we had more people that were coming by. When my other son was small, he was sort of a squirmy baby. He didn't like for anybody to hold him. He wouldn't cry but he would move constantly. I don't think people really like to hold a child unless they feel secure in holding him and he never really kept still for anybody.

Body Size and History of Illness

Conventional culture demands specific attributes of boys and girls. When self-image coincides with social expectations, the fit is easier. Two dimensions of self-image are height and weight relative to other boys of the same age. Frail boys might be more reluctant to engage in rough-and-tumble play or, once engaged, might be less adept. The "feminine" boys in our study were about five pounds lighter than the comparison group boys of the same age (table 3.8). However, they were not shorter.

Another dimension of self-image is healthy versus sickly. This, too, affects peer relations and activities. Boys who have a greater history of physical illness might be reluctant to engage in rough-and-tumble play. A history of hospitalization or major illness could also promote more parental protection of a son.

Our data provide support here. The "feminine" boys were more often hospitalized at a younger age, generally prior to their second birthday, and they stayed in the hospital longer than did hospitalized "masculine" boys (table 3.8). However, most boys in both groups were not hospitalized.

While early hospitalization rates differ for the two groups, there is only a trend for mothers of "feminine" boys to report having given more "special attention" to their sons for illness or injury in the first year, and no reported difference in the extent of their anxiety over the boys' welfare during that period. However, there was a trend in which more special attention from the mother was associated with a more positive maternal reaction to a son's early cross-gender behavior ($r = .16$, $p = .06$). And the extent to which sons were reported as requiring special attention in the first year was positively associated with their subsequent role-playing as a female ($r = .22$, $p = .03$) and negatively associated with the extent of their rough-and-tumble play ($r = -.20$, $p = .03$).

Parental Preference

Whether mother or father was preferred by the boy was highly correlated with the extent of his "femininity" ($r = .48$, $p < .001$), with more "feminine" boys preferring mother. Further, the extent to which the child watched his mother's application of cosmetics, in contrast to watching his father shave, was also highly correlated with the extent of his "femininity" ($r = .74$, $p < .001$).

These rawboned data outlining features of the mother-son and father-son experience are fleshed out in the next section, which consists of interview transcripts with parents and children.

INTERVIEWS

Our families have written these next sections. Sons recall their mothers and fathers from boyhood years. Mothers and fathers tell us, at the time their sons were first evaluated, about what was happening (and not happening) between parent and child.

Mother-Son

Each example begins with a central feature of the parent-son relationship and the son's sexual identity status as a boy and then during young adulthood. Examples are selected to illustrate diversity. In each example R. G. represents the author.

Example 1: Mother Cross-dresses Son and Treats Him as a Girl*

("FEMININE" BOY, HOMOSEXUAL MAN)

MOTHER'S REPORT AT INITIAL EVALUATION

MOTHER: When he was little I used to dress him. Maybe it was my fault. I don't know.

R. G.: Tell me about that.

MOTHER: He was very, very tiny at the time. I used to dress him like a little girl. I wanted a girl so bad.

R. G.: How would you dress him?

MOTHER: I would put little girls' clothing on him. (I would never take him out anywhere like that.) At the time I didn't think it would hurt him, because he was very tiny, only a couple of months old.

R. G.: What sorts of clothing would you put on him?

MOTHER: Little dresses, little hats, little slippers, a girl's blanket.

R. G.: How old was he when you first dressed him like that?

MOTHER: I guess till he was about nine months old.

R. G.: What made you stop dressing him as a girl?

MOTHER: I realized to myself that he wasn't a girl, that he was a boy, and I was supposed to dress him like a boy. So I stopped. I said to myself, "Why kid yourself? He isn't a girl. He's a boy."

R. G.: What was his reaction to being held as an infant?

MOTHER: Oh, he loved it. He was always smiling.

R. G.: Do you think he seemed to enjoy being held more or less or about the same as your other children?

MOTHER: More.

R. G.: Would you say you held him more, less, or about the same as your other boys?

MOTHER: More.

R. G.: Why do you suppose this was so?

MOTHER: Well, for one thing, they told me I couldn't have any more children, and I wanted to keep him a baby, and I still do, I guess, more of a baby than the others.

*Reported more extensively as "Reuben," chapter 5.

R. G.:   To what extent would you hold him when he was an infant?

MOTHER: Oh, a long, long time. Gee, most of the time I would spend holding him, because my other two—they were big already and they didn't need my attention that much, or they would go outside and play with my little sisters.

R. G.:   How would you rate the amount of time you had available for him in the first year compared to your other boys?

MOTHER: More.

R. G.:   Why was that?

MOTHER: He was a delicate baby. I watched over him constantly whatever he did—if he'd fall. My kids never had a scratch on them when they were little. I was always right after them, but with him it was more. I had more time with this one that I did with the other two.

R. G.:   Why?

MOTHER: Well, it's just that he's my last and I know he's not going to be little forever. I guess that's why I spend more time with him than I did with the other two. Of course, the other two I knew that someday there would be another one, but with this one, they told me right after he was born that I couldn't have another one, and I guess this is why I spend more time with him.

SON'S REPORT AT AGE NINETEEN

R. G.:   Do you know whether your mother wanted a boy or a girl when you were born?

SON: She wanted a girl, she told me that, so I said, "You kinda got one."

R. G.:   When did she tell you she wanted a girl?

SON: When I told her that I was gay.

R. G.:   She never told you that before?

SON: No.

R. G.:   What did she say?

SON: Well, when I told her, she started cryin' and she said, "I've been waiting for you to tell me for a long time." And she started cryin' and she goes, "Well, maybe it's my fault because I was frustrated, I was very lonely." She started cryin' and saying "It's my fault 'cause I always wanted a little girl so bad," and I said, "It's not."

Example 2: Mother Promoted Son's Interest in Fashion Design

("FEMININE" BOY, HOMOSEXUAL MAN)

SON'S REPORT AT AGE TWENTY

R. G.:   Do you think your mother should have objected more to your early feminine behavior?

SON: No, I really don't because my mother has always given me the opportunity to make up my own mind and she figures, "Well, if you

bump your head once you're gonna know not to go that way again."
She's kinda let me make up my own mind and make my own decisions,
even as a young child.

R. G.:   Do you remember your mom bringing you here the very first time?

SON: Yeah, I remember it.

R. G.:   Why did your mother bring you here?

SON: Because she thought that I was very unusual. I guess she just thought
that maybe she had done something that was wrong so she was going
to try and correct it. I was unusual, and I wasn't your typical little boy
you know, I had my own feelings.

R. G.:   Do you think she was worried about you?

SON: Yeah, definitely, but I think it was more of her conscience talking
than mine.

R. G.:   Did she try to change you after she brought you here? Did she try
to make you more masculine or discourage you from doing some of
the feminine things?

SON: I think there was a slight discouragement, but it didn't last for long
because I've always been that type of person that if I'm going to do
something and I want to do it, I'm going to do it.

R. G.:   How does your mom feel about your current plans to go into
fashion design?

SON: I asked her, "Mom, did you ever really think that years ago when
you gave me dolls and stuff to play with that I'd be a hair designer?"
and she said, "Yes, that's why I promoted it." She's known I've always
liked to dress up, even as a little kid when I would dress up in her
things, just releasing creative energy, actually. And she said, "I believe
you'll go far in fashion design." She loved what I had on for Christmas,
red and black with a big hat, she loved it, and she said, "Oh, you look
like you're coming from Europe."

R. G.:   So you think she feels that she helped promote your interests?

SON: Oh yes, there was some definite direction on her part at an early
age. I would say from the age of walking and talking, she's always sort
of pushed me in the direction that she thought I would be successful
or enjoy.

R. G.:   Why do you think she did that?

SON: Just because I feel that she'd want the best for me, she does want
the best for me.

R. G.:   Most mothers wouldn't push their sons in the direction of fashion
design.

SON: Well, I'm sure that she saw at a young age that I was semi-feminine,
I mean a little bit more feminine than most boys. And she wanted a
girl when she had me. When she was pregnant with me she was hoping
for a girl because she already had two boys, so I feel that she still had
fantasies of me being a girl after I was born. Maybe that had something
to do with her pushing me in that direction, but I told her at Christmas,

"I thank you mother, for not bringing me up in another environment and for subjecting me to the finer things in life."

Example 3: An Idolized Mother

("FEMININE" BOY, HOMOSEXUAL MAN)

SON'S RECOLLECTIONS AT AGE TWENTY-TWO

SON: The only woman that I've ever, I hate to say, been in love with, 'cause I don't know if its the right way to use it—I idolized my mother.

R. G.:   Tell me about that.

SON: She was just always there. Our family was always open and if we were running around naked it was no big deal. My mom was just always the prettiest lady and she was always on the go and she was always doing this, that, and the other. She was so business and she was so fashionable, I idolized my mother, I loved her. I do love her. But, I'd never want to have any physical contact with my mother.

R. G.:   You've never felt any sexual interest?

SON: No. Just out of what's going on inside of her head. She'd share all her thoughts with me. We used to talk about everything. We didn't hold back. My mother and I used to do drugs together. I'd come home and if we needed some pot I'd go get some pot from somebody. We weren't ever mother and son. It wasn't like mom and son it was like come on, sit down and let's gab. We were close at times, and then there were times where I'd tell her things because we had such a good relationship I just felt like I could tell her anything. I'd tell her I'd want to dress up as a woman. I'd have a chance to do a drag show or something and she just turned the disgusting knob on me, you know, "That's sick." My mother, she can't make up her mind.

R. G.:   Was she also positive about it sometimes?

SON: Yeah, that's what I never really understood. I mean it was like, "Hey it's okay," and then it's, "What are you doing? This isn't right."

R. G.:   When was she positive?

SON: I think mostly when she didn't have a husband. Anytime in our life when it was just me and mom everything was smooth sailing until somebody got into the picture, and then it was a total turn in personality.

Example 4: Mother's Son, Father's Daughter

("FEMININE" BOY, HOMOSEXUAL MAN)

MOTHER'S REPORT AT INITIAL EVALUATION

MOTHER: I felt guilty, I tried to make up for my husband not being there, so I was with him constantly—not overprotective. They could have killed themselves, and I wouldn't have gotten up off the chair if they were doing something. But, I was constantly with them, until I found a nursery school, and then I had a horrible time trying to get him to nursery school. He'd scream and kick and cry and everything. He was sick as a baby. He was in the hospital when he was three months old. He had acute bronchitis, and then he was behind glass. He was an allergic child. He had eczema all over him. If they'd go out to the pool I had to stay in with him because he couldn't be in the sun. I think I used to hold him in my arms and hold the bottle, when I fed him. It was hot so I don't think I held him a lot, loved him up a lot.

SON'S RECOLLECTIONS AT AGE NINETEEN

SON: Well, my mother would say that I was probably always her favorite child. My mother and I—my sister is more my father's girl, she's daddy's girl, I'm momma's boy, that's how it is, more or less.

R. G.: How did that happen?

SON: What I would assume is that she was probably more the ideal of what he thought his child should be because—

R. G.: Was she into sports?

SON: Probably, yes.

R. G.: What makes you sure that she was his, and you were your mom's kid?

SON: In relation to our relationships now, that is how it appears that it would have been, because to this day my sister is more—well, my father and I really don't speak at all at this point in our lives, which is fine. And my mother and I are as close as ever, I can tell her anything, I have complete trust in her, and my mother and I are very much alike—extremely.

R. G.: In what way?

SON: Well, we're both very idealistic as far as love goes; we both have the kind of thing where we give a lot almost to the point where we get screwed over in the end, you know, we're so—at least I know I am, I will trust anybody. My mother and I are very close and my father and I, we don't speak.

Example 5: Mama's Boy

("FEMININE" BOY, HOMOSEXUAL MAN)

SON'S RECOLLECTIONS AT AGE TWENTY-TWO

SON: I'm going to go ahead and say this—my mother is a very dominating woman. She always has been and as far as I remember when I was a child she was always very dominating. "You do this, you do that, you do it my way." She's always been that way and still is.

R. G.: How did that show itself when I first saw you?

SON: Well, I never really thought about it back then, until I grew older; then I grew more aware of what she was doing. I was basically around my mother all my life and my real father, when they were married, traveled on the road. I never did see him hardly at all, so it was basically my mother—has always been that way.

R. G.: How close were you to your mother?

SON: I was very, very close. I'm still close to her. I did not, certainly, cling on her—they use the term "mama's boy," I don't know if I really was a "mama's boy," I know I was very close to her, but I didn't totally depend on her as far as a parent figure, because, like I said, when I was younger I had my stepfather. I'll bring up an instance—I remember right before I was to see you the first time as a kid, I found a letter in my mother's jewelry box. It was written by my grandmother and I had found this out—that I was going to come to see you—through this letter that she had hidden, and my grandmother was discussing it in the letter, and I remember the term she used, "Well, he was always a mama's boy." I don't know if that's getting off the subject.

R. G.: What do you think she might have meant by a "mama's boy"?

SON: I just clung to her, I just ran to her.

Example 6: Mistaken Identity

("FEMININE" BOY, HETEROSEXUAL MAN)

SON'S REPORT AT AGE EIGHTEEN

SON: Well, I just learned some startling information. My mother is not really my mother. The woman who I have been referring to as my aunt is my mother, but she didn't want any more children, she already had a son. I was gonna be put up for adoption, but my grandmother didn't want to see me go out, she wanted to see me stay so she asked my "mother" if she would take me and my "mother" did. My "mother" got me when I was three days old, she's all I've ever known.

R. G.: How is this woman who's your "mother" related to your biological mother?

SON: Sisters.

R. G.: So your aunt is your biological mother. How did you feel when you first learned that?

SON: I didn't believe it. When my mother told me I laughed. I said, "You gotta be kidding, why do you want to tell me this?" She finally convinced me and I had this feeling of not being wanted, God, nobody wanted me. But, she's done a good job of raising me, I'm practically an adult, so why get all upset?

R. G.: She's been your mother.

"MOTHER'S" REPORT DURING THE SAME SESSION

MOTHER: Yes, he knows, I just told him. He's a little confused about it, he says it's kind of a shock.

R. G.: I imagine it is.

MOTHER: It is a shock.

R. G.: At least a surprise.

MOTHER: Yeah, because he just never suspected, you know.

R. G.: You've been a good mother to him.

MOTHER: Oh yeah, we've been very close.

R. G.: You have been his mother since he was three days old?

MOTHER: Yeah, I went to his hospital and got him. So he understands.

R. G.: And his biological mother, has he had contact with her as he was growing up?

MOTHER: Yes.

R. G.: Did she have any influence on his early behaviors?

MOTHER: No. She just erased it like it never happened, you know, some people can do that, well she was gonna give him up to institutions. She just accepted it as if he was my child, I think she really believed it, psychologically she psyched herself out that it was mine.

Example 7: Super-Mother

("FEMININE" BOY, HOMOSEXUAL MAN)

MOTHER'S REPORT AT INITIAL EVALUATION

MOTHER: When he was about seven months of age I noticed the peculiar hand wiggling identical to that of our fifteen-year old boy. The older boy was diagnosed as having a case of early infantile autism and I noticed this boy would stare at objects and wiggle his hands.

R. G.: And later?

MOTHER: When he was about fourteen months old he learned how to walk and I would place him out in the back yard, and he would walk past a hedge and visually self-stimulate himself, and out of the corner of his eye he would walk back and forth looking at the hedges. Backing up a little, when he was still an infant he would be sitting in his infant seat and looking out the window staring at the trees, like hypnotized, wiggling his hands and staring at the leaves.

R. G.: What sort of personality did he seem to have as an infant?

MOTHER: Well when I saw this peculiar behavior I said to myself well we've got another autistic child. But personality-wise, he was a smiling, responsive baby, and cuddly, and when he was seven months old and elicited this peculiar hand wiggling I kind of started a program of my own to counteract this autistic behavior. I insisted on eye-to-eye contact and a lot of cuddling and a super-mother type relationship.

R. G.: Tell me more about the super-mother relationship.

MOTHER: Well, I just tried to develop a strong person-to-person relationship with him to counteract his tendency to relate to objects as opposed to people. He seemed to get more enjoyment from objects than people so I forced myself upon him—in his little world.

R. G.: Beginning at seven months?

MOTHER: Yeah. I would hold him—just being a mother—loved him, you know, as opposed to letting him sit in a playpen all day long and play with toys. I would pick him up a lot and toss him up in the air and patty-cake and teach him, try to work with him to look at books with him and develop a relationship with him.

R. G.:   To counteract the autistic symptoms there was more handling?

MOTHER: Yeah. I tried to push eye contact on him. Particularly when he was looking at the leaves on the tree, I'd pull the table over and get him to look at me and I'd start the patty-cake with him.

Example 8: Lesbian Mother

("MASCULINE" BOY, HETEROSEXUAL MAN)

SON'S RECOLLECTIONS AT AGE TWENTY-ONE

R. G.:   The fact that your mother slept in bed with another woman, did that sound sexual to you?

SON: Yeah.

R. G.:   Unusual?

SON: Well, yeah, I didn't think it was normal or something. I can't really remember exactly. When you're that young you're really impressionable. Probably not normal.

R. G.:   You don't find out about two women very easily.

SON: No.

R. G.:   It's not talked about that much.

SON: Especially back then.

R. G.:   What was your mom's attitude in the way she raised you, in terms of conventional boy-girl type things?

SON: I think I was pretty well rounded.

Some sons' recollections of mother fit that predicted by theory: She was "very close," or "idolized." But other reports were not remarkable and did not clearly distinguish the mothers of homosexual and heterosexual men. And, a homosexual mother did not yield a homosexual son. The question of why some boys become "feminine" and some become homosexual will not simply be answered by men's statements beginning, "I remember Mama..."

Father-Son

The first transcript differs from those that follow. It could easily have been included in chapter 9 on theories of homosexuality. However, strictly speaking, the theory is not so much the subject's as mine. Fantasies of the absent father are *interpreted* as following a developmental sequence leading to male sexual partners. The transcript is included here because the development of erotic reality from pre-erotic fantasy appears within the context of father deprivation.

Example 1: Missing Biological Father

("FEMININE" BOY, HOMOSEXUAL MAN)

SON'S REPORT AT AGE TWENTY-TWO

Catching Up on a Lost Father-Son Relationship

R. G.:   Why did you decide to go out of town to college?

SON: Well, my real father lives there. My parents divorced when I was two years old. I had never seen my father before, I had never heard from him, so basically, I looked him up. I went down there for a visit and I got reacquainted with my father.

R. G.:   That was the first time you had seen him—when you were eighteen?

SON: Almost nineteen.

R. G.:   Wow, what was that like for you?

SON: Strange, very strange, and it didn't turn out to be very good. I don't know if it was his guilt feelings or his problems, or maybe it was part of me. We could not get along at all. There were just too many hard feelings, mainly between me, I don't know about him, but maybe his were more or less guilt and mine were more or less anger, resentment, and stuff like that.

R. G.:   Had he made any effort to make contact with you from the time he separated from your mom?

SON: No. No child support, no Christmas card, no birthday, nothing whatsoever.

R. G.:   How did you know where to find him?

SON: I was always curious. When I was fourteen years old I made a long distance phone call to him completely on my own without my parents knowing about it. I had nothing really to say. I was just petrified and just scared; I was talking to a total stranger and I didn't know what to really say.

Relationship with Biological Father

R. G.:   In those first two years when your mom was still married to your father, to what extent was he there?

SON: I can't remember then, but as far as being there he just wasn't hardly there, he was traveling. His job permitted him to do that and required him to do that, so I guess I was more or less stuck with my sister and mother. And maybe that's where I ended up getting a lot of my mannerisms.

Relationship with Stepfather

SON: Seems like when I was younger I was pretty close to my stepfather. Seems like now I don't know if we are really close. It's hard to pinpoint. No, we are really not close.

R. G.:   Looking back to about the time that I might have first seen you, how would you describe your relationship with him then?

SON: Well, I was involved with him, like in Scouting. I was in an organization called the Indian Guides. We did a lot of father-son outings, camp-outs and stuff like that. It seems like when I was younger I was much closer to him.

Reflection on the UCLA Experience

R. G.:   Were you angry that I stopped seeing you at UCLA many years ago?

SON: Well, I didn't think about it. I just said, "Okay, you are not seeing him anymore." But when my mother called me last week and told me you wanted to see me after all these years, I felt very uncomfortable. I said to myself, "Well, why in the hell does he want to see me after all these years?" You are just going to bring up the past.

A Parallel?

R. G.:   You know, I just got a feeling when you said that.

SON: But then I said, "Will it hurt?" I thought, maybe he is concerned, maybe he would just like to see how I am doing and what I've done with my life. And I said, "I guess it really wouldn't hurt."

R. G.:   You know, the sense that I got when you were saying all these things was that I wondered whether you had the same feelings when you had made some contact with your father—your biological father—and were anticipating seeing him again after all those years. Why I would want to see you? What it would be like?

SON: No, I'm not using that...

R. G.:   I was wondering whether the feelings were similar.

SON: No, there wasn't any resentment, really, it was just more or less strange, you know, that he hasn't seen me in all these years—what does he have this time to say?

R. G.:   Did you have any feelings like that when you went to see your father after all those years?

SON: I felt—I always had resentment, even when I went—it was just bottled up inside, and I was finally able to take my aggression out. From what my mother told me about him, and my grandmother and my stepfather—and from the things that he did, I resented him. Not only the fact of things that he did, but the fact that he didn't want to have anything to do with me, just like I don't exist. There were no phone calls, no child support, no nothing.

R. G.:   I haven't made any phone calls...

SON: But I'm not trying to make it seem—I was just curious as to why all of a sudden your curiosity. But then I looked at it and I started to analyze it and I said, "Well, maybe he is curious and cares about what's going on in my life."

Emergence of Pre-erotic Boy-Man Imagery

R. G.: Well, I am. I want to ask about how your sexual interests have evolved over the years.

SON: I remember when I was very young, like six, seven, eight years old, I used to fantasize about me and a strong he-man. As far as having sexual overtones to it, I can't recall.

R. G.: What do you mean, fantasize about strong men?

SON: Just a male figure.

R. G.: Do you remember in that fantasy whether there was any kind of physical touching or caressing or holding?

SON: Yes.

R. G.: Tell me what that was like.

SON: Maybe just holding hands. No kissing or anything like that. Basically just holding hands or the person was holding me in his arms.

R. G.: Up until about what age did you have that fantasy?

SON: Maybe twelve or eleven.

R. G.: What form did the first fantasy about males take?

SON: Just basically touching, kind of a strong man. I don't know, maybe like a father figure or something like that. More or less a father and son taking a walk or a father hugging a son. Maybe at that certain age. But as I got older they did become a little different.

R. G.: How did they evolve?

SON: More physical.

Transition of Boy-Man Imagery into Erotic Fantasy

SON: As I grew older—I was nude, he was nude, there was sexual contact.

R. G.: Fill out the picture a little more about what was going on in the fantasy.

SON: It was basically the same, at thirteen and fourteen, but it seemed as I got a little bit older and older then it became, like, more kissing, more touching, and more caressing. As I got older it became more physical, it became more sexual.

R. G.: Were you fondling the person or was the person fondling you, or both?

SON: It seems like the person was always fondling me. It was more like I was getting the attention.

R. G.: As it got more sexual, how old were you?

SON: It seems like it was fully developed when I was sixteen or seventeen—when it really became intense. It seems like in my fantasy I'm more or less partaking in it too. It was more or less that they were doing it, but I was also doing it.

R. G.: And the person remained older and bigger?

SON: Always bigger and older.

R. G.: Do you remember if that was sexually arousing?

SON: I don't think so at that time, but as I got older it did.

R. G.:   Did that fantasy give you an erection before the fantasy turned into a more sexual one with kissing and fondling?

SON: It felt good, but there wasn't anything sexual about it. I got more of an erection when I got older and there was more physical contact.

Interpretation of the Fantasy

R. G.:   You said you were holding the male, and maybe it was a father figure. Why do you say that?

SON: I guess basically, maybe, I'm looking for a father figure. I had one, I still do, but as far as being close, I grew farther apart from my stepfather, but these feelings became stronger, and I guess the fact, too, that my real father was gone—I guess it was more a sense of rejection on my part. I had a mother, the female part of it, but I didn't have a male part, and I felt rejected, and I felt that they didn't want anything to do with me.

R. G.:   So you are saying that at the time you became more distant from your stepfather the feelings about males became sexualized?

SON: Yes. I guess it was just the fear of rejection. It wasn't necessarily rejection, it was just not a close bond anymore, and I can't pinpoint the cause or the reason why. It was, more or less, I felt that my real father doesn't love me, I felt that at the time, and my stepfather doesn't love me, so I guess I was looking for an affectionate male.

Evolution of the Fantasy into Interpersonal Experience

R. G.:   And how has the fantasy evolved from the time you were sixteen?

SON: There is oral sex involved, kissing, caressing.

R. G.:   To what extent is the being held part still there?

SON: It's still there. It's very strong. That's part of the fantasy, just being held. It's more or less like being accepted, being loved. And the kissing part is a feeling of love, not a feeling of rejection.

R. G.:   Have you acted on the fantasy, in terms of having real sexual experiences with males?

SON: I've had three experiences.

R. G.:   Beginning when?

SON: About twenty years old.

R. G.:   What was that like for you?

SON: The very first time, of course, after it was over with, I felt very guilty, very dirty, and I thought, "God, what did I do?" But then, yet at that period of time, my very first experience was with an older man—there was also a sense of fulfillment. Like a desire had been fulfilled.

R. G.:   How much older was the man?

SON: Fifteen or twenty years older.

R. G.:   Is that about the same age as in your fantasy?

SON: The experiences that I've had, I have had about five or six—

SON: The experiences that I've had, I have had about five or six—all these men have been older. In fact, the last person I was involved with was forty years old and I had just turned twenty-two.

R. G.:   Is that the same age differential as you have in your fantasy?

SON: Yes, usually.

Example 2: Father Present More for Brother

("FEMININE" BOY, HETEROSEXUAL MAN)

SON'S REPORT AT AGE EIGHTEEN

SON: With my father, I think we have the same bad points and very different good points, and that makes it difficult to appreciate each other's good points, and we nag each other with our bad points. I think basically he sees a lot of qualities in me that he probably had as a kid, and I think I see qualities in him as an adult that I can see developing in me.

R. G.:   What kinds of points?

SON: A tendency to be very hardheaded, very stubborn, a tendency to try and deal with problems by ignoring them. But I don't think it's anything like where one of us is going to move out or kill each other.

R. G.:   Do you remember your relationship with your dad when you were a little kid?

SON: Not an awful lot. There are very few things I remember doing with my father. Every year when we had a birthday we got special days which was when he would take us somewhere on our own.

Let's see, what else do I remember? I remember he was never there. I mean, still, he works a lot, he works an awful lot, and when he lived away, he always commuted in on the weekends and we saw him on weekends and mom was always there.

R. G.:   If you had to compare the extent of closeness you had with him as a boy compared to most of the other kids you knew growing up with their fathers, how would it be?

SON: Compared with other people, I know we weren't close. If I was not close with my father, I was closer with my mother, whereas many of my friends were not close to their mother and they were closer to their father, so it evened out. Yeah, we weren't very close.

R. G.:   Can you compare your relationship with your dad when you were a little boy and what your brother's was like?

SON: I used to think he had a much better relationship with my father, I think there was a period when he did. I think both of my parents sort of had a tendency to play favorites. I think my father played favorites with my brother and my mother with me. I think two or three months ago I saw him for the first time really have a fight with my father and that was always my charge. For some reason I was never jealous of him for having a better relationship.

Example 3: An Intermittent Father, but Brother Developed "Masculine" Behaviors

("FEMININE" BOY, HOMOSEXUAL MAN)

MOTHER'S REPORT AT FOLLOW-UP

MOTHER: He was eight when we split.

R. G.:   Has somebody served in a father role for him?

MOTHER: No.

R. G.:   Nobody?

MOTHER: I had a Big Brother. What happened was one of the pediatricians told me that he needed a father and I carried on like a wild woman, saying "What do you people want from me? You know, I'm divorced and you tell me my kid needs a father, like I'm supposed to go out and find a father for him? When his own father was living in the same city and didn't have time for him and you're all yelling at me like it's my fault." So someone suggested Big Brothers and it worked well.

   But now, this boy's real brother is a tough kid. Very aggressive. He does all the swaggering and he's got the macho image, he's cool. He gets in trouble.

R. G.:   Where does he get it from?

MOTHER: I don't know. I wish I did know. But he is really, he can be really obnoxious and he always, by the way, called this boy "fag" for years, for years.

R. G.:   How old was his brother when he first called him "fag"?

MOTHER: He had to be four years old by then, so that's a long time.

R. G.:   What was he seeing in an eleven-year-old brother?

MOTHER: He was doing the feminine hand gestures kind of things.

R. G.:   How much did his father keep seeing this boy after you separated?

MOTHER: He saw the children very little, when he lived in LA. After he left, I don't think he saw them for two years. He saw his daughter.

R. G.:   So from eleven to twelve years he didn't see him at all?

MOTHER: And then it was maybe once a month, occasionally once every other week. He did not see them during the week.

R. G.:   And during the time you were married, how much contact did he have with them then?

MOTHER: Very little. It wasn't just his work. Since then I've met too many young lawyers who are also fathers and they found time for their kids. That's cop-out crap, that you don't have time. He really didn't want to make time for the kids.

Example 4: Minimal Father-Son Contact; Brother was a Role Model

("MASCULINE" BOY, HETEROSEXUAL MAN)

MOTHER'S REPORT AT INITIAL EVALUATION

R. G.:   To what extent did his father spend time with him during his first year?

MOTHER: Very little, I think he might have seen him twice in a year.

R. G.:   Was there any other man, as a father substitute, with whom he had some contact during the first year?

MOTHER: No, not during his first year, he didn't have any. I got married when he was about three years old—I remarried. But, it just didn't work out.

R. G.:   During the first two years in which you were not married, to what extent did he have contact at all with adult men?

MOTHER: Not very much. It was mostly just me.

R. G.:   Your older boy is how much older than he is?

MOTHER: Seven years.

R. G.:   During his years three, four, five, when you were remarried, to what extent was your new husband able to spend time with them?

MOTHER: Not very much.

R. G.:   Why?

MOTHER: Well, he was drinking a lot. He wanted a family and I wasn't prepared to have any more children, I didn't feel that I should have any at that time. I felt I should wait and see if things turn out right or not. I guess he sort of resented the fact that I wouldn't go along with him in that matter. So we'd go out as a family once in a while but he drank quite a bit with his other friends.

R. G.:   To what extent was your father available to him during the first couple of years when your son had no biological father around?

MOTHER: No contact.

R. G.:   The first three years that you weren't married, to what extent were you dating?

MOTHER: Not very often. I didn't have the time to date. So I didn't.

R. G.:   I'm trying to get a picture of the exposure to adult men your infant son had in the first three years.

MOTHER: Well, the thing is, in the first three years I had all the bills— I was carrying most of it. I put in quite a bit of hours at work. I hardly ever went out, it was from work to home, from bed to work to home to bed, that was about the extent of it, feed the kids, play with them a couple of hours—so I didn't date that much during those years. I was too tired to have any social life.

SON'S REPORT AT AGE EIGHTEEN

SON: My father is nowhere in the picture. He calls once every five months or something like that. Right now he's had a heart attack and he's gotta really take it easy. He's gotta watch what he eats, especially spicy stuff, and so he's really having problems.

R. G.:   You've been seeing him rarely, every five months or so?

SON: I don't see him very often. When I do I really don't like seeing him—like he's never been there. I feel I grew up through the environment of my friends.

R. G.:   In what way did your friends contribute to your growing up?

SON: I was very naive when I was young, and they used to play a lot of jokes on me. My brothers used to watch out for me and tell me, "Don't be dumb, be wise, even though you're not, pretend you are." I was just really dumb and they used to play a lot of tricks on me. Eventually it entered my mind, I soaked up everything that they do to you.

R. G.:   Was there someone, as you were growing up as a little kid, who sort of substituted as a father for you?

SON: I followed my oldest brother. Everything he did, I did; he bought an album, I bought an album. That made me feel grown up. Anything he did was right because he was a big example to me. I guess I really never needed one of those Big Brothers. He made me grow up. I sneezed the way he did, I coughed the way he did.

Example 5: A Doting Father*

("FEMININE" BOY, BISEXUAL MAN)

PARENTS' REPORT AT INITIAL EVALUATION

MOTHER: I want to tell you something. He's had a too-devoted father. This is my impression because he spent more time with him than any man will spend with a child. But, this is something he's wanted all his life and he loves children, he always did, and he just flipped.

R. G.:   This is your first child?

MOTHER: His first child and he adores him.

FATHER: But by the same token, I say whip his can just as hard as my father would do it and often enough that he knows he's got a father in the house, I'll tell you that.

MOTHER: He knows he's got a father, he sure does.

Example 6: Father Favors "Masculine" Boy, Questions Paternity of "Feminine" Boy

("FEMININE" BOY, HOMOSEXUAL MAN)

FATHER'S REPORT AT INITIAL EVALUATION

R. G.:   How about your own relationship in the first couple of years to the two boys?

---

*Reported more extensively as "Joseph," chapter 5.

FATHER: I would have had more time for the other one. I probably did have more time for him.

R. G.: Why was that?

FATHER: Had better hours, didn't have to work as much.

R. G.: During what years?

FATHER: Oh probably from the time he was born until he was a year old, or going on to two years old. I know he was very young when he was acting like a sissy, when I thought he was sissy and I thought the other one was all boy. I thought, well the little one's all boy. And the other's not.

R. G.: Did you try to dissuade him from any of these things?

FATHER: No, maybe,—maybe I harbored some resentment for him being that way. Possibly ... I probably did, 'cause when they were three or four I can remember, like when the baby was three he could hit a baseball, and this older one couldn't even pick up the bat. There was such a difference between them that I felt a stronger attachment for the little one than for the older.

R. G.: How about your own feelings toward the two boys?

FATHER: I like the little one better.

R. G.: Why?

FATHER: Because he acts like a boy. As far back as I can remember the baby was my favorite kid. It had to be for the way he acted. Also, I had problems about the older one's paternity. I remember asking his mother about it. She was fooling around with another guy. She told me I got her pregnant, we were gonna get married and she ran off with another guy and left him and wanted me to marry her. She called me up. I was a teenager, it was my first piece of tail. I thought it was great.

R. G.: Yeah.

FATHER: Of course she was a beautiful girl. I went off with her. Then I was sure I was the one that got her pregnant. Maybe I doubted it, he was six months old when I had some time to think about it. Now I'm sure if either one could pick up any sense of rejection or favoritism or anything like that, that the older one would be the one that would pick it up.

Example 7: Neglectful of a "Feminine" Son, Attentive to a New Son

("FEMININE" BOY, HOMOSEXUAL MAN)

FATHER'S REPORT AT FOLLOW-UP

R. G.: To what extent were you able to spend time with your son during his first year?

FATHER: Very little. I was going to school and working. It seemed like he was always asleep when I got home. Couldn't wake him up. So I would say, very little.

R. G.: Compared to your new son now, how were the eighteen months you had during his first year and the first year with your new boy?

FATHER: About a hundred times more.

R. G.: Now?

FATHER: Yes. There's quite a difference in my wife's attitude, I think, too—because my present wife likes for me to have the baby. In fact, it is more or less a ritual that he's fed by dad every night. We just have a lot of time, it seems like. Of course, I'm not going to school now, either. I have a lot of time.

SON'S REPORT AT AGE TWENTY-THREE

SON: I have a younger half brother now, and the relationship is just what I wish mine had been.

R. G.: Tell me about the difference.

SON: Well, when I was growing up my dad didn't have a lot of free time, he was always working. He wasn't in a position where he was financially set to spend more time, and I remember going to Cub Scouts and things, and my stepmom would be taking me instead of my dad because he had to work.

R. G.: Do you remember consciously wishing that there was something different back then, or is it in retrospect now that you see that?

SON: Back then I knew it was there but it wasn't that overwhelming, I think because I had two sisters and then the guys next door, we all kind of played around, and if my dad wasn't around, his dad was around, so he was always there, but not my father.

R. G.: When did you become aware that there was something deficient in your relationship to your father?

SON: I think ever since my half brother was born.

R. G.: How old were you then?

SON: Eleven or twelve. He would just do things and spend a lot more time than he would with me.

R. G.: How did you feel seeing it?

SON: Rejected, hurt, envious. In fact I still am. Recently, I visited my father and we talked—it was an hour drive from the airport to his house and we talked the first twenty minutes and that was it, there was nothing else to say to each other.

Example 8: Father's Favorite

("FEMININE" BOY, HOMOSEXUAL MAN)

SON'S RECOLLECTIONS AT AGE TWENTY

R. G.: Did he treat you differently from your brother?

SON: Yeah.

R. G.: How?

SON: He gave most of the attention to me.

R. G.: How come?

SON: Because I was the baby and I was his favorite.

Example 9: An Available Stepfather

("FEMININE" BOY, HOMOSEXUAL MAN)

MOTHER'S REPORT AT INITIAL EVALUATION

MOTHER: His real father left when he was six months old, and my present husband and I started living together. He would play with him in the morning and the evenings when he came home. So there was quite a bit of contact.

R. G.: How much?

MOTHER: I would say about an hour in the morning and two hours in the evening.

R. G.: Your husband took to him pretty readily?

MOTHER: Oh yes, pretty much so.

R. G.: And how did your son respond?

MOTHER: Beautifully.

R. G.: How much residual contact has there been with his biological father?

MOTHER: Very little. He will pick him up on weekends, and then it's really a fight to get him to go with him, because our son will want to stay home and he'll want to stay home with him, and his real father wants him to go with him down to the park or he wants to take him out bike riding. And the boy doesn't want to go with him. My son just didn't want to go with him. I think mainly because his father degrades him so.

R. G.: How much contact with his stepfather do you think your son has had compared to most boys?

MOTHER: I'd say about average. If it's a working father, of course. My husband takes care of him in the mornings. He does everything with my son in the morning.

R. G.: Such as?

MOTHER: Well, he fixes him breakfast, my son's in there while he's shaving, he dresses the boy for school, most of the time he takes him to school. I just leave them alone in the morning. There's time together for them. Then when he comes home in the evenings, he plays with him. He usually dresses him for bed.

Example 10: Absent Father; Mother Teaches Son "Masculinity"

("MASCULINE" BOY, HETEROSEXUAL MAN)

MOTHER'S REPORT AT INITIAL EVALUATION

R. G.: To what extent did your son have contact with males during his first two years?

MOTHER: Not very much at all. From six months my father was around
   but that was about all. My father, well, I guess he played with him, I
   guess it was a normal grandfather-grandson relationship, he would
   be climbing over him, playing with him and that was all.

R. G.:   Was your father working or was he retired?

MOTHER: He was working.

R. G.:   Would he and the boy interact some, play together?

MOTHER: My father wasn't the playing type. He was older.

R. G.:   What about on weekends?

MOTHER: Well, he was usually gone on Saturday and Sunday. My father
   was old, and he didn't have that much patience to be around him or
   be with him. He would see him in the evening and that was mostly
   about all.

R. G.:   Did your son have any contact with his father?

MOTHER: No. We were separated since he was six months old and he
   hasn't seen him since.

R. G.:   During those first couple of years, when essentially there were no
   men around except your father, did he seem to show some mixed
   feelings as to whether he preferred boy toys and activities or girl toys
   and activities?

MOTHER: I don't remember him ever going for girl toys, it seemed to
   me that he was always wanting a boy's type toy like a gun, something
   like that; he never did, no I can't ever say that he did.

R. G.:   One of the reasons I'm asking these questions is that with the
   exception of your father in the first year, there were no adult males
   around. I'm trying to get some idea where he learned to behave like
   a boy.

MOTHER: Well, my brother was really the only male image that he had,
   'cause my brother kinda came around, but he didn't live at home. But
   you know, he's admired my brother and always looked up to him, and
   my brother was the only one who played games with him. But it just
   wasn't all that often, 'cause my brother is always going to school or
   doing something.

R. G.:   Do you think you and your mom tried to consciously train your
   son to be a boy?

MOTHER: I'm sure I did. I don't know whether my mother did or not,
   but I'm sure I did.

R. G.:   In what way?

MOTHER: Well, 'cause I would bring boys' toys into the house, and I
   bought him the toys. I introduced him to boys rather than girls. Well,
   of course the boy next door really was there, so there really was no
   problem with girls, but I guess probably the main thing was seeing
   that he always wore boys' clothes and he always had boys' toys.

R. G.:   Would you in some way label them as being a boy's toy, like "Here
   is a boy's toy"?

MOTHER: No, I just took it for granted that he knew. But if we went to a store and if he pointed to anything that I thought was the slightest bit feminine in a toy or something, I'd say, "No, that's for girls." He didn't carry on or press it and say, well he has to have it. He just accepted it. "Why don't you look at this, that's for girls." I'd direct him more towards a boy's toy.

These transcripts teach many things, not the least of which is caution. One boy thirsts for his father, a deprivation that finds its way into an imaginary companion in childhood, a physically comforting man in adolescence, and a sexual partner in adulthood. But another boy, deprived of a father-son relationship from early childhood, seeks only female sexual partners. A homosexual man with a heterosexual brother reports having envied the relationship between his father and his sibling. But another homosexual man describes his relationship with his father as positive. And a heterosexual man describes his relationship with his father as negative.

While a preponderance of evidence suggests that less father-son shared time and a poorer father-son relationship are more common in the lives of "feminine" boys and homosexual men, there is too much variation to characterize these patterns of development as simply responses to the question, "Where's papa?"

4

Cross-gender Boyhood; Homosexual Manhood

"Feminine" boys, as portrayed in chapter 1, are far more likely to mature into homosexual or bisexual men than are most boys. Two-thirds of the sixty-six males in the original "feminine boy" group have been interviewed in adolescence or young adulthood. Three-fourths of them are homosexual or bisexual. Only one of the males in the group of conventionally "masculine" boys reports being homosexual or bisexual.*

The sexual orientation of these men is summarized in three ways. The first is sexual fantasy. Each person described fantasies that excite during masturbation. They described the erotic images of nocturnal emissions, or "wet dreams." They described the types of pictorial pornography that induce erections. The men compared the percent of the time that erotic content involved male or female partners during the past year. From these statements a score was given on a seven-point continuum of sexual orientation, as developed by Alfred Kinsey. On this continuum, 0 represents exclusive heterosexual fantasy, 3 is an equal degree of heterosexual and homosexual fantasy, and 6 is exclusive homosexual fantasy (Kinsey et al., 1948). Thus, if 85 percent of fantasies involve males and 15 percent involve females, the score on the seven-point scale would be 5—the proportional distance between 0 (100 percent female partner imagery) and 6 (100 percent male partner imagery).

The second way sexual orientation is summarized is sexual behavior. Behavior scores derive from a pattern of postpubertal interpersonal genital experiences. An occasional or serendipitous experience does not a

*The "masculine" twin described in chapter 8 is currently bisexual in behavior.

TABLE 4.1. Kinsey Scores for Fantasy and Behavior

	Exclusively Heterosexual or Incidentally Homosexual (0–1)	More Than Incidentally Homosexual (2–6)
	Fantasy	
Previously "feminine" boys (n = 44)	11	33
Previously "masculine" boys (n = 35)	35	0
	Behavior	
Previously "feminine" boys (n = 30)	6	24
Previously "masculine" boys (n = 25)	24	1

pattern make. For a behavior score to be given, there must be a series of experiences leading to orgasms with a single partner, or a sequence of solitary experiences with transient partners. The percent of orgasmic experiences with males or females was also transformed into a score on the seven-point scale of sexual orientation.

Erotic fantasies typically evolve earlier in life than interpersonal genital experiences. Therefore, with some younger males we can derive sexual fantasy scores but have no basis for their placement on the continuum for sexual behavior.

The seven-point scale for either fantasy or behavior can be partitioned into two sectors, each describing diverse patterns of erotic arousal and experience. Kinsey and his coworkers (1948) reported that about a third of all males have at least one postpubertal orgasmic experience with another male. This experience hardly constitutes a homosexual orientation. On the seven-point continuum for behavior this would be designated 1. Similarly, occasional ("incidental," in the language of Kinsey) homosexual fantasies would be designated 1. Beyond a score of 1, where there is more than occasional homosexual fantasy and/or experience, there is bisexuality. Thus, cutting the continuum into sectors of 0–1 and 2–6 describes two groups of people with quite different patterns of sexual orientation (table 4.1). However, this bifurcation, while useful in distinguishing two groups of men, suffers from lumping different categories of people within the 2–6 range. A predominantly heterosexual though more than incidentally homosexual man (rated 2) is substantially different in sexual orientation from an exclusively homosexual man (rated 6). Therefore, a third way of partitioning sexual orientation is to segregate persons into 0–1 (heterosexual), 2–4 (bisexual), and 5–6 (homosexual) categories (table 4.2). Here, fantasy and behavior scores (when both were obtained) are averaged.

Finally, individual scores are also presented. Each male's age at initial

TABLE 4.2. Composite of Kinsey Scores for Fantasy and Behavior

"Feminine" Boys (n = 44)		
0–1 (Heterosexual)	2–4 (Bisexual)	5–6 (Homosexual)
12	14	18

evaluation, age at most recent follow-up, and most recent sexual orientation scores for fantasy and behavior are reported (tables 4.3 and 4.4). With the previously "feminine" boys for whom we have both fantasy and behavior ratings, the two are highly correlated ($r = .88, p < .001$). With the previously "masculine" boys, the two ratings are nearly identical.

Some readers may quibble with the accuracy of these ratings, but the ratings are readily made. A rating of 0 indicates no homosexual arousal in the fantasies associated with masturbation, nocturnal dream imagery, or pornography. A rating of 1 represents very infrequent homosexual arousal; the subject's report indicates that less that 15 percent of his fantasies are homosexual. For behavior ratings, while one postpubertal same-sex experience may not indicate a pattern, it does result in a rating above 0. Only when such experiences constitute at least 15 percent of experiences is a rating of 2 or more given. Thus, the dichotomy of 0–1 versus 2–6 is easily constructed.

For the remaining scores there are also good anchor points. When a subject reports an absence of heterosexual content in masturbation fantasies or dreams, and when heterosexual pornography is ignored or not arousing, a rating of 6 is given. When a subject reports "about the same" to the frequency with which males and females are involved in fantasies or interpersonal behaviors, a rating of 3 is given. A rating of 5 is the counterpart of 1, described above. This leaves only 2 and 4, which are hardly confusable. When subjects are asked to quantify their experiences by a proportion or percent, there is less room for interviewer bias.

While some ratings might be judged by other raters to be a point different, the overriding link found here between extensive boyhood cross-gender behavior and later bisexuality or homosexuality would not be modified. Nor would there be a substantial effect on the reported associations between early-life variables and later sexual orientation.

REPRESENTATIVENESS OF THE FOLLOW-UP SAMPLE

Not every one of our boys, whether previously "feminine" or "masculine," was later reevaluated for sexual orientation. How representative of the full groups are those who remained for study? Dropouts ("experimental mortality") (Campbell and Stanley, 1963) are inevitable in a fifteen-year study. *Selective* dropping out occurs when the loss of families is not random but rather is a unique characteristic of the dropouts.

TABLE 4.3. "Feminine Boy" Group

Person	Age at Initial Evaluation	Age at Most Recent Follow-up	Sexual Orientation Score (Fantasy)	Sexual Orientation Score (Behavior)
A	8	18	0	—
B	7	16	4	—
C	10	19	0	0
D	4	14	0	—
E	9	22	2	2
F	8	20	6	6
G	10	21	5	5
H	7	14	0	—
I	6	19	5	4
J	5	17	0	—
K	6	17	6	—
L	8	19	2	—
M	5	18	1	0
N	7	21	5	5
O	10	23	6	6
P	7	17	2	1
Q	4	18	4	—
R	4	16	5	4
S	8	21	2	2
T	6	18	0	—
U	6	20	6	6
V	8	20	4	—
W	10	20	5	5
X	10	20	6	6
Y	7	16	0	0
Z	8	19	6	6
AA	6	20	2	6
BB	6	24	5	—
CC	5	16	2	0
DD	6	18	6	4
EE	8	20	4	4
FF	5	20	1	—
GG	7	18	5	6
HH	10	21	4	3
II	6	21	5	4
JJ	10	22	4	4
KK	7	21	6	6
LL	5	17	0	0
MM	4	18	4	—
NN	5	14	0	—
OO	10	21	5	5
PP	8	20	4	4
QQ	5	19	5	5
RR	8	23	4	2

Notes: A dash indicates insufficient subject experience to provide a rating.
RR is the co-twin described in chapter 8.

The first reassuring note is that our rate of dropping out was comparable in both groups (about one-third). However, biasing factors may operate differentially in this selection for one group. The reluctance of parents to bring their sons back, or of the sons to return, may be related

TABLE 4.4. "Masculine Boy" Group

Person	Age at Initial Evaluation	Age at Most Recent Follow-up	Sexual Orientation Score (Fantasy)	Sexual Orientation Score (Behavior)
A	5	15	0	—
B	8	16	0	0
C	10	18	0	—
D	7	14	0	—
E	4	19	0	0
F	6	20	0	—
G	10	19	1	0
H	10	20	0	0
I	7	18	0	0
J	6	17	0	0
K	7	18	0	0
L	7	19	0	0
M	4	15	0	—
N	6	17	0	—
O	8	16	0	0
P	8	17	0	0
Q	7	16	0	0
R	10	19	0	0
S	6	15	0	—
T	8	13	0	—
U	10	19	0	0
V	7	15	0	0
W	6	17	0	0
X	4	18	0	0
Y	4	16	0	0
Z	6	17	0	0
AA	10	24	0	0
BB	8	21	0	0
CC	8	18	0	0
DD	8	17	0	0
EE	5	16	0	—
FF	4	15	0	—
GG	8	16	0	0
HH	10	21	0	0
II	8	23	1	2

Notes: A dash indicates insufficient subject experience to provide a rating.
II is the co-twin described in chapter 8.

to patterns of emerging sexuality. However, two influences could operate at cross-purposes, canceling out bias. Some parents and children would feel embarrassed or guilty about the emergence of atypical sexuality and thus be reluctant to return. For others, concern about the son's atypical sexuality might motivate them to return and to seek professional guidance.

Some specific features of the "feminine" boys more likely to emerge as homosexual or bisexual men are described in the next section. To assess the representativeness of our follow-up sample, we looked for the presence of these factors in the previously "feminine" boys who remained in the study and those who dropped out. No differences were found. Thus, the percent of previously "feminine" boys who evolved as homosexual or

TABLE 4.5. Correlation between Boyhood "Feminine" Behaviors and Later Homosexuality ("Feminine" Boys Only)

Behavior	Sexual Fantasy		Sexual Behavior	
	r	p	r	p
Female role-playing	.24	.07	.30	.07
Doll-play	.36	.01	.22	NS
Female peers	.26	.07	.25	NS

bisexual for whom we have direct follow-up data should not be significantly different from those not available for follow-up.

Arguably, repeated interviewing about one's sexuality could influence one's sexuality. Therefore, we compared the sexual orientation of persons interviewed on several occasions between puberty and young adulthood with those seen prior to puberty and not again until young adulthood. Of these previously "feminine" boys seen more than once between puberty and young adulthood, half are in the heterosexual group, and half in the bisexual or homosexual group. Of those seen only once between puberty and young adulthood, two-fifths are in the heterosexual group and three-fifths in the bisexual or homosexual group. This difference is not statistically significant. Repeated interviewing is not associated with a greater degree of homosexual orientation.

SPECIFIC BEHAVIORS IN BOYHOOD AND HOMOSEXUALITY IN MANHOOD

A major question in this long-term study is whether there are features that distinguish which "feminine" boys become homosexually oriented.

One specific cross-gender behavior of the "feminine" boys is related to later homosexual fantasy. This is female-type ("dress-up") doll-play. Role-playing as a female during boyhood and a female peer group tend to be correlated. For sexual orientation behavior scores, the link with earlier female role-playing tends to be significant. However, for doll-play and female peers, the correlation is not significant (table 4.5).

The extent of early cross-dressing is not associated with sexual orientation, and orientation is not significantly related to the frequency that a boy stated his wish to be a girl, or to the degree of his rough-and-tumble play, within the "feminine boy" group (Green et al., 1986).

On the other hand, looking at both groups of boys combined, cross-gender behaviors were highly correlated with later homosexual orientation. This is to be expected in that only "feminine" boys emerged as homosexual. For female role-playing and sexual fantasy scores, $r = .63$; for female role-playing and sexual behavior scores, $r = .71$; for doll-play and sexual fantasy scores, $r = .64$; for doll-play and sexual behavior scores, $r = .64$; for female peer group and sexual fantasy scores, $r = .68$; and for female peer group and sexual behavior scores, $r = .75$ ($p < .001$ for all correlations).

Some of these variables may be associated with the boy's age at evaluation. Female role-playing and doll-play are less typical of a nine-year-old than of a four-year-old. Further, if a nine-year-old plays with dolls, the chances are that he also played with dolls at four. However, the four-year-old may have "outgrown" doll-play by nine. Thus, these correlations have also been controlled for age at evaluation, reducing the possibility that the association found between these early factors and later sexual orientation is a function of the age at which the measures were taken.

There is also the question of whether we should account for the person's age at the time the most recent sexual orientation scores are obtained. As described toward the end of this chapter, a few males became increasingly homosexually oriented as they matured through adolescence. Thus some of the young adolescent males who are now heterosexually oriented may in time evolve as more homosexual. If so, not controlling for age at follow-up could distort the associations between the earlier life events and later sexual orientation. On the other hand, the changes noted in the boys who became more homosexual with increasing age may have been specific to them. Furthermore, several of the older homosexual males who were not evaluated during early to mid-adolescence were actively homosexual during those years. Had they been evaluated then, the association between age and sexual orientation would be significantly reduced. Thus it may be neither necessary nor appropriate to control for the age at which most recent sexual orientation scores are obtained.

However, for completeness of presentation, correlations controlling for age at follow-up are also noted. When reported in this way, the correlations between female role-playing or doll-play and sexual orientation are no longer significant. The correlation with a female peer group remains a trend for sexual fantasy scores ($r = .25$, $p = .07$) but is not significant for sexual behavior scores ($r = .23$, $p = .14$).

The statistically derived "extent of femininity" measure was strongly associated with later sexual orientation for all the boys ($r = .67, p < .001$). However, within the "feminine boy" group only, the association was not significant ($r = .13$, $p < .10$ for sexual fantasy scores; $r = .06$, $p > 1.0$ for sexual behavior scores). (The lack of range of both the extent of "femininity" and the sexual orientation scores within the "feminine boy" group may operate against the correlation being significant, as noted in the previous chapter.)

THE EARLY FATHER-SON RELATIONSHIP AND LATER HOMOSEXUALITY

The extent of father-son interaction during the son's earliest years was significantly associated with the son's later sexual orientation. Considering

TABLE 4.6. Correlation between Father-Son Shared Time and Son's Later Sexual Orientation

	Fantasy		Behavior	
		All Families		
	r	p	r	p
Year 1	.34	<.01	.45	.001
Year 2	.28	.01	.40	<.01
Years 3–5	.28	.01	.31	.02
		"Feminine Boy" Families		
Year 1	.42	<.01	.44	<.02
Year 2	.29	<.05	.34	<.06
Years 3–5		NS		NS

both groups combined, less father-son shared time in the son's first year was associated with a more homosexual orientation. Less father-son shared time in the second year was also associated with a more homosexual orientation. This association was maintained for years three to five. Controlling for age at which sexual orientation scores were obtained, these associations remain significant.

For the "feminine" boys only, father-son shared time in year one was associated with a more homosexual orientation. For year two, the associations are borderline significant. For years three to five, the associations are not significant (table 4.6).

For all the boys considered together, the father's moving from the household before the son's fifth birthday was associated with a more homosexual orientation ($\chi^2 = 5.9$, $p = .01$). When boys separated from their father before age three are compared to those separated between ages three and five, there is no distinction between the groups in regard to sexual orientation. Thus, the significant component in the association between father-son separation and later sexual orientation appears to be whether the separation from biological father occurred by the fifth birthday.

The father's desire for a girl during the pregnancy is associated with the son's later homosexual orientation for the full group of boys. For the "feminine" boys only, there is a trend in the same direction, controlling for age at which sexual orientation was assessed (table 4.7).

The father's desire for a girl during pregnancy was also associated with his spending less time with his son during the first five years ($r = .22$, $p < .03$ for both groups combined; $r = .31$, $p < .04$ for the "feminine boy" group only). As noted before, less early father-son shared time was associated with the son's later homosexual orientation. When both variables (father's desire for a girl and father-son shared time) were entered into a multiple regression computation to assess their association with later

TABLE 4.7. Correlation between Parents' Desire for a Daughter during This Pregnancy and Son's Homosexual Orientation

	Fantasy		Behavior	
	Fathers			
	r	p	r	p
All Families	.40	<.01	.62	<.001
"Feminine Boy" Families	.32	.07	.36	.09
	Mothers			
All Families	.21	.06	.22	<.10
"Feminine Boy" Families	.19	<.10		NS

sexual orientation, only the father-son time variable remained significant (p = .02), both for the groups combined and for the "feminine" boys only. Thus, father-son shared time appears to be the mechanism whereby the father's desire for a girl or boy may relate to later sexual orientation.

THE EARLY MOTHER-SON RELATIONSHIP AND LATER HOMOSEXUALITY

The extent of the mother's desire for a girl during the pregnancy tends to be associated with the son's sexual orientation for the full group of boys. For the "feminine" boys only, there was also a trend in that direction for fantasy and a nonsignificant association for behavior (table 4.7).

This variable was not associated, however, with any other early mother-son variable (such as mother-son shared time). Thus, the data do not inform us as to the manner by which this variable might have been developmentally significant. By contrast, the link between the father's wish for a daughter rather than a son and the extent of early shared time provides a clue as to how the wish may have impacted on the young boy.

PRE- AND EARLY ADOLESCENCE

Not yet old enough for a man, nor young enough
for a boy; as a squash is before 'tis a peascod, or a
codling when 'tis almost an apple. 'Tis with him in
standing water, between boy and man.
                                        Twelfth Night, I:v.

A developmental study needs to examine events intermediate in time between entry as a boy and exit as a man. During those intermediate years, several factors were examined to compare "feminine" and "masculine" boys as a group, and "feminine" boys who evolved as heterosexual with those who evolved as homosexual or bisexual.

Not every boy was compared in the same way. Some families left the study shortly after their initial evaluation and returned only when the son was in young adulthood. For these families, we have interview material covering the intervening years but no standardized questionnaires completed during those years. Thus, about one-third of the long-term follow-up sample is not included in these intermediate period analyses. Furthermore, the child's age at the time of initial evaluation poses a problem for interpreting intermediate data. A boy first evaluated at age five would have seven years for follow-up prior to adolescence, whereas a boy turning twelve at initial evaluation would have one.

Variables reassessed with questionnaires during intervening years included those that had earlier discriminated the "feminine" and "masculine" boys: peer group composition, doll-play, roles taken in fantasy games, dressing in women's clothing, statements of wanting to be a girl or woman, and participation in rough-and-tumble play and sports.

Early follow-up information was combined into two principal age groups: up to year twelve; and between years thirteen and fifteen, the remaining preadolescent and early adolescent years. For brevity, the first period is referred to as age twelve and the second as age fifteen. At the time of early follow-up, several features continued to distinguish the previously "feminine" and "masculine" boys.

PREVIOUSLY "FEMININE" VERSUS PREVIOUSLY "MASCULINE" BOYS

While popularity in school, by the boys' self-reports, did not distinguish the groups at age twelve, at fifteen the previously "feminine" boys described themselves as less popular than most boys. Popularity in their neighborhoods at age twelve also did not distinguish the groups, but again, at fifteen, the previously "feminine" boys described themselves as relatively less popular.

Descriptions of the boys' social milieus were slightly different. At age twelve, there was a trend for the previously "feminine" boys to describe themselves less often as members of a clique, a difference that became significant at age fifteen. However, for describing themselves as having a small circle of close friends, or as being a loner, there were no differences.

As earlier, sports participation continued to distinguish these males. At ages twelve and fifteen, the previously "feminine" boys continued to participate less.

A female peer group clearly distinguished one group of boys during childhood (see chapter 1). The difference in peer-group composition

TABLE 4.8. Early Follow-up: Homosexual/Bisexual "Feminine" Boys versus Heterosexual "Feminine" Boys

	Homosexual/Bisexual Subgroup	
	To Age 12	Ages 13–15
Doll-play	More	—
Female role-playing	More	—
Called "sissy"	More	—

Note: A dash indicates no group difference.

lessened with adolescence. By ages twelve and fifteen, the gender of the boys' best friend no longer discriminated the groups. Nearly all boys mentioned a male. But at age fifteen, the boys' second-best friend did distinguish the groups. Nearly all boys who mentioned a female were previously "feminine" boys.

HOMOSEXUAL OR BISEXUAL VERSUS HETEROSEXUAL PREVIOUSLY "FEMININE" BOYS

Sex-typed Behaviors

In addition to comparisons of the "feminine" and "masculine boy" groups, comparisons were made between previously "feminine" boys who evolved as homosexual or bisexual and those who evolved as heterosexual.

These two subgroups did not differ at ages twelve or fifteen in the extent to which they participated in sports, the gender of their best and second-best friends, or in their social milieu.

However, at age twelve, the continuation of some cross-gender behaviors was associated with later emergence of homosexuality. There was an association between later homosexuality and the following factors: both parents' reports of continuance of doll-play ($r = .5$, $p < .01$); boys' continuing to role-play as females ($r = .5$, $p < .05$); and fathers' reports that the boys were still being called "sissy" ($r = .5$, $p < .05$). For age fifteen, these relationships no longer held (table 4.8).

Parental Relationship to Son

Parents reported their approaches to sons' cross-gender behaviors with a series of graded questionnaire responses. For example, with respect to doll-play, a parent could record his or her approach as always permitting it, permitting it only when alone, gently discouraging it, or always forbidding it. The extent to which parents' responses were permissive or negative to a series of behaviors was then compared with sons' later sexual orientation scores.

TABLE 4.9. Early Follow-up: Parents' Approach to Son Associated with a More Heterosexual Orientation ("Feminine Boy" Group)

	Mother's Approach		Father's Approach	
Son's Behavior	To Age 12	Age 13–15	To Age 12	Age 13–15
Recreational games with girls	–		–	
Role-playing as female	–	–		
Doll-play		–		
Cross-dressing, actual		–		–
Cross-dressing, improvised		–		
Sports play	+			
Rough-and-tumble play		+	+	+

– indicates a more negative approach in association with a more heterosexual orientation.
+ indicates a more positive approach.

Mothers: Age Twelve

With regard to sons' continuing preference for playing recreational games with girls, mothers' more negative responses were associated with more heterosexual scores at later follow-up ($r = -.4$, $p = .05$). For mothers' approach to sons' role-playing as a female, a more negative approach tended to be associated with a more heterosexual score ($r = -.5$, $p = .06$). For mothers' reports of their approach to sons' playing sports with other boys, a more positive approach was associated with a more heterosexual score ($r = -.4$, $p = .04$) (table 4.9).

Ratings of the amount of time mothers spent with sons were consistent with earlier reports. Less mother-son time tended to be associated with an atypical sexual identity—in this case with a more homosexual score (for time shared during weekdays with son without other children, $r = -.3$, $p = .09$; for weekdays with son and other children, $r = -.5$, $p = .01$; and for weekends, with or without other children, $r = -.3$, $p = .07$). However, there was essentially no association between the amount of mother-son shared time and the extent to which the relationship was rated by the mother as close or distant.

Fathers: Age Twelve

With respect to a son's playing recreational games with girls, a father's more negative approach tended to be associated with the son emerging with a more heterosexual score ($r = .4$, $p = .07$). A father's approach to a son's rough-and-tumble play was also associated with the son's later sexuality: when fathers were more encouraging, sons emerged with a more heterosexual orientation ($r = -.5$, $p = .04$).

Interpretation of these associations is problematic. A father may be more encouraging of a son's participation in rough-and-tumble play because the boy shows more interest. Or the son may show more interest because his father does. Or a father may be more encouraging when the son shows less interest. Therefore, we examined the extent to which boys were reported to participate in rough-and-tumble play and the parents' approach. When boys were rated as below average in interest, fathers tended to report more encouragement ($r = .3, p = .09$). This association was stronger for sports (below average interest, more father encouragement [$r = .5, p < .01$]).

There was a reversal of the earlier relation between minimal father-son shared time and sons' atypical sexual identity. For time spent during the weekday, either alone or with other children, less father-son time was associated with a more heterosexual score ($r = .5, p = .01$). For weekend time spent between father and son, without other children, there was no relationship. However, for weekend time spent with the son and other children, less time was again associated with a more heterosexual score ($r = .4, p = .03$). Fathers' reports of weekday time alone with the son were similar: more time was associated with a more homosexual score ($r = .4, p < .05$), but for weekend time shared with the son there was no relationship with later sexuality.

This change in pattern may be explained by the ratings of four boys who spent very little time with their fathers during this age period and who had heterosexual (0) fantasy scores. Three of these boys were in early adolescence when last seen and had not yet evolved patterns of interpersonal genital sexual behavior. One has become reluctant to return for another follow-up interview. As noted in the next section, there is a tendency for some boys to enter adolescence with heterosexual scores, at least for fantasy, and then to migrate to a more homosexual orientation.

In support of the earlier finding of distance between fathers and "feminine" sons is a series of related findings. First, mothers' estimates of the quality (as opposed to the quantity) of the father-son relationship were consistent with earlier reports. When mothers saw the father-son relationship as more distant than that between most fathers and sons, the son emerged with a more homosexual orientation ($r = -.5, p = .01$). This rating included fathers who had separated from their families and were no longer available for follow-up, as well as those still living with their children. Among fathers who were available for follow-up, there was a weak trend for them to rate themselves as more remote in their relationship with sons who later emerged as more homosexual ($r = -.3, p = .13$). Second, we examined the reported quality of the father-son relationship relative to the extent of their time spent together. There was no association between the amount of shared time and whether the relationship was close or distant.

Mothers: Ages Thirteen to Fifteen

Mothers' approach to cross-dressing was associated with sons' emerging sexuality. "Absolutely forbidding it," as opposed to "generally discouraging it," was associated with a more heterosexual orientation ($r = -.8$, $p < .01$). Similarly, mothers' more negative attitude toward sons' improvising feminine clothes was associated with a more heterosexual score ($r = -.6$, $p < .05$). Mothers' more negative approach to sons' role-playing as a female was also associated with a more heterosexual orientation ($r = -.5$, $p = .02$), and their approach to the boys' continuing doll-play tended to be similarly associated: a more negative approach, a more heterosexual score ($r = -.6$, $p = .06$). By contrast, mothers' reported positive approach to rough-and-tumble play was associated with a more heterosexual development ($r = .6$, $p = .03$) (table 4.9).

The association between mother-son shared time and sexual orientation was not consistent with the data at the time of initial evaluation or early follow-up (age twelve). Less time tended to be associated with a more heterosexual orientation. A possible explanation for this new pattern is that the young adolescents emerging as heterosexual were moving from the home environment into the world of teenage parties and dating, along with continued sports activities, while the adolescents emerging as homosexual were more likely to remain at home.

Fathers: Ages Thirteen to Fifteen

Fathers' more negative approach to sons' cross-dressing (forbidding it rather than discouraging it) was associated with a more heterosexual score ($r = -.7$, $p = .01$). Fathers' reported approach to sons' participation in rough-and-tumble play tended to be associated with sons' sexuality: a more encouraging approach, a more heterosexual development ($r = .4$, $p = .09$) (table 4.9).

Again, there was the "paradoxical" relationship between father-son shared time and sexual orientation. More father-son weekday time without other children present was associated with a more homosexual orientation ($r = .6$, $p = .01$). Time spent between father and son with other children present was similarly associated ($r = .4$, $p = .02$). There was no association for time spent together on weekends, with or without other children.

SHIFTING SEXUAL ORIENTATION

Before reporting extensive interview data following males to different patterns of sexual orientation, a word about the fluidity of adolescent sexual orientation is in order. Movement back and forth on the sexual continuum was apparent in eight boys. One boy was bisexual (rated 3) in fantasy at age twelve although already engaging in heterosexual behavior. By age thirteen-and-a-half, his fantasy had shifted to nearly exclusive heterosexuality (rated 1) and at fourteen to exclusive heterosexuality. His first homosexual experience did not occur until fourteen and then constituted only a small fraction of his interpersonal sexual experience (rated 1).

The second boy maintained a bisexual, though predominantly heterosexual, fantasy rating of 2 throughout the adolescent years fourteen to eighteen (without any interpersonal sexual experience) but then moved to a bisexual, but predominantly homosexual, orientation in fantasy (rated 4). This was maintained for the next four years (still in the absence of interpersonal sexual experience).

The third boy entered adolescence as bisexual, in both fantasy and behavior (2 for fantasy, 3 for behavior), but at age fifteen moved to heterosexuality (1) for both fantasy and behavior. He then shifted again, this time to predominant homosexuality (5 for fantasy, 6 for behavior) and remained there through age twenty-two.

The fourth boy reported nearly exclusive heterosexual fantasy and behavior at fifteen but a year later was bisexual (4 for fantasy, 3 for behavior) before moving to a predominantly homosexual orientation (5) at age twenty.

The fifth entered adolescence as bisexual (3 on both parameters) and maintained this orientation through age eighteen. At twenty-one, he was exclusively heterosexual, an orientation that was maintained through age twenty-three.

The sixth entered adolescence as exclusively heterosexual in fantasy and maintained this orientation through age seventeen (in the absence of interpersonal sexual experience). At eighteen, his fantasy shifted to bisexual (3) and at nineteen moved to predominantly homosexual (5), along with predominantly homosexual behavior. At twenty, both fantasy and behavior were exclusively homosexual.

The seventh was rated exclusively heterosexual both at puberty and during early adolescence (in the absence of a behavior rating), but then moved to a bisexual orientation at seventeen (4 for fantasy, 3 for behavior), and on to a predominantly homosexual orientation at nineteen (5 for fantasy, 4 for behavior).

The eighth evolved through adolescence with some bisexual fantasy (rated 2) but was exclusively heterosexual in behavior. However, at age twenty-one, his fantasy content moved to nearly exclusive homosexuality (5) and his behavior to exclusive homosexuality.

Thus, with six men the shift was toward the homosexual end of the continuum and with two toward the heterosexual end.

Next, extensive interview transcripts, describing early gender-role behavior and later sexual experience, bring life to these numbers.

5

Sexual Identity Spectrum

This chapter contains interviews with boys from both groups of families and descriptions of their behavior given by parents. My purpose here is to flesh out the skeleton of statistical analysis with human experience. Some readers will welcome the opportunity to listen to the words of people as they evolve a sexual identity; others will find it tedious. Still others will relish reading my interviews with the confidence that comes from knowing that they could have done better.

Robert Stoller instilled in me the conviction that interviews are the raw materials from which we weave the tapestry of clinical psychiatric research. He observes, "Unfortunately, data (in this case the exact quotations of what the [subjects] have said) can be dull. Still, I see no way around it. I believe that much of the disbelief (or extravagant belief of the impossible) that exists regarding the psychological roots of normal or abnormal behavior is due to a worker not demonstrating his data. However,... the audience is almost as much at fault, because it does not expect the facts, does not miss them" (Stoller, 1968, 278).

These transcripts reflect the shared experiences of many years. To select less than a dozen people from several dozen, and hundreds of pages from thousands, was taxing. Those I have selected are not the most salacious, nor are they the wittiest. However, they do reveal a fair picture either of early extensive boyhood "femininity" or of conventional "masculinity," a variety of early life events associated with these behaviors, and prominent details about later-life experiences at diverse points on the sexual identity spectrum.

The editing of these transcripts has included elimination of gross redundancies and extraneous remarks, correction of confusing syntax, and deletion of identifying personal details.

"FEMININE" BOY, TRANSSEXUAL MAN: TODD

Todd is exceptional in our study. He is the only previously "feminine" boy who currently wants sex-change surgery. Why should he have emerged as transsexual? Although he received inconsistent messages from his parents regarding early cross-gender behavior, some other boys received more positive reinforcement. Some other boys also received more attention from their mother and less from their father. Yet his desire to be a girl remained throughout boyhood and during adolescence. Further, Todd's current wish to become a woman does not appear to derive from a moral rejection of homosexual attractions. He wants to be a "normal woman."

TODD'S MOTHER DESCRIBES HIM AT AGE SEVEN

Reason for Consultation

MOTHER: Oh, I don't know, now that I'm here, I don't know. He's started changing in the past couple of months. He doesn't have his tendencies like he used to.

R. G.:   Tell me what you were concerned about.

MOTHER: He had this girl image; he wanted to be a girl. He talked like one, he acted like one, he did not want to be a boy, he did not like himself. He was surrounded always by girls, very feminine girls, that liked to play with dolls.

Onset of "Feminine" Behaviors

MOTHER: When he was two, he was always in my jewelry, my purses, always in the closet for my shoes, wanting to dress like me.

R. G.:   How often?

MOTHER: All the time. Until he was six years old. I never saw him play with a car; it was always with a doll. Or he'd make his own paper dolls. He's very creative.

R. G.:   Over what period of time did that continue?

MOTHER: Till six.

Reaction of Others

R. G.: Were there any people that he was exposed to in the beginning that thought it was funny or cute or encouraged it in some way?

MOTHER: I don't think anybody ever encouraged it, no.

R. G.: Were there people who laughed at it and thought it was funny and cute?

MOTHER: When he was littler, yes. I would think my parents, his grandparents.

R. G.: How often would that be?

MOTHER: Not that often, 'cause they live in another state.

R. G.: See, what I'm trying to understand is that you say you and your husband from the very beginning discouraged it. Yet he continued doing it. Is he always disobedient of your wishes?

MOTHER: Oh, no. He's always been a good child.

Brother's Influence on "Femininity"

MOTHER: I feel it was for attention, 'cause after his brother was born he didn't receive as much as before he was born.

R. G.: How old was he?

MOTHER: Three, and he was extremely jealous of him, and he still is to a degree.

R. G.: Did the feminine behavior begin before the birth of this brother or about that time?

MOTHER: I really can't say, 'cause I worked till his brother was born. But I know that he started liking purses and jewelry before his brother was born.

Female Identity and Role-Playing

MOTHER: He wanted to be like me.

R. G.: Did he say he wanted to be a girl?

MOTHER: Oh, yes. He never played the man role, he was either grand-mother, mother, or sister, but it never was the husband, the daddy, or the brother.

R. G.: Beginning at what age?

MOTHER: Three.

R. G.: What were your feelings about it when it first began?

MOTHER: "You're a boy; why don't you like being a boy?" And it was, "I don't know." It's still that "I don't know."

R. G.: What reasons would he give?

MOTHER: He would never give a reason, just, "I like being a girl." I'd say, "What's wrong with being a boy?" "Just don't want to be a boy, want to be a girl."

Peer Group

R. G.: When he was three and four and doing his female role-playing, what other children were around him?

MOTHER: Girls. We lived in a house and beside us was a big apartment, and it was just little girls, always little girls to play with, one little boy, but he just didn't like him. And then, of course, she [another mother] had a little boy his age, but they hated each other.

R. G.: How did the other children respond to his role-playing as a girl, cross-dressing, using jewelry, and so on?

MOTHER: The girls accepted it.

"Affection" for Mother

MOTHER: He always wanted to kiss me so he could get lipstick on him. That's another thing, that when he was as little as two years old, I was hesitant about kissing him any more 'cause he took me one day and held me and said, "This is how you're supposed to kiss," and he twisted his head a little bit and grabbed hold of me and he wouldn't let loose; and he kept kissing me and I just, it turned me off, you know. And I never let him grab hold of me; if he wants to kiss me, he is to kiss me like a child is supposed to kiss his mother. Not like an adult to an adult. And that could have been where my affection more or less stopped with him, 'cause I was hesitant about getting close to him after that.

TODD'S FATHER DESCRIBES HIM AT AGE SEVEN

Father's Concern

FATHER: A year ago he was quite obsessed with dolls and female clothes and stuff. Ever since we've moved he's seemed to have gone away from that. I don't know if it's just that he's getting older or the children that he played with. He doesn't spend as much time wanting to play with dolls as much as he did before. Before he'd talk a lot about how he wanted to be a girl and how he should have been a girl. He acted sort of cheated that he wasn't.

R. G.: How do you mean?

FATHER: Well, he just wanted to be a girl. He would say that. He would play with girls and he wouldn't participate in boys' games. He still is hesitant to play things like baseball or anything like that. He doesn't get any thrill from it.

Father's Awareness of "Feminine" Behavior

R. G.: When did this begin?

FATHER: Just a couple of years ago, to my recollection. He wanted to play with dolls, his mother's shoes, high heels. He seemed quite obsessed with that, high heels and slippers. He'd constantly get those out.

R. G.:   Beginning at what age?

FATHER: About four, about three years ago.

R. G.:   What other feminine things were there at that time?

FATHER: He liked to play house a lot with a couple of kids around here. He liked to dress up with shoes and clothes that some of the girls would have. He got some little dolls or something and he liked to dress them. He likes to put a dress on that, but he's got two types of doll now. He's got one he says is a boy and the other is a girl. Before that he just had one and would put a dress on it. He insisted at that time that it was a girl. That's all. Never has consideration about a boy.

Father's Reaction

R. G.:   What was your feeling about it initially?

FATHER: Anger mostly. I thought he did it because it did have a tendency to make me mad. At the time it seemed like that. I didn't really think he was doing it that way, but that's what it seemed like. I would come home from work in the afternoon, and he would be walking around with the shoes or slippers on.

R. G.:   With respect to the feminine interests, was there ever a time when you sort of felt it didn't really mean anything, that it would just go away and you didn't take any kind of objection to it?

FATHER: Yes.

R. G.:   Tell me about that.

FATHER: Well, I was just under the impression that it was just a stage that he was going through. I don't remember far back enough if I ever played with dolls. I kind of believed I did. Probably at three or four years old. I couldn't swear to it. It's been so long. I did have a little Kewpie doll that I won at the fair one time when I was a kid. I know I grew out of it.

R. G.:   When you were first aware of this with your son putting on shoes and dressing up and playing with dolls, did you tell him, "Don't do that," or did you ignore it?

FATHER: Well, I tried both ways, neither one seemed to work. I generally got angry and then I tried to ignore. I talked to him a couple of times. I thought that would be the thing to do. Ignoring it didn't seem to help any. Getting angry with him didn't either.

A Theory of "Femininity"

R. G.:   I'm curious about the very beginning, why do you think it developed?

FATHER: He was around his mother quite often then. She wasn't working then, and he wasn't in school. I was working two jobs then. While I was doing that, she wasn't working. She was just home with the kids. We never had spent a lot of time together. Whenever I'm home, it always seems I've got a ton and a half of things to do. It's things that my son really doesn't take an interest in, like fixing the lawn mower, working with the truck or something like that. He did enjoy one time we were painting the house. He liked painting with me. That's about the only thing. We'll sit down and play games, play card games every once in a while, Fish and Old Maid.

FAMILY REPORTS, AGES EIGHT TO THIRTEEN

Age Eight

Mother's Report

He continues to say that he wants to be a girl. He doesn't give any particular reason for it. His playmates remain exclusively girls. He identifies with Cher on TV. Mother has not permitted him to join the Indian Guides because they would be scheduled to meet at her house once a month, and she doesn't like to have people coming over. He "constantly" role-plays as a female. He is always the mother.

Age Nine

Mother's Report

His best friend is a girl. He is still interested in dolls. His behavior is generally less feminine. He gets along well now with his father. He "does everything with his father. I'm not in the picture."

Age Twelve

Todd's Report

Kids call him "fag." He remains smaller than nearly all the other children in class. He is a loner. His reaction to seeing a picture of a nude female: "It's ugly. They shouldn't pose like that."

Age Thirteen

Todd's Report

He is called "fag." He is a loner: "I don't play with girls. I don't play with anybody." Sometimes he gets erections, but he "never looks" at them: "I ignore them."

Father's Report

"I don't see any problems with him. Maybe he doesn't let me see it."

Mother's Report

He's still very shy. He associates only with girls. He's called "sissy" and "girl-lover" by the kids.

TODD'S MOTHER DISCUSSES HIM AT AGE SEVENTEEN

A Theory of Why Todd Differs from His Brother

MOTHER: Well, this boy wasn't loved like his younger brother was, because I was twenty years old, and I was scared to death of him. He was sick all the time, so I never held him. He didn't get the closeness that the younger one got. I was just the opposite with the younger one and held him all the time, just loved him to pieces, and that could be it. I was scared to death of him. I'd never taken care of a child, even babysat. I had to have somebody come in and show me how to do that. [Contrary to popular theory, she reports less mother-son contact.] And then he was sick all the time, too.

R. G.: How was he sick?

MOTHER: He couldn't keep anything down. You couldn't touch him. You couldn't even hold him to feed him. You had to prop him and not move him, because the minute you moved him everything came up.

R. G.: Until what age?

MOTHER: Four months old.

Similar Father-Son Time

R. G.: And what about his relationship to his dad compared to his brother's relationship to his dad?

MOTHER: I think that was always the same, because his father's not an affectionate person at all, but he'd hold him and play with him—but he wasn't overly fatherly like a lot of fathers are. Like, some kids prefer their father over their mother, but that wasn't the case with him. He's a good father but he just wasn't affectionate.

R. G.: Was he different with either of his boys?

MOTHER: No.

R. G.: You don't see any difference between—

MOTHER: Not at all. Not on his part—on my part.

R. G.: His work hours—were they essentially the same for both boys in their first couple of years?

MOTHER: He'd go to work about seven o'clock in the morning—he never saw them in the morning. I never saw him in the morning either. And then in the afternoon—he tried very hard with this boy, and he managed the Little League and tried to get him into ball and soccer and coached the soccer team and tried to get him involved, but he just was not interested. And he made him do it—made him take one year of minor league, and finally it just dawned on us he really wasn't interested, there was no sense forcing him any longer, so we stopped when he was about ten or eleven.

Recollection of Todd's Earlier "Feminine" Behaviors

R. G.: What do you remember about your first coming here and what your concern was about your son?

MOTHER: Oh, Jesus, it seems like so many years ago.

R. G.: It was.

MOTHER: At that time I had the feeling he wanted to be a girl, but he never expressed it in any way except just—he wouldn't play with trucks, he wouldn't go outside and play, and he always preferred dolls. He just preferred the softer, cleaner, peaceful type of playing, you know— he was totally satisfied with sitting and reading a book, or drawing a picture, or playing with a doll, and I associated this quiet behavior to girls' behavior. I mean, that's the way girls acted; boys were supposed to be rough and tough and outside playing, and he never did that. So I thought he had a problem. Plus he loved beautiful things. He loved jewelry and shoes and purses, but even to this day there were never any clothes. He liked drawing clothes and he liked dressing dolls.

R. G.: How far back do these behaviors go?

MOTHER: I'd say they started at three, when his brother was born. That's when I first noticed he was different. And his artistic ability started shining at three. I mean, he did glossings that were just flabbergasting. I couldn't believe that this little three-year-old was doing this.

R. G.: And you were concerned about the behavior?

MOTHER: Yes.

R. G.: And what were your husband's feelings about the same behaviors?

MOTHER: He just couldn't understand them. He couldn't understand how a boy would act more like a girl than a boy. I guess I can't—it just was—I really can't speak for him. He couldn't understand why he wouldn't go outside and play. He'd lock the door before he'd go outside.

R. G.: Do you remember his ever actually dressing up in girls' clothes when he was a little boy?

MOTHER: He would create some fashions. He'd take a sheet and make something out of it, and walk around in my shoes.

R. G.: You said that you felt at the time he wanted to be a girl. Why would he have wanted to be a girl back then?

MOTHER: Because girls got to dress up in pretty clothes and boys were just average Joes, you know. Boys would go out and—with dirt under their fingernails and girls would rather paint 'em. There was so much he could do with girls' hair and a girl's dress, and her body, whereas a boy just never did anything and he just liked pretty things. He was fascinated with that woman on TV, Cher.

R. G.: Cher Bono?

MOTHER: He always had a thing about shoes. More than anything else, it was shoes.

R. G.: What do you remember about shoes?

MOTHER: Oh, he'd get so frustrated when he watched television that they wouldn't show the shoes. I mean, he'd be standing up at the TV set trying to look at 'em.

R. G.: How old was he?

MOTHER: Maybe he was a little bit older—six, seven, eight.

R. G.: Do you remember him prancing around in your shoes when he was small?

MOTHER: No, he really didn't do that. He went and sat in the closet and looked at them, brought them out, and there were times he did wear a pair of shoes—he'd put on the heels and walk around—but not very much. I don't think any more so than other kids—boys his age. I don't know, it was almost as if he was ashamed of doing it, because he always did it by himself and he never asked his brother to play with him. There were boys that he grew up with in the neighborhood who would come in, and he'd never play with them.

Todd's Future

R. G.: How do you feel your son's future is going to evolve?

MOTHER: I know he's going to be successful, and he's going to, like most people, I guess, find out the hard way about a lot of stuff, so I'll just let him fantasize and dream his dreams, you know.

TODD'S ACCOUNT AT AGE SEVENTEEN

Sexual Interests

TODD: Well, there's one person I really like. Do you want to know his name?

R. G.: Okay.

TODD: Edward.

R. G.: How old is he?

TODD: Seventeen. He's an athlete. So I guess I'll start going to basketball games. I hate basketball.

R. G.: When did you start having a crush on him?

TODD: A long time ago. I don't remember—in the spring, I think—it wasn't that much. And since then I've liked someone who—oh, not really anybody else. It just passed.

R. G.: Do you see some people that you get a crush on, that sort of turn you on a little bit, sexually?

TODD: Yeah.

R. G.: What are they like usually—what characteristics do they have that are appealing to you?

TODD: Good-looking, I guess.

R. G.: What are your personal criteria for good-looking?

TODD: Well, most people I like are exotic. But then there's this one guy I started liking, he's really unpopular. I don't even know why I like him. He never shaves or anything.

R. G.: There's something about him that attracts you?

TODD: Yeah, I don't know why. Well, my best friend, this girl, she and I always had different tastes.

R. G.: In what way?

TODD: She likes other people, and I go, "Oh, my God, are you kidding?"

R. G.: Well, that's good. You don't want to be competing for the same guy!

TODD: No, we never are.

R. G.: That wouldn't help the friendship very much, would it?

TODD: It wouldn't matter.

R. G.: What's held you back in terms of approaching people?

TODD: Well, they're not—they're straight. It's just really nice from way back just looking at them, that kind of thing. You don't like to make waves.

R. G.: Do you have any attractions for females too, or is it all males?

TODD: Males.

R. G.: When do you think that began?

TODD: I think I was a sophomore. It wasn't very long ago, really. I've always been, like, feminine, but I never really thought of men at all.

R. G.: How old were you when you first became aware of sexual interests in males?

TODD: Maybe fifteen.

R. G.: Before then you weren't aware of crushes on guys?

TODD: Uh-uh. I realized that I liked men better than women, probably.

R. G.: In what way?

Transsexual Identity

TODD: Just—I don't know—I just wanted to *be* a woman, so I thought that they would be the ones I would like. Like on the screen, you know, famous people like that—not real people.

R. G.: When do you remember wanting to be a woman?

TODD: Since *forever*.

R. G.: You still do?

TODD: Yeah.

R. G.: Tell me why.

TODD: I don't know. *I feel like a woman inside.*

R. G.: Tell me what you mean by that.

TODD: I just—I like to dress up. I never do, but I'd like to. They just seem better. I don't know—a better life.

R. G.: Why? I'm going to press you—in what way?

TODD: I don't know. I just do.

R. G.: When you say a better life, tell me what that means to you.

TODD: I just want to be a woman. Obviously, I guess I like men.

Aversion to Homosexuality

R. G.: You don't have to be a woman to have sex with a man.

TODD: Yeah, but it would be kinda gross.

R. G.: Why?

TODD: Because—I don't know—I think that's very gross.

R. G.: But obviously you know there are a substantial number of men who have sex with men without becoming a woman. You know that?

TODD: Yeah.

R. G.: It's not new.

TODD: It doesn't appeal to me too much.

R. G.: So one of the things is that if you were a woman you could have sex with men in a way that you would find more acceptable?

TODD: Yeah.

R. G.: That's one thing.

TODD: That's the basic problem. I want to be a woman *before* I want to have sexual relations with a man.

R. G.: Do you have strong religious feelings about homosexuality being sinful?

TODD: I don't believe in God.

R. G.: So it's not a religious thing. But there is something else about homosexuality that really disturbs you, as not being right?

TODD: I just—like I said—it's not very important really, sex is just something people do for pleasure. It's not necessary to survive except if you're going to have children, unless you're going to have a baby with them, it's not a big thing. It just happens once or twice, or whatever.

Other Reasons for Wanting to Be a Woman

TODD: I'd like to have a baby, too, but I know I couldn't.

R. G.: What else?

TODD: I don't know. If I were a woman I could act like one of them, without having to suppress it.

R. G.: What are you suppressing?

TODD: Not too much. I don't do that much anymore. I'm just like—you know—I just do what I want.

R.G.: What are you suppressing?

TODD: That I want to be a woman. I just don't go out and tell people that. Like in the future I might want to love someone, and be able to marry the person. It's just like sex is something that you are supposed to do to have children, right? I mean, I know people do it for pleasure, but I don't—maybe it's because I haven't done it, but I don't understand it. I'm frigid, I guess.

R.G.: You would like to dress as a woman?

TODD: Yeah.

R.G.: If you were left to your own devices, that's what you'd like to do.

TODD: Uh-huh.

R.G.: When you think about dressing as a woman, is that a sexual turn-on for you? Does that give you an erection?

TODD: No. And I don't need to dress like a woman to feel like a woman.

R.G.: But you'd feel more comfortable if you were dressed as one?

TODD: I wouldn't always go around dressed like one, like all made up or anything. It's just that I'd feel free that I could if I wanted. I'd probably still wear jeans because I like jeans. And I'd probably even keep my hair short, too. I don't like long hair. I'd keep my nails long.

R.G.: So, what part is important for such a drastic change?

TODD: I don't know. I just feel like a woman—not necessarily because I dress like one. If I were a woman and I were dressed the same way, I don't think I'd feel much different.

R.G.: Okay, so tell me—when you say, "I feel like a woman," what does that mean?

TODD: I don't know. I'd just be one. I'd know I was one. I'd feel happier.

Female Body Image

R.G.: When you say, "I feel like a woman," do you imagine yourself having a female body?

TODD: Yeah.

R.G.: Do you imagine yourself having a woman's breasts?

TODD: Yeah.

R.G.: Do you imagine yourself having a penis?

TODD: No penis.

R.G.: Do you imagine yourself having a vagina?

TODD: Yeah, I guess.

R.G.: Do you imagine yourself with a vagina, or not?

TODD: Well, I just—yeah, that's—I'm not sure what it is. It's just the sexual part, right?

R.G.: It's the opening and the canal inside.

TODD: Oh, yeah.

R.G.: You imagine that?

TODD: Yes.

R. G.:   So when you say you feel like a woman, you imagine yourself with a woman's body?

TODD: Yeah. I don't know how much the surgery costs. I don't know what kind of results it can have.

Promoting a Trial Period and Psychological Counseling

R. G.:   Results are variable from person to person, and it's more than just how good the technical results of surgery are. The more difficult issue is whether you or any other particular person would really do better living as a woman than as a man. That's the kind of question that it takes a couple of years of trial—living as a woman—a couple of years of meeting regularly with somebody who's experienced in counseling people who are contemplating this kind of a change.

TODD: It takes a long time?

R. G.:   In the best interest of someone who is considering a change like that, keep in mind that it is an irreversible change—you don't change back again.

TODD: I wouldn't want to.

R. G.:   Okay. But the fact is that one should be absolutely convinced, given the assumption that you can't change back, that this is the best thing for you. What most doctors do who counsel people during this transition period is require people to live for a couple of years as a woman before having the surgery, so that they can be—

TODD: How can you live as a woman if you're not?

R. G.:   Well, you dress as one, and you work as one, and you change your name, and you have different friendship groups who only know you as a woman. You may not have sex with anybody, but you're living a social role of a woman. You need to know whether that's going to be a comfortable role when you get into it and can't get out again. It's a trial period because it's happened that some people who were absolutely convinced that they should change their sex went ahead and did it without the trial period, and then had regrets afterwards. Whereas people who have given it a full trial like this, of a couple of years, and have a chance to meet regularly to share what it's like on a day-to-day basis of living as a woman, and who at the end of the trial period remain convinced that life is going to be much better for them in that way, those people generally do better after the surgery without substantial regrets. It's not something that you want to leap into. It's a one-way street.

TODD: Some of them do it when they're old.

R. G.:   Well, you're not geriatric yet. Nobody is telling you to wait until you're sixty.

TODD: Well, that's what I saw on TV once. This guy changed when he was, like, fifty or something. That was ridiculous.

R. G.:   Well, there are people who have done this at various ages, from twenty to sixty, and each individual has a different reason for why he did it at a certain age and why he waited.

TODD: I want to get it done as soon as I can.

Onset of Transsexual Feelings

R. G.:   How long have you felt that strongly that you feel you are a woman, or feel like a woman?

TODD: I don't *feel* like a woman, I *want* to feel like a woman. Do you understand?

R. G.:   No, tell me again.

TODD: I mean, I don't sit here feeling like I have breasts or something, but I want to have them.

R. G.:   How long have you wanted to have them?

TODD: Well, I suppose since I—since I was about twelve or thirteen. When I started to mature—sexually mature—I wanted to mature the *other* way.

R. G.:   Did that surprise you?

TODD: No, because I'd been going along like a girl so far, so I just kept going. Another thing—if I were a woman I would shave my legs.

R. G.:   You would?

TODD: I would. I've got hairy legs, too. If I were a man, right, I wouldn't want to shave my legs, so—

R. G.:   Do you feel you've been wanting to be a woman all your life?

TODD: Yeah.

R. G.:   You said earlier the body part came when you were around twelve or thirteen, but a few minutes ago you said that you felt you wanted to be a woman as far back—

TODD: Or a girl, at that time.

Recollection of Childhood "Feminine" Behaviors

R. G.:   How far back do you actually remember that?

TODD: I used to play with dolls sometimes, and when I was really little I used to carry a purse and dress up with my mother's shoes and hats.

R. G.:   Did your mother know about this?

TODD: I think so. I've seen a picture of me in shoes.

R. G.:   How old were you when that picture was taken?

TODD: About two or three.

R. G.:   What does it look like?

TODD: It's me with women's shoes. My brother had a wig on, too. I think it was Halloween.

R. G.:   You said you thought your mother was aware of your doing some of these girl-type things when you were a little kid.

TODD: Yeah.

R. G.: What was her feeling about it?

TODD: Well, she didn't want me playing with dolls, I don't think. As far as the shoes, that was just playing, I guess. I don't remember. I just remember the picture.

R. G.: And your father? Do you remember what he knew about it?

TODD: It wasn't private or anything.

R. G.: What about the doll-play?

TODD: I remember once I was playing at a person's house—I don't remember who it was—and I was playing behind the chair so I could do it privately, you know, and I remember getting caught and they took it away. And then I used to play at someone else's house, we used to play—but that was just a big dollhouse.

R. G.: What are the advantages of being a girl instead of a boy?

TODD: I don't think there really are any.

TODD'S MOTHER DESCRIBES HIM AT AGE EIGHTEEN

R. G.: What's your understanding of where he is sexually?

MOTHER: He still doesn't know, or I don't think he knows. There for a while, until recently, he was determined he was a girl, mentally. I found a book about Christine Jorgensen and I just thought this might be interesting to him, so I took it home to him, and boy, he became obsessed with that book. For about two months, he kept telling me I should read it and blah, blah, blah, and this is the way he thought and felt, etc., and in a moment of anger I ripped the book up. But I told him later I'd go get it at the library, but it was never mentioned again.

R. G.: What made you think he might be interested in reading that book?

MOTHER: Because he's always had this thing that he thought he was a boy outside of a girl's body. He's a boy on the outside and a girl on the inside.

R. G.: So he had told you that before you bought the book.

MOTHER: Yes. When he was young, when we first started coming here, I thought that he had the homosexual tendencies. But he doesn't. He's not gay, either.

R. G.: When did he first tell you that he was a woman or wants to become a woman?

MOTHER: About two years ago. He didn't really say that. It's just that he said that he thought he found other boys good-looking in the sense that a girl would see and would look at a boy. But it never went any farther than that. He just one day told me, sitting at the kitchen table, and that was it. It wasn't any big shock, I just knew that he had been thinking about this for years and I just thought I'd go along with him. Up until he becomes of age, maybe as they say, and then we'll take it from there. I am not for it, but I'm not closed-minded enough to be against it.

TODD'S ACCOUNT AT AGE EIGHTEEN

Evolution of Transsexualism

R. G.: How are you feeling about yourself?

TODD: The same.

R. G.: Last year you said that you had been increasingly feeling like a woman and that you were quite positive towards having medical treatments, surgical treatments, hormone treatments, to become a woman.

TODD: Mmmm, cause I just read this book. I read this book, *The Christine Jorgensen Story*.

R. G.: As you read the book, did you find yourself feeling very much like Christine, as she described her life?

TODD: Mmmm.

R. G.: In what way?

TODD: Well, in every way, except she was saying that she didn't have sexual feelings toward men.

R. G.: You have?

TODD: Yes, but other than that, it was all the same. All of it was really weird. My mother bought me that book, too. I don't know, it was like a book sale, and she brought home three books for me and that was one of them.

R. G.: One of them was *The Christine Jorgensen Story*? What do you make of that?

TODD: I don't know. I didn't know what it was until I read it. And I read it and she said, "Oh, I wish I had never given it to you."

R. G.: You think she was kind of hinting to you by having brought the book that she knew that you were feeling a little bit like that?

TODD: I guess. I don't know.

R. G.: I mean, there are lots of other possible books. She could have selected *Call of the Wild*.

Obstacles to Sex Change

TODD: I don't want sex change, 'cause there are too much problems.

R. G.: What sort of problems do you think about?

TODD: Well, there's money, then there's all the time it takes, and then like, I don't know, I want to be normal, I just don't want to do it.

R. G.: What do you mean you want to be normal?

TODD: I want to be—I don't know—I'd be different.

R. G.: You'd be different from other women?

TODD: Yeah—I don't know—I'd probably be really ugly too.

R. G.:   That book by Christine Jorgensen was written many years ago, and Christine's surgery was about thirty years ago.

TODD: Oh.

R. G.:   Let's assume that the surgery, the technique of surgery has progressed a lot over the years, so that with a good surgeon, good physicians today, in fact you would look pretty much like a normal woman. Not exactly, but pretty much like one. How would you feel about the surgery in that case?

TODD: I think I would want it. But I wouldn't think about it until I was out of college, and then I wouldn't want to do it. I want it now.

Preparation for Change

R. G.:   What generally happens is that before a surgeon would do the operation, he will want you to be living as a woman for about two years, you see, and he will want you to be on female-type hormones for about two years, so that you have a fairly realistic experience of what it is to live as a woman prior to surgery.

TODD: I don't want to live like a woman for two years.

R. G.:   Why?

TODD: 'Cause it seems like a waste of time, and—I don't know—would I get dressed up and stuff? And fool people. It's too weird.

R. G.:   About the fooling people?

TODD: Yeah. I don't know what to do.

R. G.:   Well, the reason for the period first is that the medical profession wants to do reversible things before the irreversible. We want people who think they might want to have the surgery, which is irreversible, to first try on the real-life test, to experiment with what it's like on a day-to-day basis, to present oneself to the world as a woman. It takes practice in terms of use of cosmetics, dressing, walking, relating to people. It takes a lot of practice and time and trial. There are some people who during the year or two find that it feels increasingly comfortable and they like it, and they go on for the surgery. There are others who find that it's not all that their fantasy said it was going to be, that they are disappointed with it, and they decide not to have the surgery. But the time to make a decision that surgery is not for you is before the surgery, not after. Can you imagine yourself with a female genital area?

TODD: I guess.

R. G.:   And when you think about that, how does that make you feel?

TODD: Just like a woman, I guess.

R. G.:   When you think about your penis being gone and your testicles being gone, how does that make you feel?

TODD: Like a woman, not like "No!" or anything.

R. G.:   Does it frighten you?

TODD: No.

R. G.: It makes you feel like a woman?

TODD: Yeah, but I don't know if I'd feel normal. That's what I keep thinking. I will always know that I used to be a man.

R. G.: Well, that's true. You would always have that history, that you were, in fact, at one point in your life, a male, and that's true of every person who ultimately decides whether to have the surgery. The question then becomes whether living as a woman, knowing you were a man, is better than continuing to live as a man. And that's the decision that some people make in one direction and others make in the other direction. But I think you've put your finger on a very important issue.

Sexual Identity

R. G.: Which would you rather be right now if it could just magically work out? Would you rather remain a man or would you rather be a woman?

TODD: A woman.

R. G.: A woman.

TODD: But I would like to have been born one. You know, I don't want to go through all these problems of being one.

R. G.: Why would you rather be a woman. Or have been born one?

TODD: Cause I feel like one, you know what I mean?

R. G.: I don't. Tell me how you feel like one.

TODD: I just do, I don't know why. I just identify with them. I don't know if I think like them, I don't know what they think like, but you know, I like men and everything.

R. G.: But there are men who like men who feel like men. How do you feel like a woman?

TODD: I don't really know. I just do. I like to dress like them, act like them.

R. G.: How is it different when you feel like a woman?

TODD: I don't know. I've never felt like a man, so I don't know.

Ideal Woman

R. G.: How would you look as your ideal woman?

TODD: I want a nose job. I hate my nose, so after that's fixed, I think I'd be all right. I'm going to grow my hair long, I'm going to try, but, I don't think I'd keep it that way forever, I'd cut it eventually.

R. G.: Can you imagine your body?

TODD: Just normal, not like exceptionally, you know, wonderful or anything, just normal.

Evolution of Transsexualism

R. G.: Do you feel that compared to a year ago, your wish to become a woman is stronger, weaker, or about the same?

TODD: It's the same, but it's like, I don't think about really doing it as much. It's not as serious. I still want to but I don't want to go through all the pain or problems and the this and that. I'm too lazy.

R. G.: Well, I think you've got a realistic view on things. There are difficulties, and some people decide that the difficulties are worth it, and some people decide that they are not, and only you can decide that. I think you can do some additional reading. You might have the opportunity to talk with some people who have gone through it, to share your concerns with them, to see the extent to which they feel that it was or was not worth it. The extent to which they feel your worries are well founded or not too much to worry about. I think the way that responsible people make that decision is by regularly sitting down with a professional counselor who has seen lots of people who feel the way you do, to meet with you regularly, and discuss the pros and cons, so that whatever decision you finally make is a well thought out one.

TODD: You mean, like, weekly or something like that? I'm sure I could—yeah, I could, I guess. It's just I don't—what would we talk about?

R. G.: You talk about what you're feeling, about how the days are going, about what the trial period of living as a woman is like, what your expectations are, how life will be different for you as a woman. It's important to understand and appreciate those things beforehand, while you are preparing for it; you may or may not decide to go through with it after you have a fuller appreciation of it. The possibility also exists that your thoughts about sex with men as a male may change over time. Now, you also have my number, so that you can call me. I want you to keep in touch with me so that you can continue to tell me what's going on.

TODD: You mean, just call to tell you something?

R. G.: Tell me what's happening with you. Call me collect and talk to me.

TODD: I don't have much to say.

R. G.: Whatever is going to be happening in the next few years for you, whatever you do, the decision obviously is going to be yours, but I want you to have a lot of feedback from people who are very experienced in talking to people like you. And I am, and other people are as well, and I want you to know that I'm here to help you in making your decision. It will be your decision, but I want to feed things back and forth with you.

Vocational Goal

R. G.: A last question: What do you want to do professionally?

TODD: I only want to act.

R. G.: You want to be an actor?

TODD: No, an actress.

"FEMININE" BOY, HOMOSEXUAL MAN: BOBBY

Bobby was a small boy, non-athletic, and teased by other boys. He was very feminine manneristically. Early sexual experiences with females were disappointing. By contrast, early sexual experiences with males were physically and emotionally gratifying. Bobby has come to terms with being homosexual.

INTERVIEW WITH BOBBY AT AGE FIVE

After Taking the It-Scale for Children (a test in which a child holds a neuter stick figure "It" and makes a variety of sex-typed play and activity choices)

R. G.: What about those things that It was playing with?

BOBBY: Well, there were children and there were lots of things. There were Indians and some clothes.

R. G.: What kinds of clothes and kinds of toys were they?

BOBBY: There was a teapot, tea set, and a doll, and a carriage, and a tractor.

R. G.: And what kinds of toys did It like best?

BOBBY: The purse—carriage.

R. G.: Are those the things It likes to play with?

BOBBY: Yes.

"Its" Sex ("It" is presumed to become a reflection of the child's sexual identity)

R. G.: Why do you suppose It liked to play with those? Make up a story about it.

BOBBY: It was a girl.

R. G.: It was a girl?

BOBBY: Yes.

R. G.: Okay, go on. That's a good start. What are some of the things a little girl would like to do that maybe a little boy wouldn't like to do?

BOBBY: Play with the tea set and enjoy that, and play with the purse and a carriage and a dress.

R. G.: Why do girls like to play with those things? Do you know why?

BOBBY: Because they're better.

R. G.: What would happen if a little girl instead of wanting to play with girl things wanted to play with things like a fire truck, guns, toy soldiers? What would happen if girls wanted to do the things that boys usually do?

BOBBY: I don't know.

R. G.: Do you think anybody would get angry?

BOBBY: No, not exactly.

Awareness of Parents' Attitude toward "Feminine" Behavior

R. G.: What if there was a little boy who wanted to do things that girls did? How would that be?

BOBBY: That wouldn't be very good. Because he's just being bad.

R. G.: It would be bad?

BOBBY: Yes.

R. G.: How would the little boy know that was bad?

BOBBY: His mother would tell him.

R. G.: Would anybody else tell him that it's bad?

BOBBY: His friends.

R. G.: What would his friends say?

BOBBY: That he's acting like a girl.

R. G.: They would tease him, huh?

BOBBY: Yeah.

R. G.: What about daddy?

BOBBY: He'd say, "Stop doing that."

Role-playing

R. G.: Let's make believe I'm a little boy and I said, "I want to dress up like a girl, I want to make believe I'm a girl."

BOBBY: That's not right.

R. G.: Why isn't it? I feel like doing it.

BOBBY: Because you aren't a girl.

R. G.: Why can't I make believe I'm a girl?

BOBBY: Because you're not a girl and you shouldn't wear dresses.

R. G.: But what if just for a little while I want to make believe I'm a little girl? Is that okay?

BOBBY: Yeah.

R. G.: Will you tell anybody? Will you tell my mommy if I make believe I'm a girl?

BOBBY: No.

R. G.: Will you tell my daddy?

BOBBY: No. You shouldn't do it very often.

R. G.: What if I want to do it?

BOBBY: You're not a girl.

R. G.: What if I want to be a girl? Do you think I should be allowed to do those things if I want to?

BOBBY: Yeah, but you shouldn't.

R. G.:   I shouldn't? Why not?

BOBBY: Because you're just not a girl, but it's okay.

Could I Change Sex?

R. G.:   If I really wanted to become a girl, would that be possible for me?

BOBBY: No.

R. G.:   Why wouldn't it be possible?

BOBBY: Because you just can't turn into a girl.

R. G.:   What if I let my hair grow very long so it comes down past my shoulders, and what if I wear dresses all the time, and girls' shoes with high heels, could I become a girl that way?

BOBBY: Well, the only thing is you'd have to have a different voice.

R. G.:   What if I raised my voice real high and sounded like a girl? And my hair was long, and I wore a dress? Would I be a girl then?

BOBBY: Yes.

R. G.:   Are you sure about that?

BOBBY: Yes.

R. G.:   Wouldn't I have to do something about something else to become a girl?

BOBBY: No.

R. G.:   Would anybody be able to find out that I'm really not a girl?

BOBBY: Not if you grow your hair long.

R. G.:   Nobody would ever find out?

BOBBY: No.

R. G.:   What if I got sick and had to go to the doctor to be examined? Would the doctor know that I was really a boy, or would he think that I was really a girl?

BOBBY: He'd know you were a boy, but I don't know what he'd do.

R. G.:   How would he know that I'm really a boy?

BOBBY: 'Cause he'd know your last name.

R. G.:   What else would tell him?

BOBBY: Your first name.

R. G.:   Well, what if I changed my name? What if I called myself by a girl's name?

BOBBY: He wouldn't know.

R. G.:   He wouldn't know? What about when he examines me to see where I'm sick. Would he know then?

BOBBY: I don't know.

Anatomic Differences

R. G.:   Well, let's say he makes me take all my clothes off, okay? And I'm laying down on the table, on the examining table, and I have all my clothing off, would he know I'm a boy then?

BOBBY: Yes.

R. G.: How would he know that?

BOBBY: It's a bad word and I better not say it.

R. G.: I don't think it's a bad word. You can say anything you want here. What word would you like to be able to say?

BOBBY: From the wiener.

R. G.: From the wiener? I would still have a wiener, and that's the way he'd know that I'm really a boy?

BOBBY: Yes.

Gender Constancy (chapter 2) Has Been Achieved

R. G.: So what you're saying, then, is that even though I grew long hair and wore dresses and changed my name and raised my voice real high, that wouldn't make me a girl. I'd still be a boy.

BOBBY: Right, so that's why boys can't be girls.

R. G.: Even though they want to be very much.

BOBBY: Yes.

R. G.: That's right. I think you've got that pretty clear in your mind.

BOBBY: Yes.

BOBBY'S MOTHER DESCRIBES HIM AT AGE FIVE

Onset of Bobby's "Feminine" Behavior

R. G.: Why don't you tell me why you brought your son here?

MOTHER: Well, I'd say about the time I separated from my husband, he started behaving strangely. He started running around with all kinds of hand movements, and dressing up in little girls' clothes—things like that—and I thought, well, maybe it's just a stage he's going through, and I didn't—

R. G.: How old was he?

MOTHER: A little over three. I didn't think too much of it, and I asked my pediatrician, who is *no longer* my pediatrician, what I should do about it. He said, "When he reaches puberty and he starts wearing dresses, *then* you know you've got a problem."

Fantasy Characters with Whom Bobby Identifies

MOTHER: His favorite characters are Cinderella, Snow White, and he loves the Wizard of Oz, and copies the girl. Everything is girls this, girls that, and this psychologist told me that if he wanted to do those things, just send him to another room. That didn't work.

R. G.: Does he like to draw pictures?

MOTHER: Yes. Girls—only girls. Practically refuses to draw pictures of boys. And if he ever does, I'm in the picture, too. It's always me. He says, "I don't know how to draw a boy." I've showed him many times. "I can't do it. I can't do it. I can't do it."

Cross-Dressing or Improvising Women's Clothes

R. G.:   What about dressing up in girls' clothes?

MOTHER: He loves to do that. I've had problems with him at the school that he goes to in the afternoons. He's in a sports club type thing for kids from five to twelve, and the little girls, of course, play dress-up. He's always in with the girls playing, and they've tried to get him away from the clothes, and even made him a sailor suit so that he would have something if he wants to dress up, at least he can dress up in boys' clothes. And at home he's always putting on a blanket, you know, as a cape. He has put on my bathrobe, my nightgown, and things like that. No underpants or brassieres. I've caught him in a slip every once in a while—you know, a half slip that looks like a skirt. He puts on my shoes. I thought it was a little normal stage. A lot of kids like to dress up.

R. G.:   How often would he dress up?

MOTHER: I couldn't put it down in numbers, but it's quite often. He's got that cape on almost every day in some way or another and flies around the room. He's the Wicked Witch of the West. And I tell him, "If you've got a cape on, be Batman—be Robin." No, he's got to be the Cat Woman.

R. G.:   When did he first begin dressing up?

MOTHER: I guess it's about two years now—when he was four.

R. G.:   What was your feeling the first time you saw him dressed up?

MOTHER: I probably thought it was cute. I really don't remember the first time, but you know, it's just one of the normal things kids do, and I probably didn't think too much of it. Of course, when I catch him in my clothes, you know, anything of mine, I tell him to take it off, its *mine*. But, with the cape and things like that, I probably didn't pay too much attention to it at first. [Here, the mother suggests a mixed message about the cross-dressing: ownership, not gender, is the basis of her objection.]

Bobby's Strong Need to Cross-Dress

R. G.:   Have you ever put your foot down and said, "No, you absolutely cannot dress up?"

MOTHER: Yes. He does it behind my back. It's just something—a compulsion—he's got to dress up. One thing I did do a couple of weeks ago. I told him that if he promised to behave just like a good little boy is supposed to behave, that I might get him a puppy. The very next day he had on a skirt in school. I told him, "Look, you blew it. That's it. No puppy. You can't have it," and he told me, "You forgot to remind me that morning." I said, "There's no reason for me to remind you every morning that you're a little boy, and you're supposed to behave like a little boy."

Mannerisms

MOTHER: The way he walks—swinging his hips, and to top it off, he has a slight lisp, which drives me crazy.

"I Am a Girl!"

R. G.:   Has he ever said to you, "I want to be a girl!" or "I am a girl?"
MOTHER: He has more or less said that he would like to be a girl.
R. G.:   Do you recall exactly what he said?
MOTHER: "I am a girl."
R. G.:   When does he say that?
MOTHER: I think it's usually when he's got the girls' clothes on. He hasn't said it too many times—five, six times altogether. I just told him, "You're not a girl. You're a little boy!" What else can I say to him? I don't know what else to say.

Role-playing as a Mother

MOTHER: Usually he plays like a baby, or he says he plays a little boy, but I know from overhearing some of the games they're playing that he plays a sister, or he wants to be the mother, and the other kids tell him, "No, you're a boy. You're going to be the father or a brother," or something like that, and he'll give in, but I have heard him say he wants to be the mother.

Peer Group

R. G.:   With whom does he generally want to play house?
MOTHER: Well, there are quite a few kids in that building. He seems to pick out the little girls to play with. There are some younger and some older. The older ones—he kind of clings to them a little bit more, rather than the younger ones.
R. G.:   Predominantly he plays with girls?
MOTHER: Yeah. I told him, "Go out and play with the boys. Go ride your bike," and when he plays—when he tries to go play with the boys—they tease him and make fun of him and they don't want to play with him.

Playacting and Role-taking

MOTHER: He loves the Wizard of Oz. He knows every word to the entire story. He's always picked up the words and can sing all the songs, ever since he was two years old. He's known words from any song he hears. Sometimes he'll throw in a little Cinderella or Snow White—something like that—only most of the time it's Wizard of Oz, and he usually plays Dorothy or the Wicked Witch.

R. G.: Does he improvise costumes?

MOTHER: Yeah, he'll find a stick or a broom to be the Witch, or he'll try to find a pair of my shoes that are like Dorothy's shoes—you know, the magic shoes that she has—and throws on a cape, or finds something that would look like girls' clothes while he's playing it.

R. G.: How would you compare the amount of playacting and role-taking this boy does compared to other kids his age?

MOTHER: He seems to spend an awful lot of time doing it, whereas most kids you see outside playing during the day, doing something. He seems to play at being somebody else besides himself, more times than he is himself.

•

Bobby was seen in a group with other "feminine" boys, once a week for an hour. The boys were primarily involved in play activities and learning noncompetitive sports skills. They talked about doing girl-type and boy-type things and sometimes criticized each other for cross-gender behaviors in a manner similar to the criticism they received from other boys. The mother was seen weekly in a group with other mothers of "feminine" boys. The goal was for mothers to share accounts of their attempts to dissuade their sons' cross-gender behaviors that caused the sons social distress. They also pointed out to each other ways in which they appeared to be encouraging cross-gender behavior (Green and Fuller, 1973[b]).

The group sessions continued for about a year. The boy's behavior remained very "feminine," and peer group teasing continued. The mother decided not to seek additional formal therapy. She remarried and hoped that the new father would influence her son toward a more "masculine" identification. The boy was seen for follow-up about every two years. In early adolescence he had sexual relationships with both females and males.

INTERVIEW WITH BOBBY AT AGE SEVENTEEN

Emergence of Homosexual Orientation

R. G.: When was the first time you became aware of the desire for a male?

BOBBY: Well, my first fling that I ever had I was like seven. I kissed a lot with this guy. That was the extent of it. He only used to kiss. It was closemouthed, very chaste. He was a wonderful kisser. I didn't know how to kiss, so I didn't know that you're supposed to breathe through your nose or anything like that and kissed until I turned blue. I was about seven or eight and I didn't feel bad about it or anything like that. I didn't feel like I was doing something forbidden or wrong. I felt very comfortable with it. Then when I was nine I had sex with a girl. I didn't know what I was doing but just sort of lay there. I knew the specifics, but that was it.

R. G.: But your attractions to men were earlier.

BOBBY: Yeah, well I did that once but—I'm not sure if it was because he was a boy or not.

R. G.: But you also had sex with a girl a couple of years later.

BOBBY: Yeah.

R. G.: So why didn't those experiences at a fairly young age, males and females—why did one assume prominence and the other go away?

BOBBY: I liked girls. I got along with girls a lot better than I got along with boys. But I was being referred to, I guess, as their friend, never their boyfriend. I needed that and I still do, I need the affection. I wasn't getting rejected all the time, but I wanted to be like everyone else in school, and so I would ask girls to go with me and things like that. Most of the time they said no, but I was always everyone's friend. I had a lot of friends that were girls and not a lot that were guys.

R. G.: You said that you didn't think that the pressure, the labeling of you as being different or sissy or anything, contributed to your becoming gay. Why?

BOBBY: Because if anything I would have . . . I feel I would have fought against such a thing because it was these people that were teaching me to hate. I had such pent-up anger and frustration. If anything, you would think that that would turn me away from it and I would go out and prove that I wasn't. So when I finally said, "You are," that hurt the most because everything that they had been calling me turned out to be true. I held it against my peers because they knew before I did. Even though in the back of my head I'd said to myself, "Well they're just being vicious and they don't know shit."

Heterosexuality versus Homosexuality

BOBBY: I tried. I had relations with girls and everything like that when I was in seventh grade, but in ninth grade I had my first relationship, real, with a guy. There was quite a difference that I could see.

R. G.: How?

BOBBY: I knew it felt good on me so I knew what to do on him, number one because it was generally physical. It was somebody who showed me affection, and I latched on to it. It was not a very good relationship, because he just turned around and said, "Well, this isn't for me," and I went, "Oooh," and just got really crazy about it because I thought, well, why not? It's good for me. Why isn't it good for you?

R. G.: Is there a difference in the emotional part, not just the physical part, but the emotional part of a sex relationship with a woman versus a man?

BOBBY: Yeah.

R. G.: In what way?

BOBBY: I felt stronger for him. I felt what I thought at the time as love, deep affection, because I really cared about him. And girls—I heard the guys say, "They're just easy lays," and everything like that, and I didn't want that. I wanted something that meant something. I wanted a relationship that meant more to me than just getting off, and I found it with him. I found that there was a much stronger and deeper feeling.

BOBBY'S MOTHER DESCRIBES HIM AT AGE SEVENTEEN

Mother Acknowledges Bobby's Homosexuality

MOTHER: Well, he is a confirmed homosexual, there is no question about that. He's accepted it. I've pretty much accepted it, and I'm learning to live with it; obviously he has, and he doesn't seem too unhappy in this role. He's getting to the point now where he can explain it to other people also and say, "Yes, I am a homosexual." So he's a little more comfortable with it himself, and I've been able to say, "Yeah, he is gay," which makes it a little bit easier being able to realize that I'm never going to have grandchildren, and that could have been, but, you know, he says, "Look, you want a grandchild? I'll get you one." He's willing to oblige me in any way possible.

R. G.: When did this transition take place?

MOTHER: I think—well, we sat down and really, really discussed it about six months ago, and I said, "Look, I got to know one way or the other. What's it going to be?" And he said, "I'm gay, that's it. No ifs, ands, or buts about it." He's tried a male/female relationship, and he tried it with the wrong person, somebody that he's been very close with since he's about seven or eight years old, the one he calls his sister. And that was the wrong one to try it with, and it was very unsuccessful.

R. G.: In what way?

MOTHER: Well, he said it was nothing. And he didn't reach a climax; he doesn't know whether she did or not, but he said he didn't. And he has had homosexual relationships. He's been going to some discos that basically cater to the gay clientele, and he had a few relationships. Not as many as he would like, I'm sure, but he has had a few.

R. G.: How many partners, would you guess?

MOTHER: That I'm aware of, I would say probably in the last year maybe five altogether. I'm sure there are times that I don't know about. I mean, we do talk a lot, but we don't talk all the time.

R. G.:   And are these one-night stands, or are these relationships that continue for some duration?

MOTHER: It's been kind of half and half. He's had I think two or three relationships that have lasted more than a week or so, and he's always the one that gets himself hurt in the relationships. They break off with him rather than him breaking off with them, and I think that's one of the reasons he wanted to see another psychiatrist too. It was to find out why he's always the one that's getting hurt, and I'd like to know that too. I told him, why should you be different from everybody else?

R. G.:   Just because you're homosexual doesn't mean that you're not going to have the same problems that heterosexuals have.

MOTHER: Right, that's right.

R. G.:   Why should they get off easy?

MOTHER: Right, they are no different from anybody else.

R. G.:   What was happening that told you he was gay?

MOTHER: It was just coming to a head, I mean, nothing but males calling on the telephone all the time, and he had these giggling conversations that last for hours. I think he's got a phone growing out of his ear! They would just talk and talk and say, "Well, did you see what this one did," and he came home with hickies on his neck one night, you know, and I said "Look, enough is enough, I just want to know, let's talk." We talked and talked and talked and he said, "I really think that I am." He said, "I'm thoroughly convinced. I'm learning to live with it, and you have to accept it too."

Mother Accepts Bobby's Homosexuality

R. G.:   That's pretty important for him.

MOTHER: Oh yeah, I know that. I mean I can openly say to people, "My son is gay," and it's not as difficult for me to say it. But before, just the thought of it made me—thinking that he might be—it was a horrible thing for me to get over, and I had a bad time.

R. G.:   How have you been able to make that change?

MOTHER: That's the way it is, there's nothing I can do to change it, and I'm not blaming myself. I don't know what caused it, but I don't think it was me. It's a combination of things. So I have to live with it.

R. G.:   That's very important for him. The worst thing that happens sometimes with gay people is that they are totally alienated from their family and they become runaways. He is real lucky to have you as a mother.

MOTHER: He thinks so, and lots of his friends do too, which makes me feel good. They can talk to me. I'm the neighborhood mother, I guess, with an O not a U, and yeah, they can all get along with me. All of his friends say, "Why can't my mom be like you?"

INTERVIEW WITH BOBBY AT AGE SEVENTEEN-AND-A-HALF

Vocational Interests

BOBBY: I'm taking acting courses. Taking drama helps me express myself in a lot of ways so I can communicate with people. We did the Shakespeare Festival, we did *Twelfth Night*, and I was in that. But right now my career goal is I'd like to be a flight attendant, because I love to travel.

R. G.:   It's a good job. You get to travel a lot, and you also get major discounts when you are flying and not working.

BOBBY: Yeah, you can take your family and all that. Send my mother to the Bahamas.

R. G.:   One way ticket to the Bahamas?

BOBBY: Yeah, just one way.

Sexual Interests

R. G.:   What's been happening with you romantically? What's your sex life like these days?

BOBBY: It's all right, I guess. I'm not as sexually active as a lot of people I know. Probably because I'm more particular. I haven't been seeing anybody for a while.

R. G.:   Why is that?

BOBBY: A lot of times I get negative attitudes about myself, which I'm sure all adolescents do.

R. G.:   Adults too.

BOBBY: Yeah. When it comes to a romantic life, I'm a romanticist—I want the candlelight and the flowers and the whole bit, and there are a lot of people who don't want to give that. I used to fall in love really easily—I would take somebody's idea of friendship and interpret that as love or what my vision of love was, and then I'd turn around and go, "Here I am," and they would just back away.

R. G.:   What kind of person are you looking for?

BOBBY: I'm not the kind of person who goes out and says six-feet-two, green eyes, dark hair, moustache. Really it's not so much the physical aspect but somebody that I can relate with intellectually, someone who can understand what I'm feeling. I feel that I'm a more understanding person than a lot of people. Personality and emotions are important, because once you get over the physical aspect, there is all this feeling underneath.

R. G.:   What about the physical part?

BOBBY: It depends on the person and what their likes and dislikes are, because I'm open-minded about a lot of things. I'm not into leather or anything like that. You have to respect a person for what their likes and dislikes are. One thing I love after sex is just cuddling up to the person and being warm, because there is the warmth afterwards. And I know a lot of people who roll over and that's it. Or people who will leave.

R. G.: What do you like the most, sexually?

BOBBY: It depends on the person and how I feel towards him. There was one time when I met this guy and I went home and we didn't have sex—nothing—he just put his arms around me and fell asleep, and that is such a feeling of closeness that it's more feeling between us than if we had had the sex. It depends on the person. I love oral sex.

R. G.: Giving, receiving, or both?

BOBBY: Both.

R. G.: What about anal sex?

BOBBY: It's all right. I've given and received. You have to be in the right frame of mind, I think.

Sexual Preferences

R. G.: What else do you like to do sexually?

BOBBY: I'm going to start to blush. I used to love to get head. I mean that would be it. And a lot of times it was me doing that, and I wouldn't care about the other person reciprocating because, well, I was enjoying it just as much, and then I started getting it back. Then I was getting anal sex. My sexual patterns used to get kind of predictable because I would fool around and then I would lie there and get hot. I wasn't feeling unfulfilled, but I'm starting to expand my repertoire. Now I like to give anal sex as well as receive it. Although I do have a higher preference for giving than getting.

R. G.: Do you ever get involved in things like bondage or any kind of masochism?

BOBBY: I did once. I got picked up by this guy and got real drunk. He claimed he was really into it and I said, well whatever. So what I did was—the only thing I did was he tied me up. He had my hands behind my back and bound my feet. We rolled around in bed and kissed each other and that was the extent of it, and then he untied my hands, and then he beat off and that was it. But there wasn't no beatings or whippings or lick-my-boots or anything.

Sex with Males versus Sex with Females

R. G.: You've had sex with women?

BOBBY: Mmm.

R. G.: What's the difference having sex with a woman and having sex with a man for you?

BOBBY: For me, sex with men—if something happens or doesn't happen it doesn't matter.

R. G.:   What do you mean, if something happens?

BOBBY: A lot of times you hear about sex with women, if the guy doesn't come, that's it, forget it, and sex with a man, if a guy doesn't come or anything like that, it's okay. I think a lot—I don't know what the word is—too much is put on the orgasm. If it happens, it happens, if it doesn't, it doesn't. It doesn't lessen the act or the feeling that's behind it. But the thing is when you are making love with a girl or a woman, you have to be in charge and you are the big thing, and I feel more taken care of with a man. It's more relaxed.

R. G.:   Is the feeling when you are having an orgasm with a woman and having an orgasm with a man different?

BOBBY: Mentally, but not physically. Physically it feels the same, but mentally in some cases it will put a bond between two people and in other cases it's just, okay, you're done, that's it. With a woman I'd have to really love the girl before I would make love with her, but with a man it's—see, men are brought up to be stronger, so that's why two men automatically, almost upon first meeting, they will have sex, because they're both technically raised in that frame of mind. I'm a romanticist, one way or the other, whether someone is wining or dining me, or I'm wining or dining someone else, it's a personal thing. I'd have to really feel something for the woman, because mentally that puts an emotional bond between you.

R. G.:   Do you think you will ever have sex with a woman again?

BOBBY: Probably. If the situation arises—but the woman I'm with has to understand.

R. G.:   Understand what?

BOBBY: I'd say to the woman, "You'd have to understand that this is not—not really what I'm used to." I'm always afraid of being compared with someone else, and I'm sure women do that in their minds.

R. G.:   Why do you think you would come out on the short end of a comparison?

BOBBY: I've got this tiny sense of fear, and I don't know whether it's being afraid of a woman herself or what. I'd have to tell this girl that she'd have to understand that if I couldn't get it up, if she didn't excite me, it was not her fault, it was nothing that she did or didn't do.

Cross-dressing

R. G.:   What about your interest in dressing up, in cross-dressing?

BOBBY: I did it for Halloween this year. The first time, and I had fun. I went out in public. I was scared to death. I was petrified. My hair was longer and I had my bangs curled up in the front, pulled back so it was really curly in the back. I found this dress at a garage sale. It's great. Big padded shoulders and the quarter-length sleeves and this collar that went down in a V across the front, and then it had a wide lapel and it stood up in the back. So I went out and bought shoes and got tights and everything, and I was head to toe in black, with three strands of pearls. My friend and her lover dressed me up and did my makeup and everything, and I went out. I did it two nights because the first night I went to a Halloween party and no one knew who I was. Then I went dancing the night after that. I had fun. My feet were killing me. I don't know how women can do it.

R. G.:   Was it a sexual turn on to dress up?

BOBBY: No, it wasn't, but I liked the feeling. We were driving. The first night I drove by myself and I was rigid. I was scared to death. I thought for sure a bunch of surfers would pull up beside me, see me, and just beat the shit out of me. Then the second night I wasn't driving, and I felt much more at ease. We were driving by, and we drove by a family. You know husband and wife and the three kids in the back and the dog, the whole bit. I waved and they waved back and they were none the wiser.

R. G.:   Did you feel like a woman?

BOBBY: No. Not really. I walked—I practiced for it. I learned how to walk in the shoes and everything like that because I told myself, if you're going to do it, go all out. But I still felt like a man. I went there and I was attracted to this guy in a tuxedo, and I went and attacked his bod, and it was fun.

R. G.:   Do you ever have any conscious wishes of wanting to be a woman?

BOBBY: No.

R. G.:   That's really gone now?

BOBBY: Yeah, as far as I know.

Heterosexual versus Homosexual Opportunity

R. G.:   Do you think when you were a young teenager you had an equal opportunity to try out sex with females and males?

BOBBY: Not really. In later years, in junior high and early high school, tenth grade, I was going through a lot. I was always a friend with the girls, and it would never go any further than that. I was everybody's brother and I was no one's boyfriend. I was never the one that went out with anybody. I was everybody's shoulder to cry on, and a lot of girls would tell me about their problems that they were having with their boyfriends. I knew and saw the kind of guys that the junior high girls that I knew were going out with. They were the macho type, the ones that were bigger and more muscular and more masculine in a sense than I was. So getting along emotionally with a woman has never been any problem, but as far as anything physical, I never had the opportunity and I still don't—I was never offered—well, not offered, that's kind of a lousy word—everyone was running around with everybody else, and I was doing the same thing, only I was sleeping with a different sex.

R. G.:   Were guys hitting on you?

BOBBY: In high school?

R. G.:   Yeah. Or were you hitting on guys?

BOBBY: They were hitting on me. When I started having sex, I went through a period where I was sleeping with everybody. I was very loose, and I kinda regret that, but I think that everybody when they go through a coming-out stage does that because they realize that all this sex is available. But it stopped probably when I was around fifteen.

Desire for Sex Change

BOBBY: I remember I was in ninth grade, someone came up to me and they asked—I came unglued they said, somebody suggested that when I grew up I would have a sex-change operation, and this was ninth grade, we were all so smart, and I had thought about it years earlier because I had heard about it with Renee Richards when she first had her operation and it was a thing in the news. I thought that maybe that could be an answer, but I remember in ninth grade when the two of them approached me, I said, "No, that would never happen." I wasn't about to tell them that that was something that I had thought of, at that point it was a very negative thought. I thought, "No, I'd never do that," and ever since then I've never had the desire to be the opposite sex. If I was to wake up tomorrow and be a woman, I wouldn't kill myself, but—

R. G.:   Do you have a fantasy of being a female when you are having sex?

BOBBY: No. Nope. I can't picture myself being a female. The only advantage they have is that they can have multiple orgasms.

R. G.:   Some of them.

BOBBY: Some of them. Good.

Coming Out as Gay

R. G.:   When do you think that you became firmly convinced that "I am gay" was a clear statement? "This is the way I am; this is the way it's going to be?"

BOBBY: There were two stages. There was one stage when I said that "I am gay, and *I* have to accept it," and then there was the stage when I said, "I'm gay and *everyone else* has to accept it." And the second one was the year before last, when I was going into eleventh grade. I had firmly said to myself, "I am a homosexual and I understand it, and I've accepted myself, and now it's everyone else's turn." When I first said to myself that I was gay, I was almost fifteen. And I was upset. I was upset because I knew from now on that society would be on my back; that's a big worry. The thing that bothered me most was, I realized that all these names that people had been calling me were *true*. And that really upset me. Just thinking that these people that I didn't like were *right*. I moved. I came into a new high school here with a low profile, and I said, "I'm going to get myself together," and I did.

R. G.: It sounds like you've done a good job, too.

BOBBY: Thank you. It's not been easy, but I took time to understand myself and understand my feelings and attitudes and I've accepted myself, and now I've got to say this is the way I am, and now I'm going to let other people deal with it because I've dealt with it. I'm going to be dealing with it for the rest of my life.

Recollection of Earlier Visits

R. G.: Looking back now with all the fourteen or fifteen years of hindsight, do you think it was a good idea that your mom brought you here, or do you think it was a mistake?

BOBBY: I thought it was neat. I did. I had no idea why I was coming and—

R. G.: No idea?

BOBBY: None. I took a lot of ridiculous tests and they were fun. I enjoyed my visits, and then being up on the roof with the other kids in the group was fun because it was intended to be fun for the kids. I enjoyed myself. And I've always—I've never felt any—I don't remember ever having a feeling of not wanting to come to the sessions, and that's the way it should be.

R. G.: Did it affect your behavior in any way?

BOBBY: No. I don't think so.

R. G.: The reason your mom brought you here and her worry at that time was the extent of feminine behavior that you showed. She thought you were unhappy, you were being teased. Do you think that your sessions here in any way affected the extent of your feminine behavior?

BOBBY: Not really. I remember being asked by you, "Why are you acting this way?" But I didn't have a grasp of—I never—I don't think so. If it did it was minor.

R. G.: Your feminine behavior obviously diminished over time. Was that a natural process of getting older, or was it the fact that your mother was putting her foot down about things?

BOBBY: I think it's my mother saying, "No, you should not act this way," and it was myself realizing that people in school and socially are gonna look down on this, you don't do it. . . . I still have my moments.

"FEMININE" BOY, HOMOSEXUAL MAN: REUBEN

Reuben's mother is a striking example of a woman who wanted a daughter during the pregnancy with a son and treated her newborn as though he were a girl. Reuben's boyhood behaviors were markedly "feminine." As a young adult he is primarily homosexual. He recalls his mother's wish that he had been a girl.

REUBEN'S MOTHER DESCRIBES HIM AT AGE SEVEN

Reasons for Seeking Consultation

MOTHER: Well, I came today for one thing because of a suggestion from my doctor. I talked to him about it, and I told him my son is becoming more and more acting like a girl. And I had told him—I told my son—that it wasn't very nice, that he was a boy and he was not supposed to be dressing like a girl. Maybe once in a while he could play like that, but not all the time.

R. G.: What have been the things that you have been most concerned about?

MOTHER: He puts on a long T-shirt, one of my husband's long T-shirts, or my son's, and he acts like he's a girl—like a miniskirt—and then he sits down and kind of tucks it under, kind of tightens it under him.

R. G.: How often will he do this?

MOTHER: Quite often. Daily—at least once or twice daily.

R. G.: What else?

MOTHER: Dolls. He dresses them up, and he undresses them, and he puts the clothes right back on again.

R. G.: Are these boy dolls or girl dolls?

MOTHER: Girl dolls.

R. G.: And how often does he do this?

MOTHER: Every chance he gets to get hold of a doll.

R. G.: Has he shown any interest in makeup or cosmetics?

MOTHER: Yes, he has. He likes to put on my lipstick, and he watches me closely to see how I put mine on, and then he tries it.

R. G.: What else would you say is feminine about him?

MOTHER: Walking like a girl. He usually puts his hands on his hips and starts walking like a girl, or starts moving his behind real sissylike. He does that quite often, too.

R. G.: Does he always walk this way?

MOTHER: No, he walks like a boy, too.

R. G.: Which do you feel he does more of?

MOTHER: A girl.

Onset of "Feminine" Behavior

R. G.:   How long have you had any concerns about this?

MOTHER: This just started this year.

R. G.:   In looking back, what was the very earliest that your son showed any indication of this kind of behavior?

MOTHER: Quite a few years back—I'd say about four years old.

R. G.:   What was the earliest thing?

MOTHER: I noticed that he liked to play with dolls a lot, but I didn't figure that would, you know, all boys like to do that, but then when he started using T-shirts or putting on my things, well, then I started noticing a little bit more.

R. G.:   When did you first notice his interest in doll-playing?

MOTHER: Since he was very little—very little. About three.

R. G.:   How would he get the dolls at that time?

MOTHER: Oh, he'd just get them by the little hands and walk them.

R. G.:   How would he have *access* to them?

MOTHER: Well, I used to have a couple of dolls myself, and he used to play with my dolls.

R. G.:   They were yours? These are ones you had when you were small?

MOTHER: Yes.

Mother's Attitude toward "Feminine" Behavior

R. G.:   How do you feel about his behavior?

MOTHER: Well, I feared maybe there is something wrong with him. At first I didn't, but now I think I do, and I want to correct it.

R. G.:   Is your son aware of how you feel about this?

MOTHER: Well, now he is, yes.

R. G.:   How did he become aware?

MOTHER: By me telling him that it wasn't right for him to be doing that. Once in a while it's fine when he's playing, you know, but I didn't want to encourage it, and I didn't want to discourage him about it, too, because the way I felt it could go in deeper in him and maybe hurt some way.

R. G.:   What was your first feeling about the dressing up?

MOTHER: I didn't think about it. I just thought it was child's play and that's all.

R. G.:   And what approach did you take to it?

MOTHER: I talked to him about it. I told him it wasn't right for him to do that—that he wasn't a girl, he was a boy.

Approval of Doll-playing

R. G.:   And how do you feel about the doll-playing?

MOTHER: I don't mind it. I don't see anything wrong in it.

R. G.: Is your son aware of how you feel about the doll-playing?

MOTHER: I think he does know. I think he knows there's nothing wrong with it.

A Mixed Message

R. G.: And how do you feel about the cosmetics?

MOTHER: I don't like him to get into my cosmetics, so I tell him keep away from them.

R. G.: Why don't you like him to do that?

MOTHER: Well, it's my stuff, and things that are mine I don't like my children to get into.

R. G.: And what is his reaction to your feeling?

MOTHER: I guess that's why he stays away from it when I'm there. And when I leave, that's when he gets into it.

R. G.: What has been your approach to his using makeup?

MOTHER: I tell him that that's girls' stuff, and little boys just don't use it. They don't use makeup. If they do use it, it's when they have a television program or something they have to put makeup on, otherwise they don't.

R. G.: How do you feel about his feminine mannerisms or his way of walking?

MOTHER: I don't like it, but after all he is my son and this is the way I feel—if he's going to turn out like that, well, I'll do the best I can to help him out.

R. G.: Do you think your son is aware of how you feel about his walking?

MOTHER: I don't think so.

Behaviors Evoke Positive Laughter

R. G.: What was your feeling when you first became aware of how he was walking?

MOTHER: I thought he was just kidding, so I laughed about it.

R. G.: And what was his reaction to that?

MOTHER: He started doing it more until finally it did get to me, and I told him to stop it.

R. G.: And what was his reaction to that?

MOTHER: He just laughed about it and continued, and says, "Look, Mommy, look, Mommy," and just kept on doing it.

Role-playing as Female

R. G.: Does he play house or mother/father games?

MOTHER: He plays house a lot.

R. G.: Do you know what role he takes?

MOTHER: He takes the mother.

R. G.:   Is this always?

MOTHER: Yes, always.

R. G.:   What does he do?

MOTHER: He gets, like, a doll, or a stuffed animal, and pretends like he's the mother. He spanks it if it's mean, or if it's bad, or he says, "You know Mommy doesn't like for you to do this," or "Mommy doesn't like that."

R. G.:   Does he playact or take on make-believe roles?

MOTHER: Yes, he does. He does that quite often, too.

R. G.:   What roles does he take?

MOTHER: He takes the mother role—a girl's role.

R. G.:   And what's your feeling about his role-playing as mother?

MOTHER: I don't see nothing wrong with it.

R. G.:   Does he ever make up costumes?

MOTHER: He'll get a T-shirt or something that belongs to me and put it on—a blouse or something, and pretends he's a girl. He loves jewelry. He likes anything that's hanging down his neck, or a bracelet. He'll get anything—a piece of string, and get a button or something, and just hang it around his neck.

R. G.:   Compared to other boys his age, how would you estimate the amount of interest he has in playacting?

MOTHER: I'd say it's more. Because my other three sons, they weren't like him. They liked to play with dolls, but not quite that often, and they always liked to go out and play. They never liked to stay around with me. They were more tomboyish.

Miscellaneous Features

R. G.:   Does he comment on your clothing?

MOTHER: Yes, he does—all the time. He also likes to touch my nylons when I put them on; he likes to touch my legs with his hands, and the dress that I've got on, he'll put his hands on it.

R.G.:   Does he draw pictures?

MOTHER: Yes, he does.

R. G.:   What kind?

MOTHER: Girls.

R. G.:   What are his favorite toys?

MOTHER: Dolls.

R. G.:   To what extent does he participate in rough-and-tumble play? Wrestling or fighting?

MOTHER: He doesn't. He doesn't care for that.

R. G.:   To what extent does he participate in sports?

MOTHER: To my knowledge he doesn't like to very much at all, unless he really has to. Like if he is in school or something, then I imagine he would, but when he is at home he won't.

R. G.: Who's his best friend?

MOTHER: I guess I am.

R. G.: Does he seem to prefer boys or girls as playmates?

MOTHER: Girls.

Mother's Preference for a Girl

R. G.: When you found out you were pregnant, did you have a preference for a boy or a girl?

MOTHER: I wanted a girl. I wanted a girl so bad that I prayed every night so hard for a girl. Even when he was a boy, everybody said he looked just like a girl, which he did. Everyone called him a little girl.

R. G.: What do you mean by that?

MOTHER: Well, anybody who would see him, they'd say, "Oh, what a cute little girl, what a cute little girl." Everybody would say what a cute little girl because he did look like a girl. He had dark curly hair, *she* did, he did, look like a girl. And as a matter of fact, when he was little I used to dress him—maybe it was my fault—I don't know.

R. G.: Tell me about that.

MOTHER: He was very, very tiny at the time. I used to dress him like a little girl. I wanted a girl so bad.

R. G.: How did you feel when you had the boy?

MOTHER: I wasn't crazy about the idea, because I wanted a girl so bad.

R. G.: Why did you want a girl?

MOTHER: Because I never had any girls, and I wanted a girl of my own. Then my family—everybody said I hope you have a girl, I hope you have a girl—everybody, my mother, my dad—wanted me to have a girl, and I wanted a girl real bad.

Father's Preference for a Girl

MOTHER: And my husband wanted to have a girl. I guess that was the whole thing, there, that he wanted a girl so bad, too.

R. G.: How did he react when the boy was born?

MOTHER: He wasn't crazy about the idea.

R. G.: What did he do?

MOTHER: He just started going out more often and staying away from home.

R. G.: You felt it had something to do with the fact that you had a boy?

MOTHER: Yes.

R. G.: Why do you think so?

MOTHER: After him, I couldn't have any more children, so when he was four years old my husband took off. He left the home, and this girl that he was with—she had a girl from him.

Mother's Cross-dressing of Son

R. G.:   How would you dress him?

MOTHER: I would put little girls' clothing on him. I would never take him out anywhere like that. At the time I didn't think it would hurt him, because he was very tiny, only a couple of months old.

R. G.:   What sort of clothing would you put on him?

MOTHER: Little dresses, little hats, little slippers, a girl's blanket.

R. G.:   How old was he when you first dressed him like that?

MOTHER: Oh, he was about three or four months old.

R. G.:   And over how long a time did you do that?

MOTHER: I guess till he was about nine months old.

R. G.:   What made you stop dressing him as a girl?

MOTHER: I realized to myself that he wasn't a girl, that he was a boy, and I was supposed to dress him like a boy. So I stopped. I said to myself, "Why kid yourself? He isn't a girl, he's a boy."

Infant Features

R. G.:   What was he like as an infant?

MOTHER: Real tiny. Real delicate. He was a beautiful child. He had the body and the face—everything—of a little girl, very dainty.

R. G.:   What would you say about his face that was like a girl's?

MOTHER: His eyes, his eyebrows, and his hair.

R. G.:   What about his eyes?

MOTHER: His eyes were just like a little girl's. Just beautiful, just beautiful. Eyelashes real long, just like a little girl should have.

R. G.:   What sort of personality did he seem to have?

MOTHER: A little girl's.

R. G.:   In what way?

MOTHER: Well, to myself, I see him like a little girl. I see him like a little girl. I wanted a girl so bad, but to me he *was* a little girl. And also, when he was born he had milk in his breast, and I rushed him down to the doctor, and the doctor laughed at me and said, "Don't you know that a lot of little boys have milk in their breasts?" And then I felt relieved, but at the time it scared me half to death, you know.

R. G.:   What did you think it meant?

MOTHER: I thought it meant that he was a boy and a girl at the same time.

For additional transcript material describing the relationship between Reuben and his mother, see pages 78–79.

Illness

R. G.:   Was he ill at all during the years three, four, and five?

MOTHER: Yes, he was ill quite a bit.

R. G.:   What was the trouble?

MOTHER: He's had pneumonia two times—he was hospitalized.

R. G.:   How long was he hospitalized?

MOTHER: One time he was hospitalized for a month. Other times about three or four weeks, and the other time he had diarrhea real bad, he was hospitalized then, too, for, I think it was closer to a month. He almost didn't pull through it.

R. G.:   How old was he then?

MOTHER: He was about two.

Special Attention

R. G.:   Did this require any special kind of care from you?

MOTHER: Yes, I had to watch what he ate, I had to be very careful what I fed him. I had to protect him quite a bit from going out too much without a coat or something.

R. G.:   And how old was he about that time?

MOTHER: He was about two, two-and-a-half.

Others Also Cross-dressed Reuben

R. G.:   You mentioned dressing him in girls' clothing during his first months. As far as you know, has anyone else ever dressed your son in girls' clothing?

MOTHER: Yes, my sisters. They used to dress him quite often, too, in little girls' clothes, because they used to love to see him the way he looked. He was about two or three months.

R. G.:   Did this continue over some period of time?

MOTHER: Oh, until he was about one.

R. G.:   What would they put on him?

MOTHER: Little girls' things—little dresses—little hats.

R. G.:   Why would they do that?

MOTHER: Because they thought the way I did—that he was just adorable as a little girl.

R. G.:   How often would they do that?

MOTHER: Quite often—every time they had the chance. His eyelashes were so long they used to say, "Give me your eyelashes—they don't belong to you—give them to me."

R. G.:   After his first year, has anyone dressed him in girls' clothing?

MOTHER: Yes, my mother-in-law did once. I found out about it. She dressed him up to see how he would look like a little girl, and everybody just laughed about it.

R. G.:   How old was he?

MOTHER: Over a year. I think he was two years old, or he was going to be about two.

Father-Son Relationship

R. G.:   I want to ask you some questions about his dad and the kind of relationship they had. To what extent was his father able to spend time with him during his first year?

MOTHER: Well, not very much. He didn't spend very much time with the kids.

R. G.:   Why?

MOTHER: He just didn't feel up to it, I guess.

R. G.:   What working hours did he have?

MOTHER: Well, from eight in the morning until about nine o'clock at night. Other times he worked at other jobs, but he didn't come straight home.

R. G.:   Was your son awake before his dad left in the morning?

MOTHER: Some of the time, yes.

R. G.:   And would he be awake when his dad returned in the evening during his first year?

MOTHER: Oh, no, he'd be asleep by then.

R. G.:   How about on Saturdays?

MOTHER: Well, on weekends he usually took off somewhere. He made some excuse, he was always leaving the house. He was hardly ever home on weekends. He was away from the house mostly, you know, anytime he could, you know, anytime he had the chance to.

R. G.:   And what about his second year?

MOTHER: Well, about the same, because clear up to the day he did leave us he never changed. As a matter of fact he got worse.

R. G.:   And how would you compare the amount of time that he spent with this boy compared with the other kids?

MOTHER: The same, because he didn't spend time with the other kids either.

R. G.:   Compared to most fathers, how would you rate the amount of time he spent with him compared to what most other dads would spend with their kids?

MOTHER: He wasn't a father to him at all.

Grandfather-Son Relationship

MOTHER: My father always cuddled my children. Always held them up in his lap and everything. "My little boy," he used to say, "my little boy this" or "my little boy that."

R. G.:   Did he have the same ideas about this boy being a little girl?

MOTHER: No. He used to get mad. He used to get mad because I would dress him like a little girl.

R. G.:   How often would your father see him?

MOTHER: Quite often.

R. G.:   During his first year?

MOTHER: Oh, yes, well, clear up to when he was about three years old.

R. G.:   Would he be there every day?

MOTHER: No, we usually would go over to their house just about every day.

R. G.:   He would be home? He wasn't working?

MOTHER: Yes.

Mother's Androgyny

MOTHER: A lot of times I wished I would have been a boy, and a lot of times I wished I would have been a boy because I could have beat the shit out of my husband. That's why, and a lot of times I'll say it, out loud, that I wish I would have been a man.

R. G.:   When will you say that?

MOTHER: When I'll get real angry, you know, when I get angry.

R. G.:   When might this occur? Can you give an example?

MOTHER: Like, for instance, like when my husband couldn't fix something for me, you know, that's a man's job—and I used to get angry and say, "Well, gee, you can't do anything, let me do it, you can't do it. I'll do it." I used to go ahead and do it.

R. G.:   Would anybody else be around when you would say this besides your husband?

MOTHER: Well, my kids.

R. G.:   They would hear you say this?

MOTHER: Yeah, uh huh. Also, my dad used to comment on that. He wished I would have been a boy. I used to hear him say that all the time. Also, my mother too, because my dad used to call me out to help him out, and my mother used to say, "Well, she should have been a boy, you know, you keep him out there all the time anyway." When she needs us in the house then she used to get quite a bit of argument about it because my dad used to have me outside all the time.

The family moved and left no forwarding address. Contact with the family was lost for several years. The son was relocated and returned for an interview at age nineteen.

INTERVIEW WITH REUBEN AT AGE NINETEEN

Recollection of Earlier Visits

REUBEN: All I remember is being in this room with a strange person showing me little figures of my family and trying to get my opinion on each and every one of them. I remember playing with them. You know, asking me questions while I'm playing with them on the floor.

R. G.:   What do you remember about why your family came to see me?

REUBEN: She said she took me because I wasn't behaving like a normal kid.

R. G.:   Did she go into detail what she meant by that?

REUBEN: She was afraid I was drawn more to men when I was younger than I was to girls.

R. G.:   How did she mean that?

REUBEN: I hung around—what did she say? She said I hung around girls all the time when I was a kid and I was drawn—looking more at men in the park.

R. G.:   Were you looking at them romantically, sexually?

REUBEN: Yeah, yeah.

R. G.:   At what age?

REUBEN: Seven or eight.

R. G.:   And what do you remember about that time?

REUBEN: I remember she was right about it.

Early Attraction to Men

REUBEN: I remember being drawn to men more than women. I felt like I—I didn't know what that feeling was, but it was there.

R. G.:   What do you mean by drawn?

REUBEN: It was just an attraction when I was a kid, I didn't know why I felt that way and why I was looking at that certain person. It was just all odd to me.

R. G.:   Do you remember feeling that you were in love with the person?

REUBEN: Yeah, when I was a kid, yes.

R. G.:   Do you remember feeling any sense of wanting to have some kind of physical contact with the person?

REUBEN: Yes.

R. G.:   What kind of physical contact would it have been?

REUBEN: Just to be near that person and touch that person. That was it.

Early Emergence of Erotic Feelings for Males

R. G.:   Okay, now that you're older, you obviously know what sexual feelings are and what sexual attractions are. Looking back to seven or eight, do you feel that you had some sexual attractions for men?

REUBEN: I feel that I did, but I just didn't know what they were.

R. G.:   Why do you think they were sexual attractions?

REUBEN: I just know. I know now because of experiences that I can identify with that same certain feeling that I had back then, but I just didn't know what it was then.

R. G.:   And what's the earliest that you remember those feelings?

REUBEN: Seven.

Current Sexual Orientation

R. G.: What sort of sexual experiences and feelings do you have now?

REUBEN: I've come to know myself to say that I know what I am.

R. G.: What kind of sexual feelings do you have?

REUBEN: Men and women.

R. G.: Tell me a little bit more.

REUBEN: I know that I am a bisexual. All I know is that I am attracted to men and women, and I have been out with both and I enjoyed it.

R. G.: As a bisexual, which attraction do you think is stronger, the attraction towards men or women?

REUBEN: Men.

R. G.: Let's say on a one-to-ten scale, ten would be attractions only to men and one would be attractions only to women. What number would you give yourself?

REUBEN: Probably an eight.

Early Sexual Awareness

R. G.: When did you become aware that the feelings for men were sexual?

REUBEN: About thirteen or fourteen.

R. G.: And how did you become aware that they were sexual?

REUBEN: Fooling around a little here and there when I was in junior high, and they became stronger and stronger as I became older.

R. G.: Who were your first experiences with?

REUBEN: My best friends, kids my age. You know fooling around when you were a kid.

R. G.: Sometimes kids do that for more of an experimentation or a game, or sometimes it is a very strong and romantic feeling.

REUBEN: For me it was a very strong and romantic feeling.

R. G.: And your romantic feelings for females, when did you become aware of them?

REUBEN: The same age. It was back and forth. I had girlfriends, but yet I liked boys. So I had both. As I grew older I always had both. I was afraid of coming out of the closet, so I went towards the women first, and when I finally admitted it to myself, I didn't want to give up the women yet either because I enjoyed being with women.

R. G.: When you were a kid and you had feelings for boys and for girls, did that worry you, or confuse you?

REUBEN: Well, it confused me a lot. I was very young. When I turned thirteen and fourteen I kind of grew to understand it. I didn't ask why. I was confused. It hurt because I wasn't considered normal.

R. G.: And when you became thirteen, fourteen, you began having sexual experiences with men and with women?

REUBEN: Yeah.

R. G.: How did you feel?

REUBEN: More confused. But the reason is I heard people say this and that about marrying, you know, and I was scared.

R. G.: Did you know of anybody or did you think there were other people like you, who were bisexual, or did you think you were the only one?

REUBEN: I thought I was the only one in the world.

R. G.: When did you realize that you weren't alone?

REUBEN: About fifteen. It was just overhearing everybody on TV, the media and just reading about it.

Recent Sexuality

R. G.: At present, let's say in the last year, are your experiences still bisexual, or are they all gay?

REUBEN: They're mostly gay. I would honestly say I go with women more out of companionship, and men more out of a sexual relationship.

R. G.: When do you think it became stronger in terms of being primarily gay rather than bisexual?

REUBEN: When I was sixteen and I came out of the closet. I heard people say it isn't wrong to feel that way. I tried more and more to understand myself and let myself not feel so guilty every time I done something. I have a lover for about six months now. We are living together. I've come out of the closet a lot. Everything seems to be going fine.

Sexual Preferences

R. G.: What do you like to do sexually?

REUBEN: I would say just feel him, touch him, you know, be on top of him, him be on top of me. Just sort of get passionate, I'll kiss him and hold him and touch him.

R. G.: What about oral-genital sex?

REUBEN: Oral sex. Anal sex is very difficult because of his size.

R. G.: He's too big for you?

REUBEN: Way too big. I've never had that problem before. I don't really care for that either. Unfortunately, he likes it all the time, and there's no way hardly we ever do it.

R. G.: Is that causing a problem in the relationship?

REUBEN: Yes. He's a very active person. Every time I turn around, he's there. And me, I'm one time a day; he'd like to five.

R. G.: Do you like to do anal sex if you are inside of him?

REUBEN: I didn't like it before because I felt like it was making me be the dominant one, but with him I'm doing it more or less out of pleasing him, and it feels good. I never looked at it the way I look at it now. I'm not overly impressed with it, but I like it.

R. G.: What about manual stimulation: masturbation, your hand on his penis?

REUBEN: I usually do myself and he usually does his for the reason is we both—I think I know how I like it better than he does, you know, how would he know, and vice versa. We try different positions and masturbate on each other.

R. G.:   What do you think about when you're having sex with him?

REUBEN: Sometimes I fantasize about other people.

R. G.:   Males, females, both?

REUBEN: Males. And I would think that he would probably too. I fantasize about him having anal sex with me, doing it to me, but its not hurting so much.

Anatomic Sexual Identity

R. G.:   Do you ever fantasize that you're a woman and having sex with him?

REUBEN: No. I fantasize about being a woman but not—

R. G.:   But not when you're having sex?

REUBEN: Yeah.

R. G.:   Tell me when you fantasize about being a woman.

REUBEN: I see a girl walking down the street, and I look at her and say, "You can do this to make her look better and do that," that's what I think about most.

R. G.:   You imagine yourself as a woman at that time?

REUBEN: I've always felt that I should have been.

R. G.:   Why?

REUBEN: Because I guess I can identify with them more than a straight guy could.

R. G.:   In what way?

REUBEN: Because I'm not afraid to show my feelings or emotions or anything like that, and they identify and maybe see that and I can sense it.

R. G.:   Do you think it would have been better if you had been born a girl?

REUBEN: No. Sometimes I wish I were a girl, and the reason too is it's very hard for me, like when we're in a grocery store or somewhere and he, you know, wants to hold my hand, he wants to put his arm around me. And we've honestly thought about it and just said, "Oh, let's do it," and then we thought about it sensibly and said, "No, is it really worth the hassle?" It's not, and it's very frustrating sometimes.

R. G.:   Why does that make you wish you were a girl? Why not just wish that *he* were a girl?

REUBEN: It's hard to imagine him being a girl: five-eight, 150 pounds. I don't know. None of these questions are easy.

Mother-Son Relationship

R. G.:   Looking back, do you feel that there was anything different then about, let's say, your relationship to your mother, compared to most boys and their relationship to their mother?

REUBEN: I would say the relationship to my mother would probably be the reason for me being this way, because when stepfather came in when I was two, my mom set down the rule that nobody touches my kids, nobody tells my kids what to do. So he never told us what to do.

R. G.:   You have brothers?

REUBEN: I have two brothers.

R. G.:   And what's their sexual orientation, as far as you know?

REUBEN: Straight, all the way.

R. G.:   Why do you figure that they turned out straight and you didn't?

REUBEN: I have no idea. I've always tried to answer that myself.

R. G.:   In terms of the father figure that you just mentioned, is there a difference?

REUBEN: One of my brothers was closer to my stepdad and the other brother was closer to my mother.

R. G.:   Did your stepdad treat the three of you differently?

REUBEN: Yeah. I was envious. My stepfather treated the little one better because he was more like him himself. My real father treated the oldest one better because he was more like him. I got treated the best by my mother because I was more like my mother.

R. G.:   How were you more like your mother, and how were they more like their fathers?

REUBEN: My brother was crazy. He always used to get in trouble. That was my father's favorite. He'd see a bike and he'd take it. Same as my father when he was a kid. My real dad—I couldn't never understand why my brother would love him at all because I always hated him. I turned out like my mother I guess because I was so close to her all my life. I grew to know her and I grew to be like her.

Recollection of Parental Reaction to Boyhood "Femininity"

R. G.:   As best as you can remember, what was your mother's attitude towards some of the girl-type behaviors that you did when you were younger?

REUBEN: All I can remember is one time she yelled my ears out because I guess I got caught kissing a boy when I was maybe seven or eight. She didn't like it at the time, and then I knew it was wrong. After that I knew I never wanted to get caught again. Her reaction then was, "Don't do it. It's not normal."

R. G.:   And what about some of the other behaviors? Some of the play things you were doing?

REUBEN: That didn't bother her. It never bothered her. She used to tell me to do what I wanted to do.

R. G.: Specifically what girl-type things do you remember her just not being bothered about and saying, "Do what you want to"?

REUBEN: Playing with dolls, playing house.

R. G.: These were dress-up dolls like Barbie dolls?

REUBEN: Barbie dolls.

R. G.: How old were you?

REUBEN: Eight or nine.

R. G.: Did your biological father know about your interests when you were a kid in terms of doll-play and things like that?

REUBEN: He never stuck around long enough to know.

R. G.: Did you know whether your mom wanted a boy or a girl when you were born?

REUBEN: She wanted a girl, she told me that, so I said, "You kinda got one."

R. G.: When did she tell you that she wanted a girl?

REUBEN: When I told her that I was gay.

R. G.: She never told you that before?

REUBEN: No.

R. G.: What did she say?

REUBEN: Well, when I told her, you know, she started cryin' and she said, "I've been waiting for you to tell me for a long time." And she started cryin' and she goes, "Well, maybe it's my fault because I was frustrated, I was very lonely." She started cryin' and sayin', "It's my fault 'cause I always wanted a little girl so bad," and I said, "It's not." I go, "It's nobody's fault, I don't know what it is, but I don't know if I can change."

"FEMININE" BOY, HOMOSEXUAL MAN: STEVEN

Steven was a "feminine" boy with a female identity who cross-dressed extensively. His relationship with his biological father was nonexistent. Early on, his mother strongly disapproved of his cross-gender behaviors. These behaviors modified during later childhood, and his appearance was androgynous.

Steven's sexual orientation is now primarily homosexual, but his view of the homosexual life-style is not very positive. He says he does not like men. Steven is unique in our study in that cross-dressing has been sexually arousing, although he is not primarily a transvestite.

STEVEN'S MOTHER DESCRIBES HIM AT AGE NINE

Initial Concerns

MOTHER: His kindergarten teacher noticed that something was wrong because he got in the girls' line instead of the boys' line at the drinking fountain.

R. G.: What else?

MOTHER: He started, initiated, cross-dressing when he was about three.

R. G.: How did you react to that?

MOTHER: He got nothing but static from me.

R. G.: Did it continue?

MOTHER: Yes.

Mother's Early Attitude toward Steven's "Femininity"

MOTHER: We lived at our apartment, and a woman and her daughter moved in with dolls and all that shit. I didn't remember being horrified right at the outset. But it seemed I was very uptight about it.

R. G.: How about the other woman?

MOTHER: No, she wasn't. She said, "Let it flow, if he's having a fantasy let him flow with it. You know it's not going to hurt him." That's still really tough for me. In fact, she's still my best friend, and we were considering moving in together last summer. And I finally had to tell her that my fear was that it wouldn't be good for my son. Even though I wasn't worried in any particular way.

R. G.: So when she said, "Don't worry about it," did you stop objecting?

MOTHER: No, I kept on objecting. I remember getting incredibly anxious.

R. G.: At what age was this?

MOTHER: He was three when he first started doing that stuff. It always bothered me. I remember a contest of wills going on. "You will *not* do that. You will be a *boy* and will be boyish." I can remember from age five and six him saying, "I want to be a *girl.*" Then, my saying, *"No,* you can't." Then, him saying, *"Yes,* I can."

Father-Son Relationship

R. G.: During his earlier years, did he have much contact with adult males?

MOTHER: No.

R. G.: Was there any adult male figure?

MOTHER: For his first three years, it was my father, but he's a very quiet, passive man.

R. G.: How much contact was there?

MOTHER: Not much. My father really liked him a lot, but he was working all day and didn't see him that much. And my brother was there intermittently. He was in the military.

R. G.:   Generally it was a feminine environment?

MOTHER: Exclusively feminine. And when he was about five, I introduced this new man into his life that became his stepfather. And then
the summer he was six I got married.

R. G.:   And what kind of things might he do with this man in his first year
when he was introduced into his life?

MOTHER: A couple of nights a week they would see each other. The
man was very much the authoritarian, and he believed that children
should go to their bedrooms when their fathers came home from work.
And he didn't tolerate any misbehavior. And all he had to do is look
at my son and he would wither. Me, too—all he had to do is look at
me and *I* would wither. He was really a terrifying kind of person. So
there was no warmth, virtually. Although I must say, my son certainly
seemed to like him more, more than was warranted. I don't understand. He wanted to please him, I think. He would do things and try
to think of things that would please the man even though he was
afraid of him.

R. G.:   You were married to this man for how long?

MOTHER: Two years.

R. G.:   Are you in a relationship now?

MOTHER: I'm having a relationship right now with a man who my son
unfortunately likes very much. And he's told me he wants him to be
his father. I won't—I would never marry him. But he wants—he wants
to marry me and he's sort of—he loves my son. I told my son that
we're not going to get married. He didn't like it.

R. G.:   How often does he see him?

MOTHER: Once a week maybe. My son wants a father. He's told me. In
fact, I saw this man last summer and then after I stopped seeing him—
he wanted no part of the Cub Scouts! Yuck, and I couldn't tell if it
was because it was so Mickey Mouse or if it's because he didn't have
a father to be a den thing with.

STEVEN'S MOTHER DESCRIBES HIM AT AGE ELEVEN

Steven's Current Behaviors

MOTHER: I can't think of one feminine thing he's done in almost two
years.

R. G.:   Is he still showing feminine gestures?

MOTHER: No, not noticeable to me. His sibilant *s*'s that used to bother
me so much, I don't hear any more.

R. G.:   Does he get along well with both boys and girls?

MOTHER: Yes. He's never had a lot of boyfriends, but he's always had a
few good boyfriends, and he does now too. They tend to be the same
kind of boys. They're not really rowdy. He gets into very imaginative

games and conversations with them, and they talk about the books they've read. He doesn't go out for sports.

R. G.: How do the kids relate to him? As far as you know, do they call him a sissy?

MOTHER: No. He's in the sixth grade now, and the director of the school told me at the beginning of the year that he was a little bit effeminate at times. I guess he had some of those gestures. And I told her some of my fears—some of the things we had been through— and it never came up again. And nobody ever seemed to notice it.

Early Heterosexual Arousal

MOTHER: I've got something really funny. He loves to read *Playboy,* and he told me that when he sees the naked women he gets boners. And I remember feeling very glad about that. It relieved me. "Aha, my kid's normal!"

R. G.: How old is he now?

MOTHER: He's eleven. He seems so much more grown up to me now. There's still very little rough-and-tumble. I'm living with a man. We've been living together ten months, and he and my son are very very tight. And my son is crazy to wrestle with him. He hangs on him and pulls him to the ground all the time. There's an incredible amount of physical contact between them, which I really love.

R. G.: Has your boyfriend's presence had an effect on your son's behavior?

MOTHER: Not in terms of whatever masculine and feminine means. They've just gotten very close. They have the same interests. They go off to the bookstores and spend a day reading. You know, they're very similar, and my boyfriend identifies with my son a great deal because he lost his father when he was a kid.

INTERVIEW WITH STEVEN AT AGE SIXTEEN

First Homosexual Experience

STEVEN: I met this guy. I fell head over heels in love with him. We went to bed one night. He was handsome, moderately feminine. Sex was different from what I expected; it was a letdown, less intense. But this guy couldn't make a commitment. I think his instability attracts me.

R. G.: What about girlfriends?

STEVEN: I thought I was in love with one. That didn't work out. But she's still my best friend. It wasn't really a sexual relationship. Only one time. Intercourse with her was a big disappointment.

R. G.: Tell me the difference for you in having sex with a male or a female.

STEVEN: I can be more passionate, rough with a guy. You sort of know what to do, what hurts. With a girl it's different.

R. G.: Which do you prefer?

STEVEN: It depends on my mood. I have to know the guy on a friendly basis.

STEVEN'S MOTHER DESCRIBES HIM AT AGE SIXTEEN

MOTHER: He was having this boy over a lot to sleep. I looked into the room, and they were lying on the floor in a sleeping bag. I said, "I know you two are lovers." And he said, "It's all right, Mom; I'm not a homosexual. I'm bisexual. I've slept with girls, too." He told me that girls turn him on more than guys. "There's nothing wrong with it," he said. "Some of your best friends are lesbian."

R. G.: How do you feel about this?

MOTHER: I told him the only thing I couldn't stand would be if he were a queen.

STEVEN'S MOTHER DESCRIBES HIM AT AGE EIGHTEEN

Acknowledgment of Steven's Bisexuality

MOTHER: I told him I was going to come see you, and he was real interested in that. He said he wished he could be here, and I said, "Do you have anything you want me to tell him?" and he said, "Sure, the way I'm feeling these days is real strongly bisexual." He said, "Up here [at school] it's real easy to take out girls, and so I'm kinda doing that," and he said, "I don't feel real strongly about making a statement about my sexual identity yet, because I just don't feel like I know what that's going to be." He said there is an active gay movement up there he could join, and he's resisted that all along. He knows that I would still rather he not be gay.

R. G.: And he knows you will accept the fact that he is, if that's where he decides to settle.

MOTHER: Yeah, he knows that, I mean, that's basically the understanding between us. He knows I'm not going to reject him.

R. G.: He may well still be quite undecided where his primary orientation is. There are people who live out their lives essentially as bisexuals, which doesn't mean that they can't make up their mind. It means that they have more options than many other people, that they are responsive to males and females. And it depends on the particular circumstance where they are in their lives, whether they decide to marry at that time or decide to have children. That may tilt it in terms of at least a predominant life-style for that period. For some men that may work, for others it doesn't.

Steven's Relationship with Males and Females

MOTHER: You remember when he was a little boy, that he always wanted to play with girls, and now all of his best friends are young women. He has no sexual relationships with them, mostly, that I know of. They're his best friends, so in a way it's exactly the same. He has two close male friends that he's had for the last five years, but I think that the relationships that he has with these two guys are just ridiculous, it's a very hostile kind of relationship. It's not sexual with either one. They hang out together and fight all the time. I don't understand it.

R. G.: What else about relationships?

MOTHER: A couple of years ago we had a really long talk, and he told me that he felt a lot of pain and a lot of sorrow, that he could not seem to and never had been able to make friends with men, with boys, real solid friendships, the way that some guys are friends. He said, "I don't know how to do that, and I wish I could. I feel the loss." That was sad to me—that felt sad, because in his case I think there are two separate issues. It's—however he is sexually is almost independent of a problem area which I see him as always having had, which is an ability to be close to men.

R. G.: On the other hand, most men have an inability to be close to women.

MOTHER: I know. And I can't help but feel that he felt bad about that— he felt inadequate. The only time I know that he really fell in love— really, he's been in love twice—when he fell in love, the kind of falling in love that knocks you out, was with a boy. At the same time, for about two years, he was very much in love with this girl, although it was never really consummated sexually the way it was with the boy.

R. G.: What do you mean, wasn't consummated?

MOTHER: Well, I had the sense, and I wish he were here to talk to you about her, the passion—it wasn't as passionate as it was with the boy, but he was incredibly tied to her.

R. G.: What else?

MOTHER: I think he has real complicated relationships with women. The relationship with this one woman is very complicated, and a lot of it, I think, has to do with his responsiveness to women who are rejecting, and of course I consider myself responsible for that. I mean, there's always been a tension between us. In this conversation that I was mentioning, he also said that there was a point in his life, he couldn't remember just exactly when, maybe five years or so ago, he said this realization that he was in fact a male came to him and he said, "I'm a boy." He said to himself, "I'm a boy, I don't have to put on skirts when my mom isn't here, I don't have to do that anymore." He said when he was a young boy, when he was real little, the thought of just being around women's clothing and stuff was so exciting, because clothing was so soft and everything connected with women was so much more sensual than male stuff—footballs and stuff like that— which is true.

Steven's Explanation of His Sexual Orientation

MOTHER: He also said, with regard to how he grew up, "Look, let's face it, I never had a father." He was never close to his stepfather, my second husband was just a disaster, and then the man that we lived with who was so good to him, died, and he said, "All of your best friends were always wonderful," and I have a lot of really great women friends. He said, "All of the best people in my life—the people that I've liked most of all—were women."

R. G.: But why should that make one identify with the women rather than be exuberantly heterosexual and go out and capture one and live with her forever?

MOTHER: Yeah, I wish I knew.

R. G.: We can argue that from both sides.

MOTHER: I know.

R. G.: You can take someone who is now gay who says, "The reason I'm gay is that all women in my life were bitches. From a very early age on, I realized that they were just castrating bitches, and I wouldn't go near them."

MOTHER: Right, and so what have you got?

R. G.: That's one of the pleasures of psychiatric research.

MOTHER: You come up with circles, each time.

INTERVIEW WITH STEVEN AT AGE TWENTY

Current Homosexuality and Problems with the Gay World

STEVEN: I'm living in a house with three other people, one of whom is my lover.

R. G.: Tell me about your romantic interests since I saw you last.

STEVEN: It got to the point where I realized that *they*, society, wanted me to polarize, and part of it was just that I was basically reluctant to make a stand pretty much on anything, politically or sexually, but people are just too threatened. I was really surprised to find out that homosexuals as well were biased against bisexuals, you know that was like a big realization for me—that straights and gays don't like the bisexual.

R. G.:   There's no democracy in this world.

STEVEN: None, you know, and so I've basically been experimenting— not experimenting, but realizing and experiencing what it's like to come out, but, see, I have such a different experience. I have such a different experience than most in my group, because I was confronted with it—with my homosexuality—at an early age, not quite eight. Is that when I first started seeing you—I was about eight?

R. G.:   At that time you were involved in homosexuality?

STEVEN: Something was of concern—I was different from the rest of the boys.

R. G.:   In terms of interests?

STEVEN: Uh hum.

R. G.:   You weren't sexual yet?

STEVEN: I don't think so. Anyway, you know, I never had the sudden trauma—like my roommate just came out to his mother, you know— he's, like, twenty-four years old, and big deal—and I couldn't really relate to that. And on the sexual level as well. I see myself as definitely being a minority of one. Like recently, one of the big issues that I've come up against is the issue about cruising—anonymous sex. I know I was aware of it when I was around sixteen or seventeen, one of my first boyfriends would tell me about his little affairs down under Santa Monica pier. I was like shocked, and it was always like somewhere in the back of my mind, and then, as I started getting gay friends, be- coming close with a lot of gay men and realizing that it's a significant part of their life, once again I started thinking, "I'm the oddball again." Then I started questioning: "Why haven't I followed them? Why hasn't my past led me to a couple of bathrooms or a park or beach or what- ever?" You know, I just walk with my friends and they say, "I'll be right back," you know, and then, "I just got a blow job." And I went with my friend one night and I said, "You've got to find out what it's all about," so I went down with him one night to their local hangout, and I think it was like two o'clock in the morning, and these men that just hang out under the piers—and I was just sitting there on a piece of driftwood just sort of looking over there and this guy sort of walks by a piece of driftwood and he, like, positioned himself, you know— and then he walked by me, and then my friend walked away from me, and I'm left alone now—and what if this guy comes up to me on the piece of driftwood?

R. G.:   Did he?

STEVEN: No, he didn't. Basically, I'm just scared, I think. It must be the danger that's so appealing in it, because I don't think they're getting an emotional release or gratification at all. In fact, I can't imagine that the act itself would be that pleasurable. I have friends who are addicted to it. We had this big confrontation one night, which I got kind of upset, and I said, "How can you do that?" They came back with, "Oh, you're not really a homosexual, you're not really gay, you don't know about this—it's part of what being homosexual is about."

R. G.:   It sounds like they are trying to put their value system onto you.

STEVEN: But apparently I've missed out on where it's really at, you know, my friends go, "That's where it's at, that's what its all about." I can't accept that—I just can't.

R. G.:   You know, there is a comparable phenomenon in the straight world, too, people who are involved sexually with a lot of anonymous partners at large swinging parties—

STEVEN: Yeah.

R. G.:   The "lovers" are essentially disembodied, so its not an exclusive priority of the gay world. It goes on in the straight world too.

STEVEN: I know there are gay men who don't do that, but I haven't met many myself.

Bisexuality

R. G.:   You started saying something about prejudice against bisexuals, and then you dropped that.

STEVEN: Well, I suppose that I considered myself bisexual in high school. I knew that I was—I recognized my femininity and realized that people would call me gay because I am feminine and I have mannerisms of a homosexual, so that's it. But I've never been revulsed by a female. I've had sex with women; I've enjoyed it, but, I don't know, it doesn't seem to work, somehow.

R. G.:   What do you mean by that?

STEVEN: Maybe I just don't feel comfortable enough in that bisexual identity—maybe I just run from a more extreme version of bisexuality, but, you know, I've told that to some of my gay friends and they're shocked—they're shocked! *I'm* sick. I am sick for having sex with a *woman*, they are *not* sick for having sex in a *bathroom*.

R. G.:   You don't know any bisexuals?

STEVEN: Yeah, but most of them are nervous type people. I'm attracted—this is something I never tell people—I'm quite attracted to several women. I like the more masculine women than feminine ones. I know I have been in the past, but, see, you cannot—you can't approach—I mean, a dyke is like good friends, right? You can be good friends with them because you know there's not going to be the sexual bullshit between you, but yet at the same time you start getting interested in her, you know, and you can't cross that line.

R. G.:   It's not necessarily always the case.

STEVEN: That's true.

R. G.:   There are women who identify as lesbian, who also have sex with certain men who are appealing to them, just as there are men who are identified as gay who have sex with women on occasion.

Earlier Homosexual Experiences

R. G.:   When did you have your first male-male relationship?

STEVEN: When I was sixteen. Physical?

R. G.:   Yeah.

STEVEN: Well, I played around when I was—just boy games, sex games with boys—about ten.

R. G.:   What did you do?

STEVEN: Well, we—it was two—it was at my grandmother's house, if she left during the day. The two neighbor boyfriends would come in and we'd have intercourse. We were too young to really know why we were doing these things. We didn't ejaculate. And we'd dress up in my grandmother's clothes and prance about.

R. G.:   How many times did you do that?

STEVEN: Oh, about four or five times. It happened right before I left, I'm sure it would have gone on. And then it didn't happen again until—I think I was a late bloomer, what you call a late bloomer, because I don't remember really having desires. Some of my friends just turned to cruising out of desperation, you know, they get so horny, "I've gotta do it." It's never really bothered me that much.

R. G.:   Did you also have sexual attractions to females then?

STEVEN: Yeah, uh huh, but there wasn't that secret, you know, urge or mystery thing—it made the man so much more special than when done with the woman.

R. G.:   Which do you think came first: awareness of attractions to males or females?

STEVEN: To males.

R. G.:   Okay, at ten you had some sex experiences with males. Trace through if you can your awareness of sexual attractions up to sixteen.

STEVEN: Well, I discovered masturbation when I was about thirteen, and that summer I was really into it, maybe even twice a day, you know, just totally went for it.

R. G.:   When you would masturbate, what did you think about?

STEVEN: I remember I got my hands on a pornographic magazine that I found in one of my mothers friend's house, and I would jack off to the pictures of the guys—they weren't guy-guy stuff, it was just men-women, but I would always get a hard-on with the male and jack off to that, usually the male. All right, I think I might have stuck a few objects up my ass, but I didn't, like, turn on that much. And then shortly afterwards I met my first boyfriend. I couldn't bring him to my house, and we couldn't go to his house, that's for sure, because his parents were, like, traditional Catholics. He was so paranoid he didn't want his parents to see me because he was afraid they could see faggot, you know, no doubt about it.

Earlier Heterosexual Experiences

R. G.: Which was more pleasurable, your first experience of sex with a girl or with a guy?

STEVEN: The guy, because she was a virgin and she was, like, "Ow, ow, ow," and I was fucked up, I couldn't understand what was going on and I just came. It was really stupid. We didn't use any sort of protection at all. When I've had sex with a woman I've never—I've been lucky, I suppose.

R. G.: When did you first have sex-play with a female?

STEVEN: Probably about sixteen. And then one night I went out to a party with my best friend, who is a girl, and we took Quaaludes for the first time, and my mother's friend's girl stayed at our house and she was a dyke but I didn't know it at the time, and I remember her trying to come on—like she asked me once if she could spend the night in my room and I said, "Why," and she goes, "I don't know." Yeah, I definitely felt scared about sexual feelings and things like that, I think I was pretty much just generally afraid, as I'd get really wary whenever I felt like a woman was coming on.

R. G.: What were you afraid might happen?

STEVEN: I was afraid that I would have to—that I was *so expected* to do this trip, and I was confident in that respect. I don't think it was pure performance anxiety, actually, but it came out just like—I don't really wanta do it—and there was something about, something I didn't like about the women, some kind of feeling about them. Of course, no guys ever came on to me, so I couldn't really compare it, I didn't really know what was going on. Anyway, the three of us took a Quaalude for the first time and decided to go to bed together and it was just like, "Oh, okay." I do remember going down on one of them and liking it a lot.

Memory of Childhood Evaluation and Its Effect

R. G.: What do you remember about being here?

STEVEN: I knew that I was being watched, that I was being observed—that you would be looking for signs of effeminate behavior, so I was always on guard, but I would encourage the other little boys—like, we would play Cinderella or something, and I would want to be Cinderella and the child—I would be the father.

R. G.: Looking back now, many years later, what's your feeling about your mother having brought you here?

STEVEN: I think it was good, I'm glad that she did. For a long time I thought that it wasn't good, you know—I certainly didn't tell anybody. "Where are you going?" "Oh, out," you know, no one could know, but it was good. I feel good about having gone through it. I really don't know much about your research or what you've done, but I think it's basically good.

R. G.: Why do you think it was good to come here?

STEVEN: Because I think it's a crucial issue, I think it's important, very important, it's something that's not being looked into very much—but I do wonder why there were no girls—I remember that's one thing, it was like, "Why are there only boys here?" You know, "Do girls ever"—I remember asking my mother, "Well, why isn't it wrong then, when a girl puts pants on and plays with trucks?"

R. G.: Why do you think it was good that you had the experience of being here?

STEVEN: Because it was brought to my attention, I think, my deviance was brought to my attention at an early age, and for a while I thought that was good. It scared me emotionally, somehow, but I think it's made me stronger personally in some ways.

R. G.: What ways?

STEVEN: Talking about what's going on in my mind—why do you like to dress up in women's clothes, what do you think about women, things like that.

Erotic Cross-dressing

R. G.: To what extent, if any, are you still interested in dressing up?

STEVEN: I like to wear jewelry. I like rhinestones—I've been into buying rhinestones, bracelets, necklaces. I use makeup on occasion, and I like to wear furs. I like to dress up, but I don't feel that I have the urge to dress up as a woman. I don't fantasize that. But I have kept a lot of my liking for feminine accoutrements. I mean—a love of dressing up, the act of dressing up and going out, you know, and being outrageous.

R. G.: Is the dressing sexually arousing?

STEVEN: I've dressed in skirts recently at my friend's house, and one of the negligees—and that definitely was an erotic attraction, the negligee.

R. G.: That gave you a hard-on, being in the negligee?

STEVEN: Uh hum, wearing it, looking at myself in the mirror.

R. G.: That gave you a hard-on?

STEVEN: Uh hum. The skirt didn't, really, it was just fun wearing it. Yeah, I'm still learning—I still have a desire to wear a dress, but, see, I just don't know if it means that I want to be a woman, it's just, you know, men can't do that.

R. G.: Prior to this time that you put the negligee on and got a hard-on, have you ever been sexually aroused by cross-dressing before then?

STEVEN: Yeah, I used to—yeah, when I was like, about—oh, I suppose I cross-dressed actively until I was seventeen, eighteen, and I'd come home from school and my mom would be at work, and she had this box of old clothes, and I would dress up usually—the whole thing, all the way: nylons, skirt, blouse, bra, and I'd put tits in them, and I'd be too afraid to wear makeup because there would be marks, you could tell—and I would masturbate in drag, imagining myself a woman giving head. And that was definitely very erotic.

R. G.:   What age did you begin masturbation along with the dressing?

STEVEN: About fifteen, I would say, until about eighteen.

R. G.:   Before fifteen were you dressing up and getting sexually aroused?

STEVEN: It's hard to say. I know I got some kind of special feeling when I dressed up, but I can't definitely identify it as sexual—I can't recall getting an erection.

R. G.:   Do you ever imagine yourself as a female when you're dressed up?

STEVEN: Yeah, sometimes I do.

R. G.:   When?

STEVEN: Usually when we're out, like at a party or quite drunk, or quite dressed up.

R. G.:   How seriously do you think about being a woman? Have you ever thought about taking hormones and having a sex-change operation?

STEVEN: No. I know some people, some men, who do that to a point— who'll dress up, go in drag, and take hormones. I've seen men with big tits and a cock.

R. G.:   Are these natural breasts or are these—

STEVEN: No—they're just like rock hard. They don't move.

Lesbian Identity

STEVEN: I do think, though, if I were a woman I would be a lesbian, because I don't like men very much.

R. G.:   A lesbian has sex with a woman. Why can't you have sex with a woman as a man?

STEVEN: I keep thinking that it would be—my life would be so much easier if I was just straight, and I do love women, but I'm not spurred on—I don't fantasize, erotically fantasize, about women. I know I want to have children someday.

R. G.:   But you say you don't erotically fantasize about women, but you would as a lesbian—a woman erotically attracted to other women.

STEVEN: Yeah, I know.

R. G.:   How can that be?

STEVEN: Because if I were a woman, I don't think I would like to do the role that I would have to play and have a sexual relationship. I think I would resent the attitude that I would get from the man—thinking along the same lines of why am I not homosexual, why don't I just get into a woman. Man is a fuck, you know, I associate love with some sort of pain or some sort of hurt or something. It just seems like I set myself up so many times to get hurt badly; maybe its because they are capable of hurting me, but I don't know. Sometimes I just know that I will get hurt; I know it won't work out with my pursuing this, but I do it anyway, and I'll get really depressed. But I haven't gotten depressed enough to become heterosexual, which sounds strange to me, thinking that I would have to turn to heterosexuality, probably out of depression.

"FEMININE" BOY, HETEROSEXUAL ADOLESCENT, HOMOSEXUAL MAN: SAUL

Saul's behavior in early childhood was extensively "feminine." His preschool sexual play was with a girl, but he wanted to marry a boy. Cross-gender behaviors diminished considerably by adolescence, and in his early teens he was actively heterosexual. However, considerable energy was expended suppressing homosexual arousal throughout the teen years. Then, in young adulthood, a homosexual experience eclipsed his previous heterosexuality.

SAUL'S PARENTS DESCRIBE HIM AT AGE SIX

Reason for Consultation

FATHER: He has dressed up like a lady for a number of years. He used to do it with pretty great frequency. Now it is considerably less, I would say. Whether this is the result of parental implied criticism I don't know, but nevertheless, he does it less. He used to use all kinds of things—different types of clothing he used to wear, and still does to some extent imitate the ways of women.

R. G.: What do you mean?

FATHER: When he is dressed up he sometimes—when he is not dressed he will go kind of like this [gestures in a feminine way].

Onset of Cross-gender Behavior

R. G.: How old was he when he first began to dress up in girls' clothing?

FATHER: I would say probably about two or three—definitely between two or three.

R. G.: Do you remember how you felt the first time you saw it?

FATHER: I haven't been much concerned with it until fairly recently, so I don't think I was in the beginning either—when he was a little one.

R. G.:   Whose clothing would he wear?

FATHER: Initially he would wear his mother's clothing, but still mostly it's hers—slips, undergarments. Also he likes long, silky things, pajamas.

R. G.:   What about men's things?

FATHER: We try to get him colorful and interesting men's clothing, like he had a pilot's outfit for Halloween, and I bought him Indian clothes. It was hinted to us that perhaps he was an imaginative boy. He was interested in color, so we tried to get him interested in colorful clothing that would fit into a man's role, but we really haven't done this enough, I think. He will wear high heels—walk around in the house in high heels.

Core Identity

R. G.:   Will he say "I am a girl" or "I am a woman"?

FATHER: No. When he was littler, he did say he loved to be a lady when he grows up, but not any more. Recently he has definitely decided that he is going to be a man when he grows up.

R. G.:   Would he give any reason for wanting to be a woman?

FATHER: I don't know. Over the last year it has dropped off—when he was four.

R. G.:   Did he increase his behavior after his sister was born?

FATHER: He increased a number of things. An increase in babyish behavior, including women's behavior.

R. G.:   (to mother): Do you agree?

MOTHER: Definitely. There was an increase of infantile behavior and wishing verbally to be a baby, and this was his way of coping.

R. G.:   Did he ever state he wished to be a girl before the child was born?

FATHER: I would think there was some of it before, yes.

R. G.:   So it was an increase of previous behavior rather than completely new?

MOTHER: No, it wasn't new behavior at all.

Peer Group

R. G.:   What about preferred playmates?

FATHER: Females usually.

R. G.:   At what age?

FATHER: Probably this is conditioned by the availability. Our next door neighbors had two little girls his age, and he has also had boy friends, but he seems more relaxed with girls, or boys below his age. Although I might say that he has always had, still has, fairly good boy friends.

Role-playing

R. G.:   What about the mother/father or family games in which he had to take one or the other kind of role?

MOTHER: He is very imaginative in general, very imaginative in his play, and he has been since the time he was a little child—from the time he was under two. I was amazed at this ability to pretend and take on roles. This is something that he loves to do. He gets great pleasure from this. He is fantastic at accents—at languages. He is very inclined this way. He used to play a lot when he was little, and he usually was the woman. He went through a very brief cowboy stage, and he liked his Indian suit, but for the most part he really takes the role of a girl.

R. G.:   Beginning when?

MOTHER: Just around two.

Playing as Mother

MOTHER: He would wear my shoes, and he would take my purse, and he would say, "Mommy going to the market." He had a very special relationship with my mother, and he had an imaginary playmate, and she is a grandmother. He created her with my mother. Anyway, where this was most marked was in nursery school last year, when he was four. He did a tremendous amount of playing house and dressing up. That was without any shadow of a doubt his favorite thing to do—to dress up and to play in the house. He always dressed up like a lady, and whenever I came to get him, I would see him in these elaborate outfits, and my heart would really sink. That's when it really began to bother me, was in the year between four and five. I did express concern to his nursery school teacher, who at that point told me I should investigate why it was bothering me. That it was my bag. This was the peak between four and five. I was most uncomfortable with it and handled it most inconsistently.

R. G.:   What was inconsistent?

MOTHER: My reaction to it. He was dressing up at home, and the fact that I was unable to hide my displeasure. This year in kindergarten he also still enjoys going into the house. He just is invariably the mother. They have begun telling him he has to be the father, and at kindergarten conference they said he has no idea how to be the father. He says, "I don't want to be the father. I don't know what a daddy does." They said he has no idea what to do in that role, and they do a lot of playacting. He always chooses a feminine part. They don't let him have it, and also he is getting laughter from the kids. The thing that disturbed individual teachers the most was that the children were drawing pictures of each other and a girl drew a picture of him with a dress on and held it up proudly, and everybody and he were pleased, and all the other children were pleased, and nobody said, "But he has a dress on." That was what really disturbed the teacher enough to contact me.

Toy Preference

R. G.: Tell me about playthings and preferred toys.

MOTHER: He went through a fantastic car and truck stage. At two, all the time with trucks. He loved them. His favorite books were about trucks, blocks, cars, and trucks; and he also wore my shoes. Never dolls. Occasionally—in other people's houses. He did not have a mother role that way. At the same time he was interested in cars and trucks, he loved outside play—very muddy—he loved mud, sand, and dirt. He wore my shoes and took my purse and went to the market. I didn't think anything of it. He got to the stage where he loved to dress and undress, and I did go out to a rummage sale looking for dress-up clothes, because I had always thought, "Isn't it fun? Wouldn't it be fun to have a big box of dress-up clothes?" I bought a whole bunch of crazy hats, and I did look for men's hats, but I could not find any men's hats at the rummage sale. So here was a box of clothes; there was nothing interesting for men, and I really didn't think too much of it. He liked jewelry too. In retrospect, I am feeling guilty. I didn't feel guilty or concerned at the time.

Games

MOTHER: Between two and three, kids of the neighbors used to come over and they used to play house. He loved to play with sand and mud, but the sand and mud thing was cooking. It wasn't so much road building. He loved to make pies and soup, and he very quickly dropped out of cars and trucks. His six-year-old friends still like cars and trucks. He doesn't. He liked imaginative games, running around, things like that.

Attention to Mother's Fashion

R. G.: Does he ever comment on your clothing?

MOTHER: Very often. He really notices any new article of clothing. If I put eyeliner on, which I don't always do, he always comments. If I have a permanent, a haircut, if my hair looks funny.

Pictures Drawn

MOTHER: He is very good artistically, and he used to draw very, very elaborately. They were usually me. It was amazing, very elaborate, tremendous details of the face, beautiful dresses, flowers, earrings. He would very rarely draw men, and when he did it was just nothing—a stick and a blank face. No hands, and that used to disturb me. They spend a lot of time asking the child to tell stories, and then they write it down, and he draws a picture. They were always about women and ladies and marriages and things. This began to disturb me, and when I became unable to deal with the dressing up, I became even more afraid to curb the dressing up because I saw this tremendous desire underneath, and I didn't want to make him feel guilty. So I didn't say, "We don't do that," because I was afraid. I began to feel this tremendous desire. He got teased at school, and that was very powerful. In a way I was glad, but in a way I feel fearful about making him feel guilty about a desire that is still there. I feel that it is now at a point where it is more than just changing behavior. I don't know. He often said, "I want to be a girl." He knows he isn't going to be. He knows he is going to be a man. He plans occupations, masculine occupations.

R. G.: Never says, "I am a girl"? Always "I want to be"?

MOTHER: "I would like to be." He would really love to put on my nightgowns and negligee next to his skin.

R. G.:   You said all this began around two. Looking back in retrospect, is there anything prior to two that you would like to look at now with a different insight?

MOTHER: I consider this very normal two-year-old behavior. I still do not consider this abnormal.

Infant Appearance

R. G.:   Would people comment to you what a beautiful child—what a beautiful girl?

MOTHER: No, yes. They never said he would make a beautiful girl. They always said what a beautiful child, in grocery stores and things. He always got that kind of comment. He had huge eyes, but I never heard anyone said he would make a pretty girl.

Mother-Son Contact

R. G.:   What about your own physical contact with your son?

MOTHER: Very close, but I don't think excessive. I enjoyed holding him, and he wasn't the kind of baby who pushed you off. He was a very cuddly baby. He loved to be cuddled. I loved to give him a bath. I loved to put oil on him. I used to massage him. I used to stretch his body out. I got pleasure from it. He got pleasure from it. I wouldn't say it was excessive.

Husband-Wife Role

MOTHER: My husband makes a lot of decisions, but they are not decisions the boy sees. I wouldn't say I run the whole show. I run the show that

my boy sees. I don't think I overrule. I really think this is the way we
have mapped out our lives, and you know, this is my area. I think
pretty much my husband doesn't care about these things, and this was
something that came out in our kindergarten conference, you know,
the importance of his seeing daddy's role in the family. I really feel
that I would like to become less important in his life, and I would like
my husband to become more important.

R. G.:   In terms of modeling in the family and decision-making responsibility and authority, how does he see things?

MOTHER: I think this is very important.

R. G.:   How?

MOTHER: In terms of what actually goes on between them—very little.
And one thing is that we recently realized that they spend a prescribed
amount of time every night before he goes to bed, but we realized
that the quality of this contact has not changed in three years. It's a
ritual. It's the same thing, and it's been mostly me nagging at my
husband. He has been trying to be more creative about the kind of
time he spends, what he does, and trying to do more appropriate
things.

R. G.:   What happens when you are both present and decisions have to
be made? What happens then?

MOTHER (to her husband):   What would you say? (Silence.) (To R. G.):
My opinion is it is me. This is something we are working at now.

R. G. (to father):   Does your wife make decisions by default, or might you
suggest something and it will be overruled?

MOTHER: It's not the overruling. It is that he views this as my domain,
and not his. He doesn't wish, he doesn't choose to make decisions in
this whole area.

MOTHER: It's not the overruling. It is that he views this as my domain,
and not his. He doesn't wish, he doesn't choose to make decisions in
this whole area.

Heterosexual Rehearsal

MOTHER: There was one incident—it wasn't an incident, it was over a
couple of weeks when he was two—that really threw me. There was
a little girl next door who was four when he was two. At the time of
two he was masturbating—in a fantastic way—I had never been around
kids and I did not know. I mean, I knew and expected kids to masturbate to the extent that they played with their penis or held themselves or something, but he would go down for his nap; he would take
off his diapers, and he would do the most fantastic things; and I just
used to sit there and watch. It was fascinating. He was having a wonderful time. He would take cars and trucks and run them up and
down his penis, and he would take something soft, something cold,

something hard, and always taking textures and would get this tremendous erection and it would go down and he'd bring it up and have the most wonderful time. The little girl next door came and started playing "doctor" with him, and "doctor" consisted of her stripping him, him lying down flat, completely passive, and her manipulating him until he had a big erection. And I kind of didn't make a big deal out of it and wanted to leave it alone. The woman next door was horrified and really lambasted her daughter; and my attitude was, "Leave it alone and it will go away."

Later, it was very funny—a whole bunch of kids were sitting on the steps talking about what they wanted to be when they grow up. Somebody wants to be a fireman, policeman. One kid said,"I want to be a doctor," and my son at age two said, "I want to be the one who is *sick*." Okay, so we used to laugh and think, "Oh, my God. Our kid is going to be passive all his life," and laughed and joked.

The boy's parents were seen about seven times during the next fourteen years. They reported much less "feminine" behavior in their son. The father reported spending more time with him. Both parents' concerns about their son's "femininity" dissipated, and they were confident of his emerging heterosexuality.

INTERVIEW WITH SAUL AT AGE NINETEEN

R. G.: I haven't seen you for a long time, so maybe in a general way, before I get specific, you can tell me what you're like, what your interests are, how you spend your time.

Acting and Theater Interests

SAUL: Well, right now I'm studying film, and that's what I want to do is go into film, and I'm also very interested in the theory aspect. I have a lot of academic interests and a lot of interest in the performing arts.

R. G.: Tell me about your interest in films.

SAUL: I definitely want to do more work in theater, and I want to do more work on my acting, but ultimately what I want to do is direct films, more than acting.

R. G.: Do you enjoy acting?

SAUL: Yes, very.

R. G.: How far back do you remember an interest in acting?

SAUL: Probably around the sixth grade.

Social Interests

R. G.: What kind of social life do you have?

SAUL: A good one. Like sometimes I surround myself with a lot of people, and then sometimes I spend a lot of time alone.

R. G.:   What about dating relationships, romantic involvements?

SAUL: It's always been good for me, and I've been involved in relationships for a real long time, but I've had problems with it, in terms of
making commitments. I haven't had any real long relationships. The
longest one I've had is the one I'm in right now, which must be close
to six months. I've had plenty of relationships, but I don't know if the
quality has been that good. But I feel good about the relationship I'm
in now, and I feel good about future relationships. I think I'm growing
and learning.

R. G.:   Tell me in what way.

SAUL: Well, I went through a period of being really anti-intellectual, and
I saw myself as this kind of laid back, stoned out, mellow hippie, and
so I went out with girls that were like that. I went out with girls that
were like—they had dropped out of high school, I was still in high
school, and they had no intellectual interests whatsoever, like the far-
thest thing from the kind of people my parents would like, basically.
And I just get really bored, in every relationship I'd get really bored.

Recollection of Earlier Social Contacts

SAUL: I think when I was younger I was more into being by myself
because there were so few people I knew that had the same interest.

R. G.:   Were you sort of a loner during those years?

SAUL: Sort of, but never really intensely, I mean I always had friends;
I always had people to be with, but they were like the outsiders, they
were kind of scared kids, weird kids.

R. G.:   It wasn't a clique?

SAUL: No, at times I was in cliques and at times I was way out there. I
always felt separated up to when I went to high school; I always felt
like I was outside even when I was known.

Sexual Relationships

R. G.:   When did you have your first sexual relationship?

SAUL: Well, my first girlfriend was the summer before I went into eighth
grade, and that was a really intense relationship. I mean, that was the
first time I had sex, and then after that, I didn't—I wasn't involved
for a while, for probably two years.

R. G.:   And somewhere before eighth grade makes you about twelve,
thirteen?

SAUL: And then the next relationship I had was when I was fourteen.

Same-sex Erotic Fantasies

R. G.:   At the time that your sexual feelings were starting to emerge, were
there any same-sex feelings?

SAUL: Yes.

R. G.: To what extent?

SAUL: I'd say equally. Yeah, I guess equally, but then I started realizing that that wasn't the way that things were supposed to be.

R. G.: What do you mean?

SAUL: I mean I just knew—it just kind of dawned on me that that isn't acceptable, the yearnings decreased a lot, and now I still have those feelings, but in a real ambivalent way. I still feel attracted to men, not so much the adult men but to people my own age that I'm close to, but any time the ideal opportunity for having sex happens, I get really turned off and really scared. Sometimes I feel all right with men, sometimes I don't.

Fear of Homosexuality

R. G.: Do you think you get turned off because you are scared?

SAUL: I just get this feeling, really strong feeling in my gut of nervousness.

R. G.: What would happen?

SAUL: Well, I think it'd probably be great, I mean I'd really like it to happen, but I just have to get over those feelings.

R. G.: Do you know guys who are gay, guys in your age-group?

SAUL: No, I don't know any guys my age who are gay. I know a lot who are bisexual, and I know a lot who are like me, like they could be bisexual but they're really scared of it.

R. G: Tell me more about what part of it scares you.

SAUL: I know it's not a moral thing, and it's not a thing that people find out because I talked about it a lot. I love my parents. Well, I mean I'd even mentioned it to them, they know, but it's more—

R. G.: When you shared this with them, what was their reaction?

SAUL: I never really shared it to them, I just made a little comment and they pretended they didn't hear. But it's more of a gut reaction thing, it's more of a physical thing which is weird because I know at times I felt physically attracted, definitely. It's just a nervousness.

R. G.: So when you first became aware of sexual feelings, they were about equally divided?

SAUL: Yes.

R. G.: This was when you were about eleven?

SAUL: Yes.

Evolution of Heterosexual Experience

R. G.: And then about a year later you began a relationship with a girl. How did that evolve, and why did it evolve for this girl rather than some guy?

SAUL: Well, I didn't know any guys that would be into it. And it was— why did it evolve with this girl? I don't know, it was just real spontaneous. We really liked each other, we spent a lot of time together, we got really close, and it happened.

R. G.: When you were having sex with her, did you ever imagine she was a guy?

SAUL: No.

Masturbation Fantasies

R. G.: Do you remember how old you were when you first began to masturbate?

SAUL: Ten or eleven.

R. G.: And do you remember what you used to think about in terms of sexual daydreams?

SAUL: It was women and men, and it was usually people around—like people I rode the bus to school with.

R. G.: Let's say out of ten times that you masturbated, how many times did you imagine a female?

SAUL: Probably about seven or eight female.

R. G.: And what percentage of masturbation fantasy now involves males?

SAUL: Now very rarely with males—I mean only two other times that I remember, last year.

R. G.: When was there a change, a drop-off?

SAUL: The drop-off was like when I was about twelve or thirteen like probably about a year after I started masturbating.

R. G.: Why do you think that was the case?

SAUL: Because at first I realized that it wasn't cool to be attracted to men but I didn't stop. But then a while afterwards, I guess when I started being around girls more and being into it and talking about it with the other guys, I guess that's when it happened.

R. G.: Did you share with the other guys the fact that you were having fantasies about males?

SAUL: I didn't do that until—I started doing that maybe a year ago, just real close friends. I talked to more women friends about it because they're really—

R. G.: More understanding about it.

SAUL: Yeah, because it seems like more women are willing to admit that they have those kinds of feelings than men, even though a lot of men do.

Current Erotic Fantasies

R. G.: How about pictures of attractive men or attractive women, to what extent is there a relative turn-on looking at a male model in a fashion magazine or a female model in a fashion magazine?

SAUL: I could probably go twice as much to all females. I'm not really receptive to looking at pictures of a male fashion model and saying

"Wow, he's sexy," but I can appreciate aesthetically, like if I see pictures of a dancer, I can say he's really beautiful, but I don't have a physical attraction.

R. G.:   Do you get erections sometimes around attractive men?

SAUL: I have a few times.

R. G.:   When that happens, how do you feel?

SAUL: Well, the first time it happened that I can remember is last year, probably about six months ago, I was really glad because it was this person that I was really infatuated with and I was really attracted to. I knew he was attracted to me, but I didn't know—every time we got in a situation where something could happen I got really turned off and got away as quick as I could. I really wanted to have sex with him, but I was worried that if we did I wouldn't be able to get it up, and so then I didn't. One time I masturbated and I thought about him, and I was really glad, but nothing ever happened, nothing came of it.

R. G.:   Why was that?

SAUL: I don't know, it was weird, it was like he was really attracted to me and he was really open about it, and I was really freaked out and intimidated, but then I started getting interested, and then I told him and after that I got turned off.

R. G.:   Would you change anything about your sexual relationships?

SAUL: No, I feel really good about my sexuality.

Recalled Childhood Behaviors

R. G.:   Let me go back to when you were a younger kid. What do you remember about your interests?

SAUL: I remember playing tag. I remember once when everyone in the class got together and made a huge sand castle. I was never interested in sports as long as I can remember. I used to say it was because I was just not a competitive person, but I don't think that was it. I think that probably a lot of it was that my dad never had any interest in it, and I never got the basics, and I was always scared to ask him how to coordinate. So it was only when I got older that I really learned to use my body fairly well.

R. G.:   Did other kids tease you or give you a hard time for not being interested in sports?

SAUL: No, I mean they were really supportive, like I remember a lot of times people teaching me how to play sports that I hadn't known how to play. I would play, and I'd play with them at recess for a couple of days and then I'd get bored with them. I just found it very boring and dull, but I remember having friends that were real jocks, and they were always trying to get me to play and I just never wanted to.

R. G.:   Do you remember whether most of your friends were boys, girls, or a mixture?

SAUL: I remember that there was some kind of attraction to playing with the girls, but when I think of who were friends of mine in those days, I think of certain specific guys.

R. G.:   Do you remember what sort of things you liked to play?

SAUL: I'm trying to think if I liked playing with dolls, but I can't really remember ever doing that. I'm sure I did.

R. G.:   Why?

SAUL: Well, I think everyone does, and I know that I wasn't—when I was young I wasn't really antigirl, I remember enjoying being with the girls and that's probably what they were doing, so I think I probably did but can't remember for certain.

INTERVIEW WITH SAUL AT AGE TWENTY-ONE

Further Reflections on Boyhood "Sex-typed" Interests

SAUL: I remember kids had to do with violence and I was always very opposed to violence and aggressivity, and I remember the kids would go out and kill snails and I would try and protect the snails. And when people wanted to play war, I didn't want to play war. I didn't have a natural interest in sports, and it was very forced. I mean, I had to say, "Okay, you really should go play football," and then I would try and play a little bit, but I never really liked it, and I never really got into it.

R. G.:   Do you remember doing specifically feminine things?

SAUL: I guess I really liked playing games, like acting games or make-believe, like that. I was always putting on little plays or was really interested in dressing up, and I think I enjoyed wearing women's clothing to some extent.

R. G.:   When was that?

SAUL: It's pretty vague. I'd say it was really early. I remember in kindergarten.

R. G.:   Do you remember that people would object to your dressing up as a girl and making believe you were one?

SAUL: Yeah, I remember once in nursery school. That's the only thing I remember. The only specific memory I have is like there is this dress-up. Like costumes, and they're all women's clothes, and I remember once wearing a skirt or something and the teachers were mad at that. "You can't play with that."

Influence on Current Behaviors

R. G.:   Do you think having some feminine interests as a kid has influenced you today?

SAUL: Well sure it has, definitely. Well, one thing all those experiences created in me, or that maybe was even the cause of those experiences, a great sensitivity to personal interactions, and the way things work. And always feeling a bit outside of the normal patterns of behavior and always feeling like—less and less as I grew older, but definitely feeling very much apart from other people.

Emergent Homosexuality

R. G.:   Do you feel it's influenced your sexuality?

SAUL: It's a really complex issue. More and more I've come to identify myself as gay, and I know that is behavior that is associated with gay people. I really don't understand what—I can't say whether that was the cause or the effect. And I don't know whether straight people exhibited that kind of behavior as children. Actually, I was just think- ing about it a couple of days ago. About why—about issues of effem- inacy and homosexuality. What I was thinking was whether that effeminacy and being attracted to that image of women and playing the role of women came less from a real desire to be a woman than from the fact that knowing, on a certain level, that I was gay all my life, and having no acceptable model or image of how to be a man and be gay, and feeling well, if I want men, if I'm attracted to men, then I have to be a woman. I don't know how much that operates with other people, but I think it operates, I think, it did operate—

R. G.:   Are you talking about when you were much younger?

SAUL: Yes.

R. G.:   Are you feeling that it still operates with you?

SAUL: Not at all now. As a child, yes. I guess that it's just that real literal thing of the way a child's mind operates.

R. G.:   It's a black and white universe. If you're going to be in love with a man, you must be a woman, 'cause Mommy's a woman and she's in love with a man.

SAUL: Yeah, exactly.

R. G.:   There's not too many grays, and there's no model of homosex- uality. Everything is heterosexuality.

SAUL: I remember being really attracted to these images of being a woman, and now, I mean, I couldn't imagine myself as a woman or wanting to be a woman.

R. G.:   What do you mean, that you have come to identify yourself more as gay?

SAUL: Well, just in the sense that I've always. . . . When I was thirteen or fourteen, I thought homosexuality was disgusting and unnatural. And then I began to accept it and I began to think that I was interested in exploring gay relationships, in addition to straight relationships. And then I thought, I'm bisexual, and then it just went through this whole process, and then I realized, when I finally did have a real relationship with a male, which was only very recently, I realized that it was, for me, much more fulfilling than any of the relationships that I had had with women. Because I had had all these relationships with women a lot, and I always felt, you know, I guess I'm just a person who doesn't really get into relationships, who doesn't really feel a lot or doesn't really, you know, can never—always have to be independent and never really be into relationships.

R. G.: Deficient heterosexuality?

Heterosexuality versus Homosexuality

SAUL: Right. And then I got involved in a relationship with a man, and I realized all these things.

R. G.: What was different with a man?

SAUL (long pause): It was more of a gut-level thing. It meant more to me and I felt more.

R. G.: Try to tell me how.

SAUL: What I felt, I felt more intensely. Sexually and emotionally, and psychically. It was just more fulfilling, and it hit me more on a gut level. It was much less superficial.

R. G.: Do you think, in any way, that that could have been the result of that individual male versus other women you've been with, or is it really a generic thing, that any male, or most males, would be like that versus the way most females would be?

SAUL: I know that I'm more sexually attracted to men. But I don't know whether it's a more generic thing or not, because it's the one relationship I had that was the only one that really felt that way. And I had had other relationships with men that were just, you know, nothing special. So I can't say. But I feel, I really feel that I'm emotionally and even in a spiritual way attracted to men. Because that kind of bonding means a lot more to me in a really deep level.

Late Onset of Homosexual Behavior

R. G.: How is it you feel that this is a relatively late evolution in your identity? You are twenty-one now. It sounds like this has happened primarily in the last year.

SAUL: Yes it has. On a certain level I always knew I was gay, and I always felt that it was just—that it was really reprehensible. I mean, I could accept it in other people, but not in myself. It was like my worst nightmare, my worst fear, and I was just going to do everything in my power to deny it and to prove that it wasn't true.

R. G.: Why?

SAUL: Because. . . . It's hard to get in touch with it now, because I really moved through it. Partly because all the images I had of homosexuality were very negative. And that's what I always thought, and then I realized there was an extra charge on it too, which did come from my family, which was a real fear of disapproval from my parents, and a feeling of shame, and a lot to do with the disapproval of my parents, as well as just no positive role models. You know, the gay people that I saw in society were all very negative to me and I felt very, very repulsed by them. Since then, I don't feel that at all. You know, the people that I used to think, "Oh, I never want to be like them, I never want to have anything to do with them." And now I realize they're really sweet people. I had this terrible fear of effeminate men. I just couldn't stand them. So what was the original question?

R. G.: I was wondering why it evolved relatively late for you, as opposed to some guys, when they are twelve or thirteen, they know they're gay and that's it.

SAUL: Because I had such a negative charge on it, and I felt such a strong desire to prove it wasn't true. I couldn't feel good about myself unless I could prove I was straight. Now, since I feel the opposite, if I was all of a sudden to turn straight right now, I wouldn't feel good about myself. I've even thought about going into therapy, to be changed and all that, but now it's the last thing I want to do.

Homosexual Fantasies

R. G.: What percentage, if I could quantify it with you, what percentage of your current sexual fantasies, not behaviors, but just sexual thoughts, are about men and what percentage are still about women?

SAUL: I'd say about 90 percent about men.

R. G.: That's a pretty dramatic shift from a couple of years ago.

SAUL: I know. And it was—I used to force myself to fantasize about women while I masturbated, you know, but those images weren't exciting.

R. G.: When you say force yourself, you mean you would put the other ones away?

SAUL: Yeah.

R. G.: You wouldn't let them go into consciousness?

SAUL: Right.

R. G.: It's interesting, though, that there are some types of therapy, behavior modification therapy, that talk to the idea of utilizing only heterosexual images during masturbation because it's conditioning. The sexuality and orgasm, being a pleasurable response, is going to reinforce the heterosexual imagery.

SAUL: It's ridiculous.

R. G.: It doesn't do that?

SAUL: No, not at all.

R. G.: It doesn't work that way?

SAUL: No, because the imagery is like the spring of your sexuality, not the other way around.

R. G.:   Say that again. It's the imagery that's the spring?

SAUL: Yeah. Like the wellspring. I mean where it comes up from really deep inside. Images determine your sexuality, not the other way around. Because I really tried, I really had to force myself to fantasize about women. I got to the point where I—I mean I had sex with a lot of women and I learned how to make it really pleasurable for her even though I wasn't enjoying myself. And I learned how to perform. Looking back, it seems so ridiculous that I didn't just give up long ago, earlier, because it was never really that pleasurable, and it was like, "Now I have to do this for her." But I just hung in there for years.

Homosexual Relationships

R. G.:   How did you find your first male lover?

SAUL: He was someone I'd worked with over the years in several places and that I'd known for a long time. I'd known he was gay for a long time, and one day I just started looking at him in a different way and putting out energy to him like I was interested, and then we started going out and seeing each other.

R. G.:   Are you involved in a relationship now? With a male?

SAUL: Uh-huh.

R. G.:   How is that relationship going?

SAUL: It's kind of in a difficult period right now, but it had been very good for the last month or so.

R. G.:   How do you find the difficulties in a male-male relationship? How are they similar or different from the difficulties of a male-female relationship?

SAUL: It's the same. You can't win for losing. It's exactly the same issues. Except every time, every relationship I'd been in had almost the same issues with women. Now, I have the exact same issues, except switched. Everything he says to me or does to me, except that I said and did to them.

R. G.:   How is it that you're not saying the same things to him you used to say to women? Why is the other side of the coin coming back to you now?

SAUL: Because with this relationship, my whole conception of relationships and attitudes towards relationships has been completely reversed, and from a perspective of saying always, "Well, I'm really independent, I don't want to be tied down, I'm afraid somebody is trying to possess me and losing my freedom," always saying that. Now, it's like I really want that intimacy, and I really want to be with someone. And it's really kind of ironic. I've affected so many people's lives that way, and so many people that were really close to me always listened to this ideology I had about relationships. It was really because I was gay and wasn't into these straight relationships. I'd been spouting off for so long, "It's ridiculous, you just gotta be independent." So in a way—

R. G.: They got you. They got you.

SAUL: I deserved it.

Boyhood Homosexual Awareness

R. G.: Do you feel that you had some erotic interest, in embryo form, as a very young boy for males?

SAUL: Yes.

R. G.: Why do you think so?

SAUL: Well, it depends I guess on how you define erotic. One thing I do remember from kindergarten or first grade was that everyone, the kids on the block, saying who they were going to marry. And I said, "I'm going to marry Gary," who was the next-door neighbor. And people said, "You can't do that!" But it was a feeling of I did want to marry Gary, I did want to. I'd like to bond with him, I'd like to be with him.

R. G.: How does that differ from real good-chum/buddy relationships that boys have? You must have had those too.

SAUL: Yes.

R. G.: Guys that you felt really close with and you want to be with.

SAUL: I think there are elements of that in the straight, good-chum/buddy relationship, because I know the people I was good-chum/buddies with that I was totally in love with. It felt kind of the same way towards me, but they were straight and it was just that I wanted it to be more. There was an erotic component to that too.

R. G.: There was?

SAUL: It was a real kind of hip subculture where there was a lot of touching and affection. I remember specifically with one boy that I was really in love with that we were really chums. And we'd walk around (this was in eleventh grade) with our arms around each other, we'd hug each other, we'd kiss each other and I know that he had an erotic—it had an erotic element for him. But it was always, "Yeah, we're good buddies," and it was not like, "I want to make love to you."

R. G.: How early do you remember an erotic and genital response to males?

SAUL: Third grade.

R. G.: That makes you about eight or nine.

SAUL: Yeah, it could have been third or fourth.

R. G.: Before puberty?

SAUL: Yeah, a little before puberty.

R. G.: And when do you remember your earliest erotic feelings for females?

SAUL: Well, I remember that I had sexual play with females at a much younger age where I had an erection. I don't know if that—yeah, I mean I played. Prior to puberty, I had sex with a boy when I was probably a year before puberty, and I had sex with a girl when I was in nursery school.

Early Homosexual Priority

R. G.: When you first became aware of a sexual attraction to people that was not play, but you looked at someone across a room and you got kind of a genital erotic response, when did that first begin for a male and when did it first begin for a female?

SAUL: Well, systematically, as a regular thing, at puberty for males. But before, I mean before I really knew what sex was, probably around the time about a year before puberty. And for a woman, not until much later. Not until maybe age thirteen or fourteen.

R. G.: So your earliest sexual orientation was really homosexual?

SAUL: Yeah, it was just immediate. I remember feeling that there were certain boys that I just felt—God, I'm feeling really drawn to them, and imagining not sexual opportunity, but like being naked with them. And I don't remember if I had an erection, but I remember that it was something I had to suppress, and I felt really guilty when those boys exhibited friendship towards me, I felt really ashamed of myself, like I wasn't deserving of their friendship because I felt that these images kept coming up that had to be suppressed. Then at puberty it was like every male I saw was very strong. And with the women, it was really a very self-conscious thing that I imposed on myself. I would look at a woman and say, "Wow, she's really beautiful." It was always very aesthetic and never really gut-level lust. It was always aesthetic appreciation—even during sex.

"FEMININE" BOY, BISEXUAL MAN: JOSEPH

Joseph had a strong father, perhaps too strong. While the identification gap between many of our "feminine" boys and their fathers resulted from father's aloofness, Joseph's father seemed a "tough act to follow." His presence, coupled with a mother who was encouraging of early cross-dressing, may have provided the necessary ingredients for both facets of Joseph's sexual orientation.

JOSEPH'S PARENTS DESCRIBE HIM AT AGE SIX

Disagreement over Initiating Consultation

R. G.:   In a general way, why have you come here today?

MOTHER: Well, I think we *shouldn't* be here today.

R. G.:   You should *not* be here?

FATHER: Frankly, I'm beginning to feel the same way she is. I think it may stem back from something I think is a physical impairment in my son. He had a bad foot. He's improving, I admit, he's improving over a period of time and wore a brace up to a year ago. Now, things developed that he would never play with more than one child at a time. He couldn't stand any competition. He would go with no other but a girl—a girl who was quite dominant, incidentally—and he would be with her continuously.

R. G.:   Anything else?

FATHER: He wanted to wear dresses, and we've kind of told him he was a boy and all that, but if we would just kind of leave him alone, I think he would have a tendency to wear dresses, you know, parade that way.

MOTHER: When he says he loves to wear dresses, it's not to go out in. He is a highly imaginative child. He has seen two weddings, which impressed him tremendously. He's very much in view of the Cinderella-type things, and he only wanted to be part of either the wedding ceremony or the bridal procession. Also this idea of wearing the costume. He's always in that imaginary world of his, and the dresses that he's talking about were only during his playtime at home. He doesn't dress and go out.

FATHER: Yes, as she says, he at one time was very Snow White and Cinderella folk, and they reflect—all the stories we read, the hero is always a girl. Even now at the age of six he still likes a wand. He's hepped up on Batman right now, and he's got a Superman costume, so he'll put on the Superman costume. Oh, the other thing, the clincher that prompted me to go ahead and do this, is I went to his schoolteacher and I said, "Have you noticed that my son has feminine traits?" She said, "Now that you mention it, all his stories, you know show-and-tell, etc., seem to be about a mother and her girl."

R. G.   (to mother): And your feeling? How do you feel about it?

MOTHER: Well, until my sister came to visit, which was about a month ago, I told my husband that I feel his is a perfectly normal, healthy attitude. The only thing he was not accepting was that he happens to have a son who is not, who isn't much of a ball-playing, outdoorsman. Really, his personality is so adjusted, and he happens to have a son that is very imaginative, who loves to listen to music, who likes to read, who is not evidently going to be a ballplayer—

FATHER: Because of his foot primarily, I think.

MOTHER: But I think this is a son who is very much counter to what he expected in a son. I really feel in my heart that these things are part of the attitude. Now he has a definite idea of what a boy should be, and I think his son is going to be a very normal, healthy boy. It's just that he's going to go along lines that his interests do not extend to.

R. G.: How long have you had the concerns that you've expressed today?

FATHER: For a very, very long time.

R. G.: How long?

FATHER: Since childhood.

R. G.: Not longer than six years.

Onset of "Feminine" Behaviors

R. G.: What was the very earliest that you noticed any feminine behavior?

FATHER: I'd say two-and-a-half.

R. G.: What was the first thing you noticed?

FATHER: His desire to be a fairy godmother or a Cinderella or a Snow White. He would never take the part of the Prince or anything except the heroine.

MOTHER: He was very set in his characters.

R. G.: How often would he do that?

FATHER: Quite often.

MOTHER: Yes, every day. If he could get away with it every day, he'd do it every day.

Other "Sex-typed" Behaviors

R. G.: Has there been anything else you think might be feminine behavior that you had some concerns over?

MOTHER: Nope.

FATHER: Every once in a while he'll go through some very feminine motions.

MOTHER: He loves to dance.

FATHER: But his motions can be very, very effeminate.

R. G.: How far back does that go?

MOTHER: Always when he danced.

FATHER: I know he danced, but he'd swish around and he'd make like a girl, but too damn realistically—too damn well.

R. G.: How early was he able to do that?

FATHER: We got pictures of that, remember?

MOTHER: Yes, when he was threeish.

FATHER: And, boy, it was sick. It was too damn realistic, and at three years old, where he puts on this wig and dressed in this dress my wife gave him. It was a very fluffy thing that he was wearing.

R. G.: Does he play with dolls?

MOTHER: No.

R. G.: To what extent does he participate in rough-and-tumble play? Wrestling, fighting, tag—that type of thing.

MOTHER: With his dad.

FATHER: None at all, only with me. That's because I push him.

R. G.: Okay, how about sports?

MOTHER: He's a terrific swimmer.

FATHER: Oh, yes, his mother happens to be a terrific swimmer. He has been swimming since two-and-a-half, three. He is an excellent swimmer. But of course this is a noncompetitive sport. He'll dive, he has no fear.

R. G.: How do you feel about his participation in rough-and-tumble sports?

FATHER: With me, he loves it. He hits me every time. She objects to this, she thinks it's a terrible thing to have a boy do that. I look forward to it because I want to see this happen. I want him to be aggressive.

MOTHER: I say I don't like the idea of his just going over and hitting you. I don't think a child should hit his father. I don't mind if it's at a time when it's a rough-and-tumble play, but he'll come over any old time and hit him, and I don't like that.

FATHER: Generally speaking, when he hits me, I'll hit him back. I'll give him a shot and we'll start a little action going for a while, and then we'll break it off.

R. G.: How do you feel about his participation in sports or lack of?

MOTHER: Oh, I would love to have him participate in sports. I try to have him do things, but it doesn't work out.

Initial Attitude toward "Feminine" Behaviors

R. G.: When he first began doing feminine things at three, what was your feeling about that behavior?

FATHER: I went like this [raising hands], but I lived with it. My wife accepted it as a very, very normal thing.

R. G.: Did you?

MOTHER: Yes, I did. I think all children go through the stage of putting on costumes.

FATHER: Continuously the same thing—never related to a boy. In fact, just now as we were walking up the stairs, he said, "Daddy, who did you want, a boy or a girl?" I said, "Gee, I don't know, I'm very happy with you." And so I said, "What would you have rather been?" and he didn't answer me on that either way.

R. G. (to mother): What was your approach to the early feminine behavior that you felt was normal?

FATHER: She used to buy him wigs.

MOTHER: I went along with it. I felt that whatever stimulates the imagination. I didn't think there was any difference about whether if he would ask about a certain book that I would try to get it for him. If he were interested in certain music I would try and get him records, and if he were interested in certain costumes I would try and get him that.

R. G.: What did you buy him?

MOTHER: I bought him a yellow make-believe wig with braids.

FATHER: A Hansel and Gretel—

MOTHER: Yes, a Hansel and Gretel type thing which I remember as a child having in the house. I enjoyed it so much I bought him one. Yes, it's true, I remember it so well. And then I had gotten him—oh, he wanted a crown like Cinderella, so I had gotten him some tinsel that had been a Christmas ornament and made it into a crown. This was the extent, and the rest he improvised with whatever was around the house. [Joseph's parents showed me a picture of him with a blond wig, his mother's gown, a magic wand, and a crown; it was from the family album.]

FATHER: And capes, you know, he always likes his cape.

MOTHER: He takes his blanket.

FATHER: And the fairy godmother. The one that was great was the Witch of the East, what's his name, oh, the Wizard of Oz. He's very much impressed with that.

MOTHER: All I do know is that he improvised costumes with whatever materials were around the house. He used his security blanket constantly for the cape. The only thing I ever did buy him was the one wig, and I did make him a crown out of the tinsel.

FATHER: And you made him wands continuously.

MOTHER: However, he constantly begs me for the wands after they've broken. And I kind of set it aside now and say, "I think we've really outgrown wands."

Peer Group

R. G.: Do you think he prefers boys or girls for playmates if he has a choice?

MOTHER: I would say girls.

R. G.: How about the age of kids?

MOTHER: Older, always older. If they would accept him.

FATHER: When he went out looking for a friend he had to find a younger one—the kid across the way. It was only when they called him that he would go, but if he had to go seek his own friends at his own level, he wouldn't go down the street where there was a rough-and-tough boy.

Sleeping Next to Mother

FATHER: In our place where we lived, apparently he couldn't get a good night's rest. He'd get up at any hour of the night or any hour of the

morning, and because he was either scared or something, we've permitted him into our bed. And of course he'd snuggle up to his
mother, and it was warm in there and delicious, and of course my
wife couldn't sleep. It was very funny. We switched one night because he always comes in at one time, and I'll never forget this, he
couldn't have been more than two, two-and-a-half. He just comes in
and then puts his cheek on my arm, and right away he jumps up and
runs around to the other side. Right away he knows where he wants
to be, which frankly I don't blame him, she smells a lot better than I
do.

MOTHER: And I was the one who was constantly telling my husband this
was wrong, and I wanted him in his own bed, and he insisted that we
bring him in, and every opportunity I'd bring him back.

FATHER: You're right, I've got to admit that.

R. G.: How often would he come in?

MOTHER: I'd say three or four times a week.

R. G.: Beginning at what age?

MOTHER: Oh, I'd say twoish. As soon as he got out of his bed.

R. G.: Continuing to what age?

MOTHER: Until about five, about a year ago.

Father-Son Relationship

MOTHER: I want to tell you something. He's had a too-devoted father.
This is my impression, because he spent more time with him than any
man will spend with a child. But this is something he's wanted all his
life, and he loves children, he always did, and he just flipped. He
delivered his own child, and since then he's been unbelievable.

R. G.: How did you get to deliver your own child?

MOTHER: We didn't make it to the hospital. We did it in a gas station,
breech yet.

R. G.: How did you manage that?

FATHER: She did a magnificent job.

MOTHER: I directed. We were on our way to Holy Cross Hospital, couldn't
make it. Stopped off and it was over so quickly I couldn't really tell
you that much, one foot came, the other came out and then a pair of
testicles came out and he yelled, "Hey, we got a boy." He's had constant
adult adoration and attention since he was born.

FATHER: Too much. He had a grandmother whom he loves very, very
much and who loves him beautifully. He's got two sisters-in-law, particularly, who love him very, very much.

MOTHER: She happens to love children. They are very close.

FATHER: And, again she happens to be right—he's had much too much
adult life. The reason incidentally that we put him into the nursery
school at the beginning. We felt that he was not getting enough sports.
I've been trying to work with him, and he's improving.

R. G.:   This is your first child?

MOTHER: His first child and he adores him.

FATHER: But by the same token, I say whip his can just as hard as my father will do it and often enough that he knows he's got a father in the house, I'll tell you that.

MOTHER: He knows he's got a father, he sure does.

EARLY FOLLOW-UP

Age Thirteen

Father's Report

Joseph shows no feminine behaviors but still throws a ball like a girl. His male friends are aesthetic. He also has female friends. He no longer gets teased.

Age Fifteen

Father's Report

"I don't think he gets excited about girls. He's still very artistic. He shares his mother's love of beauty. He uses language that is effeminate. He gasps at beautiful things. Also, he still throws a ball like a girl."

Mother's Report

"I think he's doing great! To me, he's real special. My husband used to be worried about his interest in hair. I was never worried about that. I just thought it was because he was around a lot of girls. He's a great mimic. But my husband wanted an athlete."

Joseph's Report

He is taking dancing lessons and singing in a play. He wants a career in dramatics. His best friends are same-age males. He had a crush on a girl during the past year. He gets an erection when looking at a picture of a nude female, and sometimes when looking at a picture of a nude male with an erection. His masturbation fantasies are of making love with a female, or of another male and a female, or of a female masturbating. He sees himself eventually marrying and having children.

JOSEPH'S FATHER DESCRIBES HIM
AT AGE SEVENTEEN

Current Concerns about Joseph's Sexuality

FATHER: He's getting to be a hell of a nice kid. Very, very much taken up in theater arts, completely enswamped, engulfed, in that. I'm just concerned about the sexual area.

R. G.:   Okay, why are you concerned?

FATHER: All right, here's the story. Maybe I'm relating to myself, but then I could be completely wrong. Two years ago, I think it was, some little gal finally got him and got into bed with him.

R. G.:   That's pretty young. That's about the ripe old age of, when, fourteen, fifteen?

FATHER: Fifteen. Which was when I started. He doesn't know that. I always try to tell him that—in other words, I don't want to bring up the fact that I was fooling around.

R. G.:   Fifteen is young.

FATHER: All right, fifteen is young. Listen, a buddy of mine didn't go until twenty-one, and then he made a pig of himself the rest of his life. I'm not knocking it. The only thing that I am concerned about is the fact that she threw him over for another guy in a couple of months or so.

R. G.:   He might as well get used to that.

FATHER: Well, if he takes it for that, of course. But as long as it hasn't done him any harm. See, he does like different girls, but he doesn't do—make out—with them. In other words, certain girls that will go after him he doesn't like. But he has *Penthouse* in his room.

R. G.:   I'm sure he's not just buying them for wall decorations.

FATHER: Yeah, I think he did buy one for that.

R. G.:   The fact of the matter is that if it's there, then obviously that's the best clue you have that he is sexually interested in females.

FATHER: If I even seen the kid with an erection I'd feel all right. When I was a kid I had an erection all the time. The guys, he's hugging, kissing—but friends—just absolute friends, you see.

R. G.:   Well, there are friends like that.

FATHER: Well, that's okay, and again, there's nothing wrong with it; it's just that he's secret with me.

R. G.:   Did you used to share sexual stuff with your parents?

FATHER: I never discussed anything.

R. G.:   I *still* don't.

FATHER: Anyway, that's my only concern. See, it all started, of course, when he was a kid—with the dolls, and then the makeup.

R. G.:   Okay, what's your worst fear?

FATHER: My worst fear is that—that he'd be a homo, or he'll be a—you know, it's a funny thing, as I get older with the kid, I'm not so concerned with him, yet there are times with his relationship with certain guys—I'm wondering what the hell is going on.

R. G.:   Let's make up a few scenarios. Let's say it turns out that during adolescence he has some sexual experiences with males and he has some with females. How would you feel about that?

FATHER: I'm an adult enough person to understand this. That doesn't mean that I myself at one time may not have been attracted—in fact, when I was a kid about eight years old we played in the fields, some guys tried to bunghole me or something, and then there was another time with a brother and sister. You know, I go through these little scenarios too. There was one time in my life I might have been a little attracted, but I never fulfilled it. And these things are not that bad in my mind, as long as I understand where I come from, and if this is the situation, how does one treat it? How does one handle it? I love the kid, I don't want to scar him. As long as he comes out all right.

Reassurance about Joseph's Sexual Options

R. G.: During adolescence there is a fair amount of sexual experimentation. If you read the Kinsey books, one of the more startling statistics that came out of the Kinsey volume in 1948 was that something like 37 percent of adult males had engaged in a same-sex experience leading to orgasm after puberty. Thirty-seven percent, so obviously it's very common. And for the vast majority of these people, they did not go on to become exclusively gay. So that's one thing. Also, I'm sure, since you're not living in a social vacuum, that you're aware that bisexuality is far more commonly talked about, and maybe even practiced. It is certainly more openly acknowledged.

FATHER: Right.

R. G.: There's a psychiatrist colleague of mine who has written a book called *The Bisexual Option*, in which he argues that being bisexual is a far more human-potential-fulfilling experience than either exclusive heterosexuality or exclusive homosexuality. Bisexuals have not cut off from their relationships one dimension of sexuality and caring and affection and love—half the human race. He argues that people who have this flexibility, who really can relate depending on the individual, regardless of gender, have a far healthier outlook and a far healthier existence. This is not written by some wild person on a mountaintop, but by a clinical psychiatrist. That is a potential that more and more people are exploring. From what you've said in terms of his having an interest in *Penthouse* and things like this, an exclusively homosexual lifestyle just does not seem to be fitting. Where his sexuality will finally sit on a continuum, I don't know. Sexual orientation is a continuum. It's not an either/or, heterosexual/homosexual thing. People in different times of their life move some points one way and some points the other way. Where your son will be in five or ten years is still an open question.

FATHER: All right, let's take the other alternative. Sometimes a guy gets turned on to this type of scene, and it becomes a question of whether or not of changing it back.

R. G.: Ok, say you've got somebody who is bisexual. Then the question is, what is the motivation for change? Why would somebody want to change? Let's say somebody is in a marriage, a heterosexual marriage, and the bisexual part is causing some marital stress. Can you, in fact, help enhance the heterosexual part and suppress the homosexual part? Well, Masters and Johnson wrote a book in which a number of married bisexual men were involved in therapy because the homosexual part was unsatisfactory to them in some way, and Masters and Johnson reported dramatic changes in these people, who were highly motivated to be exclusively heterosexual.

An Attempt to Maintain a Solid Father-Son Relationship

R. G.:   The important thing is that if homosexuality does occur and you become aware of it, the most tragic thing that can happen is alienation between a kid and a parent.

FATHER: Absolutely.

R. G.:   He needs support no matter what he does with his life, whether vocationally, sexually, socially.

FATHER: Let me ask you something. If I find that this is happening—

R. G.:   If it's not problematic, what a teenage or young adult wants to hear from the parent is that you love him or her as a parent, and an ideal kind of statement, if you feel comfortable with it, is "You're old enough to know what the world is like in terms of heterosexuality, bisexuality, homosexuality. What I really do care about is that you be happy. It's the quality of a relationship that's of much more concern. As a parent, I know that just being heterosexual doesn't guarantee happiness. It's really the quality of a relationship that you're in, and I really hope that you're able to find a partner or partners that make your life fulfilling." If you can believe that and say it with conviction that goes with the belief, then I think you've done a magnificent job as a parent, and I think a kid is very lucky to have a parent like that.

INTERVIEW WITH JOSEPH AT AGE SEVENTEEN

Current Sexuality

R. G.:   How are things going?

JOSEPH: Pretty good. I've been thinking a lot sexually. I don't know if I'm bi or not. I've been thinking a lot about it. I find that I fantasize about both men and women, and it scares me a lot sometimes. Because I keep saying to myself that I really want a wife and kids, but is it my deep-down preference that I'm gay? Is it possible to overcome that, let's say chemically you are gay but you really want a wife and kid, I mean, is there, like, a psychological thing you can go through to change it?

R. G: I'll try to answer that, but let me just hear more about what you are feeling, why you think you are bi.

JOSEPH: Well, about three years ago, two years ago, I had a girlfriend, and we would try and everything. I was rushing it, and therefore I was more in bed with her thinking I had to do this now, and it wouldn't happen.

R. G.:   You wouldn't get an erection?

JOSEPH: Yeah. I would get half an erection. It would be a mental block, and she was just as inexperienced as I. In addition, my dad would always tell me stories, like "How are things going with Diane," "If you need any condoms, call me," and stuff. I would buy them myself, it didn't matter, but he would always—I always felt a pressure from him about how he started. He would always say how he started at sixteen and how he went with all these women and he lived the high life, so there would be pressure from that. "Oh, I have to beat out my Dad." So that was part of it. Then, also being very self-conscious, as an actor, I'm very much aware of my own body. I know what I look like, I spend a lot of time grooming to make myself look as good as possible. Therefore I notice other men's bodies, too. I get excited. So I've been beginning to wonder. I want more than anything a wife and kids—I really, really want that.

R. G.:   How much heterosexual experience have you had?

JOSEPH: Well, I have had petting, a lot of petting, but not to the point of going to bed with them. Yeah, a lot of petting.

Sexual Fantasies

R. G.:   When you masturbate, what do you usually think of?

JOSEPH: Usually of men more than women.

R. G.:   What percentage of the time would you say you think of men?

JOSEPH: About seventy to thirty.

R. G.:   What's going on in your fantasy?

JOSEPH: Well, mainly getting head.

R. G.:   Is it somebody that you know or somebody that you make up?

JOSEPH: Both. People that I've seen, and there has been someone that I know. I have gotten head from a guy once, that really excited me.

R. G.:   How old were you?

JOSEPH: Sixteen.

R. G.:   And that was just one time?

JOSEPH: Yeah. We were both pretty, really, drunk. And he admitted that he was bi, and I said, "What the hell."

R. G.:   What about wet dreams?

JOSEPH: I fantasize more about women in dreams than I do while I'm awake masturbating. I fantasize about men more when I am awake.

R. G.:   These are sexual dreams?

JOSEPH: Yeah, they are sexual, definitely. They are based on experiences that I've had.

R. G.: You look at pornography?

JOSEPH: Meaning magazines?

R. G.: Centerfolds or people actually involved in sex-play?

JOSEPH: Yeah, sure.

R. G.: Have you seen gay magazines?

JOSEPH: Yes.

R. G.: Let's take them one by one. Let's say you look at a centerfold of just a nude female—not the same picture—ten times. How often would that give you an erection?

JOSEPH: It depends. I'm into big breasts. I don't know—about four or five.

R. G.: What if you looked at a photo of a nude male, like a *Playgirl* centerfold?

JOSEPH: About three or four. I really get into it when it is men and women together. It's interesting—I can either fantasize about being the male or the female.

R. G.: Which do you think turns you on more, all other things being equal—an attractive female or an attractive male?

JOSEPH: I think the men.

R. G.: And in actual experience you've really had more heterosexual activities. You were in bed a number of times, at least, with this one girl.

JOSEPH: Two or three.

R. G.: And in terms of homosexual experience, there has been only one. But the fantasy exists.

JOSEPH: The fantasy is there.

Concerns over Bisexuality and Reassurance

R. G.: Are you worrying about bisexuality primarily because you want to get married and have kids or because you think there is something wrong about being bisexual—that there is something wrong with being gay?

JOSEPH: I'd rather be bisexual than be gay—for one, just because I really want a family. I don't think it's necessarily wrong, it's weird—like, it doesn't turn me on, per se, to see two guys together, but it depends. But maybe it does subconsciously, and it comes out when I am masturbating or when I am tipsy or something. But I really do want a wife and children very, very much, and it scares me when I am unable to get an erection when I am with someone.

R. G.: But you do find women to be attractive?

JOSEPH: Yeah.

R. G.: You know, the situation that you described in which you were inexperienced—the situation in which you felt a lot of pressure to perform—is the absolutely ideal situation where you fail. That's something called performance anxiety, which is a technical term for when you feel under pressure, you feel anxious, and that's incompatible with being sexually aroused and getting an erection. I mean, it's just impossible. Most guys, irrespective of what their fantasy life is, in their initial experience with girls, have essentially the same kind of experience that you had. It seems to me that if you do find women attractive, it means that at the time that you would want to, and you feel relaxed, you will have no difficulty having heterosexual intercourse. The issue of integrating a bisexual lifestyle as opposed to maintaining an exclusively heterosexual one is something that some people do. You will have to find what fits most comfortably.

JOSEPH: Part of it is, I don't know if it's true, but homosexuality is like a fad, you know—the whole area we live in here in L.A. could be influencing it a lot.

R. G.:   Personally and professionally I know people who are married and have children and who are bisexual. It's a question of how you negotiate to be open with your wife about this and go into a marriage and family situation with everybody's eyes wide open. "This is who I am. Can you accept that?" There are some women who can and some who can't. If five years from now there is a woman whom you find very compatible and you would really like to have a family with her—and you still are continuing to have homosexual relationships and fantasies as well—then it's up to you. Do you want to be open with this person or not? The situation isn't really that different, for example, with heterosexual monogamy. There are some men who go into a marriage knowing that they really can't be monogamous, and it's a question of then deciding whether it's appropriate to tell their prospective wife that they are not going to be monogamous, and hopefully reach that understanding beforehand. Or whether they are just not going to talk about it. So what I'm saying is, if the interest in wanting a conventional family remains, from what you've told me, I don't see why that is not a possibility. Many of these people that I know don't find that the bisexual part interferes with the heterosexual part. They say that it's like two different channels on a television set. It's not like you have two different channels coming over on the same number. It's a question of switching channels, so they don't interfere with each other—you don't get a blurred picture so you can't see anything clearly. It is possible for some people to go from one channel to another and have a good picture on both channels.

JOSEPH: I almost think it's neat being bisexual, if in fact I am. Yeah, exactly, like, why should I be restricted?

INTERVIEW WITH JOSEPH AT AGE NINETEEN

Current Sexuality

JOSEPH: Well, this is something that's been on my mind fifty zillion times a day—you know, sexuality. I thought I was bisexual, the last time. But the threat of "gay" is pressing against me, and it scares me. It scares me for two reasons: first, from what I observed from other people and people I've talked to, it seems like such a much more lonely life; two, the whole mental and family-oriented thing in the sense of being an only child of my parents and there's still a strong commitment to all that stuff.

R. G.:   Go on.

JOSEPH: The threat of coming out and saying that I'm gay—I don't know if I am, because I think women still do attract me. I've had relations with both, and I like both. I don't think I could ever be happy being totally straight, and I don't know if I could be totally happy being gay. I think I could be happier being totally gay than totally straight. I don't think it's like a disease; I just think it's a preference, decision. What's bad also is I definitely want kids. I've talked to people—you know, who have gay friends, who are married and have children. They just say it's a very fulfilling thing and have whatever you want on the side. I told my parents—my dad—two years ago. He just asked me and I said I thought I was bi. We haven't really discussed it.

R. G.:   What percentage now—say in the last year—what percentage of your sexual contacts have been male, what percentage female?

JOSEPH: A lot more have been male; 70 percent male.

Advice to Bring Father up to Date

R. G.:   How much would you like your father to know?

JOSEPH: I don't know, because I haven't made a full decision yet, and I don't really know if until I've made a decision if I want to talk to him about it.

R. G.:   Maybe he could benefit from just knowing that. Knowing your dad over the years, I'm quite sure he was really concerned—more concerned by his not knowing. I think he would benefit enormously from your just telling him where you think things are so he doesn't have some mysterious cloud hovering over him. I think if you were to tell, and it's the truth, that you don't have a commitment to being exclusively gay and that you have some interest in having a family and children, that you are bi—you know, bi runs a spectrum. I think he needs to be reassured rather than being left in the dark.

JOSEPH: Does he ever talk to you that he thinks I'm gay?

R. G.:   He tells me he's worried about where you are. I feel responsibility

to his worry and to your confidentiality, and the way for me to deal
with that is to have you tell him just enough so he feels better. It would
be good for him, and it certainly isn't going to harm you.

"FEMININE" BOY, HOMOSEXUAL ADOLESCENT, HETEROSEXUAL MAN: LARRY

*The adolescent route of Larry's sexual orientation is the reverse of Saul's. Larry
was markedly "feminine" in boyhood. He evolved from homosexual
experimentation in his early teens to an actively homosexual lifestyle by his mid-
teens. But like Steven, Larry found many features of the gay world wanting.
Consequently, he actively suppressed his homosexuality during late adolescence
and commenced an affair with an older woman. As a young adult, his sexual
experiences remain heterosexual.*

LARRY'S PARENTS DISCUSS HIM AT AGE NINE

Reason for Consultation

FATHER: At an early age you don't pay too much attention to those
things. One thing was that he liked to put on female clothing, especially
his mother's clothing, and at first we thought it was just like playing
with dolls as a child. Later on we thought it should have diminished,
and it didn't, and it was brought to our attention that this could be a
problem even at that age.

R. G.:   What's your feeling about this?

MOTHER: Very similar. He was playing with dolls, playing dress-up, playing school in nursery school at the age of three. By the time he was
four it didn't diminish. The interest seemed to grow in dolls, and he
has an older sister who had these little Barbie dolls, and he used to
take them and dress them up. As he got into his fourth year, we started
to take things away from him. It isn't as apparent perhaps to others
that he is still identifying so strongly, because he doesn't show us
anymore. I think he has sort of gone underground with the female—
I think he's sort of changed his tactics.

FATHER: That could be. For example, I've gone into him when he's
playing school, and now he's playing the part of the male teacher
rather than the female teacher.

R. G.:   Formerly, he played the female part?

FATHER: Right. Formerly he always played the female part.

Mother-Father Roles

FATHER: Another thing which may or may not be material, two years ago there was a big change that took place in our family. Up until that time, in order to keep peace in the family, I used to always let her have her way, and they always identified with her as the dominant figure. Well, when we started going to this therapist, it was pointed out what damage this was doing to the kids by my abdicating my role as leader of the house. I immediately took what was normally my normal role. I had to. She couldn't understand that I was able to do this. This was my natural role always, but I always subliminated it because I wanted to keep peace in the family, and I thought the only one it was doing harm to was me. When I realized it was harming someone else, the roles changed. In the beginning I had to do it in a way that everyone thought was ridiculous. Every two minutes I had to say, "I'm the boss" and overly react. Now it's become a natural thing where it's no longer a problem.

MOTHER: There's been a change as far as your figure being stronger, absolutely, and I mean that definitely the children look to him now today as head of the household.

R. G.:   Tell me what it was like before.

MOTHER: They would come to me, and it was once put to them who was the boss. They'd say "Mother" because Daddy was busy, and if we were together in a situation where the child got unruly, I would be the one who would discipline them.

FATHER: Not only that, but if ever I wanted to make a decision relative to the children she would overrule it, and so I got to the point that each time there had to be a decision made, well, "Go ask your mother," but now Mother has to come to me to make a decision. I don't have to go to her.

MOTHER: I think he has come into his own again.

Earliest Signs of "Feminine" Behavior

R. G.:   Looking back, what is the earliest sign or clue you may have had concerning an unusual amount of feminine identification?

MOTHER: Well, for one thing, I would say, probably at nursery school he would dress up—age three.

FATHER: Probably right at this third birthday.

MOTHER: They had dress-up for the children. They would have all the clothes there, and he played a great deal with girls in the school. He's a handsome child, and he was a good-looking baby. A lot of people always made over him. At the beginning he was a very mild child. He was a joy.

FATHER: Not mild, he was not a discipline problem. He was always outgoing and he used to—especially with older women. He got a lot of reaction from older women, so he'd always play up to them.

MOTHER: Yes, and at a very early age he would remark, "That's a pretty dress you're wearing," and especially to the grandmotherly type.

R. G.: How old would he be at that age?

MOTHER: I think it was like four, very young, he would notice. He was outgoing and people, especially older women, just loved him, and they let him know it. There was one in particular who has taken care of children, a friend of the family, and he loved to sit and comb her hair when she was there. She would tell me all this, but she said that she noticed at a very young age, three or four, she felt the effeminate ways, the things I wasn't even aware of.

R. G.: Did she describe what she meant?

MOTHER: Oh, I think it was mainly the gestures with the hands. I don't notice that even now.

R. G.: You say up until two years ago you weren't aware of any of this?

FATHER: No.

R. G.: You had no awareness of his dressing up as a girl?

FATHER: Yeah, but I didn't know that it was that important.

Wish for a Daughter

MOTHER: We both wanted a girl. His sister and I wanted a girl for the third one, and my husband wanted a boy. I remember my first reaction to having a boy. My son doesn't know about it. When they said it was a boy, I said, "Oh, you mean I haven't got a girl?"

Sister Treated Him Like a Girl

FATHER: One thing, our daughter, who is now fifteen, ever since she heard about this she has been blaming herself. She has a guilt complex because when he was younger—she wanted a sister—she used to treat him like a sister, and she thinks that this is why he has gone this way.

R. G.: How would she treat him as a sister?

FATHER: She would do his hair, play dolls with him, and she'd dress him up as a girl.

MOTHER: She was telling me she once dressed him up, with a bonnet and so on. He was two years old maybe, but I feel that there is no connection.

FATHER: In her mind she feels like she started it. I tell her not to worry about it, it wasn't that, it was my abdicating the role of the father that did it, and she shouldn't worry about it.

R. G.: Were you aware at the time that she was treating him like he was a sister?

MOTHER: No, I've never heard her say this to me. I just heard her tell me that she dressed him up. Whether she did it more than once or twice, I remember one time only, and I felt that it was really ludicrous that she could feel that.

Female Role-playing

R. G.: You mentioned his taking the role of the female teacher. When did this begin?

MOTHER: I would say probably when he was around four, three, three-and-a-half. He played house then, and he was the mother. He would play at nursery school, he would play at home, and he would even get his brother who was four years older in on it, and his brother is much more the shy one. And so he usually took the role of the mother. Then he played with girls a great deal, and now he plays with boys, but he has a short span of getting along with children. That may be another problem, but he will still play with a girl too.

FATHER: He's an excellent mimic.

MOTHER: I remember one time there was something on the TV and he got up—we had a little coolie hat—and he put it on and he wrapped himself around with a bedspread, and he came hobbling in like a Chinaman and he said, "Me Chinese, me Chinese." It was four or five years ago and it was really very funny. We don't know if he's going toward acting or this is really part of him.

Female Playmates

R. G.: When did he begin playing with girls?

MOTHER: Right from the beginning.

FATHER: We never thought it was that unusual at the time. One thing that stands out in my mind one time, and this was three or four years ago. This girl was calling him "Fagala," and I got angry and said, "Stop calling him that," and she said "Oh, you've got an evil mind."

Photographed with a Pocketbook

MOTHER: When we left the Valley he was about five or six. I remember we came across a photograph of him. He was about four years old, and he was standing holding my pocketbook with a group of older boys. These aren't boys that he played with particularly. He was standing there with this pocketbook.

Wish to Be Female

R. G.: Has he ever said "I am a girl" or "I want to be a girl?"

MOTHER: He said to me—when he was younger—something about he'd like to be a mother.

FATHER: I have had direct discussions with him on it, and when his other doctor made such a big issue out of it, and in the beginning he admitted that it would be easier to be a girl—that it would be preferable to be a girl.

R. G.: Did he give any reasons why?

FATHER: I don't know whether this is my hang-up or his, but because he thought that the girls were the bosses. This is my reaction. That's why I said I don't know whether it's my hang-up or his.

MOTHER: When he was four, five, when he was playing house, I sometimes would ask about the role he took as mother, and I said, "You know when you grow up you're going to be a father like Daddy," and he would say something like, "No, I'm going to be a mother like you."

R. G.: What would you say?

MOTHER: I would say, "No, you're going"—I mean, I wouldn't argue.

R. G.: Did he ever say "I am a girl"?

MOTHER: No, I don't think he ever stated it as such. He liked the pretty things. I thought at one time he was just noticing the pretty clothes to be flattering and to get attention from older women, but I think also that maybe he liked the pretty things. I know when I would dress up to go out, he would notice it and make nice remarks about it, you know, "Oh, what a pretty dress, Mommy." The other boy, I sometimes don't quite understand, was brought up in similar circumstances and even more so because my husband had not made the change by that time, yet he never seemed to have this tendency.

Cross-dressing

R. G.: Let me go back now to some of the women's clothing. Can you tell me the kinds of clothing that he would wear?

MOTHER: Mainly it would be my things—shoes, sometimes hats.

R. G.: What was the first thing he chose of yours?

MOTHER: I don't think it was mine, I think it was at nursery school. They would have a big box of old clothes, probably hats and high heels and dresses.

FATHER: He would put on nail polish. I stopped him from doing that. One time he had nail polish on—and again, I became aware of these things less than two years ago—I told him no more nail polish, that was it, scrub them off.

Parental Approach to "Feminine" Behavior

R. G.: It sounds like you had some concern a long time ago about feminine behavior because you asked people about it. What was your approach as you continued to see some of it?

MOTHER: Well, at first I was afraid to say anything. I thought, well, what if I let him know that we feel this is odd or peculiar behavior, feeling that something's different about him. I remember asking his first doctor should we allow it or not, and he said, "No, don't allow it, just tell him, you know."

R. G.: And did you follow that advice?

MOTHER: Yes.

R. G.: What did your boy say or do?

MOTHER: That's when I feel that he went underground with it, and certainly since then—many times he will take a towel, for instance, and wrap it around his head turbanlike, but long enough so that it would look like a braid down his back, so that he was affecting long hair.

R. G.: What has been the attitude of your daughter and your other son towards his feminine behavior?

FATHER: They make fun of him.

MOTHER: They were calling him Sally. "Come and listen. He's playing Sally."

Interest in Pornography

FATHER: I've never known him to have an erection. One thing that happened that I think is cute—maybe not. For his birthday I wanted to get him something, and he said he would like me to get him a *Playboy* Magazine. I said, "Fine, I'll get you one." She was all upset about it, and so I started talking to him about it. "Why do you like *Playboy* Magazine? We'll get it and look at it together." And he said something about that he liked to see the girls and their titties, and he said it gives you a—he didn't say hard-on but something to that effect— and I haven't gotten it for him yet. I haven't run into a place where I could get it, but I intend to get it and she's all shook up about it.

MOTHER: Well, I don't think this is the type of thing that you approach a nine-year-old with. At this age I don't think this is particularly a healthy thing to arouse him sexually. I don't think it's accomplishing anything, and to be honest, I think he is doing this because he thinks this is great, this is going to show that he's manly.

Larry was seen every two years for reevaluation. "Feminine" behaviors diminished. His relationship with his father remained distant. He entered psychotherapy with another therapist when he was fifteen. During early to mid-adolescence he was actively homosexual. However, at seventeen he began to live with a woman twenty years his senior. The relationship was sexual.

INTERVIEW WITH LARRY AT AGE EIGHTEEN

Emergent Heterosexuality

LARRY: I wanted to stop the homosexuality.

R. G.:   Why did you want to give it up?

LARRY: It wasn't good for me. I'm sociable, active; it was not an accepted thing. People would turn their backs on me at ritzy social parties. I don't feel it's wrong to be gay, but there's a better life outside that. It's more accepted and easier. I wasn't really happy.

R. G.:   Tell me about your sexual attractions.

LARRY: I'm not turned on to men, but I think they're attractive. I don't get turned on looking at a girl either, not unless I'm in bed. I've turned away guys; it could be in two years I'll go back, but not at this point in my life.

R. G.:   Tell me what the sex was initially like with your female partner.

LARRY: At first I came too fast. Maybe I wanted to get it over with, but then I grew to like it.

R. G.:   What is the difference between sex with a male or a female?

LARRY: With a woman you don't have to use lubricant. It's easier to get in.

R. G.:   Do you have oral-genital sex?

LARRY: If she takes a shower first, otherwise no. After screwing I have to run to the shower. I can't stand the smell.

R. G.:   When you have sex with this woman, do you sometimes think about men?

LARRY: At first I did, about this one guy. Now I don't think about anything during sex.

R. G.:   What do you think your future sexuality will be?

LARRY: I don't miss the men. But I could go right back. I'm not sure. If a guy comes along and wants to set me up with clothes, a car, I don't know. I might take him up on it.

Transition to Heterosexuality

R. G.:   Tell me about how the transition was for you, from being gay to moving in with this woman.

LARRY: I just said, "If I'm going to do it, I'm not going to do it, you know, go bi for a while, then go straight; if I'm going to do it I'm going to do it cold turkey, and I'm going to cut it right then and there." And then it just dragged on for, I don't know, about two or three months, and then it just—I would be with a woman and almost call up and then I'd hang up, and I go, "No, I can't do it," and I'd go get high or something so I'd forget about it and then I just really tried, you know, and it finally stopped, and then when I went out with a girl I was wondering, "Jesus, it's been such a—I mean I went for like six months without sex." I'm wondering if I'm ever going to be able to get erected, I mean, shit, six months, and maybe I won't get turned on by her, but maybe I won't get turned on by a guy, and then I'll be impotent for the rest of my life. There was a lot of things that I had to resist, a lot of attractions, a lot of people approaching me and not going for it, where I would have before instantly. So it was very difficult.

R. G.: I want to back up a minute to that transition period, where you said you cold turkeyed yourself before getting involved with women.

LARRY: Before, I was involved with women at the same time, you know, off and on being very close and just one night, everybody getting so loaded that everybody's horny and everybody fucks whoever's around. I don't know, I just worked my way out of it. I moved in with a girl, and I think that's right around the transition period. I moved in with her and I started to be around her more, and then I started getting closer to her, and I started getting sexually stimulated and attracted to her, you know, because she was so much my personality, which I guess I really needed at that time, which was good for me.

R. G.: There was a period of six months that you weren't having sex with anybody. Were you resisting?

LARRY: I wasn't resisting a woman.

R. G.: No, but you were resisting attractions to the men, you were pulling yourself away—

LARRY: Right—okay. I resisted men, but I didn't also want to immediately pick up and move in with a girlfriend, because I think I would be using her as a test.

R. G.: What about sexual fantasies, like masturbation, during those months?

LARRY: God should strike my head with lightning if I ever masturbate. I don't like to masturbate, I'm sorry, I'm odd. I don't like it. I wanted to wait. I wanted to resist both only because I wanted to know basically for myself. I wanted to come out where one day I'll know, and then I'll know that I can do this. And I didn't want to test it out with a girl and then all of a sudden it failed. I didn't want to get involved with a relationship immediately, and the fact that it broke up was because *of*, you know, I don't want that. I just kinda blocked it all out of my mind, you know. I was thinking, well, maybe I couldn't get hard, maybe I can, maybe I can't, maybe I can. After six months—I don't know what happened. I went out with two of my friends, and they're the beer-drinking, go-out-and-pick-up-a-chick-and-fuck-her, drop-her-off-on-the-corner kind. And I just—it was so weird to me to do that, because they just called me up and they said, "You get in here." They were really carrying on. They came in and they said, "You know, you've been here too long, you've been refusing to go out with us, you've been working so much, fuck everything," and they dragged me out, literally, like put on my coat and just like said, "You're going." So we went out to a—I think we went to a bar, some dance place that was predominantly straight—and this girl walked up to me and she said, "Do you want to dance?" and I said, "Sure." She was very aggressive. So I started dancing with her, and she was a very beautiful woman, very beautiful. And I looked at her and I just said, "God damn, she's beautiful," because I was just—I mean that was my comment, I would think that, straight or gay. And then I just really saw how beautiful she was in a different light, you know, and I'm going, "Now's the time, this is it. This is the one that's gonna get screwed, you know, this is it," and I just said okay and I went for it all the way, you know, [click] hang on, and then I started seeing her, and then I'd go, "I got a hard-on," so then my confidence was right.

R. G.:   Nothing succeeds like success.

LARRY: Yeah, it's like there's my plateau, stepped up another one. I'm proud of my discipline and my willpower that I have now. And after that a few guys approached me, and I thought I didn't even have the slightest—or maybe I could, but I just went, "Guys, I'm really flattered, but I've been there but I've left that now." They go, "Oh, come on, once you're gay you're never straight, once you're gay you never go back." And I said, "Well, I'm gonna prove that to you."

LARRY'S MOTHER DESCRIBES HIM AT AGE EIGHTEEN

MOTHER: I think my son's doing much better. I don't know whether this relationship is with a mother figure or a sex figure. I was hoping it would be sex. I don't believe in sex before marriage, but knowing his problem I thought it was better. He told me he's had sex with men. I'm against him having sex with men. It's against Catholicism.

INTERVIEW WITH LARRY AT AGE TWENTY-ONE

Breakup of the Heterosexual Relationship

LARRY: I broke up with my girlfriend of two years, and I'm on my own again. There's nothing else, really, that's—just been a lot of struggling and a lot of bullshit, a lot of hassles, fighting, arguing, freaking out. It was a very odd situation. My parents are really glad because she was older than me, and so my parents just kinda freaked out about all that. They couldn't handle that at all, and it caused a lot of conflict in the family.

R. G.:   What was the relationship like?

LARRY: It was just great. I mean we didn't get along—we had a lot of personality conflicts, and the age may be just chronological, a lot of problems just because of acceptance.

R. G.:   How was the sexual part of your relationship?

LARRY: We had sex all the time, and there were some points that I just wouldn't have sex with her because I just couldn't stand her. I was having sex with other girls but—there's just that little thing of, "Okay, now I'm really committed, let's see what it's like to have a girl on the side, you know, let's go through the fighting of that." I had to have a taste of that.

R. G.:   How was that?

LARRY: Oh, it was funnier than hell.

R. G.:   Did she find out?

LARRY: No, I'm too clever. And it wasn't anything romantic with the other girls—it was just going on having a good time with someone who was more or less my age, because there were certain things I couldn't do with my girlfriend.

Mother's Concern over Larry's Sexual Orientation

LARRY: My mother asked me that when I broke up with my girlfriend, she goes, "You know, now that this is over, do you think you'll be going back to it?" and I said, "My god, from three years 'n' plus, I've been straight, I haven't even gone back to that or thought about even looking at it." It was a heavy-duty scene. In fact, I even think I started crying. I said, "You know, I have made so many goddamn efforts, and I've changed my life for the better, and you guys still—you know, drop it." I said, "Jesus Christ, can't you ever give me just a hug and a kiss and just praise me and say, 'You know, I believe you, you did it or whatever.' " and she just looked and she says, "Yeah, you're right, I'm really sorry." The gay feelings were there a long time ago, you know, the feeling of it was there, I mean before even the last time I saw you. The last time I saw you, it must have been weak or subsiding, and just the—if it's brought up it's when it's brought up, and that's when I think about it, and it's like I'm glad I'm not because I'm really fulfilling my life now, and it's brought out, they all know it.

Negative View of Homosexual Lifestyle

R. G.:   Let's talk about the extent of sexual interests in people as males or as females. How would you compare those two at this time?

LARRY: The only tushes I look at are the ones that wiggle in nylons. There is no way I'm ever gonna give that up because that's what I've wanted all my life, even when I was participating in homosexual activities. If somebody comes up to me for advice, I can advise them well and I can say, "Yes, I have experienced; yes, I have been there, and let me tell you, it's not a good scene." You know, some people think it works out fine. I don't know any gay couple that I've known for all my life, and the ones I know now that get along, they are vicious little motherfuckers. I mean this guy—I was over a friend's house and he told me—that was the first night he told me he was gay, and I said, "Great." And then, right then his ex-lover came in and just started ripping the place apart—I'm just sitting there—and then he thought I was the new culprit, and I said, "Don't look at me," I said, "he just told me that," and he goes, "Sure, sure," and then he came to hit me, and I slugged him and said, "Fuck off." It was a very raging scene. I said, "I don't have time for this, you guys are freaks." I think of the way my life used to be and I just go, "No, you cannot," because I see old gay men that are just so lonely and so unhappy, and they try so hard and they get so much rejection, and everybody's got that little thing about hiring gay people. There's one in my apartment building right now, and I look at him—he is so pathetic, he just had a triple bypass and there was nobody that cared about him, you know—and I really felt sorry for him, not because he was gay but just because he was so alone and he didn't choose another life, but I left a nice note on his door and I said, "Welcome home, hope you're feeling better."

R. G.:   That's very nice.

Homosexual Temptation

R. G.:   How much of you still wrestles a little bit with the homosexual temptation?

LARRY: I don't think about it. I was approached and I was not tempted. I was just curious. I kind of challenged my feelings. Usually I'll just put up a defense and I'll just break it immediately. In terms of attraction now, I can still look at a guy and say, "Yeah, he's very good looking." But I don't say, "Oh, God, I'd like to be able to lay next to that or cuddle up to that." That's not where I am.

But there was this one guy who did approach me, and I kind of let the thing go. Not feelings, my defense. And I was really stoned and drunk and he was going for it. He was touching my leg and stuff. He never touched me on my dick, but he got close, and then I just said, "Wait a second, you know, no." And he said, "Fine," and he just left. And he went on to somebody else, and I just kept to myself the rest of the night, thinking about, why did I do that? It bothered me, but I didn't say—I didn't go through a whole traumatic thing. I said, "Well, I think I've reached my goal." And I know, it's like an alcoholic, once you drink you're always going to drink, and once you're gay you may have a tendency to go back to it. Afterwards I felt really good about myself. The next day I was really encouraged about that feeling.

"FEMININE" BOY, HETEROSEXUAL MAN: RICHARD

The developmental progression from cross-gendered boy to homosexual man is not a perfect fit. In early childhood, Richard cross-dressed, role-played as a female, had primarily female friends, and did not want to have a penis. By late childhood, he was engaged in sports and relating comfortably to boys. Possibly his shift in core identity and gender-role behaviors is explained by his mother's strong preference for a boy, her early discouragement of his "feminine" behavior, and his father's progressively improved relationship with him. In young adulthood, Richard is actively heterosexual. One more point: when five years old, Richard had wanted to marry a girl. By contrast, Saul, who also abandoned cross-gender behaviors, and who is now homosexual, had wanted to marry a boy.

RICHARD'S PARENTS DESCRIBE HIM AT AGE FIVE

Reason for Consultation

MOTHER: He prefers to play with girls. He wants to have a rather exclusive hold on me, and he just can't tolerate it if I pay any attention to his sister or any other child. Also, his wanting to participate in girls' activities and not in boys' activities, and dressing up in girls' clothing—wanting to put on makeup and doing things that are generally more passive, assuming the role of a female when they play house. I think that he's got a problem. I think we need help.

R. G. (to father):   What have been the things that you have been most concerned about?

FATHER: My difference would be that I don't think he has a problem—he may have a problem, and on the other hand I am away working most of the day and some of the things that she has picked up, I obviously haven't. I do notice that his activities center on preferring to play with girls, but on the other hand there are just more girls to play with in the neighborhood.

MOTHER: There are also a lot of boys, too, dear, that he goes to school with. And the new boy that moved in. But he prefers the girls. There are as many boys as girls, but he prefers girls.

R. G.:   What other behaviors are you concerned about?

MOTHER: Well, if there is a choice of games to be played, it's always house. One day a little boy came over, and he is the same age, and they were playing together for a while, and my son wanted to play house and the other boy didn't want to play house, and my son got very obnoxious and almost forced him into playing house, and they finally did. My son wanted to put on an article of my clothing and wanted to play that he was the mother and the other boy would be the father, you know. My son would be the wife and the other boy would be the husband, and it finally became so intolerable for the other boy that he said, "Well, this is a play and I'm calling intermission now." My son became furious, then the whole play degenerated.

R. G.:   How long have you had these concerns?

FATHER: About two years.

R. G.:   Since he was about three?

MOTHER: About two or three.

Parental Response to "Feminine" Behavior

R. G.:   What has been your approach so far to this behavior?

MOTHER: Well, I don't like for him to do this. I'm afraid to tell him that he absolutely can't wear this clothing, but I try to make him find another use for this garment, that is not for a female but that it's for a male, you know, that it could be a painter's garb or something like that, but no, he doesn't want to do this. It's strictly to be a female sort of thing. I don't punish him for it, and I don't really put him down. Lately I have been much more direct. I've been telling him that this is really for girls, and boys wear such and such, and would you like to wear it this way?

R. G.:   What has his reaction been to your approach?

MOTHER: He is quite negative and very stubborn. He doesn't want to go along with it.

R. G.:   When was the first time you noticed him dressing up in girl's clothing?

MOTHER: It's within the past two years.

R. G.:   What was your feeling about it when you first noticed it?

MOTHER: A negative feeling.

R. G.   What was your approach at the very beginning?

MOTHER: Very mild because I thought, he was only three years old. At the point it was not terribly important. He was playing with girls. It bothered me, but I don't think I redirected him at that time. Probably no.

R. G. (to father):   How about yourself, do you recall your first reaction to it?

FATHER: My only approach at that time was to ignore it because I didn't see anything in it. Now that we are more concerned, I also try to redirect him. No particular censure or anything like that.

R. G.:   You mentioned his interest in cosmetics—can you tell me more about that?

MOTHER: He likes to put on all sorts of eye makeup and lipstick. He will put it on like an Indian, which I encouraged him to. So he does not really make up as a female.

R. G. (to father): What's been your approach to the cosmetic use?

FATHER: Just so you don't make a mess in the bathroom.

MOTHER: Right. All he wants to do is cook or play house, and he will always take the role of the female, and it doesn't go over so good with the other kids—the other guys.

R. G.: Who is he usually when he plays house?

MOTHER: The mother.

R. G.: How often does he play house?

MOTHER: Every day, at least.

R. G.: How far back does his interest in taking the female role go?

FATHER: About two-and-a-half years.

R. G.: What was your feeling about this at first when he would play house and be a female?

MOTHER: Negative, but I kind of thought it would pass. I thought it was because he was playing with girls so much. When we lived in the other house there weren't any other boys. There was a girl but she was an older girl. She was a year-and-a-half older.

Favorite Toys

R. G.: What are his favorite toys?

MOTHER: Cooking utensils.

FATHER: Cooking ware, stoves.

MOTHER: Doll furniture.

R. G.: And when he asks for cooking utensils when he has wanted them, have you gone out and bought them for him?

FATHER: Oh, no. His desires are quite *extravagant*, so we haven't always gone out and gotten what he's wanted.

R. G.: The feminine toys he has, you purchased yourselves?

MOTHER: Yes.

Favorable Response from Outside the Family

R. G.: What have been the reactions of persons outside the family?

MOTHER: Well, one of the mothers, the mother of this girl he plays with, has always remarked that, you know, she thought it was kind of funny. She never said it in a critical way. She thought it was just funny.

R. G.: Sort of comical funny or odd?

MOTHER: Comical funny.

Mother's Wish for a Boy

MOTHER: I really wanted a boy, but I thought he was going to be a girl. When he was born and I saw it was a boy, I was ecstatic. I was very pleased because I had always wanted a boy first, and I thought my husband would want a boy first.

R. G. (to father): How about yourself? Did you have a preference for the first child?

FATHER: No.

Infant Characteristics

MOTHER: He wasn't as outgoing as his sister. He wasn't as ready to be picked up all the time as she, but I would say that basically he was a happy baby.

R. G.: What was his reaction to being held?

MOTHER: He liked it.

R. G.: Was he cuddly?

MOTHER: Not terribly. He wasn't rejecting, but he wasn't terribly cuddly.

R. G.: How would you compare his reaction to being held with your daughter?

MOTHER: She seemed to like it more. She needed it. She was a very difficult baby to begin with. But if you compare him to the average child, I'd say probably the same or maybe more. I spent a lot of time with him—doing things with him and reading to him and being with him, taking him with me everywhere I went. As far as actually holding, he was independent, actually. I actually didn't cuddle and hold him a great deal, but we had a great deal of contact.

R. G.: How would you describe his face as an infant?

MOTHER: When he was younger, people would mistake him for a girl. He had curly blond hair and he was a beautiful baby. Up until the time when he was about three, people kept mistaking him for a girl, and I was kind of pleased by it. I was pleased that he was such a beautiful child, but I would always say, "He's not a girl, he's a boy." I would tell them so that he knew he was a boy and they were wrong.

Mother-Son and Father-Son Time

MOTHER: In the second year it was mostly like going in the car and going to visit friends and shopping. I took him with me absolutely everywhere. During his second year I went back to work for one month.

FATHER: But that was during the night.

MOTHER: Yeah, I was working at night, and my husband would spend a great deal of time with him. He would get him up in the morning and feed and dress him, and on weekends he would spend the whole weekend with him because I was sleeping in the morning.

FATHER: She only worked weekends actually.

R. G.: So when you were at work—

FATHER: He would be with me, and we would be out puttering around the yard, playing.

R. G.:   How would you compare the amount of time you spent with him compared to most fathers and their sons about the same age?

FATHER: About the same, possibly a little less maybe.

INTERVIEW WITH RICHARD AT AGE FIVE

Getting to Know the Boy

R. G.:   What's the favorite thing you like to do in the whole world?

RICHARD: In the whole world that I like to do? Eat watermelon.

R. G.:   Okay. What kind of game do you like to play the very, very best?

RICHARD: I don't really know. But I know what dinner I like best.

R. G.:   What?

RICHARD: Chicken wings.

R. G.:   Uh-huh.

RICHARD: And pizza.

R. G.:   Good.

Friendships

R. G.:   Who is your very, very best friend?

RICHARD: Betty, 'cause she's my girlfriend.

R. G.:   How old is Betty?

RICHARD: Six-and-a-half.

R. G.:   What makes her your girlfriend?

RICHARD: I just like her a lot. And when I grow up I might marry her.

R. G.:   Would you like to be married some day?

RICHARD: Well, only with Betty.

R. G.:   Would you like to have little children, too?

RICHARD: Yeah.

R. G.:   Which would you like to have—a little boy or a little girl?

RICHARD: Two girls and a boy. I like girls better than boys.

Early Behavior Preferences

R. G.:   What do you like better about girls?

RICHARD: They dress up and make up.

R. G.:   They dress up and make up?

RICHARD: And I like to dress up and make up.

R. G.:   What do you like about dressing up and making up?

RICHARD: I can be a clown.

R. G.:   What else can you be if you dress up and make up besides a clown? What else could you be?

RICHARD: An actor.

R. G.: You'd like to be an actor, too?

RICHARD: Yeah.

R. G.: What kinds of parts—what kinds of roles would you like to play if you were an actor? Who would you make believe you were?

RICHARD: A cowboy.

R. G.: Do you like to dress up like a girl or put on girls' makeup?

RICHARD: Yeah.

R. G.: What's fun about that?

RICHARD: 'Cause you dress up in makeup.

R. G.: Uh-huh.

RICHARD: 'Cause you dress in girls' dresses, which I like the best.

R. G.: Why do you like that so much?

RICHARD: Because every time I wear these clothes they get tight on me.

R. G.: Uh-huh.

RICHARD: I mean, they get me hotter because the pants go all the way around you and dresses just go out.

R. G.: You like that better. Whose dresses do you get a chance to wear?

RICHARD: I never wear a dress, but I wear a bathrobe and I wear a bath towel.

R. G.: I see. Is a bathrobe or a bath towel like a dress?

RICHARD: Yeah.

R. G.: Do you make believe it's a dress when you wear it?

RICHARD: Yeah.

R. G.: So you like to wear a towel and a bathrobe and make believe it's a dress. Do you get a chance to wear a real dress?

RICHARD: No.

Perceived Parental Attitudes toward Cross-dressing

R. G.: Why?

RICHARD: Mama doesn't let me.

R. G.: Why doesn't she let you?

RICHARD: Because my sister's dresses are too little.

R. G.: What if your sister's dresses were not too little, but the same size as you, would your mommy let you wear your sister's dresses then?

RICHARD: If I was little.

R. G.: If you were the same size as your sister would your mommy let you wear her dresses?

RICHARD: Yeah, but only if I was a girl.

R. G.: Only if you were a girl, not if you were a boy. Why is that?

RICHARD: Because boys don't wear dresses.

R. G.: Why not?

RICHARD: 'Cause they look funny in dresses. And because girls are supposed to wear dresses.

R. G.: If you had your choice and nobody would know about it and you could do it in secret all by yourself, would you rather wear dresses, or would you rather wear pants?

RICHARD: Dresses.

R. G.: What happens to little boys who wear dresses?

RICHARD: Their mothers get mad.

R. G.: How about their fathers?

RICHARD: They get mad too.

Wish to Be a Girl

R. G.: Have you ever wished you'd been born a girl?

RICHARD: Yes.

R. G.: Why did you wish that?

RICHARD: Girls, they don't have to have a penis.

R. G.: They don't have to have a penis?

RICHARD: They can have babies. And—because they—it doesn't tickle when you tickle them here.

R. G.: It doesn't tickle when you tickle them there? Where your penis is?

RICHARD: Yeah. 'Cause they don't have a penis. I wish I was a girl.

R. G.: You wish you were a girl?

RICHARD: You know what? I might be a girl.

R. G.: You might be a girl? Why do you think that?

RICHARD: Well, because if girls had penises and boys had—umm—

R. G.: Vaginas?

RICHARD: Umm...umm...it would be funny then because you wouldn't know which was which because girls have vaginas and boys have penises.

R. G.: Do you like to have a penis?

RICHARD: No.

R. G.: No?

RICHARD: 'Cause every time I'm in the wash—when I—I'm trying to soak my hair to get the soap off, it tickles my penis.

R. G.: It tickles your penis and you don't like it to tickle your penis? What don't you like about it tickling your penis?

RICHARD: 'Cause it tickles.

R. G.: It tickles. Does it get big and stiff and stand up? [Richard nods.] It does? You like that? [Richard shakes head no.] You don't like that? And if you were a girl that wouldn't happen? [Richard nods.] How do you know it doesn't tickle a girl there?

RICHARD: It might, but it doesn't tickle as much as it tickles boys.

An Understanding of Anatomic Sex Differences

R. G.: Why do you think girls don't have a penis?

RICHARD: 'Cause they have to have babies. And babies don't come out of penises!

R. G.: Babies don't come out of penises, that's right.

RICHARD: Babies come out of vaginas.

R. G.: Babies come out of vaginas—that's right. Do you think girls ever had a penis when they were real little, or were they born without a penis?

RICHARD: Born without a penis.

R. G.: That's right. You think it's ever possible for a little boy to become a little girl?

RICHARD: No.

R. G.: That's right. How about a little girl becoming a boy? [Richard shakes head no.] That's not possible either, that's right. Is there anything else about being a girl that's good?

RICHARD: There's nothing else I want to say.

Reassurance about Being Anatomically Male

R. G.: Okay. You told me an awful lot. You told me how you feel about things, about boy and girl things. You know it's okay if it tickles down there.

RICHARD: It is?

R. G.: Yeah, sure, that's fine. If it gets big and stiff and tickles, that's perfectly okay.

RICHARD: But your penis doesn't go down for a long time.

R. G.: That's perfectly okay.

RICHARD: But it hurts when it doesn't go down for a long time.

R. G.: But it goes down, and it doesn't really hurt. It just looks and feels a little bit different.

RICHARD: It tickles when it goes down.

R. G.: It's a nice feeling, isn't it? You're not scared of it when it gets big and stiff, are you?

RICHARD: No.

R. G.: Good! It's supposed to do that when you tickle it. And you're lucky you have something like that, because girls don't have that. That's one big advantage of being a boy. 'Cause girls can't do that, you know?

RICHARD: Uh-huh.

R. G.: Sure they can have babies, but only boys can have a penis stand up like that.

RICHARD: I wish that boys could have boy babies and girls could have girl babies.

R. G.: Well, you know boys help girls get babies.

RICHARD: How come?

R. G.: Well, for every little child there's a father and a mother. Right?

RICHARD: Yeah.

R. G.: So you'll have something to do with the girl having a baby when you grow up and get married.

RICHARD: You mean making the baby?

R. G.: Sure, you'll help make the baby.

RICHARD: How?

R. G.: Haven't your mommy and daddy told you how that happens?

RICHARD: No.

R. G.: Well, the boy plants the seed inside the girl, and then the baby grows inside the mommy's belly like in a nest.

RICHARD: How can the seed go inside the mother's belly?

R. G.: It goes into the vagina from the daddy.

RICHARD: You buy a seed at the store?

R. G.: No, the daddy makes it inside his body and then he puts it inside the mommy's body.

RICHARD: You mean it comes outside his tushie?

R. G.: No. It comes out his penis. That's why the penis is a very special thing.

RICHARD: The seed comes out of the penis?

R. G.: The food that makes the seed grow. See, the mommy really has the seed inside her belly in her baby nest, and the daddy has the food that makes the seed grow. It's food for the seed, and that food comes from the daddy's penis and goes into the mommy's vagina, and that makes the seed start to grow, and the little baby grows from the seed.

RICHARD: You mean the little baby is a seed?

R. G.: It begins from a little, tiny seed just like a plant seed. It's called an egg, but it's just like a little tiny seed.

RICHARD: You mean the baby's in the seed?

R. G.: Yeah.

RICHARD: How can a baby be in a seed?

R. G. (undaunted): Well, have you ever seen a little seed grow into a flower? [Richard nods.] Well, it's the same thing. It starts real little, and it gets fed by the mommy and daddy, and it grows and grows to make a tiny baby.

RICHARD: Oh.

R. G.: So when you become married and you become a daddy, you'll help the mommy have a little baby, and that's why it's good to be a boy and that's why it's good to have a penis—so you can help the mommy. She needs you.

The boy was seen weekly in group sessions with other "feminine" boys, his mother was seen weekly with the other boys' mothers, and his father was seen with other boys' fathers. This treatment program lasted about a year (Green and Fuller, 1973[b]). The boy was the smallest in the group and was often picked on for his size. He was encouraged to be more assertive. He showed less "feminine" behavior in the group than some older boys. His mother worked toward not encouraging his cross-gender behaviors and interrupted a very close relationship between her son and a girl friend who appeared to enhance his "feminine" behaviors. His father

*made an effort to engage the boy in mutually enjoyable father-son activities, such
as Indian Guides.*

INTERVIEW WITH RICHARD AT AGE EIGHT

R. G.:   Do you remember why you were brought here when you were
younger?

RICHARD: I used to like to play with *other* girls and I used to fight with
other children—boys.

R. G.:   You said other girls. Did you think you were a girl?

RICHARD: Yes.

R. G.:   Why?

RICHARD: Because I had long hair. This was when I was four. And, my
sister had long hair. Then when my mommy cut my hair, it grew back
long again, so I thought I was a girl.

RICHARD'S PARENTS DESCRIBE HIM AT AGE EIGHT

Encouraging "Masculine" Behavior

MOTHER: He is playing more with his school friends—his boy friends
that come over—and sometimes he goes to their houses. I'm kind of
not letting him go because they live so far. He has to cross a street
with a signal on it. He has his school friends come over and play with
him.

R. G.:   How do you feel about those particular friends?

MOTHER: Oh, I like them, but like I said he wants to go over there and
I haven't let him go because I have never let him cross a busy street.

R. G.:   What are the possibilities of somebody else taking him?

MOTHER: Yeah, I could. This week I couldn't because the baby has been
sick, and I haven't been able to take her out. When things get better
I'll take him if he wants to go. He went to a birthday party by himself—
without him wanting me to go with him or anything.

R. G.:   It seems to me that if one of the things that you have been worried
about is that he doesn't want to play with boys, and now you are saying
that he wants to—like he wants to do everything to participate, you
should let him.

Poor Body Image

FATHER: Last night, I had been working late, and he came to me when
I came home, and I think he is becoming conscious of his slight build.
He was saying that they were calling him skinny, so I told him to just
stand up straight, and I told him he wasn't skinny, but he said, "Yeah,

but I am—look at my little arms," so I didn't know what to answer him after that.

R. G.: Objectively, is he skinnier than the other kids?

FATHER: Yeah, I think so.

MOTHER: He's not shorter, but he's skinnier.

RICHARD'S MOTHER DESCRIBES HIM AT AGE TEN

(The parents are separated.)

MOTHER: I feel very differently about him. He is okay. We shouldn't manipulate his environment. His dignity has suffered. He's taken karate lessons but he was terrified. He still will not participate in contact sports and he won't take gymnastics. He still has as many girl friends as boy friends. He plays more with the boys. He plays board games, goes bicycle riding and swimming.

He dresses appropriately except for a night jumper he wanted that his sister had. He expropriated that for himself. At Halloween he dressed as a Little Old Lady from Pasadena, which I approved of. He is no longer obsessed with the cross-dressing or doll-play. He will occasionally play with his sister's doll. I feel he changed, when I stopped leaning on him. But maybe it's my perceptions of him that have changed.

I can accept it if he becomes homosexual. It'll be all right. It won't reflect on me as a bad parent.

INTERVIEW WITH RICHARD AT AGE EIGHTEEN

Relationship with Parents after the Divorce

RICHARD: I lived with my mom when my parents got divorced, but we didn't get along too well. We got along on a regular level but she—like, I always wanted to go out late, and she always had too much control.

R. G.: How old were you when your parents got divorced?

RICHARD: Fourth grade, ten.

R. G.: When your parents first got divorced, how often would you see your dad?

RICHARD: Every weekend, pretty much all the time until I moved in with him.

R. G.: So you weren't getting along that well with your mom?

RICHARD: Yes, I mean just like normal bickering and stuff, but not too well. I hated her boyfriend so much, I never got along with him at all and I was getting in fights, like physical fights, I'd fight with him.

R. G.: When did he come into your life?

RICHARD: Ever since they were divorced. I never got along with him. He was a jerk. Now my mom realizes that he's a jerk.

Sports Involvement in Adolescence

R. G.: How have your interests evolved?

RICHARD: I played sports in tenth grade and then eleventh grade I played, but in twelfth grade I didn't have time. In seventh, eighth, and ninth grades I wasn't involved in any after-school sports, but in school we played. It was normal—football, soccer, baseball, softball. Training, working out. Still play tennis, you know, from time to time.

Interest in Cars

R. G.: How do you spend your other time?

RICHARD: I come home from school usually and I go to work. Usually every Friday and Saturday I go out on a date or just with friends. I don't really do anything when I get home from school. Cars are really a big interest of mine. I have four years back of every *Motor and Road Track, Sports Car Graphic,* stuff like that.

Current Sexuality

R. G.: Tell me about your social life. What are your romantic interests?

RICHARD: Let's see, my first girlfriend that I can remember was in ninth grade. My first girlfriend—ninth and tenth grade—and it didn't work out that good. She was weird. She wasn't like, into guys, yet she wasn't ready for a relationship, really. I have had pretty good luck after. I got my values real mixed up. I was a little bit too materialistically concerned with things, and I went out with this one girl whom I'd been seeing off and on for a while. She's a snob. Now I'm going out with a girl who's really smart. We'd rather spend time together than anywhere else. I mean, girls I've been out with in between—went out with this fifteen-year-old girl—then she was fourteen and I was sixteen—I couldn't see anything coming out of that relationship. She was really smart for her age. But you know, just different interests.

Initial Heterosexuality

R. G.: How much sexual experience have you had?

RICHARD: I've had sex. Of course.

R. G.: What do you mean, of course? Some people haven't. How old were you the first time?

RICHARD: I was almost sixteen.

R. G.: How was it?

RICHARD: It wasn't bad. It was pretty good. For her it wasn't that good. I think she put her hands over her face the whole time. It was her first time. I mean, like, I had messed around before—it was like nothing big really. She treated it as a really big thing, though. There were no bad feelings afterwards. But we didn't get to know each other too well. It kind of like drove us apart after.

R. G.: Did you have sex with her again?

RICHARD: No, only one time with her. And then after, my sex life has been pretty good.

R. G.: How many girls have you had sex with?

RICHARD: Four.

R. G.: How many times altogether?

RICHARD: I don't know. A lot.

R. G.: Sometimes guys at first have a problem getting an erection. Other guys have a problem coming too fast, faster than they'd like to come.

RICHARD: No, it's been pretty good. I mean, coming too fast or coming too slow, I've never had a problem getting an erection. Sometimes they come when they're not wanted, but they also come when they are wanted.

Denial of Homosexuality

R. G.: Some kids in their early teens also have sexual feelings towards guys. To what extent have you experienced anything like that?

RICHARD: None.

R. G.: To what extent have you ever been turned on by the thought of sex with a guy?

RICHARD: No, uh uh.

R. G.: Do you know any guys like that, guys who are bisexual, or guys who are gay?

RICHARD: No, I know people in school who you think they might be. But we're not really friends with them.

R. G.: What makes you think that certain guys are gay? What are the clues?

RICHARD: They just have no friends that are girls. Or all their friends *are* girls. Like all they do is hang around girls all the time. Weird people. Some guys dress feminine. Some guys you can't really tell, because some of my friends dress really feminine, not really feminine—it's hard to tell. I don't think there's that many gay kids.

Attitude toward Homosexuality

R. G.: What do you think about people who are gay?

RICHARD: It's kind of disgusting in a way. I mean, it's not something that I would choose. But the more I open my eyes to this, the girls I am going out with now, I have become a lot less bigoted. But I guess now I can accept them for who they are. It's still kind of gross. Because I wouldn't want it. But I guess for them it's fine, as long as it doesn't bother anyone else.

Pornography

R. G.: Have you read erotic stories?

RICHARD: Of course.

R. G.: What sort of stories?

RICHARD: Like names of them? I don't remember names, just like in magazines. *Playboy* articles.

R. G.: Have you seen X-rated films?

RICHARD: Yeah, like I've seen *Deep Throat* and stuff.

R. G.: What's your feeling about watching films like that?

RICHARD: Really stupid. In two minutes, they are the most boring things. It's just the first time I saw it, it was like a big deal. But then it's like too stupid.

R. G.: Did it turn you on?

RICHARD: Like, do I get an erection? Yes, sometimes. Sometimes it's like, you know, just stupid.

R. G.: Do you read magazines like *Playboy, Penthouse*?

RICHARD: Yeah, I read *Playboy*. Good articles, too.

R. G.: When you look at the pictures and centerfolds, does that turn you on?

RICHARD: Yes, sometimes it gives me an erection. Sometimes it doesn't. But it's always attractive to me. I mean, I don't instantly get an erection every time I see a naked girl, every naked girl. But yeah, they're very attractive. Big sights.

R. G.: Have you ever seen pictures in *Playgirl* of nude males?

RICHARD: No, I've never even seen *Playgirl*.

R. G.: Have you ever seen pictures of nude men?

RICHARD: Yes, of course.

R. G.: Does that turn you on at all? Seeing nude men?

RICHARD: No.

R. G.: How about with masturbation. What do you usually think about when you masturbate?

RICHARD: Just, like, a girl, usually.

Recollection of Boyhood "Sex-typed" Interests

R. G.: What do you remember about what your play interests were like back when you were a little kid?

RICHARD: I played board games, I guess. Monopoly, Life, stuff like that. Lincoln Logs, I remember we had Lincoln Logs. Little wooden toys with colored Tinkertoys. It's hard to remember.

R. G.: Do you remember who some of your friends were? Boys? Girls? Mixture of both?

RICHARD: Both, I would say. When I was little, probably both.

R. G.: How do you remember getting along with the kids back then?

RICHARD: Fine, there was no problem really. I think I was more introverted then.

R. G.: Do you remember going through a phase when you were young of liking to play with girls rather than boys?

RICHARD: Yeah, like when I was in first grade, probably. But not liking everything that was girl-type things.

R. G.: What kinds of things do you remember?

RICHARD: Just like playing with dolls and G. I. Joe.

R. G.: Do you remember liking or going through a phase in which you were dressing up in girls' clothes?

RICHARD: No.

R. G.: Do you remember ever wanting to be a girl?

RICHARD: No.

R. G.: Do you ever remember being called sissy for any reason?

RICHARD: Not really, just like normal. Of course, you get called sissy sometime, but never, I wouldn't be called sissy all the time. I didn't like going to school like in kindergarten, just afraid of going to school, then it was fine like in first grade; it was fine.

R. G.: Do you remember what you were afraid of?

RICHARD: Just starting in school, like being away from home, something new. And having to walk home from kindergarten. I remember that was a pain, but I adjusted after a while, and ever since it was fine.

Relationship with Parents

R. G.: What do you remember about your dad then when you were little?

RICHARD: Oh, God, my dad was weird. He's always just been like an outsider in the picture. My mom's like the dominant force in the family—not dominantly but the visible. Both of my parents—neither of them were dominant—but my dad was kind of never involved.

R. G.: Tell me more what you mean by that.

RICHARD: He just was never—he never really cared like what my grades were then, or interested in what I was doing. Maybe he was, but this is what I remember, and what I remember could be different from reality, but it's my reality. I don't think that he was really too interested, you know, now he is—now he's very interested.

R. G.: So you remember your mother as being the dominant parent in your life when you were a little kid?

RICHARD: No, she wasn't dominant; she was just the parent, you know, and my dad, too. I mean, they were both my parents. Like my dad

was in Indian Guides with me, normal dad stuff, but my mom, she's
not domineering at all or dominant.

Future Sexuality and Lifestyle

R. G.:   Do you see yourself someday getting married and having a family,
or being a bachelor?

RICHARD: Married, with a family. I wouldn't be like that happy, married
forever. You get bored. This girl's the only one I've no signs of bore-
dom at all. Definitely, a great relationship. With the other I got so sick
of her, so materialistic. I need someone who's, like, good for my growth
too. You know, not like impair it. 'Cause she just like added to my
materialistic needs, and it kind of bothers me that I'm materialistic
sometimes. You know, I don't want to be, I want to direct it towards
a more philanthropic way, you know, like DeLorean. He said opening
up his plant in Ireland would give jobs to the unemployed Irish—and
it would be like Henry Ford, a great philanthropist, a rich man. But
he didn't do that at all. It was all bullshit. But that's something I can
see myself, running my own car company like the American dream.
Like Ford.

"MASCULINE" BOY, HETEROSEXUAL MAN: MARTIN

*Martin's childhood behaviors were conventionally masculine. Although his
parents divorced when he was five, he continued to have extensive contact with
his father. He also became very close to his mother. Martin recalls viewing his
parents having sexual intercourse. He reports that this experience served as a
model for his later heterosexuality.*

MARTIN'S MOTHER DESCRIBES HIM AT AGE NINE

Lack of Concern over Sex-typed Interests

R. G.:   Has there been anything at all about your son's behavior which
has been of concern to you?

MOTHER: When we got a divorce, he went through a lot of changes. He
became more sensitive to my moods and feelings. He seemed to worry
a great deal, and he was only five. He would worry while I was at work

and things. He was just terribly sensitive to my moods and feelings, as though he were trying to protect me, and that bothered me. I was hoping that it wouldn't continue for very long.

R. G.:   Has your son ever gone through a stage of any kind of feminine development during which he liked to do girl-type things—any girlish behavior?

MOTHER: No, I can't honestly say that he has.

Early Behaviors

R. G.:   Has he ever gone through a period of liking to dress up in girls' clothes?

MOTHER: No.

R. G.:   Nothing like wearing your high-heeled shoes?

MOTHER: Well, he's put things on, but no more than picking up my husband's articles of clothing.

R. G.:   Or cosmetics or your underclothing?

MOTHER: No.

R. G.:   Has he ever said that he'd like to be a girl, or that he is a girl?

MOTHER: No.

R. G.:   Did he ever go through a period of liking to play with female-type dolls, such as Barbie?

MOTHER: No.

R. G.:   Does he play house or mother-father games, or has he played these games?

MOTHER: Yes.

R. G.:   What role would he usually take in these?

MOTHER: The father.

R. G.:   What does he usually dress up as for Halloween?

MOTHER: Usually something yucky like Dracula or Frankenstein or Superman. He was a pirate this year; it's usually something sort of aggressive, something that he can act out, not something passive. Lots of props.

R. G.:   Does he playact or take on make-believe roles?

MOTHER: Yes.

R. G.:   Does he imitate characters from TV?

MOTHER: All the time. I can't remember too many women; it's always men, male characters.

R. G.:   How would you compare his interest in playacting, role-taking, with most boys his age?

MOTHER: Well, it may be just—he may be a bit more interested in it when he's at home, because he's an only child and he has a lot of time alone.

R. G.:   Does he improvise costumes for these roles?

MOTHER: Sometimes.

R. G.:   What sort?

MOTHER: With his blanket or—it isn't frequent. Mostly, it's with props: trucks, cars, little men, things like that, but not costumes.

R. G.:   Does he seem to show any unusual interest or fascination with types of cloth, textures?

MOTHER: No. Oh, satin, yes—he's a freak about satin.

R. G.:   In what way?

MOTHER: Well, ever since he was little, he's had to have satin on his blanket, and he takes it and rolls it around his finger and makes a point with it. He can't go past a piece of satin without fondling it and standing right next to it if he's talking to you. He can't pass it by.

R. G.:   Does he comment on your clothing?

MOTHER: Not very often, no.

R. G.:   Does he comment on his dad's clothing?

MOTHER: Yes, more often than mine.

R. G.:   What sort of things does he say?

MOTHER: He'll like, if I buy him something—my husband is rather conservative, and if I buy him some things that are a little bit sharper, more modern, he likes that. He likes anything that he gets himself that is similar in any way to his dad's, such as boots or plaid cuffed pants or anything that my husband has. There's a certain, "Gee, I have one like you." But that's about his only interest in clothing.

R. G.:   Does he draw pictures?

MOTHER: Sometimes. He doesn't like to draw because he doesn't think he's good at it.

R. G.:   If he does draw pictures, what types are they?

MOTHER: They're usually mechanical things.

R. G.:   Are there people in these pictures?

MOTHER: Sometimes.

R. G.:   Are they usually males or females?

MOTHER: They're almost all male.

R. G.:   What are his favorite toys?

MOTHER: He likes his Big Jim, and he likes trucks and his bicycle. He likes his books, but not as much as things that he can wheel around the floor. He makes caves with his blanket and garages and things—those kind of boy toys, trucks and tractors and things.

R. G.:   With whom does he usually play?

MOTHER: Usually the boy across the street or by himself.

R. G.:   Who would you say his best friend is?

MOTHER: A boy at school.

R. G.:   Does he generally prefer boys or girls as playmates?

MOTHER: Boys, although lately, this last year, he's taken a fancy to an older girl.

R. G.:   When children were first available to him as playmates, while he was growing up, were there primarily boys around or girls, or was there a mixture?

MOTHER: Mostly girls when he was small, real young.

R. G.: When did boys start to come into his life?

MOTHER: When he was about three-and-a-half, he went to a school full time, and that was when he had more boys to play with.

R. G.: To what extent does he participate in rough-and-tumble play—wrestling, fighting, tag, etc.?

MOTHER: He loves it, eats it up.

R. G.: How would you compare his level of participation with most boys his age?

MOTHER: I think he's even more into that. He's always been extremely physical, more so than any other child I've ever come across—to the point of, when he was able to walk, he would reach a point every night—whether we had company, whether we were out—when he could feel it was coming to the end of the evening, and he would literally run from wall to wall to wall till he would drop, grab his blanket, get up and run again. He's just been very physical: climbing, jumping, running.

R. G.: How do you feel about his participation in such activity?

MOTHER: I try to encourage him to have quiet times, too. At first it was hard for me to accept, I guess, because I had just never been around little boys very much, or men for that matter. I just felt he should sit in a corner and contemplate a little more frequently, but then I came to accept that that was the way he was. I felt, and I still feel, that he has a certain amount of energy that he has to expend every day, and it's very important that he gets rid of that. It's important for his mind and his physical well-being.

R. G.: To what extent does he play war games, soldiers, cowboys and Indians?

MOTHER: He likes that very much, probably more than anything else. He likes guns.

R. G.: How do you feel about his participation in activities like that?

MOTHER: I feel it's very healthy for him.

R. G.: To what extent has he shown an interest in sports?

MOTHER: He's very interested in sports. My husband is a football nut.

R. G.: How would you compare his interest with most boys his age?

MOTHER: It's a little bit more focused for nine.

Preference for a Girl

R. G.: Did you have a preference when you were pregnant for a boy or for a girl?

MOTHER: A girl.

R. G.:   How did you feel when a boy was born?

MOTHER: I was very disappointed.

R. G.:   Do you feel that your disappointment in some ways influenced your relationship with him?

MOTHER: No, I don't think so, and now I have a terrible preference for boys.

INTERVIEW WITH MARTIN AT AGE FIFTEEN

Earliest Crush

R. G.:   Do you remember how old you were the first time you ever had a crush on anybody?

MARTIN: Nine, I think.

R. G.:   Who did you have a crush on?

MARTIN: This girl—it was like in the fourth grade or something.

R. G.:   She was about your age?

MARTIN: Yes.

Current Romantic Interests

R. G.:   During the past year have you had a crush on somebody?

MARTIN: Yes.

R. G.:   And who was that?

MARTIN: A girl, same age as I am.

R. G.:   Okay. That sort of broke up or—?

MARTIN: Yes. She's going away for the summer.

R. G.:   Will you be seeing her again when she gets back?

MARTIN: Probably.

R. G.:   You were dating her?

MARTIN: Yes.

R. G.:   Do you have sex with your girlfriend?

MARTIN: No.

Experience with Pornography

R. G.:   Have you read stories, not with pictures but just reading stories, that describe people making love?

MARTIN: Yes, in magazines.

R. G.:   What have you seen?

MARTIN: People making love, that's about it.

R. G.:   Are these a man and a woman, two women, two men?

MARTIN: A man and a woman.

R. G.:   Have you seen pictures that show two women making love?

MARTIN: No.

R. G.: Have you seen pictures of two men making love?

MARTIN: No.

R. G.: These pictures of men and women making love, are they totally nude?

MARTIN: Yes.

R. G.: You see the genitals?

MARTIN: Yes.

R. G.: When you look at pictures like that, do you get a special feeling or reaction somewhere in your body?

MARTIN: Sometimes, not most of the times, sometimes.

R. G.: What sort of reaction do you get?

MARTIN: An erection.

Wet Dreams

R. G.: You know what a wet dream is, I presume?

MARTIN: Yes.

R. G.: Do you remember how old you were when you first had a wet dream?

MARTIN: Fourteen.

R. G.: And what do you remember about what goes on in the wet dreams?

MARTIN: I remember a picture I saw, and they're moving.

R. G.: What kind of picture?

MARTIN: Just a man and a woman making love.

R. G.: Are you in the dream, or is it other people that you don't know?

MARTIN: It's other people that I don't know.

Masturbation

R. G.: Do you remember how old you were when you first learned about or began to experiment with masturbation?

MARTIN: Fourteen.

R. G.: On the average, how often would you say that you masturbate?

MARTIN: I don't know, once a year maybe.

R. G.: Once a year?

MARTIN: Yeah, maybe.

R. G.: Do you have some thoughts about whether masturbation is good for you, bad for you, normal, not normal, dangerous, harmless, what?

MARTIN: I guess it's normal. I can't see how it would harm you, but I'm just not into it.

R. G.: Do you find yourself getting horny and wanting to masturbate?

MARTIN: Yes, sometimes I feel that way. I don't know, it goes away.

R. G.: Do you have any religious feelings about masturbation as to whether it's sinful, something that shouldn't be done?

MARTIN: No.

R. G.:   On the rare times that you do masturbate, what do you usually think about?

MARTIN: Me and some woman making love.

Onset of Sexual Interests

R. G.:   When did you become aware of sexual interests in girls?

MARTIN: About fourteen, 'cause I got propositioned, you know, and I wasn't even up for it.

R. G.:   What happened?

MARTIN: It started with a game. There was a girl and a guy game where all the guys would count to a thousand or whatever, and the girls would go hide, and whoever we found we got to kiss 'em, right? And I was going with a girl in the game, and I'd find her, and it was getting late, and she was really getting into it, and she offered herself, and I'm goin', "What, really?"

R. G.:   What did she say to you?

MARTIN: She goes, "Yeah, let's go for it in my house, because my parents aren't home," something like that. I shined. I was real nervous, and I would have been fumbling and kinda new, you know, but the experience is different and I wasn't ready for it. I was into hanging out with the guys and doing those kind of things, and making out or whatever was just part of that, actually. She offered many times— she was persistent about it. She was really up for it, and I wasn't, and my friend who was with me, this one guy who just happened to overhear, was going, "You're a fool, you're a fool!" But I wasn't up for it.

Early Crushes

R. G.:   Do you remember having crushes when you were young?

MARTIN: Yeah.

R. G.:   How far back?

MARTIN: Fourth grade, third grade.

R. G.:   Do you ever remember having crushes on guys, boys, or older men, when you were a little kid?

MARTIN: No, I don't.

Homosexual Interests

R. G.:   To what extent, if any, had you any kind of sexual or romantic feelings towards males—boys, or older men?

MARTIN: No—I mean, sometimes I feel real close to some of my good buddies, you know, enough to hug them, buddy around, but not sexually, no.

Sexual Experience

R. G.:   How much petting experience have you had?

MARTIN: Not a whole lot. I felt breasts and that's about it.

R. G.:   Is this over clothing or under clothing?

MARTIN: Under.

R. G.:   And have you felt the genitals, the vagina?

MARTIN: No.

R. G.:   When you felt this girl's breast, did that turn you on? Did that give you an erection?

MARTIN: Yes.

R. G.:   And did she touch you?

MARTIN: Yes.

R. G.:   Your penis?

MARTIN: Yes.

R. G.:   And did that turn you on? Did that give you an erection?

MARTIN: Yes.

R. G.:   Do you have any questions about that, any questions about sexual experiences or sexual behaviors with other people?

MARTIN: No, not really. It's just not a definite must in my life right now.

R. G.:   If you have any questions about sex, is there somebody that you can go to and ask?

MARTIN: My mom.

R. G.:   Anybody else?

MARTIN: No. My mom and I are pretty open, we talk.

MARTIN'S MOTHER DESCRIBES HIM AT AGE FIFTEEN

Concerns about Martin

R. G.:   Are there any things about your son's behavior that worry you?

MOTHER: Yes, I think that he has a distorted sense of reality. He lives in a land that he's made up, in that he has a conception of what the real world will be like and what it will expect of him, but he doesn't see what he should go through to get there. He's not willing to make the effort to do that. It's something that we try to deal with as much as possible, and I feel it's his biggest problem.

R. G.:   Can you amplify what you mean?

MOTHER: Right now he thinks he wants to be a professional, but he's not willing to do the work in school. He thinks because he wants something, it will happen. He has not been applying himself at all. It's been hard.

R. G.:   How is he developing socially?

MOTHER: He's an introverted person who handles responsibility very well. There's this great dichotomy there. He can be just tremendous in areas of leadership, strength, organization, and ideas, and yet he has to be set up. It still has to be done by a third party, usually the mother. He has to be dragged there and pushed through the door, and then he can perform. He tends to be withdrawn and a little antisocial. He has difficulties with relationships, and yet he's a very warm child, but he's a late bloomer.

Emerging Heterosexual Interests

R. G.: How about his developing romantic interests?

MOTHER: He's pretty popular with young women, usually older than he. He has a certain sensitivity other boys his age lack, and women find that very attractive. He shows great strength. He's very gallant with his mother and other women. He started a relationship with a young girl who was graduating from high school. She's in college this year. However, there will be a lot of other young ladies. He's had another girlfriend since about January. He's seen her every Sunday night in his group meeting and called her on the phone because she lives quite a distance away. She's his age. He has also corresponded with girls from camp last summer and calls them and keeps up with them and hopes to see them again this year. I think he has real good relationships with young women. Very healthy. He's testing the water, that's what he's supposed to be doing. We do talk, which is really good.

Mother-Son Relationship

R. G.: It sounds like you've got a real good relationship with your son.

MOTHER: Yes, and we're honest with each other. We try and cut the bullshit, and not hurt either. He's sensitive and so am I, and what's nice is he realizes now how much he is like me. I think he can identify with certain things I'm going through, and as a result it's really nice for me because I have a sensitive human being who will say, "It sounds like things are a little rough for you. How are you doing?" He's a nice boy, and I worry about him. You want your children to be perfect and wonderful and have the end product well adjusted. You forget about all the shit work you have to do to attain it and maintain it.

Father-Son Relationship

R. G.: How long have you been remarried now?

MOTHER: Nine years.

R. G.: Since your son was what, about six or seven?

MOTHER: Yes, about six-and-a-half.

R. G.: Does your son have any residual contact with his biological father?

MOTHER: He doesn't see him very frequently. He did in the beginning, more than most people would, but his father is now married for the third time, and they have just recently moved, so it's quite a hardship to see him as much as he did before, and I think it shows.

R. G.: In what way?

MOTHER: It bothers my son. He likes to go there for a number of reasons. When he goes there, he's an only child and it's peaceful and quiet. They only have dogs, no children. He's got his own little kingdom there. He likes going with his dad, but unfortunately it has been getting farther between visits.

R. G.: When did it start to taper off?

MOTHER: I think it really started when he got married this last time. Maybe three years ago, maybe four.

R. G.: How available was he to your son in the first years of his life, before the divorce?

MOTHER: Very. He took care of him probably 51 percent of the time. Yes, very.

R. G.: Why was that? That's not typical for fathers.

MOTHER: I think it was just the type of person he was. I am also able to delegate, and don't define myself by it. I'm really not quite sure why, except that my husband now is that way too and has been. I tend to think I pick a particular type of individual and that I have something to do with making sure that that happens. I didn't have that kind of father.

R. G.: So he was really very available for six years, until the divorce?

MOTHER: Yes, then when I went to work and we would have conflicting shifts, it was nice for the child in that he had a parent at all times. There was very little outside child care that went on for the first few years, until I separated from my husband.

R. G.: Your son was about six?

MOTHER: Yes, about five.

R. G.: How much contact did he maintain after this?

MOTHER: Very close. He had him every weekend. Every single weekend. Then it worked out to be about every Sunday, and then it gradually became every other Sunday. During his second marriage he had a very horrible relationship. Then he had a period of time when he was single again, and he increased the time that he spent with him. Since he's married the third time it has decreased, and since he moved it's become really ridiculous. I think now he only averages seeing him about once every six weeks, for a day.

R. G.: When you first got remarried, how was the relationship between him and your new husband?

MOTHER: Pretty good, because he had known the boy since he was about three, and my son had known him, so there wasn't a big adjustment there. It wasn't really a big problem.

R. G.:   So he had a fair amount of contact with two father figures at that time?

MOTHER: Right.

MARTIN'S MOTHER DESCRIBES HIM AT AGE SEVENTEEN

View of Martin's Development

MOTHER: He's changed a lot, he's become a lot more responsible and a lot more open, I think.

R. G.:   In what way?

MOTHER: He communicates well. It's been a struggle but he does, now finally he's able to put words to his feelings. He writes a lot of poetry and reads quite a bit of it to me, and it shows—to me it shows a sensitivity that I think is sort of unique in a seventeen-year-old boy, and I considered it also a real good, I guess, catharsis for him to really get his feelings down and put words to them. He is struggling along with a present girlfriend, a relationship that's difficult.

R. G.:   What else?

MOTHER: I try very hard to let him be independent, and it's probably easier with him than it will be for my two younger ones. It's easier for me to allow him to be independent. I'm not sure why, maybe because I sort of know who he is. And he's always been a good kid, a good-hearted kid. We've talked a lot about what he's going to do with his life, and all this new crisis with the girlfriends he communicates to me.

R. G.:   It sounds to me like your son is a very sensitive boy.

MOTHER: Yes, he is. That's why he's having girlfriend problems. A lot of it is that. We always used to say when he was real little, "Some girl's going to come along and put a ring in his nose and just tell him jump through this hoop and that." He's such a sweet guy, he'll be saying, "Okay, fine." He's a good kid. I'm very proud of him.

INTERVIEW WITH MARTIN AT AGE EIGHTEEN

Current Romantic Interests

R. G.:   What's your life been like since I saw you last?

MARTIN: Ups and downs. Some things more emotionally hectic, my girl-friend wants to be involved in my big senior deals, like prom—she wants to be involved with that. I don't know—just ups and downs. We had some distance, you know, got away from each other for a while and dated around. And as it is now, after some serious talking, it seems that we're gonna make a go of it, and I said, "If you're into it, hang in there, because it's good, and if you're not, don't fool yourself for me."

R. G.:   So you are seeing other people sexually also?

MARTIN: Yeah.

R. G.:   How is that for you?

MARTIN: Good, just good, just different. No one-night stands, just kinda different relationships on and off.

R. G.:   Are they very satisfying?

MARTIN: Yeah.

R. G.:   How many relationships have you had?

MARTIN: I haven't had many—three or four. And those relationships—some have been for about—they've been real, real good for about three months, and then things would change, and I just gotta get away from it, you know.

Theory of Heterosexuality

R. G.:   I'm going to ask you to make a theory. Lots of people who are always trying to develop theories about sexual behavior ask people to develop theories of how come they're a homosexual. How does homo-sexuality develop?* By contrast, I want to ask you to make up a theory of why you have evolved as heterosexual.

MARTIN: That's interesting. I think for me it might have started when I busted my mom and my dad making love, and that was really—you know, I was really young, and it's interesting that I still remember that and—let me think. They said, "We're going to go and hug and kiss for a while," and I thought that was cool, and it was about five o'clock, in the summer, and I was watching TV. And it got dark and I got lonely, and I just said, "God, they've been gone for a long time," you know. I opened the door and that was—Ahh!

R. G.:   How old were you?

MARTIN: Maybe six.

R. G.:   What did you see?

MARTIN: Well, at first, see, I peeked in. I didn't just announce myself, and I saw—well, they had blankets over both of them, so I saw him on top of her, and I had a good idea of what they were doing, and so I went back to my TV to see if I could watch it some more, and I got really lonely. So I went back, and they were done by the time I opened the door, and my dad was behind the door, and I go, "What're you doing with my mom?" And from that point, I thought that when I got older I would understand about what they were doing, and I guess that's what a man and woman do, you know, on a grown-up level. So in school, I remember, it was a big thing to kiss someone at

*See chapter 9.

school, and I just think that my attention was always focused on girls, you know, as far as sex goes. I didn't have—I never had a concept of having sexual attractions to a guy.

R. G.:   Did you know that some people did?

MARTIN: No, I never knew that until later on in life.

R. G.:   When did you first become aware of that?

MARTIN: I don't know how it came up, but I think about twelve, thirteen, when, you know, street language and all that—yeah—something like that—and I understood the concept, but I didn't know anyone and wasn't exposed to it, really.

R. G.:   And when that possibility became an awareness of yours, did that then seem like any kind of option for you?

MARTIN: No, because I was into women—just how I am, I guess. I understood what it was about, kinda—I understood the concept that guys and dolls—but that wasn't an option to me, just 'cause I didn't feel that way, and my friends didn't feel that way, and I viewed it as abnormal and something was wrong with them.

R. G.:   Do you think there's anything that your parents could have done earlier on in your life that might have influenced you towards becoming bisexual or homosexual? Let's assume that they had been different kinds of parents—you had a different relationship with them. Can you imagine a relationship such that it would have turned out that you would have had some sexual interest in guys?

MARTIN: That's a hard question. I guess they could have exposed me to their bisexuality, you know, if they were into that. They could have exposed me to—my mom could have said, "Yeah, this is my lover, so-and-so," and kiss or something, or my dad could have done that—something like that—and showed me that it was okay.

Theory of "Masculine" Development

R. G.:   Why do you think you developed conventional boyish interests? Because not all boys do. Some boys develop feminine interests, and some develop interests that are a sort of mixture—androgynous—partly boyish and partly girlish. How come you developed conventional boyish interests?

MARTIN: When you grow up with boys your own age or older or younger—like, I had friends that were from all ages, and just seeing how they act, you know, how conventional boys act and what they play, you know—cars and dolls—guy dolls and stuff—but it was more than that. I felt comfortable doing that, and I felt right, I think, and—I don't know, that was about it, I guess. I felt like I had that will to do those things. I had *enthusiasm* for those things.

These were representative transcripts of a selection of boys on their way to diverse points on the sexual identity spectrum. The examples suffer from not being as representative as some statisticians might wish, in that they are not reflections of each point that statistically distinguishes those "feminine" or "masculine" boys who evolved as homosexual, bisexual, or heterosexual. These descriptions are not easily reduced to correlation coefficients, stepwise linear discriminant function analyses, or other wonders of statistical science. On the other hand, they provide a more human picture of sexual identity development.

6

Psychological Tests, Media Preferences, Idols, and Vocational Goals

Some clinicians and researchers reduce people to factors derived from complex psychological tests. For them psychometric instruments provide the texture and color of human personality. Less exuberant supporters of psychological testing see it as providing a picture that is complementary to that obtained by clinical interviewing.

A merit of the psychological test is its standard format from person to person and the opportunity to compare the individual with "norms" derived from the larger population. A merit of the interview is its tailor-made suiting to the unique fabric of the individual's experiences. This study is replete with clinical interviewing. It would have been remiss to exclude psychological testing.

Psychological tests were administered to our subjects at initial evaluation and at follow-up. The tests given in boyhood were the It-Scale for Children (Brown, 1956) and the Draw-A-Person test (Machover, 1953). These tests have been used extensively in research on the sexual identity development of children, for both show differences between most boys and girls.

Tests utilized when the two groups were older were selected to provide a broad view of personality and to focus on specific features of personality. For the broader view, the age-appropriate Cattell Personality Factor Instruments were used (Cattell et al., 1957). These have the advantages of being geared to both teenage and adult years and of measuring several personality factors.

The Tennessee Self-Concept Scale (Fitts, 1965) was used because a measure of self-esteem should be an important dimension in persons who were stigmatized in boyhood and who may be living a stigmatized life-style in adulthood.

The Adjective Check List (Gough, 1952) was used because it measures additional self-described dimensions of personality and provides separate measures of psychological femininity and masculinity. The Bem Sex-Role Inventory (Bem, 1974) also provides measures of masculinity and femininity as separate dimensions and additionally permits classification of persons as highly masculine, highly feminine, high on both dimensions (androgynous), and low on both (undifferentiated).

While much of the clinical interviewing of the men described in this study focuses on sexual behaviors, these tests measure the men out of bed.

CHILDHOOD

It-Scale for Children

The It-Scale for Children presents the child with a "neuter" stick figure ("It"). The child holds the card on which "It" is drawn and then makes a series of selections for "It." The selections are from cards depicting sex-typed toys, clothes, and accessories, and boy and girl companions. There is also a series of four adults, one of whom "It" can be when grown up. These pictures include a conventionally depicted male and female, a masculine female, and a feminine male.

The It-Scale discriminates boys and girls as early as the third birthday. "Masculine" choices receive score points; "feminine" choices do not. Boys score about 68, girls about 33 (Rabban, 1950). Scores are not substantially influenced by intelligence within the average range (Epstein and Leverant, 1963) or by the sex of the person giving the test (Doll et al., 1971).

It-Scale scores for the two groups of boys in our study were very different. The behaviorally "feminine" boys' average score was in the range typically occupied by girls (47), while the contrast group's average score was in the conventional boys' range (74) (t = 5.81, df 93, $p<.001$).

The It-Scale is a rather "transparent" test. A sophisticated child wishing to conceal cross-gender interests can easily make conventional choices. We were thus skeptical of finding a group difference in the older half of our boys (eight to eleven years). However, even here there was a significant group difference (56 for the "feminine" boys; 78 for the "masculine" boys) (t = 3.80, df 44, $p<.001$).

Draw-A-Person

With the Draw-A-Person test, the subject is handed a piece of paper and asked to draw a person. The test may be scored simply or in complex fashion. Simply, the only scoring is whether one draws a male or a female. The sex of the person drawn first is presumed to reflect the drawer's sexual identity. From age five, about 80 percent of subjects draw a person of their own sex (Jolles, 1952). A more complex analysis, often used clinically, analyzes the maturity level of the drawing, the sex differentiation of drawings of male versus female, the relative size of male and female drawings, etc. (Koppitz, 1968). In its simple form the test is readily administered and scored by a psychiatrist. So, here I report the simple form.

The Draw-A-Person test findings were as distinctive as those with the It-Scale. While over 90 percent of the contrast group of boys drew a male first, only 46 percent of the behaviorally "feminine" boys drew a male first ($\chi^2 = 20.1$, $p<.001$).

The quality of figures drawn (beyond whether male or female) and the captions supplied may also be revealing. They may be quite elaborate for the boy's age (figure 6.1) or informative about identity (figure 6.2).

ADULTHOOD

Cattell Personality Factors

These tests are an age-graded, multidimensional set of questionnaire scales designed to provide information on sixteen personality dimensions. Thirty-six previously "feminine" boys scored differently from the same number of previously "masculine" boys on several scales.* They were more outgoing rather than reserved, more easily upset rather than calm, more tender-minded rather than tough-minded, more apprehensive rather than assured, more tense rather than relaxed, and more conservative rather than experimenting.

Previously "feminine" boys scored higher on anxiety, lower on tough-poise (meaning that they tend to "feel" rather than "think" their way through problems) (Krug, 1981, 13), lower on independence, and higher on neuroticism. Scale differences such as tender-mindedness and tough-poise can be construed as consistent with some qualities shown by these young men during earlier years. Their scoring as more easily upset, more tense, more anxious, and more neurotic could reflect social ostracism experienced during childhood.

Twenty-six previously "feminine" boys who are now homosexual or bisexual (from 2 to 6 on the scale of sexual orientation) scored differently from the ten who are now heterosexual (0 or 1 on the scale) on two factors: higher on tender-mindedness and lower on leadership.

---

*All group differences are analyzed by t-tests, with $p = .05$ or less, unless noted otherwise.

FIGURE 6.1   A four-year-old boy's picture of a female, drawn from fantasy (not copied).

FIGURE 6.2   A nine-and-a-half-year-old boy explained why he drew a female: "I tried a man, but I couldn't do it."

Tennessee Self-Concept Scale

This test consists of a hundred potentially self-descriptive terms, to be ranked by the subject on a five-point scale ranging from completely false to completely true.

Scores of thirty-five previously "feminine" boys compared to twenty-six previously "masculine" boys showed a few differences. The previously "feminine" boys scored lower on the subscales of self-satisfaction (self-acceptance) and physical self (which reflects a person's opinion of his body, state of health, physical appearance, skills, sexuality); and personal self (or personal worth), and higher on the neurosis subscale (which reflects the test-taker's similarity to neurotic patients). The groups of men did not differ on the subscales of moral ethical self (feelings of being a good or bad person), family self (feelings of adequacy as a family member), social self (sense of adequacy and worth in social interactions), general maladjustment, psychosis, personality disorder, personality integration, or the number of "deviant signs" (an indication of psychological disturbance).

There were no differences between the groups of previously "feminine" boys who are currently homosexual or bisexual and those who are heterosexual.

Thus, the formerly "feminine" and "masculine" groups differ on measures of self-acceptance and how they regard their body with respect to general state of health, physical appearance, physical skills, and sexuality. Considering the stigma of having been a "sissy" or of currently being homosexual, it is not surprising that these men have a less positive self-image. Considering the extent to which they were not adept at sports during boyhood, the fact that more were hospitalized in early childhood, and their current atypical pattern of sexuality, it is not surprising that a scale reflecting body state, skills, and sexuality would show these males to have a lower self-image.

As Gordon Allport observed some thirty years ago, "A child who finds himself rejected and attacked on all sides is not likely to develop dignity and poise as his outstanding traits. On the contrary, he develops defenses" (Allport, 1954).

Adjective Check List

This list consists of three hundred adjectives commonly used to describe a person's attributes. The individual taking the test indicates which adjectives from the list are accurate self-descriptions.

The thirty-one men in our study who had been "feminine" boys, compared to the twenty-five who had been "masculine," scored higher on the scale of succorance, or being more apt to solicit sympathy, affection, or emotional support from others. Adjectives which contribute to a high score are *appreciative, demanding, emotional, immature, self-centered, self-pitying, submissive,* and *whiny.* Those that yield a lower score include *aloof, confident, dominant, independent, indifferent, individualistic, mature, self-confident,* and *strong* (Gough and Heilbrun, 1965, 11).

The men who had been "feminine" boys scored higher on abasement, or the tendency to express feelings of inferiority through self-criticism, quiet, or social impotence. Adjectives contributing to a high score include *anxious, cowardly, despondent, gloomy, retiring, self-punishing, spineless,* and *timid.* Those that lower the score include *aggressive, arrogant, boastful, egotistical, hard-headed, independent,* and *self-confident.* Persons who score higher also appear to have problems of self-acceptance (1965, 11), making this difference consistent with a finding from the Tennessee Self-Concept Scale.

The men who had been "feminine" boys also scored higher on deference. Adjectives which contribute to a high score include *appreciative, cautious, cooperative, gentle, obliging,* and *peaceable.* Those that lower the score include *opinionated, tactless, aggressive, boastful,* and *headstrong.*

The men who had been "feminine" boys tended to score lower on dominance ($p = .06$). Adjectives which contribute to a low score include *dependent, easygoing, fearful, lazy, mild,* and *shy.* Those that elevate the score include *aggressive, ambitious, confident, determined, forceful,* and *outgoing.*

Several scales that might have been predicted to discriminate the groups did not. There was only a very weak trend for the previously "feminine" boys to score lower on self-confidence ($p = .18$) and dominance ($p = .12$). On "readiness for psychological counseling" there was only a trend for them to score higher ($p = .08$). Considering that there are twenty-three test scales, these last "trends" are probably artifacts of the number of scales tested, with more scales increasing the probability of finding group "differences." Other scales which showed very little or no numerical difference between the groups included personal adjustment, achievement, and aggression.

Next, we compare twenty-two previously "feminine" boys who evolved as bisexual or homosexual with the nine who evolved as heterosexual. The homosexual/bisexual subgroup scored lower on dominance, higher on readiness to receive counseling, and tended to score higher on abasement ($p = .08$) and lower on heterosexuality ($p = .06$).

Subsequent to the development of the original Adjective Check List scales, separate "masculine" and "feminine" scales were derived (Heilbrun, 1976). Of the three hundred adjectives, twenty-eight "masculine" items, and twenty-six "feminine" items were extracted, based on score differences between samples of "masculine" males and "feminine" females. Some "masculine" adjectives are *aggressive, autocratic, dominant, inventive, self-confident,* and *shrewd.* Some "feminine" adjectives are *considerate, dependent, excitable, frivolous, sensitive, timid,* and *worrying.* When scores on the standardized masculine and feminine scales (that is, standardized by number of adjectives checked; ACL Manual, 64, 93) were compared, previously "feminine" boys scored significantly higher than the comparison group on the standardized feminine scale, but not significantly lower on the standardized masculine scale.

The twenty-two previously "feminine" boys who are now homosexual or bisexual differed slightly from the nine who are now heterosexual. There was a tendency for more "feminine" adjectives to be checked by the bisexual or homosexual men (17.2 versus 14.7; $p = .10$). Again, there was no difference in the number of "masculine" adjectives checked, but there was a trend for the "M-F" score to be higher for the bisexual or homosexual men (-5.20 versus -0.78; $p = .06$).

Thus, the Adjective Check List provides evidence of developmental continuity between cross-gender behavior in boyhood and sex-typed self-descriptions in manhood. It also suggests more "psychological femininity" for the homosexual men.

Bem Sex-Role Inventory

This is a sixty-item test where the individual indicates on a seven-point scale the extent to which each item is a valid self-description.

For the thirty-five previously "feminine" boys versus twenty-two previously "masculine" boys, there were no differences in the percent of subjects scoring as masculine, feminine, androgynous, or undifferentiated. Comparing the twenty-five previously "feminine" boys who are currently homosexual or bisexual with the ten who are heterosexual, there were also no differences.

Thus, scores on the Bem Sex-Role Inventory are not consistent with the differences found on the separate masculine and feminine scales of the Adjective Check List. Two possible reasons for the discrepancy are the different self-descriptions asked of the respondent and the different manner of scoring the tests.

TEST SCORE SUBSCALES THAT SEPARATE THE GROUPS

These test results were also analyzed to determine whether any subscales, taken as a cluster, discriminated the men. Three subgroups were formed: previously "feminine" boys who are now homosexual or bisexual; previously "feminine" boys who are now heterosexual; and previously "masculine" boys who are now heterosexual. This division was to determine whether score differences were more characteristic of previously "feminine" versus "masculine" boys, or of currently heterosexual versus bisexual or homosexual males. A discriminant function analysis was performed (described in chapter 3). Due to the interrelation of subscales, different individual subscales that distinguished our groups (as described above) may not differentiate groups when the subscales are considered conjointly.

On the Cattell tests, previously "feminine," currently homosexual or bisexual males scored higher on the first function or cluster of scales, which included those for tender-mindedness, a warmhearted and outgoing manner, and overwroughtness and fretfulness. There was a gradient for the three subgroups in their scores on this function; the "feminine" boy, homosexual/bisexual males scored highest, followed by the "feminine" boy, heterosexual males, and then the "masculine" boy, heterosexual males. Thus, neither earlier gender role status nor current sexual orientation was more strongly associated with this function. On the second function or cluster of scales (a less powerful discriminator of the groups than the first), the previously "feminine," currently homosexual or bisexual males scored similarly to the previously "masculine," currently heterosexual males. The scales in the function characterizing these groups describe persons who are shy, dominant, and calm. These scores were less characteristic of the previously "feminine," currently heterosexual males. Thus, for the second function there was no clear pattern regarding earlier gender status and current sexual orientation. These two functions discriminated correctly 76 percent of the three groups.

On the Tennessee Self-Concept Scales, previously "feminine," currently homosexual or bisexual males scored higher on the function composed of scales for neurosis, family self, and identity, and lower on the scale for self-criticism. The neurosis and family-self scales were previously defined. The identity scale reflects on the manner in which a person sees himself. Low scores on the self-criticism scales indicate psychological defensiveness rather than a healthy capacity for self-criticism. The second, weaker function included contributions from the number of deviant signs and the scales of personality integration, identity, and social self. Previously "feminine," currently heterosexual males scored highest on this function, while previously "feminine," currently homosexual or bisexual males and previously "masculine," currently heterosexual males scored lower and similarly to each other. Thus, no clear pattern relating gender role or sexual orientation emerged. These two functions classified correctly 72 percent of the groups.

Finally, on the Adjective Check List, currently homosexual or bisexual males scored higher on the first function, characterized by the scales of succorance, nurturance (inclination toward behavior that benefits others), and change (seeking of novel experiences). Previous gender role status per se was not associated with these scores, since previously "feminine" and previously "masculine" heterosexual males scored similarly. On the second function the discriminating scales were heterosexuality (characterized as seeking the companionship of peers of the opposite sex), intraception (attempting to understand oneself or others), and lability (spontaneity and flexibility). Previously "feminine," currently heterosexual males had the highest score on this function, while previously "feminine," currently homosexual or bisexual and previously "masculine," currently heterosexual males had lower scores, respectively. No pattern relating to gender role or sexual orientation emerged here. These two functions correctly classified 60 percent of the groups.

(A more extensive report of these psychological test results can be found in Green, Williams, and Mixon, 1987.)

Finally, an editorial point about males who live their lives at varying points on the continuum of psychological masculinity or femininity. Scoring as highly masculine may not be the social ideal for men; Charles Manson, Idi Amin, and Adolf Hitler would probably have had more masculine scores than John Lennon, Martin Luther King, Jr., and Franklin Roosevelt.

MAGAZINE PREFERENCES, MASS MEDIA IDOLS, AND VOCATIONAL GOALS

Magazine preferences for the two groups during adolescence and young adulthood differed. *Gentlemen's Quarterly* (*GQ*) is a magazine devoted to men's fashions, featuring an array of young adult, decorous male models. The seven men who named *GQ* as their favorite magazine had been "feminine" boys. Six were currently homosexual or bisexual men. One previously "feminine" boy selected *Vogue*, a women's fashion magazine. The four men who selected *People*, a glossy, gossipy weekly, were previously "feminine" boys, three of whom were homosexual or bisexual men. Sports and science magazines were more often selected by the previously "masculine" boys.

While there was not a great difference in the types of movies preferred by the two groups, there was a difference in the gender of their favorite movie or television idol. Females were more often mentioned by the "feminine boy" group. At ages thirteen to fifteen, thirteen of sixteen males who selected a female were in the "feminine boy" group. At age sixteen or older, fourteen of sixteen who selected a female were in the "feminine boy" group.

Vocational goals also distinguished the groups. At ages thirteen to fifteen, *all sixteen boys* who aspired to be actors were previously "feminine." Five of the eight who wanted to be doctors were previously "feminine." By contrast, all boys who wanted to be lawyers, athletes, engineers, or pilots were previously "masculine." At age sixteen or older, all seven boys who aspired to be actors were previously "feminine"; one aspired to be an "actress."

The contrast in vocational goals was not nearly as sharp between the "feminine" boys who were to emerge as heterosexual versus those who were to emerge as bisexual or homosexual. Eight of the sixteen boys who wanted to be actors at ages thirteen to fifteen emerged as homosexual or bisexual, as did one of the five aspiring doctors. At age sixteen or older, all three men who wanted to be models were in the homosexual/bisexual subgroup. Three who wanted to be writers or filmmakers were in the homosexual/bisexual subgroup, as were all three aspiring teachers. Only one previously "masculine" boy wanted to be a model, and none writers. Three wanted to be teachers and three computer scientists. The previously "masculine" boy group also included aspiring athletes, a housepainter, a truck driver, and an underwater welder.

The association between boyhood "femininity" and an interest in acting is not a new finding. It was described some twenty years ago in my pilot study of "feminine" boys conducted with John Money (1966). In that earlier sample, nine of twenty boys showed a striking capacity for role-taking and stage acting. We noted:

It is commonly accepted that many homosexuals are found in the entertainment field, as in the acting profession. While there has been no adequate survey to verify this belief, reference to its authenticity runs the gamut from the classic psychoanalytic works of Otto Fenichel to a recent essay in *Time Magazine*. Fenichel said: "The percentage of homosexuals seems to be higher among actors than in most other professions" (Fenichel, 1945). *Time* said: ". . . in Hollywood, you have to scrape them off the ceiling" (*Time*, 1966).

Two immediate explanations emerge for the coincidence of homosexuality and a career in theater. One is that both derive from a common or related feature of early life, and the other is that the theater, because of the presence of many persons with "alternate life-styles," provides a social sanctuary for homosexuals. Certainly the stigma is less than it would be in the field of neurosurgery (Messer, 1979).

In the earlier study we saw the playacting of those boys serving as both an "extension of effeminate role-taking" and "a device that gave a certain respectability to behaving as a girl." For those boys, drama "was a roundabout and socially permissible excuse for feminine dressing. . . . Dressing up was replaced by costuming and makeup" (Green and Money, 1966).

With this new, larger group we also have data on the relative extent of participation in role-playing games, specifically playing house. The "feminine boy" group participated more (chapter 1). For boyhood participation in playacting generally, the "feminine" boys also participated significantly more ($t = 7.5$, df 104, $p < .001$.) And again, in this new group, interest in acting as a career began early in life, before the social sanctuary of such a career would be apparent to most boys.

Example

MOTHER: SON AGE SEVEN

In school he takes a part in each play. He's not one of these children that lets others take the parts. He is in each and every one—he does love to playact, and this is part of his personality.

SON: AGE EIGHTEEN

SON: Just Friday I got the lead in the musical this year. It's very exciting. And I'm applying to theater school.

R. G.:   When you were younger, did you have any interest in theater or acting?

SON: Role-playing. I have a very vivid imagination, and I would have my favorite record and I would sing it every day. I would memorize all the words. So I was always interested in it. I thought it was very magical—the whole thing, I loved it.

An additional impetus to some of these boys gravitating toward acting and theater may be peer acceptance. These boys find approval in drama classes and acting schools, where they can share their interests with others, a commonality previously denied them because of their aversion to rough-and-tumble play and sports.

CONCLUSION

Males who are distinctive in sex-role attributes in boyhood remain psychologically distinctive during young manhood. How they remain distinctive is partly a function of continued sex-typing. Some tests that discriminate them in adulthood are those that typically separate males and females. But others are general personality variables. These may relate to the social consequences of having cross-gender attributes earlier in life or to their current homosexual life-styles.

The question, "Is homosexuality a mental disorder?" sparked a debate in the 1970s that generated nuclear heat but only candlelight. Part of the debate focused on psychological test results. When I reviewed these about fifteen years ago, there was no strong evidence supporting the homosexuality = mental illness equation. Our new data reveal that most of the psychological test differences shown by our groups of homosexual or bisexual men and heterosexual men are consistent with the effects of having experienced a stigmatized lifestyle. Others reflect differences on attributes for which judgments of desirability are value judgments, such as independence versus dependence or aggressiveness versus passivity. These differences do not paint a picture of mental disorder. Furthermore, clinical interviewing and hours of conversations do not reveal any, in either group, as overtly psychotic. Each group has its share of characterological personality disorders and neurotic disorders. Each has men who are making it interpersonally, romantically, sexually, and vocationally. Each has men who are deficient.

The boyhood "femininity" of most of our males has dissipated (chapter 5). How it remains, varies. One man wishes to be a woman and three continue to cross-dress periodically. However, interviews with others do not reveal gross residual "femininity."

What is not heard in the interviews in chapter 5 is that some men talk with a body language that our culture defines as "feminine" or labels "effeminate." They speak as though they were players on a stage, not as idlers on a street corner. What cannot be seen in chapter 5 is that, during the interview, some men in the previously "feminine boy" group sit upright with legs crossed rather than slouched with legs spread. They are groomed carefully and dressed stylishly rather than carelessly and casually. When entering the office, they walk with steps half a foot apart rather than a full foot. They idolize Judy Garland, not John Wayne. They read *Gentlemen's Quarterly*, not *Road and Track*. They would rather be on the stage at Stratford than on the football field at Dallas.

But there is also overlap. Some of the previously "feminine" boys are indistinguishable in appearance and manner from some of the previously "masculine" boys. These men are neither coarse, nor fine; neither "macho," nor "swish." What they do *in* bed is not apparent from their style *out* of bed.

7

Psychotherapy and
What It Did

To treat or not to treat? Considerable controversy has surrounded the diagnosis and treatment of extensive cross-gender behavior in children. Prior to its inclusion in the American Psychiatric Association's list of mental disorders in 1980, there was no official recognition of extensive cross-gender behavior as a psychiatric syndrome, and less official rationale for treatment.

The first plank in the diagnostic platform of the new "gender identity disorder of childhood" is strong discontentment with being a boy—a cross-sex *identity*. Later planks are cross-gender *behaviors*, such as cross-dressing. Therapeutic interventions directed at these two types of "symptoms" differ considerably, as do their immediate and long-range implications.

Discontentment with being a male, beginning during childhood, is heard repeatedly in the histories of male-to-female transsexuals (chapter 1). The developmental road of the adult transsexual is pocked with psychological potholes. Even if the person eventually obtains sex-change surgery, the long-term outcome remains guarded. And the scars of years of conflict can never be removed. For the child, discontentment with being a male cannot be alleviated by sex-change surgery. Therefore, psychological intervention directed at increasing comfort with being male has a commonsense rationale, for both the short and the long term.

Gender-role behaviors, on the other hand, are cultural artifacts. The demands that boys play with trucks, and girls with dolls, that boys wear pants and girls dresses, can be seen as whims of tradition. If so, should psychotherapy be directed at unfastening culturally deviant links between anatomic sex and gender-role behaviors? Cross-gender-role behaviors may be the only signal of major discontentment with being male. As such, they represent more than benign nonconformity.

Controversy resulted from the evaluation of the boys in this long-term study. Some critics claimed that the findings would be used to reinforce patterns of rearing children in stereotypical sex roles. Controversy also resulted from some parents electing to modify their sons' extensive cross-sex identity with professional treatment. This was labeled "homosexual genocide."

Most parents in our study elected not to seek therapy for their child's cross-gender behaviors, but rather to try gently to discourage the behaviors as they occurred. On the other hand, a minority of the parents entered their sons into a formal treatment program.

Should parents have the prerogative of choosing therapy for their gender-atypical son? Suppose that boys who play with dolls rather than trucks, who role-play as mother rather than as father, and who play only with girls tend disproportionately to evolve as homosexual men. Suppose that parents know this, or suspect this. The rights of parents to oversee the development of children is a long-established principle. Who is to dictate that parents may not try to raise their children in a manner that maximizes the possibility of a heterosexual outcome? If that prerogative is denied, should parents also be denied the right to raise their children as atheists? Or as priests?

The "pro-treatment lobby" was fueled primarily by the fervor of George Rekers and other UCLA psychologists. They argued that they were treating cross-dressing behavior not only because it was a stimulus for social criticism, but also "to prevent adult transvestic sexual difficulties." Further, "for the gender-identity-disturbed boy (where the boy expresses the desire to be, or the belief that he is, a girl), there is the added need for treatment since he is at high risk for adult transsexualism" (Rosen et al, 1978, 124).

Social stigma was another basis for intervention, with therapy designed "to alleviate the present state of discomfort and to prevent future unhappiness" (127). To these clinicians, not to intervene is wrong: "Psychologists must take seriously the complaint of the parents regarding the child's behavior, since the parent is the legal agent responsible for the well-being of the child. . . . It would be unethical for the psychologist not to assist the parents . . . in providing intervention techniques currently held to have the greatest therapeutic potential" (130).

Addressing themselves to a possible homosexual outcome, these psychologists asserted, "If a parent brings a child to a psychologist and asks that the possibility of homosexual development be prevented, is this not an ethical and professionally proper goal for the psychologist? We conclude yes" (132). Earlier, Rekers and his colleagues categorically stated that "once parents and professionals have concluded that a boy has a gender disturbance, a therapist cannot ethically refuse to treat the child" (Rekers et al, 1977, 9).

Gay activist attacks on the Rekers program were not cushioned. It was called "pernicious," and "the most insidious attempt to stamp out the development of gay identity in young children" (Morin and Schultz, 1978, 142).

Less strident and more scholarly objections to treatment noted the imprecision with which "gender problem" boys are identified (Wolfe, 1979). It was pointed out, for example, that some boys whose behaviors are not conventionally "masculine"—perhaps because they have motor-skill behavioral deficits—are nevertheless content being males. This last criticism correctly addresses the *significance* of the gender-type behaviors to the boy. However, its author went on to state, "At this juncture no compelling evidence exists to support the belief that effeminate behavior in childhood will affect later sexual preference" (Wolfe, 1979, 567). In fact, by 1979, there was already a substantial body of evidence linking cross-gender behavior in boyhood with homosexual behavior in manhood (for example, the studies of Bieber, Evans, Saghir and Robins, Zuger, Lebovitz, Green, Green and Money, and Money and Russo [cited in chapters 1 and 10]).

Time has not honored the dire prediction of the Rekers group for the consequences of withholding therapy. Transvestism has not been the outcome of any previously "feminine" boy in our untreated sample, and transsexualism has evolved in only one. Nor has therapy achieved the goal of aborting homosexual arousal or "temptations" (Rekers's current term; Rekers, 1982[a], 131). My interviews with two males who went through the Rekers treatment regimen in boyhood find both to be bisexual. One is reported extensively below.

Kenneth Zucker (1985) has pointed out scientific inconsistencies in the various treatment reports by the Rekers group as well as alternative explanations and interpretations of their findings. To me, the basic strategy of Rekers's treatment model, which is based on operant-conditioning, can be faulted in that it ignores the *motivation* behind the child's behaviors. While specific "feminine" behaviors are punished and "masculine" behaviors rewarded in that treatment model, this approach ignores reasons *why* the boy prefers traditionally "feminine" activities. Why has he chosen to play with dolls and not trucks? Is it only that he has been previously "conditioned" to make these preferences? Simply conditioning the boy so that he obtains rewards for alternate behaviors and is punished for earlier preferences may make the child *look* different. But to what extent is self-concept changed?

I have even more difficulty with the moralistic basis that has recently been revealed behind Rekers's attempts to "treat" these children. That basis is described in his books, *Shaping Your Child's Sexual Identity* (1982) and *Growing Up Straight* (1982). The goal of treatment is to promote "real masculinity, which should be affirmed in every young man in order to prevent them from being strongly tempted by the sexual perversions" (Rekers, 1982[a], 112). Homosexuality is "an unfortunate perversion" and a manifestation of "promiscuous and perverted sexual behavior" (1982[a], 85). Rekers states that "persons afflicted with these abnormal sexual conditions have historically realized that their sexual conduct is...a sinful yielding to temptation" and that "homosexuality has been sold to the unwary public as a right between consenting adults" (1982[a], 87–88).

My treatment strategy for reducing extensive sexual identity conflict in children, as exercised in the late 1960s and early 1970s, was summarized in my 1974 book:

> The boy's contact with his father and with his male peers may be augmented by participation in some local program such as "Indian Guides." Many of their activities are of a non-competitive nature including excursions, outdoor cooking, and handicrafts. These boys should not be hurtled into Little League....
>
> Boys feeling unable to compete in rough-and-tumble aggressive play may, with the logic of early childhood, choose the "only" alternative: being with girls and adopting their behavior. But another choice is available: they may build, draw, read, play board games, and play with boys who are not wholly sports- and roughhouse-minded. Fathers may be overly demanding of their sons, expecting them to be athletic and aggressive. The boys' inability to meet these fathers' definition of "masculinity" may cause them to view father and his activities as negative and to draw closer to mother and her activities. Such fathers can be encouraged to engage their sons in activities within their *mutual* interest and competence....
>
> Non-aggressive male peers can be invited home after school or on weekends, to provide a not-so-threatening peer relationship for the feminine boy....
>
> Some boys reveal their feminine identifications through physical gestures. The importance of feminine mannerisms lies in its effect on peers and the resultant social feedback. A feminine-appearing boy will be labeled "sissy" and set apart from other boys....
>
> We hope we can reduce their current pain and permit them a wider range of social options in the future. (Green, 1974, 278–79, 308)

A broader social view was also taken:

> Treatment intervention...focused on helping these people adjust to their society. What can be done to help society adjust to these people? Can the behavioral scientist also be effective as a social activist? Can the researcher/therapist modify societal attitudes so that atypical sexual

life-styles which do not infringe on the liberties of others do not cause conflict for the atypical individual? (302)

Twelve boys in our long-term study entered a formal treatment program. Treatment formats included behavior modification (such as that described by Rekers et al, 1977), group therapy with the boys and with their parents (Green and Fuller, 1973[b]), individual therapy with the boys and with their parents (Green, Newman, and Stoller, 1972), and psychoanalytic therapy with the boy (Greenson, 1968).

The next section presents two treatment examples, with follow-up. Nick and his parents entered a family-based psychotherapy program with me. Kyle entered a behavior modification program, as described by Rekers and his colleagues.

FAMILY THERAPY: NICK

NICK'S MOTHER DESCRIBES HIM AT AGE SIX

Overview

MOTHER: The first thing I noticed one day at a friend's house—she has four little girls. He likes to go over there, and he likes to go back in their room and play with their dolls. He went back there and grabbed a doll and wanted to make a dress. He took Kleenex and paper towels and tore them and folded them and poked holes in them and really made a very attractive dress with these dolls. And my friend commented on it and said, "Gee, I think he's going to be a dress designer."

R. G.: How old was he?

MOTHER: He was four, four-and-a-half. You know, I don't know what I'm afraid of—if it's homosexuality. I even hate the word.

R. G.: What else?

MOTHER: I think a lot of it is that he likes the sight of feminine things. He would tie aprons around himself. I got so that I never kept aprons in the house any more, because he'd get my aprons and tie them around him—here up at his shoulder and under his arms—to make a nice long skirt, and would go around the house in aprons. He'd have to have an apron tied around up here with a nice full skirt, and then one tied around his head to make a nice flowing hood. He would go around the house in two aprons like this. Like an old lady. It got so that if there was nobody in the house I would let him do it. It got so that we were taking aprons and just sticking them places and hiding them, and even today I go around and find aprons wadded clear back on closet shelves where we had tried to hide them, just in a fit of panic.

R. G.:   How would others react?

MOTHER: His grandmother lived here, and we used to come and visit, and he'd get to her house and go right to the kitchen and get an apron and start tying it around him as a long skirt with the long hood. She thought it was kind of cute, you know.

R. G.:   Are there other things which concern you?

MOTHER: He won't play with boys. They tease him. He has said he wants to be a girl. I don't know if it should worry me or not. That's why I am here. Maybe it's something that he can grow out of. Maybe it's something that he's going to need some help to grow out of.

Relationship between Nick and His Grandmother

MOTHER: There was a strange, unnatural love between them. When he was three weeks old, Grandma said to us, "Go out for a walk." When we got back she was sitting in that old rocker. Just rocking him. I've never seen her so delighted. He was happy as a clown. I remember when he was eleven months, he recognized her from a car two blocks away, with trees and sunlight. He went like this—he was waving his arms. He stopped it as soon as we drove up and got by her. She'd visit every six or eight weeks. She'd sit and rock him. Grandmother was always out in the kitchen. She would wear an apron. If she visited, she would even bring her own apron. He tried to emulate her. The minute she would come in the house, he would put on an apron. We have a picture of him improvising an apron from a dishtowel that was taken when he was twenty-eight months. Grandma was very reserved, but with this boy she danced around the room and giggled like a little girl. Before she died she said, "Tell him how much I love him. We are tuned in on the same beam."

Genital Surgery and Additional Maternal Attention

MOTHER: He had a lot of illnesses. He has had a lot of history of ear infection.

R. G.:   When was that?

MOTHER: Oh, it started when he was less than a year. Finally with the backache, they sent me to a surgeon. He did surgery on him about a year ago. He was there three different times. He came up once for a couple of pieces of surgery through the penis with the cystoscope.

R. G.:   During those early illnesses, did he require special care in any way?

MOTHER: Yes, I guess. The fever scared me. I would have done anything to get rid of the fever. And then a lot of times, many visits to the doctor, you know, that other children don't have—and then, of course, the surgery. He's had the cystoscope and catheters and everything else up his penis, and the blood—and he had a little narrow place at the tip of the penis, all up and down that tube, and they had to cut that and widen it in some way. So there's been enough to terrify him, really.

R. G.: How did this affect the way you treated him?

MOTHER: He was sick so often that I would have done anything to keep him well. Other mothers would send their kids out in the water or out in the wet sand or out in the high wind, and here I would always have little caps tied around him. He'd go in swimming, and I'm there with a Q-Tip, you know, going around the ear. And all the other mothers— the kids running around with wet heads, you know, and I'm following him around with towels trying to wipe his ears out. I just couldn't see another earache. He was getting all this extra attention and concern. He's probably just geared to that. "Put your hat on. Zip up your jacket." Whereas my other boy can run around, and I hardly say anything. I figure if he's cold, he's going to come in and do something about it. I'm sure I've overly cautioned him.

MOTHER'S NOTES OF NICK'S PRESCHOOL BEHAVIOR

The boy's preoccupation with aprons and his relationship with his grandmother are highlighted in these preschool notes made by his mother when he was three.

Three Years, Two Months

He seems to pick out dolls to play with rather than the trikes, trains, etc. He seems to identify with me and his grandmother more than his father and grandfather. I really think it is grandmother more than me. He adores her. For the last two months or so he has insisted on wearing an apron—calls it his "dress." He stands out on the beach and likes to watch the wind blow his "skirt." He insists on wearing his dress to bed. He carefully arranges the dress so it falls in folds when he sits down. We have tried to discourage his interest in dresses.

At night, if he wants a drink of milk, he screams if his daddy brings it. He insists that *I* do. Sometimes he tends to turn on his father and will not permit him to help him or comfort him at night if he has a bad dream.

Three Years, Three Months

We went to his grandmother's. She always has on an apron, and the minute he walked in the house he found an apron and wore it the entire day. His father and I have gotten rather touchy about this and tried to pry it off him, but no luck. In fact, the next day in describing his trip and visit to a friend, the highlight of the day was that he "wore Grandma's apron."

He has been talking about his grandmother all week—he wears his apron "just like Grandma." All older ladies in books he calls "grandmother." He goes to sleep with that page of the book open so he can "go to sleep with Grandma."

At home, when watching TV, he likes the musical programs, especially with girls in long dresses, and dancing. He comments, "See their *long* dresses," and proceeds to lower his apron down to his ankles. My husband and I are both concerned regarding his obsession for dresses. He still goes around wearing an apron all day. Sometimes two aprons. He says he is "Grandma."

Three Years, Six Months

He still wears his apron around the house all day. He takes off the pajamas and wears the apron to bed all night. In school, he picked up Raggedy Ann as soon as he walked in the door—took off her apron and tried to put in on himself.

TREATMENT

The boy and his parents were seen weekly for about three years. My goal with the boy was to understand his reasons for wanting to be a girl and the appeal of girl-type behaviors. My goal with his parents was to discourage any support of his cross-gender behaviors, and to encourage boyish behaviors that were compatible for father and son. Sometimes the boy and his parents were seen conjointly, sometimes separately.

The excerpts and notes that follow are representative of interviews and treatment sessions that spanned the three years. During an early session with the boy, the irrevocability of being a boy or a girl was stressed. An office fish tank stocked with guppies became the therapist's ally.

INTERVIEW WITH NICK AT AGE SIX

Here the boy is given the Draw-A-Person test (chapter 6).
R. G.:   Could you draw a picture of a person for me?
NICK: Yes.
R. G.:   Okay, tell me when you're finished. . . . Oh, that's nice—very nice. Who is that?
NICK: Mary Poppins.
R. G.:   That's very nice. Now can you turn it over and draw a picture of a man on the other side? . . . Okay, that's a man. Who is that?

NICK: Uh—Dick.

R. G.: Who is Dick?

NICK: It's a friend of this lady here.

Interest in Cross-dressing

R. G.: Do you ever sometimes like to dress up like Mary Poppins?

NICK: Sometimes. No, all the time.

R. G.: Can you tell me how you dress up to make yourself look like Mary Poppins?

NICK: Well, I take a sheet and put it around me and then I hold it around me. Then I wrap a blue blanket around me and I look like Mary Poppins.

R. G.: What do you do when you look like Mary Poppins?

NICK: I make a umbrella out of Tinker Toys.

R. G.: Do you act like Mary Poppins?

NICK: Well—yeah.

R. G.: Can you show me how you act like Mary Poppins?

NICK: See, I go up on my foot, and then I jump off with my umbrella and go, "Whoo..."

Mother's Reaction to Cross-dressing

R. G.: Does your mommy see you play?

NICK: Yeah, and sometimes I have a baby-sitter there.

R. G.: Do you like playing more when your mother's there or when she's not there?

NICK: When my mommy's not there.

R. G.: How come?

NICK: Because she doesn't want me to play.

R. G.: Why doesn't she?

NICK: 'Cause she afraid I might go out the gate [dressed up like that].

R. G.: Have you ever gone out dressed like Mary Poppins?

NICK: Uh-uh. 'Cause every time my mommy saw me.

R. G.: I see. You think people might not understand why you dress up that way?

NICK: Because I'm a boy and boys aren't supposed to dress—go out dressing like girls. My mommy has to make me stay in the house.

Peer Group's Reaction to Nick's Cross-dressing

R. G.: You like to dress up like a girl sometimes?

NICK: Not all the time. If I dress like a girl when a friend comes over, they won't want to play with me.

R. G.: Why is that?

NICK: Well, because, see, a boy is a boy and a girl is a girl, so they want to go home.

R. G.: I see. But sometimes you like to play as a girl if you can? Can you tell me which you like better to dress up as, a girl or as a boy?

NICK: Oh, I don't know—as a boy.

Preference for Being a Boy rather than a Girl

R. G.: You know, sometimes little boys your age wonder whether it's possible for them to become little girls. I wonder if you ever think about that.

NICK: I think about that. I think that it's possible for them to become—sometimes I don't want to be a girl and sometimes I want to be one.

R. G.: What's nice about being a girl?

NICK: Uh—nothing much.

R. G.: Must be something you like about it, if you want to be one sometimes.

NICK: Well, girls don't have to fight. Sometimes girls scream, and then I scream and then I get mixed up with them.

Possibility of Changing Sex

R. G.: Tell me this, do you think it's possible for little boys like you to become little girls?

NICK: Yeah, it's possible.

R. G.: Tell me how you think it can happen.

NICK: I mean, it *isn't* possible.

R. G.: Oh, it's not possible. Do you know why it's not possible?

NICK: Uh-uh.

R. G.: Can you tell me how little boys are different from little girls?

NICK: Because girls have long hair and boys have short hair.

R. G.: Is there anything else that's different?

NICK: No.

R. G.: Try to think. Maybe you do know some of the answers.

NICK: Girls wear dresses and boys wear pants. That's all I can think of.

R. G.: Are little boys and girls built the same way, or are their bodies different in some way?

NICK: Their bodies are different.

R. G.: Can you tell me how they are different?

NICK: Uh—well, girls don't have to fight and boys do. That's one good thing about it. That's all I can think of.

R. G.: Is your mommy's body the same as your daddy's body?

NICK: Uh-uh.

R. G.: No? How are they different?

NICK: Mommy wears a dress all the time, Daddy wears pants all the time, and Mommy has long hair.

R. G.: Do you think if someone had long hair—let's say you have a boy or a man, okay, and this boy or man has long hair and wears a dress. Does that make him a girl or is he still a boy?

NICK: He's still a girl.

R. G.: He's a girl?

NICK: Uh-huh.

R. G.: You mean if a boy lets his hair grow—let's say down to here—and he puts on a dress—that turns the little boy into a girl? Or is he still a boy?

NICK: He's a little girl.

R. G.: Not really.

NICK: I know.

R. G.: You know?

NICK: 'Cause he's still a little boy.

R. G.: He's a boy who's dressing up like a little girl.

NICK: That's just got long hair down to here.

R. G.: That doesn't make him a girl, does it? Do you know why it doesn't make him a girl?

NICK: 'Cause it's just like a Beatle.

R. G.: Uh-huh. The Beatles have long hair.

NICK: It's just like a Beatle wearing a dress.

R. G.: Right, and why wouldn't the Beatles be girls if they wore a dress?

NICK: Because they play a guitar, and ladies can't play a guitar.

R. G.: Oh, some ladies can play a guitar, but there's something even more than that.

NICK: Well, they'd be wearing pants all the time if they had to go on TV.

A Lesson in Sex Differences

R. G.: It's even more than that. Something about the body is different, too, isn't it? Do you know where little babies come from?

NICK: No.

R. G.: Well, let's look at these tropical fish on my window ledge.

NICK: I have a mommy guppy and a pappa guppy.

R. G.: Do you know where the baby fish come from?

NICK: From under there.

R. G.: From under where?

NICK: See, it's right under her fat place.

R. G.: Right, the mother carries the little baby fish. Okay, now can a daddy fish carry the babies too?

NICK: No.

R. G.: That's right. So that's another difference between boys and girls—isn't it?

NICK: See, here's the fat place. And then the mama has babies?

R. G.: Right. So then that's only in the mommy fish. Now, do you think if that daddy fish wanted to become a mommy fish he could do it?

NICK: No.

R. G.: Why couldn't he?

NICK: Because he would not have the same thing that babies come out of.

R. G.: That's right. His body is different from the mommy fish. Just like the bodies of little boys are different from the bodies of little girls. Now what if the daddy fish were to dress up and look like a little girl fish?

NICK: He'd just have to paint his self ugly.

R. G.: And he wouldn't be a girl, because his body would still be different.

NICK: Yes.

R. G.: Now, is your body different from the body of a little girl, do you think?

NICK: Uh-huh.

R. G.: Have you ever seen a little girl undressed?

NICK: No.

R. G.: Have you ever seen your mommy undressed?

NICK: Yes.

R. G.: And have you seen your daddy undressed?

NICK: Uh-huh.

R. G.: And can you tell me how your mommy's body is different from your daddy's body?

NICK: Well, uh, they don't have the same kiki. A kiki is on the bottom.

R. G.: They have different bottoms. Can you tell me how it's different?

NICK: Well, the daddy has a long kiki and the mommy has a short kiki.

R. G.: Yes. And the inside's different because the mommy has a place to hold little babies.

NICK: I know, and the daddy's breast is little and the mommy's breast is big.

R. G.: That's right.

NICK: So, if the Beatles are dressed up like they're girls and they went somewhere, and they'd say, "Look at that sissy." You could tell, because they wouldn't have a big thing sticking out.

R. G.: That's right. They're called breasts.

NICK: Uh-huh.

R. G.: Is your kiki more like your daddy's or like your mommy's?

NICK: Like my daddy's.

R. G.: That's right.

NICK: Only daddy's is bigger.

R. G.: Because he's a bigger person. He's a bigger man, and you're a little man. And how about when you grow up—what do you think is going to happen?

NICK: Be like my daddy.

R. G.: You'll look like your daddy—that's right. So you do know a lot about the differences between a boy and a girl, don't you? So you know that it's more than just letting your hair grow long or putting on different clothing.

TREATMENT NOTES

In treatment today, with father and son present, I said I thought it might be good to examine again the reasons why they were coming to see me. I asked the boy if he had any idea. He said nothing. I said, "Well, sometimes boys your age think it's better to be a girl, or wished they were a girl—and people don't understand this." He remained quiet. "And sometimes boys keep thinking this way even when they get older, and maybe other people who don't understand that tease them, and it's good if we can understand why some boys feel that way." I asked him if he felt that way and he said yes.

I wondered if he had any reasons for this and he said, "Girls don't have to play rough and get hurt." I said that I thought maybe he felt that way because he remembers how he was hurt in the hospital when younger with surgery, and he said yes. I told him how I thought that was behind him now, and that, besides, he didn't have to play rough games, etc., just because he is a boy.

·

Today he had a fantasy about another "feminine" boy whom he knows I see here. He said, "He should be spanked. Or at least reminded. He probably wants to be a girl because he can wear girls' dresses and have long hair. But he shouldn't do this because children will make fun of him. Boys burn up dresses of boys. Boys can go places and have more fun."

·

Recently he was asked by a neighbor why he's coming here. He made up some reason. I asked him what he'd say if he had to tell the truth. He said, "Because I play with girls too much. And I like to wear girls' clothes." I asked him if during the time he has been coming here he understands more about why. He said no. I asked him if he still had thoughts about sometimes thinking it's better to be a girl than a boy. He said yes, but that he was "growing out of it." He wanted to grow out of it because people would make fun of him.

·

Today, father cited a vignette to show how his wife undermines him. If they are driving a car and the boy's hands are out the window, the father will tell him to put them in, "if they got into an accident," etc. Then his wife says the same thing, as if to "bless" what he's said. Without her approval, father's statement has no validity.

•

Today, father reported that last week Nick saw bulls castrated. Then people ate the organs at a barbecue. The son asked, "If my penis got cut off, would I die?" Later, the boy was in the bedroom in his pajamas. He asked, "What happens if someone's bottom got cut off?" Later in the session, mother said, "He's seen them in the bucket—all blood." Then father said, "He may not be aware that they're balls. He may think they're penises."

A Session with Mother, Father, and Nick

Today the boy began by playing with several dolls. His father said that there was something important to discuss. The boy kept on with the doll. Then there was a description of how the boy and dad got into a flailing battle and hit each other. The boy has "extraordinary rage." We wondered why he so overreacts to being hit or hurt. I wondered whether it's a residual of his pain at the hands of physicians.

I said to the boy, "Were you hurt?" He said, "Yeah." His mother doubted that there was any relation to the penis manipulations. Then she said that she was concerned over them hurting each other. When his father held him around, the boy had said, "You've got me by the penis."

Later his mother went on to relate what the boy says when being held: "You don't love me." She was holding him in her lap and asking, "What are you angry about?" He was holding a doll, playing with the dress and saying, "Momma, do you like the dress, would you like it?" She said, "Why aren't you answering me?" I said, "I think he may be. Maybe he's angry because he can't wear dresses." Mother asked him if he would like to wear a dress. He said, "Yes, around the house."

I restated an interpretation from a previous week: "The boy retreats from physical abuse and pain into being a girl. He is very fearful of injury, injury to his penis. For a five-year old boy, to lose his penis may mean being a girl. Dressing like one may prepare him for this. This could be an attempt at mastery over something feared."

•

This week, he was playing outside with a hose and jumping about like a water sprite. A new boy in the neighborhood came along and made a snide comment about the way he was gamboling about. He blasted him with water from the hose. His mother punished him for blasting the kid (rather than for gamboling about).

The boy has been recovering from impetigo. He asked his mother, "If I got a scab on the tip of my penis and I couldn't pee, would they cut it off?" She thinks he meant the scab.

The boy is going into the hospital for a genito-urinary examination tomorrow.

NICK'S PARENTS DISCUSS HIM AT AGE SIX

During a session with the parents, both the mother and the father showed great reluctance in accepting any responsibility for Nick's "femininity." They preferred seeing the causes of his behavior in disordered chromosomes or a hormonal imbalance. Intervention here was directed not so much at discounting biological contributions as at focusing on influences over which the parents retained some control. ·

MOTHER: Is there such a thing as taking a hormone count to see whether anybody's femininity—

FATHER: Like chromosomes?

MOTHER: No, I don't mean chromosomes. I've asked him that before.

R. G.:   This is a new approach to the nonexperiential genesis of feminine behavior. It doesn't have anything to do with one's environment or what happens in one's life or one's family.

MOTHER: No, I'm not ruling that out, but I can't really completely and honestly rule out this other thing also.

FATHER: You have a sexometer? I know a doctor who sells monkey glands.

R. G.:   It could be astrology, but we can't do anything about that. In today's play session your son has shown he's really afraid to do boy things. He's terribly frightened of—

MOTHER: Like what?

R. G.:   Playing anything with a ball. He is just terrified that somebody's going to hurt him. Like he's going to be terribly, terribly hurt. He's really physically frightened. I'm not sure I know why.

FATHER: He shows this a lot around the house.

R. G.:   Why should he be so frightened?

MOTHER: I'm sure I've overly cautioned him. I don't know. I'm sure that I've not let them do things that I really should have let them do because I was frightened that something might happen.

R. G.:   Has he ever really been hurt by playing ball?

MOTHER: Not that I know of.

FATHER: He never played ball!

MOTHER: My husband won't play ball with him. Damn it, I don't know what I have to do. He won't even fix the fishline for him. Last week they were coming in and wanting to fish. Well, I don't like bait or worms or fish or anything, and he doesn't either but [to her husband] of the two of us I think it ought to be you that's going to bait a hook, and not me. *That's one area where I get off the hook.*

FATHER: Maybe we can get artificial worms.

MOTHER: The other boys in the neighborhood fish. This is an activity that the kids in our neighborhood happen to do, okay? Then our kids don't fish. I think it would be great to give them something that everybody else in the neighborhood does.

FATHER: If he would have said, "Dad, I want to play ball," I would have done it.

MOTHER: Yes, but he would never say that. I'd be disappointed if he were a ball player, but he should be adequate, you know, so that if he has to he could catch a ball.

A strategy here was to pose an alternate model, other than behaving as a girl, to a boy not adept at athletics.

R. G.: My position with him tonight in play was that I can understand that not everybody likes to play ball, but I didn't think he would be hurt. I didn't understand really why he should be so afraid of being hurt. I can see where not every kid wants to play ball, but at the same time he doesn't have to do girlish things. That's something, doing sissy things, that people make fun of. He can do boyish things but not dangerous things; he's going to be very unhappy doing sissy things. He heard me. He just sat there. He was playing with a doll while I was saying it. He got a little upset and put the doll away.

MOTHER: Just this week he said to me, "Are there some men who grow up and when they get grown they want to be a woman?" I thought maybe this was something you had discussed with him.

R. G.: No, I told him that as he grows up, and if he continues to do sissy things, that he won't have many friends, and people will make fun of him, and that he'll be very unhappy. Now, he may infer from that that there are some people that don't outgrow it. He may have inferred that. My guess is that he's hoping that there are some people maybe who are like he is.

MOTHER: Yes, that's what I kind of sensed.

R. G.: You know, if he asks you again, "Are there some men who grow up and still have the idea they would like to be a woman?" you might say, "Usually they are very unhappy, because they can't be women, and so why try to be something you can't be?" See, he doesn't have to do girlish things just because he avoids boy things. There are plenty of boys who aren't athletic and competitive, but they do boyish things. When I told him that tonight, he started building. He was building things.

Instruction to the Mother to Reward Specifically "Masculine" Behavior

MOTHER: In Cub Scouts they were playing a game. It was real boyish and real good. It was fine. In a game he is rough and tough, and he is one of the last ones in there. It's a game where you eliminate people by trying to pull them over a circle, and boy, they yank them and crack them around a whip and make them fall.

R. G.: When you see him doing these things, do you tell him that you're pleased and reward him for it?

MOTHER: No, I don't.

R. G.: I think you should. Say, "Gee, that's really great. You really held your own. You really did beautifully."

MOTHER: Well, I didn't do it enough. I should do it more. I didn't really do it.

More Father-Son Involvement Encouraged

R. G.: Rather than his being in Cub Scouts, I would still rather see him go into Indian Guides, because that's father and son instead of mother and son. You've got to get these mothers out of the way. Feminine kids don't need their mothers around.

MOTHER: Just with daddies and boys.

FATHER: Well, I might look at their schedule. I hate to get involved.

MOTHER: See, he's just like my son. He doesn't like to do group-type things.

R. G.: You know, it doesn't matter what it is, as long as it is primarily involving boys and father. It should be the two of you.

NICK'S MOTHER DISCUSSES HIM AT AGE EIGHT

Nick's mother had continued to restrict his free movement into a circle of male companions. Considerable effort was expended here to persuade her to allow him further out on his tether, by pointing out the possible benefits of giving him more freedom and the possible consequences of not permitting him autonomy.

MOTHER: When I watch him come home from school, there'll be a group of boys and a group of girls getting off the bus, and then finally, all at once, he comes through all by himself. And it looks kind of pathetic, and it breaks my heart to see all these youngsters off the bus together and he's alone.

R. G.: I thought he was more integrated now into groups of boys?

MOTHER: Well he is, but the neighborhood always shifts and changes, and then they all stop at the malt shop on the way home and I don't think it's—my husband agrees with me—it's a real crummy place, and we're all trying to close it down.

R. G.: Do the kids stop in there? Do the other boys stop?

MOTHER: Oh, yeah.

R. G.: Don't you feel, though, that if you're concerned that he's not integrating with a group of boys, you're making it much more difficult for him by saying he can't stop here, that he is an exception?

MOTHER: I—I know it, but you know—

R. G.: What's going to happen to him in the malt shop?

MOTHER: It's not—there's a bunch of hippies in there.

R. G.: What does that mean?

MOTHER: Well, I know that they use dope openly in there. You know, they smoke marijuana. At least they seem to do it.

R. G.: He's not going to start taking heroin if he goes into that malt shop. But if he's isolated from other boys, then you're going to perpetuate the kind of problem you have with him. He's not going to feel comfortable in a group, in a peer group of boys. And what's left to him? Either being completely by himself, or retreating into the security of a group of girls. That's what we're trying to undo. It seems to me the dangers, the long-term dangers, of his being a social isolate are a lot more than sitting around in a malt shop.

MOTHER: The malt shop is not so innocent. You have to be familiar with what it is.

R. G.: No matter what it is, you're not going to be able to isolate him from the culture in which he is living. It's impossible. What you can do, which I think is harmful, is make him a social isolate. He's living in a culture, he's a part of that culture. Maybe 50 percent of his friends in his class, no matter what you think or do, are going to be smoking marijuana. And if you really try to isolate him from everybody else, he'll grow up as an isolate with all the problems he was having some years ago and maybe even worse.

MOTHER: Then you'd let him associate with people who smoke marijuana in a place with card playing and a pool table? There are dirty hippies in there.

R. G.: Considering the problems that he has had, I would lean over in the direction of allowing him to do the things that other kids are doing. I think in the long run that's going to have a more helpful payoff for him than protecting him from that kind of environment. He's an exceptional kid, and he needs that kind of exposure.

MOTHER: All right. But you still don't know the whole story of that crummy place.

R. G.: I don't care what they're doing. I don't care if they're performing abortions underneath the malted milk counter. The issue is that he has to become integrated into a group of kids his age. Boys.

MOTHER: You know, I don't think it's very fair. You don't really understand the situation.

R. G.:   We began this story by saying how pathetic it was to see him off by himself. I agree that it is pathetic and that it is important that he feel that he can integrate into a group of his peers, which has always been an issue with him. If he can't be with boys, he's going to want to be either completely alone, away from everybody, or else be with girls. And that's exactly where he was three years ago. You may feel more comfortable in that, and more secure, but in the long run he's the kid that loses out. These are the years he needs to form his masculine identity. If you want that, you've got to take some risks.

INTERVIEW WITH NICK AT AGE TEN

Recollections of Earlier Sex-typed Behaviors

R. G.:   Do you remember back a couple of years ago why your mommy and daddy brought you here?

NICK: All kinds of problems I had.

R. G.:   What kind of problems?

NICK: A big, fat, girly problem.

R. G.:   What do you mean, a big, fat, girly problem?

NICK: I put big, fat, girly dresses on.

R. G.:   Do you remember why you used to do that?

NICK: 'Cause I wanted to look funny. 'Cause I wanted to look like a big, fat weirdo with a girly dress on—all funny.

R. G.:   You wanted to look like a little girl?

NICK: Sometimes I'd act like one.

R. G.:   How would you act like a girl?

NICK: I'd go "Yippee," or scream.

R. G.:   Do you remember any other ways you acted as a girl?

NICK: I'd play house, and I'd have a little dolly. I threw it away.

R. G.:   When was this?

NICK: I think it was a couple of weeks ago—a little dolly. It was real ugly. I just got so mad I threw it away, 'cause I ripped all the hair off of it. I threw the whole thing away.

R. G.:   When you would play house, who would you make believe you were?

NICK: The father. Sometimes some boys would play house and no girls, and sometimes a boy would be the mother.

R. G.:   Who would play the mother if somebody had to play it?

NICK: No one would play it.

R. G.: Did you ever wish you were the mother?

NICK: No, God! 'Cause then you have to put on a dress and apron.

R. G.: It sounds as though a couple of years ago you did enjoy doing that.

NICK: I didn't though.

Wanting to Be a Girl

R. G.: Do you remember any time when you actually wished you had been born a girl?

NICK: Yes.

R. G.: What do you remember?

NICK: I think a long time ago, when I was four or five.

R. G.: When you wanted to be a girl?

NICK: Mm-hm.

R. G.: Do you remember *why* you felt that way?

NICK: At first I wanted to be a girl. Then only girl neighbors lived right next door to me, and they'd always come out to play with me and baby-sit me. Then when I was about four or five, I got all this stuff about girlies.

R. G.: What did you like about being a girl?

NICK: Well, I could baby-sit people and get lots of money.

R. G.: Were there any other reasons?

NICK: Yeah. Then I got older and thought they looked so pretty and stuff. Then, you know, nobody is mean to girls.

R. G.: What do you mean, nobody is mean to girls?

NICK: Well, like nobody pushes them all over the place.

R. G.: Who pushes little boys around?

NICK: Big people.

R. G.: Boys? Girls?

NICK: Both. Most of the times boys.

How Parents Would Have Treated Nick if He Were a Girl

R. G.: What about your mommy and daddy? Do you think they would have treated you differently if you were a girl rather than a boy?

NICK: Yes.

R. G.: How?

NICK: I would get dolls and dresses.

R. G.: Is that something that you would have liked?

NICK: No, dolls are very weird.

R. G.: How else would your mommy and daddy treat you differently?

NICK: Oh, I might have a girlie room.

R. G.: What would that be like?

NICK: It'd probably have hair-ruggings all over the floor, and dolls all over the bed and things. Maybe I would have a cat. That's why I was

always probably wishing to be a girl, because if you're a girl you get
a pet—a cat.

R. G.:   Would your mommy have been different to you if you'd been a
         girl?

NICK: I'd have to clean the house, and I don't like doing that.

R. G.:   Any other way?

NICK: I'd probably cook.

R. G.:   Do you like doing that?

NICK: Not that much. Sometimes I do—sometimes I cook a little.

R. G.:   And would your daddy treat you differently if you'd been a girl?

NICK: Mm-hm.

R. G.:   How?

NICK: *He would probably have paid me attention.* [Italics added]

R. G.:   How would that be?

NICK: Usually when I ask him things he wouldn't do it.

Sex-change

R. G.:   When you used to think you wanted to be born a girl, did you ever
         think you were a girl?

NICK: No, girls have long hair and they have dresses.

R. G.:   But what about if you'd put on dresses and had long hair—would
         you have been a girl?

NICK: No.

R. G.:   Why not?

NICK: 'Cause I wouldn't speak like one.

R. G.:   What do you mean?

NICK: I got a real hoarse voice and everything. Then when I was a girl
         my legs would get all hairy, and I'd grow a beard and moustache. One
         time I saw a lady with a moustache, and it was so weird.

R. G.:   Are there any other reasons why you couldn't grow up to become
         a lady?

NICK: No.

R. G.:   Is there anything different about your body from a little girl's?

NICK: My body grows hair.

R. G.:   Anything else?

NICK: Nothing else.

R. G.:   What about your bottom? Is your bottom the same as a girl's?

NICK: Yes, a bottom—a bottom is a bottom. A girl's bottom is the same
         as a boy's bottom.

R. G.:   Is it really?

NICK: They look different.

R. G.:   How are they different?

NICK: A girl's vagina is inside and a boy's penis is outside.

R. G.:   That's right. So that's another reason why a little boy couldn't become a little girl.... Do you think some of those girl things might come back again?

NICK: No.

R. G.: Why don't you think they might?

NICK: 'Cause I won't be asking for girls' hats.

R. G.: Do you feel now that you prefer being a boy?

NICK: Mm hm.

Nick was seen about every year-and-a-half for follow-up interviews. Some problems remained, and intermittently he saw psychotherapists.

INTERVIEW WITH NICK AT AGE EIGHTEEN

Emerging Sexual Interests

R. G.: How about your social life in terms of romantic interests?

NICK: You mean a sexual attraction?

R. G.: Yeah.

NICK: See, I don't know what to do. I hear other people—they talk about it a lot. They talk about really everything—that some girl likes a boy, or some boy likes a girl, and then sometimes I don't always feel that way towards a girl—sometimes I feel that way towards a—I don't know, maybe, I guess I have sometimes homosexual feelings. Sometimes it kinda bothers me, because sometimes I feel uncomfortable being around someone my own sex—that's always a conflict with me in having friends.

R. G.: Which sexual attractions do you find to be stronger, those toward women or those toward men?

NICK: I don't know, maybe about equal—sometimes women and sometimes men. I don't know, maybe men more I like—it might be.

R. G.: What about in sexual dreams?

NICK: I don't have them that often, I guess. Maybe I masturbate too much—maybe that relieves them.

R. G.: Do you remember any of them?

NICK: I can remember a few. One was with a girl. I can only remember about three, really. One I had recently—about a week ago—involves something like with a male, someone my own age—a boy my own age.

R. G.: What happened in the dream?

NICK: I remember he saw me, and he said something to me about some sort of sexual activity, and I went with him. I don't think I ever did it, but he was talking about it, and there was some group he had that did it, or something like that, and I think he showed pictures of what he did. But I never actually did it.

R. G.: Okay. How about the dream that was with the girl—did you have any sexual contact in your dream?

NICK: Yeah.

R. G.:   What happened?

NICK: Well, there is this little girl, and I went and I had intercourse with her.

R. G.:   Okay. What do you usually think about when you masturbate?

NICK: It's being with a woman and having intercourse and being there and having her stimulate my genitals or something like that.

R. G.:   With her hands or with her mouth?

NICK: Well, both. And then sometimes it's with a man or someone my own age, like, doing the same thing.

R. G.:   What's happening when there's a man in the fantasy?

NICK: Well, sometimes it's hugging him or kissing him.

R. G.:   What else?

NICK: I guess my penis would be in his mouth, or he would be touching me outside.

R. G.:   How about his penis inside of your mouth, is that part of your fantasy?

NICK: Yeah, sometimes.

R. G.:   Okay. How about your penis inside his rectum? Is that part of your fantasy?

NICK: Sometimes, and sometimes he is in my rectum.

R. G.:   In terms of the frequency of these various kinds of fantasies, do you masturbate more thinking about a woman or thinking about a man, or is it equal?

NICK: I think maybe it's mostly about a man. But some women.

R. G.:   What percent is about men and what percent is about women?

NICK: Probably like 60 percent men and 40 percent women.

Earliest Homoerotic Feelings

R. G.:   How far back do you think your attraction to males goes—what age?

NICK: Maybe when I was about three or four I would think of—I remember thinking of, sometimes, handsome faces of men and always have it in my mind. And then I remember, well, I think when I was just maturing and beginning puberty, maybe at twelve or thirteen, I remember I was attracted to certain men—that certain men attracted me.

R. G.:   Did you masturbate thinking about men?

NICK: At times, yes.

R. G.:   Women, too?

NICK: Yeah, also at times. I remember in the beginning when I was masturbating, I was thinking an awful lot about men.

Sexual Inhibitions

R. G.:   What would happen, do you think, if either a female or a male were to indicate to you that they had some sexual interest in you?

NICK: Well, I know a girl has at school.

R. G.:   How do you know?

NICK: Because she said.

R. G.:   What did she say?

NICK: Like, I mean, the way she acted, she said that she's—I know she's— she's very loose and has intercourse with a lot of people, and she said she liked me a lot and I was good looking and everything, but I didn't have it with her because, I don't know, I thought she was kind of fat— I just didn't really want to.

R. G.:   Were you a bit frightened?

NICK: Yeah, maybe, yeah.

R. G.:   Everybody is frightened the first time in terms of whether they can be particularly good at it, or come too quickly, or being a little clumsy—you know, everybody has that fear the first few times—it's normal.

NICK: You know, that's the way I felt, and so I didn't want to do anything silly.

R. G.:   And yet if in fact she does like you, and she is experienced, my guess is that you're probably not the first person she's had sex with for whom it would be the first time.

NICK: Yeah.

R. G.:   And she would probably understand.

NICK: That's true.

R. G.:   What would you do if some male made some indication to you that he found you to be interesting to him—sexually attractive to him?

NICK: Well, I don't know. If I wanted to have sexual relations with him now, I'd say yes. Probably just to experience it—just to see what it's like and try it. Because if I feel that way that strongly, I think maybe I should.

R. G.:   Does that scare you as much as having sex with a woman for the first time?

NICK: I'm trying to think. A male never came up to me so I don't know how I'd feel. I know I would be scared.

An Early Homoerotic Attraction

NICK: There is someone—my dad knows someone who is a friend of his, and he—this man—I think this man has a son, and I think the son is two years older than me. I met him when I was very young, about five or six, and—I don't know, there is this thing about him that I was attracted to, I guess I always wanted to meet him, and he's very good looking, very handsome. I don't know, I feel this attraction toward him and I don't understand it, and it kind of frustrates me.

R. G.:   How old were you when you first met him?

NICK: About five or six.

R. G.: What do you remember about that time?

NICK: Well, there was nothing sexually, but I remember he was very—he was older than me. He was someone to look up to. He would do things that I didn't do—he was much more bold and brave. To me he was very good looking and that type of thing, and maybe that's something I looked up to or wanted. And I wanted him for myself.

Recollection of Boyhood "Femininity"

R. G.: What do you remember about why you came here?

NICK: Well, I remember at the time that I was having difficulty—my parents thought—I was putting on women's clothes, or I wasn't doing the things that other children my age were doing. I wasn't really participating with them. I didn't care about it. I was putting on strange clothes all the time. They had doubts with me in that area and acting feminine.

R. G.: In what way would you act feminine?

NICK: Well, maybe I would copy characteristics—feminine characteristics.

R. G.: Do you remember consciously doing that?

Recollection of Grandmother

NICK: No, I don't remember consciously ever trying to. But I think at times I would, maybe, and it would kind of worry me. I remember, I think because I admired my grandmother a great deal, maybe I was copying it from her, using her as a model.

R. G.: What do you remember about her?

NICK: As a child, she was older and I think very graceful. She cooked very well, and everything about her was cool and very charming, and maybe it was her that I wanted to copy, in a certain way.

R. G.: Do you remember actually copying some of the things that she did when you were very little?

NICK: Well, I remember that I would put on aprons whenever I was at her house. I would have to put on an apron right in these drawers. I used to pull out an apron. They were always trying to hide the aprons from me. They would try to keep the door shut so I wouldn't keep taking them. I think finally they just let me do it. I went around—they have a picture of me doing—I'd run around putting flowers over my head at Easter time, with some baskets and flowers. I don't know—it must have been strange.

R. G.: What was so appealing about the aprons?

NICK: Well, it looked like a dress, you know, I think, and perhaps my grandmother wore them. Not just that—I couldn't get someone's dress—maybe the apron was the only thing.

R. G.: Is your grandmother still alive?

NICK: No, she died when I was six.

R. G.:   So if she was dead when you were six, you've got some pretty strong memories of her.

NICK: Yeah, she had this garden, this very interesting garden. She was just very different. I guess my mother was very, very harsh. My grandmother was really gentle, just different. Her movements and everything she did were different. Maybe that attracted me.

INTERVIEW WITH NICK AT AGE TWENTY

Social Adjustment

NICK: I'm having a lot of doubts now. Last semester was very terrible. I knew a lot of people. I knew almost all of them, but I never got along. I was always too hyper or too excited or very ill-content. There was no way I could ever get to socialize with anyone. A lot of people I didn't like kind of withdrew from me, or they probably thought I was strange. Everyone would form little cliques and not allow me to do anything in them.

R. G.:   What else?

NICK: I was also having sexual doubts, sexual frustrations. A lot of anxiety.

Sexual Conflicts

R. G.:   What do you mean, sexual doubts?

NICK: Well, I had homosexual desires. I would have feelings like that all the time, I wouldn't know how to fulfill them or even the other desires, the heterosexual. I was frustrated because I never knew how to fulfill them or how to solve them. I guess I've developed this for a long time, these feelings, and I've never known how.

Homosexual Desires

R. G.:   Which desires are you finding are getting stronger—the homosexual ones or the heterosexual ones?

NICK: I notice the homosexual ones are stronger.

R. G.:   When you think about the homosexual desires, what do you experience?

NICK: With a homosexual it would probably be a very handsome man or maybe a boy, say someone my age, fondling genitals or something like that.

R. G.:   What else do you think about them?

R. G.:   Do you imagine any other kind of sexual activities with a man or a boy your age?

NICK: Sometimes I think about the anal, the anus.

R. G.:   In your sexual fantasies, who would be taking the initiative—you or the other person?

NICK: I think both.

R. G.:   How often do you see somebody on the street or wherever that you find sexually arousing to you who is a man?

NICK: Several times, five or six times in a day.

R. G.:   When you have dreams at night, sexual dreams, what percentage of them involve a man and what percentage of them involve a woman?

NICK: I think a great deal of them I think about men, I mean both men and women.

R. G.:   What percentage involve just men?

NICK: About 80 percent.

R. G.:   How often do you masturbate?

NICK: Usually once a day.

R. G.:   What do you usually think about when you masturbate?

NICK: Usually I'm nude and the other person is nude, and I'm usually caressing them all over and they're caressing me all over. I'm touching their genitals and them touching mine, fondling them with their mouths or putting my penis in their vagina and fondling her all over.

R. G.:   What percentage of the time, when you masturbate, do you think about a man?

NICK: Eighty percent.

Homosexual Conflict

R. G.:   What bothers you about having a homosexual relationship?

NICK: I've never had one myself, so I think I'm indecisive about it. I'm not really bothered about religion or what society thinks. I'm not going to do it out in public and advertise it and then be disapproved. I mean, no one is going to know it. I think it's more myself. The doubts I have.

R. G.:   What sort of doubts?

NICK: If it's unnatural, I think that it might be unnatural.

R. G.:   What do you mean, unnatural?

NICK: Well it's not the way that people are made, the sexual organs are made to reproduce, and if they are used in a different way—if they were used in a way that they were not made for—I think of that. I see that they're not used in the way they're made for. Maybe I wonder more about my emotional stability.

R. G.:   What do you wonder about?

NICK: I see in having a homosexual relationship for me purely a fulfilling thing and maybe just a pleasure or aesthetic delight. I take some pleasure in viewing the body and seeing it, and then I would have a whole sensation, a whole experience, a whole feeling with it. When I do have that, I develop a taste or appreciation or pleasure in viewing a female and a male both. With both I desire a contact experience, but I'm not made to have naturally a relationship with a male.

R. G.:   You know, a lot of the sexual acts that men and women engage in don't lead to reproduction either. Whether they're using contraceptives, whether it's oral-genital sex, or mutual masturbation or anal intercourse. There are a lot of sexual acts that males and females engage in which don't lead to babies. So when you say unnatural that the organs were not made for that, well, it's true that two men or two women can't together have a baby, but much, if not most, of the sexual acts between men and women also don't lead to making babies.

NICK: I want a more romantic interest, something deeper. I've been wondering more about romance between two people of the same sex because I see myself that it's not a thing that widely happens. Maybe I look in literature and art, and you don't read about it that much. I mean, romantic relationships happening to men and women; it seems those are the most fulfilling, the ones that contain the most fruit, the most art or the most beauty. I notice, too, that those between people of the same sex always seem very strange. Either they happen only for the moment of pleasure of a certain taste, or a certain delightment in the body.

R. G.:   I think then you've read selected samples of literature, because the fact is that there are male-male and female-female couples who have been together for many years and who lead very satisfying, fulfilling lives together—at least as satisfying and fulfilling as any heterosexual couple. You may not know these people, you may not have read some of their biographies, but they exist.

NICK: Well, sometimes I think that's funny. Maybe because society does, I don't know.

R. G.:   Well, making a relationship work, homosexual or heterosexual, is difficult. It takes a lot of work. You know from the divorce rates that about 40 to 45 percent of male-female couples divorce. There is no guarantee of great satisfaction in a relationship just because it's heterosexual. Neither is there a guarantee of dissatisfaction because it's homosexual. It really depends on the individual couple.

Acting out Sexual Fantasies

R. G.:   To what extent, now, have you been tempted to, or come close to, acting out some of the fantasies, actually doing some of the things that you imagine?

NICK: Well, I don't know if I've come very close. I mean, if I were very rich, I could perhaps hire some male prostitute. It's something I don't want to do. I mean, you don't have to be that rich. I don't want to do it at all. I guess in my state right now, I think, you can't—how would you let that be known to them, or if they would want to do that themselves—even if there were homosexuals?

R. G.:   First of all, I think what you're saying is you're not sure whether the man would be homosexual, and if he was, you don't know whether he would be interested in a sexual relationship with you.

NICK: Yeah.

R. G.:   What about with women—how do you feel about approaching them?

NICK: Well, I think the same way, almost. I'm really very touchy with them. In society it's more accepted for the woman and the man, but— say there is a woman you have this desire to have intercourse with. I always was afraid of acting on that, because it would make me very foolish.

R. G.:   What do you mean?

NICK: Well, it might, you know—the woman—saying that you want to do this—it would be very startling. It is something, perhaps with some people, that means a commitment. It's not taken lightly by some people, and it might offend them.

R. G.:   Do you think that there are some women who have fairly active sex lives with a wide variety of people without making a strong commitment?

NICK: Yes, oh, yeah. But I mean, I wouldn't know if that's what they feel.

R. G.:   For a moment let's think about a hypothetical other person who has some sexual feelings towards a woman as well, and makes some overture suggesting a sexual relationship. Do you feel that the girl feels that she's being coerced by the question, or do you feel she feels free to say, "Well, I would prefer not to."

NICK: Well, I think a person—anyone—might feel coerced, and even if a girl were to come up to me, I would feel a little funny.

R. G.:   If she was not interested in a casual sexual relationship—do you think that most women would feel comfortable in saying, "I'm just not interested in that"?

NICK: Yeah, they would say that, but I would be afraid that I would insult them just in asking them. I would think that most women, if they didn't want it, they would just say no, that they didn't want it.

R. G.:   I think it depends very much on the person. It's a little bit harder with your sexual feelings for men, because with a man you're not really sure whether he's interested in a homosexual relationship. You can presume just on a probability basis that most women, obviously not all, but most women are heterosexual. But the fact is also, you could—on a probability basis—assume that most men are heterosexual. So it's a little bit more difficult to be sure with a man, unless you happen to be in an environment in which most of the men are gay, like in a gay bar. If you're interested in sex with a man and you're in a gay bar, it's very much like being with a woman in that you could feel like, well, probably these people are interested in sexuality with someone like me. Now the question is, are they interested in sexuality specifically with *me*. It's that kind of thing that everybody has to go through in terms of approaching someone with the possibility of their saying, "Well, no thank you, I'm waiting for someone else." In the same way, someone may well come up to you—either a woman or a man—and make it known to you that they're interested in having a sexual relationship with you. Then you've got the same liberty to say yes or no.

Sexual Experience

R. G.: In terms of actual sexual experiences, what have you had so far?

NICK: Touching. I remember once when I was a child with girls, I always used to pull down my pants and they would pull down their underpants. I remember one time when I was about eight or nine, I went to someone's house and there were two girls. They were taking a shower, and they were naked, and they were all running around. I saw the vagina, and they were asking me to pull down my pants, and I would do that. They would just be running all about nude, and they really enjoyed being nude in front of everybody. I remember once at a friend's house when I was about fourteen or fifteen, we would take off our clothes and walk around nude all over the place. One time the other kid and I both had erections, and we would touch each other so we could be able to reach orgasm. That's all.

Support for Emerging Sexuality

R. G.: It sounds like you have the capacity to be responsive sexually to either women or men, which I think many people would consider to be advantageous, because it allows a wider range of sexual and romantic possibilities. There are men, for example, who are only attracted to other men and wish they could be attracted to women, because there are certain things they feel they're missing with no relationship with a women. You're not one of these people. It sounds like you do have the capacity to experience sexual arousal to females as well as to males. It sounds to me like the bigger problem is that you, like many other people your age, are shy, don't really know yet how to go about initiating a sexual relationship. There are many, many other people your age who have the same self-doubts and inhibitions, fears of rejection, fears that it won't work out right, whatever. It's the same whether it's heterosexual or homosexual. You will have relationships in your life, and some of them will be more important than others, and you will find that some of them will float to the top as being important people. But that doesn't happen overnight.

INTERVIEW WITH NICK AT AGE TWENTY-TWO

Sexual Fantasies

NICK: I still feel I have a strong homosexual feeling, and also I'm attracted sexually to women.

R. G.:   Which one do you feel is stronger?

NICK: I feel maybe towards males is stronger—I mean at times they're equal—and sometimes towards females.

R. G.:   What do you think determines which feels stronger to you?

NICK: At times I'm attracted to males; I feel a stronger passion. Whereas I look at a female and a female body and see that they're rather rounded and sort of flabby and not very developed or not very interesting. And a male's body perhaps interests me more. At times it seems it's more exotic or strange; perhaps there's more detail.

R. G.:   More detail?

NICK: Well, in veins or in muscles or bones, in form. Whereas a female, it's sort of always smooth and sort of rounded. Women, they sort of sit all over the place all the time, and a lot in women doesn't appeal to me.

R. G.:   Like what?

NICK: All these women with these big teeth or big lips and smiles, or lots of those things done with their hair—enormous and overt features, all out of proportion. The same too with men, the other homosexual movements or fantasies—that doesn't appeal to me.

R. G.:   Have you come close to having real-type experiences?

NICK: It's on the edge, it's something I would like to do; I'm not close to it. Right now I have no friends and no contacts with people my own age or any other.

Theory of Homosexuality

R. G.:   Why do you feel that your own sexual interests have evolved the way they have in terms of an interest in males and an interest in females?

NICK: I guess I felt a need for fulfillment with a male, some sort of extra attention or something extra with a male.

R. G.:   Why?

NICK: I've always thought that interaction is with people that you hate at times or you find dangerous or you are afraid of—I know with animals they like that.

R. G.:   With what?

NICK: Animals can be that way. With people too. And women—I always thought women are sometimes attracted to men who are very dangerous to one another, and the same way as for example with my life I had a lot of bad contact growing up as a child. I know boys always used to make fun of me because I couldn't act right physically. I always had a lack of attention with the boys or growing up with men, I never had any playmates that were men or boys when I was young. And my father I thought was strange, our relationship. I don't think he was the type that cut himself off. I think he always tried to remain available and helpful, and really always listened to us when we talked. Maybe for me, maybe I created something with my father.

R. G.:   What purpose would having a sexual partnership, a sexual relationship with someone serve, if in fact there has been rejection in the past?

NICK: That's what I have to do, that's what I must do. That's the only way I can deal with it.

R. G.:   Why?

NICK: Perhaps the anger hurts me, and so I want to make it with something different, or I want to be recompensed, repaid or something fulfilling to make up for what was wrong. Perhaps that's it.

Reflections on Early Boyhood Visits

R. G.:   Looking back, do you think it was helpful or not helpful that your parents brought you here when you were young?

NICK: Well, I don't know—if I were in their place at the time, maybe I would have felt very much the same. I think I probably would have done the same. I can't say whether it would be helpful. If I had a child like that, I think I would be worried. I'd probably want to let them understand what they were doing, because maybe if they do that—they were probably afraid that I would wear dresses or something when I got older and be made fun of and not accepted in some way, and they were probably doing that as a measure—as a means to help me. I think I would have done the same thing. I don't know if it was helpful. I guess, looking at it overall, at least I don't have a desire to do that now.

R. G.:   Do you remember coming here and talking with me on a once-a-week basis?

NICK: Yeah.

R. G.:   What do you remember about that?

NICK: Well, a lot of it was, like relationships between myself and my parents—troubles I was having at home. Maybe it was not just the sexuality.

was relating to their hair, and then I said, well, he's just a baby, you know—it'll pass with time. But then he kept this up.

R. G.:   You say the baby-sitter's daughters were dressing him in girls' clothing?

MOTHER: And they carted him around and carried him just when they were home from school. The reason I know they were dressing him in clothes was because the older boy told us finally that they treated him like a doll and dressed him up in doll clothes and all this stuff. I probably should have asked her not to let them do it. But again, I felt, well, he's just a baby—it won't matter.

R. G.:   And over how long a period of time was this continuing?

MOTHER: I worked for eighteen months, so it probably continued that far—at least a year-and-a-half.

R. G.:   And they were with him on a daily basis?

MOTHER: Five days a week.

R. G.:   Why did they do that? Do you have any idea?

MOTHER: Well, I guess they presumed he was a baby and a doll.

FATHER: They were actually just playing with him, I think, taking care of him, doing something they want—you know, they were girls and they like dolls.

MOTHER: So shortly after that, I quit working and began to take care of him.

R. G.:   Looking back, what's the very earliest that you noticed anything that could be considered feminine?

FATHER: I would say probably wearing the shirt on his head.

R. G.:   And he was how old at that time?

FATHER: Two-and-a-half, three.

MOTHER: Two-and-a-half.

Doll-play

R. G.:   You've mentioned his interest in playing with dolls. Can you say more about that?

MOTHER: We hadn't had any dolls to this point in the house until we had our daughter, and when we would go to my sister's—she has two little girls—he would want to play with the dolls, so I didn't correct him at first. I thought, well, all little boys play with dolls, but it got to where it was an obsession. Every time we'd go somewhere where there were dolls, this is what he would want to play with. Now at home he will find other things, but when there's a doll around that's what he will want to play with.

R. G.:   How far back does that go?

MOTHER: There again, I'm sure he played with dolls at the baby-sitter's, because with two girls they had quite a few. My husband kept telling me I should do something, not let him play with them. I'd say, "Oh, well, all boys like dolls." I just kind of passed it off. But now he'll go into her room, and she has several stuffed toys—there's no dolls to speak of, but he'll take her little dresses and dress the stuffed bears, and he'll dress them in her little dresses. And I've gotten after him, you know, several times about it. He'll sneak back in and do it again.

R. G. (to father):   What's been your approach to his doll-playing?

FATHER: Well, I've stopped him from doing it a few times, but I think it's created a slight problem. Now if he has something like that and he sees me, he'll hide it—try to get rid of it. If I walk into her room and he was in there, he would all of a sudden be doing something else, you know, and so really I don't know how to approach it. I don't know what I should do.

R. G.:   When he first began playing with dolls, what was your feeling about it at that time?

FATHER: It was pretty much like hers—you know, he's a baby. It's a natural thing to do.

Female Role-playing

R. G.:   You've also mentioned that he takes the role of a female when he plays games.

FATHER: Not—not all the time, but he has done it. Like if they're going to be playing something in the room—"I'm going to be the mother and you be the father."

R. G.:   What has been your reaction and your approach to that?

FATHER: Well, I haven't seen this personally myself. His brother has seen it once in a while, and it's been mentioned to her a couple of times.

R. G.:   What has been your approach?

MOTHER: Well, I've tried to explain to him what his father's world is, because I know he relates too much to me, but I really think I haven't pushed him away from it. I've just tried to tell him, well, daddies go out and work, and he said, "Why do daddies go out and work?" I said, "Because they have to make money—that's father's role." I don't think he has really any idea of what I'm trying to explain. But I keep trying. He'll say once in a while, "Well, I want to grow up and be like daddy."

Desire to Be a Girl

R. G.:   Has he ever said, "I want to be a girl"? Has he ever said, "I am a girl"?

MOTHER: Oh, yes, he's said he wants to be a girl. He's even made up a name. It's several months ago—I can't remember what he said his name is going to be or anything, but he quite strongly wanted to let me know that he wanted to be a girl. And he wanted to grow up to be a mommy.

R. G.:   What have you said?

MOTHER: I've told him, well, no, you want to grow up to be like daddy—you want to be a man. I haven't really forced the issue.

R. G.:   Has he ever said, "I am a girl"?

FATHER: Not to my knowledge. No.

Father-Son Relationship

R. G.:   To what extent were you able to spend time with your son during his first year?

FATHER: Well, the problem was working odd hours. I was working, and as a matter of fact I traveled a lot. I was gone three weeks to a month.

R. G.:   How often were you away for that period?

FATHER: Sometimes two-week trips, sometimes three-week trips—it would amount to eight or nine of them a year.

R. G.:   And when you were home, what working hours did you have?

FATHER: A lot of hours. I was working nights, I'd go to work three-thirty in the afternoon I'd sometimes get off five or six in the morning. So naturally when I'd get up I was ready to go back to work again. A lot of times it was seven days a week.

R. G.:   What sort of things were you and your son able to do during that year?

FATHER: Well we weren't able to do a whole lot really, with him being a baby. We weren't able to do a whole lot.

R. G.:   How would you rate the amount of time you had available for this boy in his first year compared to your older boy in his first year?

FATHER: I'd say I had much more time with the older boy.

When he was five, Kyle entered a behavior modification program, with other clinicians, in a laboratory setting and at home (Rekers and Lovaas, 1974). In the laboratory, parental attentiveness or disinterest was used to positively or negatively reinforce specific "masculine" or "feminine" behaviors, such as playing with boy-type or girl-type toys. At home, a token reinforcement program was instituted. Kyle received blue tokens for "desirable" behaviors, such as play with boys' toys or with boys, and red ones for "undesirable" behaviors, such as doll-play, "feminine" gestures, or playing with girls. Blue tokens were redeemable for treats, such as ice cream. Red tokens resulted in loss of blue tokens, periods of isolation, or spanking by father. The treatment program lasted ten months.

Two years after treatment ended, Kyle was described as "indistinguishable from any other boy in terms of gender-related behaviors" (Rekers and Lovaas, 1974, 186). At age nine, Kyle was described as having "a normal male sexual identity" (Rekers, 1982[a], 138). At fifteen he was described as "indistinguishable from any other normal teen-age boy ... developing normal masculine roles, [with] a normal male identity [and] normal aspirations for growing up to be married and have a family" (139).

Kyle and his mother were not seen by me again until he was seventeen.

KYLE'S MOTHER DESCRIBES HIM AT AGE SEVENTEEN

Looking Back at the Initial Evaluation

MOTHER: Well, I am indeed still thankful the day I saw you on TV and you took me in, because I knew there was going to be a problem if something wasn't done, and I knew I couldn't handle it.

R. G.: You say that you took the initiative?

MOTHER: I did. When I saw you on TV that day, I kept after my husband until he finally let me call. It would have been easier to say, "It will go away," but I'm not that way. If there's something that I know is not right, I'll dig and dig until I get to the bottom of it. I guess my husband didn't really want to admit there was a problem. But over the years if I've mentioned this about my son having to go, he's resented it; he didn't want anybody to know about it. I did what I thought was right, and I'm not going to feel guilty about it. I'd do the same thing all over again, because I knew there was going to be a definite problem if something weren't done.

R. G.: What do you think would have been the outcome if you hadn't come to UCLA?

MOTHER: If he had not become a homosexual, I'm sure he would have been very, very fetish.

R. G.: What?

MOTHER: Fetish, you know, too feminine. Not that I think macho means rifle in a truck and a six-pack of beer and a cowboy hat. Unfortunately, this is what is macho. I don't think sports are where it's all at either. I am just as proud of my son and his art, and I don't care if it's a girl or a boy or whatever. That's something he'll have his whole life. Playing football on a football field maybe through high school and maybe, if they're lucky, college, and maybe a few professionals, but it's not a long-time thing. Art is. I'm just as proud of him as I can be. I am thankful that I took him to UCLA.

R. G.: If those behaviors had continued, why do you think he might have become homosexual?

MOTHER: Well, if it were allowed to continue as a child, his patterns would have been set by the time he was ten or twelve years old. It would have been too late for me to do anything, because he would think it was perfectly all right. I really don't know if I can tell you the difference between fetishness and homosexuality except what I've read. Fetish is to enjoy wearing women's underwear and stuff like that. But as far as sex in the bed, I don't have any idea. Had he not been on the treatment reinforcement program telling him what was right and what wasn't right, why wouldn't he want to wear women's underwear or nightgowns or whatever as he got older? As far as I am concerned, he wouldn't have known there was anything wrong with it until people started teasing him and hurt him.

R. G.:   In what ways do you think UCLA changed things for him?

MOTHER: Well, the reinforcement program. I knew there was a problem, but I didn't know how to handle it. I was frustrated; I wouldn't know where to begin to help him, and it was nothing I did or it wasn't his fault. Unfortunately, I hired a baby-sitter that didn't take her job seriously. She let her daughters—you know the story, the two little girls were playing with him like a doll. I remember his older brother came in one day, and he told me that the girls were treating the younger boy like a plaything, like a doll, and they were dressing him in girls' clothes and aprons and putting shirts on his head to make it look like long hair, and then pretty soon the younger boy didn't know the difference. So he didn't know whether he was supposed to play with the teacups or cars.

R. G.:   Was he confused as to whether he was a boy or a girl?

MOTHER: I think so. Oh, I'm sure.

R. G.:   Did he say that? Or was it more an impression you got?

MOTHER: He saw nothing wrong with picking up a doll instead of a car, and I didn't really realize this until I came to you. He thought it was perfectly all right to go pick up the dolls instead of the airplane, because he played with the girls and that's what they played with and he didn't know. How could he? So the thing is, how do I get him not to feel guilty about it? It wasn't his fault. It wasn't my fault. When my husband and I split up a year-and-a-half ago, I think he felt that was partially his fault.

R. G.:   Why?

MOTHER: Because he and his dad weren't close. But there again, that was nobody's fault. He enjoys the finer things in life; the older boy enjoys sports, but this one shouldn't feel guilty because he didn't want to go hunting or kill a deer or didn't want to play football—again, the macho. To me that's not masculine.

R. G.:   Did he get closer to your son after the time that you came to UCLA?

MOTHER: No, I think they drew further apart. But it wasn't all my husband's fault; a lot of it was my son's. He can really shut somebody out if he wants to. I mean, he can just turn them completely out. Also, I don't think his father could accept the fact that he had a son that wasn't as masculine as he would have preferred. And I am not being unkind towards my husband. Let's face it, when those guys were young, it was black and white. You had to be a jock to be a male; it was a hard thing for his father to accept. I could see the gap widening, and it put me right in the middle because I loved them both. But you know what masculine is to me? If I see a guy shed a tear, that's so much more masculine. It takes much more of a man to shed a tear than it does to shoot a deer.

INTERVIEW WITH KYLE AT AGE SEVENTEEN

Recollection of Earlier Visits

R. G.:   I don't know how much you remember about seeing me when you were a little kid.

KYLE: You had a really long beard.

R. G.:   It probably looked longer when you were a little kid. What else do you remember?

KYLE: Well, I can remember when you came to my birthday party.

R. G.:   Right, and running around and squirting each other with water, outside your house.

KYLE: Yeah.

R. G.:   What do you remember about coming to see me initially when you were about five?

KYLE: We talked a little bit.

R. G.:   And you remember me with a very long beard?

KYLE: And I thought you were kinda hunched over for some reason.

R. G.:   Well, it's good that I reappeared, if for nothing else than to dispel the image.

Recollection of Earlier Sex-Typed Behaviors

R. G.:   What do you remember about why your mom brought you to me at that time?

KYLE: Well, because I had a baby-sitter once, and like she had two daughters and like they used to have me play with dolls and stuff like that. So that's why she did, because my brother told her that when I go over there I never played with cars.

R. G.:   And that worried your mom and dad, or one was and one wasn't? Do you know?

KYLE: I think they both worried.

R. G.:   Do you remember playing with dolls?

KYLE: Yeah, I can.

R. G.:   Was there anything else that you remember that they were worried about?

KYLE: Well, she had seen a guy on TV or something, and he said he had done stuff like that when he was little and he became a groupie and was homosexual, something like that, and they didn't want that to happen to me.

R. G.:   They were worried about your becoming homosexual because of playing with dolls at age four or five?

KYLE: They didn't tell me that at four. They told me that I guess when I was about eleven or twelve.

R. G.:   Do you remember anything else back then in terms of other playing interests and things you did that might have worried them?

KYLE: I don't remember this, but my mom said that the girls used to dress me up in dresses, but I don't remember doing that.

R. G.:   Do you ever remember going through a phase in which you liked to dress up in girls' clothes?

KYLE: I can remember one time, this kid—me and him used to do it sometimes.

R. G.:   How old were you?

KYLE: I was pretty young, because those people got divorced when I was six or so, I think, and I never saw him after that.

R. G.:   And through what years do you think you did this dressing up?

KYLE: I think I stopped at four.

R. G.:   Did your parents know about the dressing up?

KYLE: Uh huh.

R. G.:   And do you remember what your mom and dad's reaction was?

KYLE: They were kinda mad.

R. G.:   Both of them?

KYLE: No, my dad was I think more than my mom.

R. G.:   What kind of friends did you have back then—mostly boys, girls, a mixed group?

KYLE: It was a mixed, because I remember all us kids from the neighborhood—I had my best friends, this boy, and there was another boy who lived across the street.

R. G.:   Some of the kids I see remember wanting to be girls when they were real tiny boys. Do you remember going through a phase of wishing that you had been born a girl?

KYLE: No. I can remember when I was about—before I started kindergarten I was afraid that all boys had to go to the army and be killed. I thought I had to go to the army and be killed, so then I wanted to be a girl 'cause I didn't want to go get killed.

R. G.:   I remember worrying about that too when I was a boy. I grew up during World War II, and I remember it also, worrying about going in the army and getting killed and thinking that girls were really lucky, they didn't have to go. Did that wish to be a girl stay with you for some time after that?

KYLE: I don't think so. After I found out everybody didn't go in the army to be killed, I don't think I did.

R. G.:   If you could be magically reborn all over again as a newborn kid, would you rather be born as a boy or as a girl?

KYLE: As a boy.

R. G.:   Why?

KYLE: Because I think boys are in an advantage in society. I think I'd like to be born over as a boy and be exposed to all-boy things and stuff when I was little so I could really, you know, be good at sports and stuff. But I like art, too, so I think if I had to pick between the two, I'd pick art.

R. G.:   You mentioned dressing up sometimes in girls' clothes when you were a little kid. Do you sometimes now wonder what it would look like or how it would feel to dress up in women's clothes?

KYLE: I had to do it when I was a freshman for initiation in a theater group.

R. G.:   How did it feel?

KYLE: I hated it, because I had to wear nylons and they were really sick.

Recollection of Behavior Therapy

R. G.:   What do you remember about seeing the other doctor?

KYLE: I can't remember really doing anything. Oh, I remember what he looks like. He had really long ears.

R. G.:   That's how *I* remember him, too.

KYLE: Yeah.

R. G.:   Do you remember doing things in any of the buildings at UCLA with him, like in playrooms where you had to play with certain kinds of toys maybe by yourself or maybe with your mom or your dad?

KYLE: Mom said they used to put me in a room by myself with toys, and I'd go pick the ones I wanted to play with.

R. G.:   Do you remember that?

KYLE: I can't remember that.

R. G.:   What did your mom tell you about that or why they did—

KYLE: She said at first I used to play with dolls, and then after a few months I used to play with cars.

R. G.:   Why do you think things changed?

KYLE: I don't think I was really exposed to cars and stuff like that with the baby-sitters, 'cause she had two girls and one boy, and the girls were always there when I was there, so I thought since dolls were there I just got used to playing with them.

R. G.:   How did your mom explain all this to you? Why you were seeing him and why you were in these rooms with all these toys.

KYLE: She didn't really explain it, so that's why I felt that there was something wrong with me.

R. G.:   And your dad, did he explain any of this to you?

KYLE: No, not really, not until I got older.

R. G.:   Looking back at it now with the advantage of hindsight, in retrospect, do you think it was a good idea that your parents brought you to UCLA, do you think it was a mistake or—

KYLE: I think it was a good idea.

R. G.: Why?

KYLE: Well, I was playing with dolls and stuff like that, and that could have led to bigger problems, and I'm glad that they got help, because I don't think lots of parents would do that. They'd be too ashamed or whatever, but I'm really glad my parents did.

R. G.: Why would playing with dolls lead to bigger problems?

KYLE: Well, that one guy who was on TV, he played with dolls and stuff, and that led to putting on dresses and stuff like that and acting like girls 'cause girls would play with dolls.

R. G.: And do you think that might have been the way that you would have developed yourself?

KYLE: Probably.

Romantic Interests

R. G.: How have your romantic interests evolved over the years?

KYLE: I went out with this girl last year for a long time, and then all of a sudden we broke up and—oh, I seem to always fall in love with some dumb girl.

R. G.: What do you mean, some dumb girl?

KYLE: Oh, not dumb, I guess. There was a girl in my freshman year, and I'd been in a festival and she stood right next to me, and so I really liked her. I liked her for a couple of years. There was another girl. I sent her flowers.

R. G.: Sounds pretty romantic.

KYLE: From a secret admirer.

R. G.: How old were you the first time you ever remember having a crush on somebody?

KYLE: Second grade. My teacher.

R. G.: What do you remember about the teacher?

KYLE: She had her hair frosted; and she came to one of my baseball games once.

R. G.: How long did you have a crush on her?

KYLE: I suppose the whole school year.

R. G.: And after that, who was your next crush on?

KYLE: Probably the next-door neighbor, and I liked her a bit—for a year or so, but I was just really young.

R. G.: When did you have your first crush on someone that you might describe as more of an adult type, you know, romantic—

KYLE: It was probably Dona.

R. G.: How old were you then?

KYLE: A freshman in high school, fourteen.

R. G.: Was that your first sort of love, romantic—

KYLE: Yeah.

R. G.: Was that a sexual crush too?

KYLE: I suppose.

Sexual Feelings

R. G.: Try to think back. When did you first ever become aware of sort of a sexual turn-on with somebody—you know, you're looking at somebody and having some kind of a sexual response in your penis, or just imagining the person without clothes on?

KYLE: Oh, that was probably junior high.

R. G.: How old were you then?

KYLE: Twelve. That was seventh grade, when everybody was talking about it and everything. We used to try sneaking into the girls' locker room and stuff like that.

R. G.: Was that around the time of puberty?

KYLE: Yeah.

R. G.: What do you remember about your very, very first sexual feelings for somebody?

KYLE: Oh, the next-door girl, I remember one time I spent the night at her house, and with that we started kissing each other and stuff, and I guess that was the first time.

R. G.: Was that a sexual turn-on for you?

KYLE: Yeah, I suppose it was.

R. G.: Do you remember getting an erection?

KYLE: I think so.

R. G.: How far did things go with her?

KYLE: I guess we got embarrassed, so we stopped.

R. G.: And how about after that?

KYLE: I never really got close to—really close to a girl until last year.

R. G.: In between that time and last year, did you have any kind of heavy necking experiences?

KYLE: There was one girl we used to—you know—I went to a movie with her once.

Erotic Experiences

R. G.: Did you have petting experiences?

KYLE: No, we just kissed a lot and stuff. I didn't really like her. I just went out with her because that's what everybody else was doing.

R. G.: Now what happened with the girl last year?

KYLE: We went to the prom and we got kinda heavy at the prom.

R. G.: How heavy?

KYLE: Pretty heavy, from the balcony.

R. G.: Petting?

KYLE: Uh huh.

R. G.:   Touching breasts?

KYLE: I did a few times, but she's really shy, so.

R. G.:   Did she let you touch her breast skin, or was it over clothes?

KYLE: One time I did touch her breast.

R. G.:   But she was kinda embarrassed by it?

KYLE: She's really religious. So after that we broke up.

R. G.:   That was it?

KYLE: Yeah.

R. G.:   Was that a sexual turn-on, or more one of curiosity?

KYLE: Well, I think my curiosity was solved with my next-door neighbor. I did touch her breast and stuff like that, and I suppose it was more of a turn-on.

R. G.:   What did you do with her?

KYLE: Oh, we just—we used to, you know, play whatever you call it, doctor whatever, and we'd look at each other and stuff like that.

R. G.:   How old were you at that time?

KYLE: Junior high.

R. G.:   Did you explore each other's body with your hands or—

KYLE: No, just looked.

R. G.:   Just sort of taking a good look?

KYLE: Yeah.

R. G.:   What's the most you've done as far as sexual experience with one person?

KYLE: That would probably be this girl, last year.

R. G.:   Tell me about that.

KYLE: She had like her top off.

R. G.:   What about below the waist?

KYLE: No, I didn't, she was having her period.

R. G.:   And how about her touching you below the waist?

KYLE: She did.

R. G.:   How was that for you?

KYLE: Do you mean, did I like it?

R. G.:   Yeah.

KYLE: I suppose.

R. G.:   Were you sexually turned on? Did you have an erection?

KYLE: Uh huh.

R. G.:   And did you have a sexual climax, or did you stop before that?

KYLE: I stopped it.

R. G.:   Is that because you wanted to stop it or she wanted to?

KYLE: She wanted to stop. She was afraid we were gonna get caught.

R. G.:   Where was this?

KYLE: It was over at my house.

R. G.:   Was anybody home?

KYLE: My mom was and her brother was there.

R. G.:   It doesn't sound like the most opportune time. Did you have a chance to go further another time?

KYLE: No.

Erotic Fantasies

R. G.:   Do you know what a wet dream is?

KYLE: Uh huh.

R. G.:   How old were you the first time you had a wet dream?

KYLE: Junior high, too. Eighth grade.

R. G.:   Do you remember what was going on in the dream?

KYLE: I think it was something about this cheerleader in junior high, and she had really big breasts and everything, so I was thinking about her a lot that summer.

R. G.:   And what about wet dreams since then, what are they usually about?

KYLE: Same girl.

R. G.:   What's going on in the dream?

KYLE: She is wearing this—the one I can remember, she's wearing this white long dress, and she starts kidding me and everything, and then all of a sudden we switch to a sauna, and there's steam all over the place and she's naked. I think I dreamed that one more than once.

R. G.:   Did you have intercourse in the dream? Or did the dream stop before then?

KYLE: Well, she takes off the towel in the sauna and everything, and then it stops around there.

R. G.:   How old were you when you first started masturbation?

KYLE: Oh, my cousin, he was the one that taught me to do it. I didn't like it.

R. G.:   He told you how to do it or—

KYLE: His brother showed him and then he told me. I didn't like it.

R. G.:   How old were you?

KYLE: I think I was a freshman. Fourteen.

R. G.:   You said you didn't like masturbation. What about it didn't you like?

KYLE: Well, when it squirted all over the place and it was messy and I didn't like it at all.

R. G.:   How about the feeling part of it, was that pleasurable?

KYLE: I suppose it would be better if there was a girl there and every-thing, but I really didn't like it.

R. G.:   You're probably aware that what guys think about when they mas-turbate is very different from person to person. Some people make up stories, some people remember pictures, some people think about real people that they've seen. When you do masturbate, what do you usually think about?

KYLE: Real people.

R. G.: What happens, what's going on in your daydream?

KYLE: I can usually just imagine her standing there.

Homosexual Fantasies

R. G.: Lots of times when guys eleven, twelve, thirteen, fourteen—when they are just beginning to discover their sexual feelings like you were describing to me, they become aware of sexual feelings about males, boys, as well as about females. Sometimes when guys are like twelve, thirteen, or fourteen, they are first getting a lot of sexual feelings— you know, wet dreams, masturbation, looking at people and getting erections. They're beginning to discover themselves sexually. At that stage they sometimes get sexually turned on by men or guys as well as by girls. To what extent do you remember going through a period like that yourself?

KYLE: My cousin, he taught me how to masturbate and stuff like that, but not very much.

R. G.: How did he teach you to masturbate?

KYLE: Well, he just started doing it, and he told me to do it, but him and his brother used to do all kinds of stuff like that.

R. G.: Would they masturbate each other?

KYLE: Uh huh.

R. G.: And would they masturbate you?

KYLE: No, I never did with them.

R. G.: Did you want to or did you feel it was—

KYLE: No, I thought it was kinda sick, if they were brothers and all that.

R. G.: And to what extent, if any, have you had some sexual feelings for a man as well as for women?

KYLE: I can't really remember very much. I remember, I think sixth grade, there was a guy who was—he was older. I didn't really have sexual feelings for him, but I liked him, I thought he was a nice guy.

R. G.: Did you have a crush on him?

KYLE: I don't think I really had a crush on him. See, he was a senior in high school, and he was nice to me, and most of the seniors in high school just push you around. He's about the only one who didn't. But I never really had any sexual feelings for him or anything.

R. G.: How about with other boys your age or guys who are older? To what extent, if any, have you had any kind of sexual feelings for them?

KYLE: Well, my cousin was the only one.

R. G.: You had some sexual feelings for him?

KYLE: I didn't have feelings for him. We just kinda messed around.

R. G.: Let's say when you weren't with him, you were by yourself, did you sometimes think about him and get sexually turned on?

KYLE: No. I would think about it and be ashamed of it.

R. G.: I'm not sure I understand what you were doing with him that made you feel ashamed.

KYLE: Well, you know, like he'd show me how to masturbate—well, I guess he *did* masturbate me, and then I would think about it and feel ashamed when I was by myself.

R. G.: You felt that wasn't a proper thing to be doing?

KYLE: Yeah.

R. G.: How often did that happen that he would masturbate you?

KYLE: About three times.

R. G.: And how old were you then?

KYLE: I suppose the last time was my freshman year.

R. G.: And when you would masturbate when you were by yourself, and you would daydream about things, would you sometimes think about him?

KYLE: Usually, if I ever thought about him, then I'd stop.

R. G.: If you in fact had or have some homosexual fantasies or feelings, would you feel comfortable enough in telling me that?

KYLE: Well, a long time ago, like in grade school, I used to have dreams, and there would be guys and girls, you know, and stuff and that used to really upset me, but I've read where it happens to all guys, all guys dream about other guys and stuff, so—

R. G.: You recognize that a lot of young guys go through experiences like that?

KYLE: I read where all teenage guys, mostly or usually, do some homosexual—

R. G.: That's very common. If you still had feelings like that now, would you feel comfortable enough in telling it to me?

KYLE: I suppose I would tell you. I've gotten comfortable.

Attitude toward Homosexuality

R. G.: Let's assume for a moment that for whatever reason, you had turned out to be gay or bisexual. How would you feel about that now?

KYLE: Well, I think it's—like lots of times I think that maybe it has something to do with hormones, because like for classes like human relations we had to study some about it, and I think that it's sort of really gross, like, you know, when I read in books stuff about it.

R. G.: What sort of thing have you read?

KYLE: I read a book called *Scruples*, and it had a thing about a guy— they were in a bathroom, and it was pretty gross.

R. G.: I'm sure you're aware that there's a lot of social controversy about homosexuality and whether homosexuals should be allowed to be schoolteachers, should hold public office, have equal opportunity for jobs, housing, the whole civil rights question. How do you feel about that issue?

KYLE: I don't think they should because—well, I believe in God and everything, and I think that it's a pretty bad thing, and I think that they should try to be helped by whatever, but I think it is pretty bad, and I don't think they should be around to influence children, 'cause children are pretty easy to influence, little kids.

R. G.: Are you saying that you feel homosexuality is sinful?

KYLE: I suppose it is. I don't think they should be hurt by society or anything like—especially in New York. You have them who are into leather and stuff like that. I mean, I think that is really sick, and I think that maybe they should be put away.

Idea of Reference (Personalizing a Neutral Event)?

R. G.: Is there anything else?

KYLE: Like sometimes—I don't know. I suppose I could be overly sensitive, but sometimes like a guy—like when I was in the airport, there was this guy that kept looking at me when I was in the restaurant, and that makes me mad when they do that because—I don't know. I guess I was afraid that it could happen, you know, I could—'cause of playing with dolls and stuff.

R. G.: Tell me more about what you felt when he was looking at you.

KYLE: I felt like punching him.

R. G.: Why?

KYLE: Because I don't really—because I guess I would be overly sensitive because I did play with dolls and stuff.

R. G.: How was he looking at you? What was special about the way he was looking at you?

KYLE: Every time I turned around, he was looking, and maybe he thought I was somebody he knew or something.

R. G.: Do you think he was gay?

KYLE: I don't know. I don't know how to even notice gay people.

R. G.: Okay, but it was something about the way he was looking at you that was sort of bringing you back to some of those thoughts.

KYLE: I suppose probably because we were also going to meet you. I might have been overly sensitive to it.

R. G.: The kind of feeling you had tonight with this guy who was looking at you and made you feel uncomfortable—what other times has that happened to you?

KYLE: I suppose I've been overly sensitive when guys look at me or something ever since I can remember, you know, after my mom told me why I have to go to UCLA because they were afraid I'd turn into a homosexual.

R. G.: Are they looking at you because they think you're homosexual?

KYLE: I don't know. Maybe.

R. G.: Why would they think that?

KYLE: I don't think they're looking at me and thinking I'm homosexual. Maybe they think that I'm attractive or something.

R. G.:   Do you think you're an attractive male?

KYLE: No, not really, but I don't know, maybe somebody thinks that.

INTERVIEW WITH KYLE AT AGE EIGHTEEN

Current Adjustment

KYLE: I just think that I don't want to be the way I am, I guess.

R. G.:   Tell me in what way.

KYLE: I guess I wish that I wasn't—I guess I am withdrawn from people a lot, and I don't want to be that way, but I really don't know what to do about it.

R. G.:   Is it different for you than other kids your age who are shy?

KYLE: I think there is something different about it.

R. G.:   How?

KYLE: It seems like other people can open up to at least one other person. I guess I don't want people to get to know me.

R. G.:   What do you think they will find out?

KYLE: Things that I don't want them to find out.

R. G.:   Like what?

KYLE: I guess about my past.

R. G.:   What are you looking at about your past that you feel is affecting the way you are now?

KYLE: Well, everything about UCLA.

R. G.:   In what way?

KYLE: I guess then I always felt ashamed, self-conscious and everything.

R. G.:   What are you self-conscious about now?

KYLE: The way I look and the way I act.

R. G.:   Tell me first how you look that you feel self-conscious about.

KYLE: I sometimes think that I look too feminine.

R. G.:   In what way?

KYLE: When I was little, I remember people used to always tell me that if I was a girl I would be a really cute girl and stuff like that.

R. G.:   Do you remember that, or were you told that people said that?

KYLE: No, I remember that.

R. G.:   Do you remember how you felt when people said that?

KYLE: I didn't like it.

R. G.:   What gives you the idea now that you still look effeminate?

KYLE: I don't know. Maybe my hair or something.

R. G.:   Do people make comments to you now that suggest that they think you look effeminate?

KYLE: No.

R. G.: Do people look at you in a way that you think they are looking at you that way because you look effeminate?

KYLE: Maybe sometimes.

R. G.: Could you give me some examples when that might be?

KYLE: I can't really remember specifics. I guess whenever people look at me, sometimes I think they are.

Last Year's Airport Stare

R. G.: Do you remember last year when I talked to you, you told me that while you were waiting in the airport before you met me that you felt that some guy at the airport was staring at you and made you feel uncomfortable?

KYLE: I just remember sitting there and a guy was staring at me. I don't want to be that way. I don't want to be. So that's why I don't think I really know who I am.

R. G.: I'm not sure I understand what you are saying.

Homosexual Concerns

KYLE: Well, I think—I think that I could be gay. I don't know.

R. G.: What makes you think that you could be gay?

KYLE: Things and stuff, but I don't want to be like that.

R. G.: Tell me what things.

KYLE: Well, like dreams I've had, and stuff like that.

R. G.: Okay. Tell me about the dreams.

KYLE: Well, they are about other guys, and I don't like it.

R. G.: How recently—when is the last time you had a dream about other guys?

KYLE: A few weeks ago.

R. G.: Tell me as much as you can remember from the dream.

KYLE: I think I've blocked it out. When I wake up, I know what I was dreaming about, you know, guys and everything, but I don't really want to remember what it was about. So I just block it out of my mind.

R. G.: How much do you remember?

KYLE: Well, I can remember who they were and stuff like that.

R. G.: Are they sexual dreams?

KYLE: Yes, I guess.

R. G.: What happens sexually in the dreams?

KYLE: I don't think anything really happens, you know. But I'm thinking it, you know.

R. G.: Does the dream progress to a point where there is sexual contact, without clothes, touching?

KYLE: Maybe without clothes, but I don't think touching or anything.

R. G.: But you get the feeling in the dream it is a sexual feeling?

KYLE: Yes.

R. G.: How often do you have a dream like that?

KYLE: Every few weeks.

R. G.: When did they begin?

KYLE: Maybe since I was seventeen or sixteen.

R. G.: Do you also have romantic or sexual dreams that include females?

KYLE: Yeah. I had some.

R. G.: What happens in those dreams?

KYLE: About the same things that happen in any of them, I guess.

R. G.: And is there any sexual contact?

KYLE: Yeah, I guess. I remember the girl ones better because I guess I want to.

R. G.: What percentage of these dreams—let's say out of ten dreams like this, how many of the ten involve males and how many involve females?

KYLE: More male, I guess. I remember those better, because I don't want to dream those.

R. G.: What would you estimate—out of ten, how many would be about males?

KYLE: Maybe six or seven.

Homosexual Drive

R. G.: Anything else that you remember?

KYLE: Yeah, I guess. But I don't want to talk about it. Because you are the first person that I've ever said any of this stuff to.

R. G.: I know that. I'm also perhaps the only person that you know that you can say it to that's not going to jump up and down on you.

KYLE: I know, but it's hard.

R. G.: It's embarrassing. I know that. But I would like you to try. I think there is a lot of advantage in being able to get something out for the first time. Is part of you that recognizes the attraction for males—is part of you wanting to act on that to see what it would be like? You're nodding yes? Okay. How strong a desire is it?

KYLE: Sometimes it is very strong. I don't know. I know there are guys that would.

R. G.: Sometimes it's pretty strong?

KYLE: But I don't want to.

R. G.: Why not?

KYLE: Because I don't want to be that way.

R. G.: Why?

KYLE: Because I want to have a family some day and all that kind of stuff. I don't want to end up like somebody going to all kinds of weird bars and everything all the time with other guys and stuff like that; I don't want to do it.

R. G.: Do you feel that that is the only way gay men have relationships, to go to bars?

KYLE: I don't think I could really love another man, really love him. I don't think I really could.

R. G.: Why do you think that?

KYLE: Probably because I won't let myself think that.

Homosexual Crushes

R. G.: Have you ever felt a crush on another man?

KYLE: Yes.

R. G.: When?

KYLE: The past year.

R. G.: Tell me about the crush.

KYLE: Well, at the junior high school there was a kid there. I guess I kind of thought that he liked me or something.

R. G.: Was he gay, do you know?

KYLE: I don't know. I just got the feeling he was, I don't know why. He was a really popular guy and everything, and always went out with girls and everything. Like I'd go there and he would come and sit down at the table next to me and everything, and he would never move, and he would always talk to me and everything all the time. I guess he was.

R. G.: And that caused a lot of conflict for you. When did you first have a crush on another male?

KYLE: Probably when I was in seventh grade.

R. G.: What do you remember about the first crush?

KYLE: I didn't like what was happening.

R. G.: Did it scare you?

KYLE: It did.

R. G.: Did it surprise you?

KYLE: Not really.

R. G.: Why not?

The Link with Boyhood "Femininity"

KYLE: Because I have been through all the UCLA stuff and all that. So I knew.

R. G.: Why should the UCLA stuff—?

KYLE: Well, because that was the reason for me to go, so I wouldn't be gay.

R. G.: Who told you that?

KYLE: My parents. Well, they didn't really say that. My mom says that. She said that the reason she called you was because she saw a guy on TV who was gay, and he said that he played with dolls when he was young, and that's what she didn't want me to be.

R. G.: Why should there be any relationship between playing with dolls or doing some girl things when you are four or five and having a crush on a male when you are thirteen or fourteen?

KYLE: I guess if you play with dolls or something like that, you are perceiving yourself as a girl, that you want to be one. I guess when you are older, you know, it's still there.

R. G.: Were you still perceiving yourself as a girl when you were twelve, thirteen, or fourteen?

KYLE: No. Well, maybe I was fantasizing once in while, but I didn't perceive, I knew.

R. G.: You knew you weren't a girl?

KYLE: Uh huh.

R. G.: But you sometimes made believe in your fantasy that you were?

KYLE: Yes.

R. G.: What years are we talking about now?

KYLE: Till now.

R. G.: Until now? Try to paint one of the fantasies—a picture—what you see in your mind when you think about that.

KYLE: It used to be that I was a girl, but now it's not. It's more about other girls.

R. G.: What do you mean, now it's more about other girls?

KYLE: It's not me—a girl—any more. It's just other girls. I don't see myself as a girl any more.

R. G.: When did it stop?

KYLE: I think about eighth grade.

R. G.: I got a little confused because you said until now, but then you said it stopped in eighth grade.

KYLE: Well, no. I don't think of myself as a girl.

R. G.: Do you still want to be a woman?

KYLE: I don't think so. But that's what I said; I don't really know myself very well. I don't know what I want.

R. G.: If you were a woman now, magically, what advantage would you have?

KYLE: I can't really think of any. Except for maybe since I am uncoordinated everything would fit my sex better if I was a woman.

R. G.: Can you think of anything else?

KYLE: I guess if I like guys, it would be easier if I was.

R. G.: Why?

KYLE: 'Cause that's the way it's normal, I guess, for girls to like guys. Not guys to like guys.

Heterosexual Crushes

R. G.: Have you had any crushes on girls?

KYLE: Yes.

R. G.: When?

KYLE: I can remember one in seventh, in junior high. And then I liked a girl, I remember I liked a girl in my junior year real well. I didn't think about guys when I liked her.

R. G.: How long did you have a crush or some romantic feelings about her?

KYLE: A few months, I guess.

R. G.: You went out?

KYLE: She couldn't go out; she wasn't old enough.

Heterosexual Experience

R. G.: Have you had some kind of petting, necking experiences with girls?

KYLE: Not with one I really liked.

R. G.: What sort of experiences have you had so far?

KYLE: I guess I've done about everything.

R. G.: Have you had sexual intercourse?

KYLE: Once.

R. G.: Tell me about the experience.

KYLE: I was really drunk. I didn't know the girl. I had never met her before except for that night.

R. G.: What do you remember about it?

KYLE: Well, I can't remember everything because, you know, it's all kind of a blur to me, since I was drunk. It wasn't really like I could feel anything or anything like that.

R. G.: Do you remember whether it was enjoyable?

KYLE: Yeah, I guess it was. Scary, too.

R. G.: Did you ever see her again?

KYLE: No.

R. G.: To what extent do you have a desire to have a sexual relationship with a woman now?

KYLE: I haven't been thinking about it.

Sexual Orientation

R. G.: If you had to compare your interest in having sexual contact with a female versus sexual contact with a male, which would be stronger?

KYLE: I guess with another man right now or lately.

R. G.: If you had to put it on a ten-point scale, and let's say one was pure sexual interest in a female and ten pure sexual interest in a male, what number would you give it?

KYLE: Probably a seven.

R. G.: What about in masturbation fantasy? What kinds of things do you think about?

KYLE: This is hard.

R. G.: I know it's hard.

KYLE: Sometimes I think about guys; sometimes I think about girls. Usually towards the beginning I think about a guy, and then at the end I think about a girl.

R. G.:   After a while it sort of switches over, and you are thinking about a girl? What happens with the girl?

KYLE: I usually have sex.

R. G.:   Do you have sex with the guys in the daydream?

KYLE: Yeah, I guess.

Homosexual Experience

KYLE: I did have a homosexual experience with a guy.

R. G.:   When was that?

KYLE: It must have been almost a year ago.

R. G.:   Tell me about that.

KYLE: It was in the convention center.

R. G.:   What happened?

KYLE: It's hard to bring this up.

R. G.:   I know.

KYLE: I was in the bathroom, and I'm disgusted with it.

R. G.:   Did you go into the bathroom knowing that there was a guy in there?

KYLE: Yeah.

R. G.:   What happened when you met inside?

KYLE: I went into the stall. He looked under there, and I guess I did what he wanted me to.

R. G.:   What happened?

KYLE: He didn't do anything to me.

R. G.:   What did you do for him?

KYLE: I can't say it.

R. G.:   Did you suck his penis?

KYLE: Yes.

R. G.:   How did you feel doing that?

KYLE: I don't know.

R. G.:   Do you recall if you were sexually turned on?

KYLE: I don't know what I felt.

R. G.:   Did you ever see him again?

KYLE: I wouldn't even know what he looked like if I saw him.

R. G.:   Okay. It sounds like you have had two brief sexual encounters, one with a woman you never saw before and one with a man you never saw before. Can you compare what your feelings are about both of them?

KYLE: I guess I was kind of numb both times.

R. G.:   The first time you were kind of drunk.

KYLE: Then I was numb. That's the only thing I know.

R. G.:   What do you mean, numb?

Homosexual Conflict

KYLE: It wasn't like I was real. And afterwards, a few weeks later, I tried to kill myself.

R. G.:   Tell me about that.

KYLE: I swallowed about fifty aspirins.

R. G.:   Did you really want to die?

KYLE: I think I really wanted to, but I knew I wasn't going to. But I really did want to.

R. G.:   Why?

KYLE: Because I don't want to grow up to be gay.

R. G.:   How strong an influence on your thinking is religious feeling?

KYLE: Not really strong, I don't think. It is pretty strong, but it's more me. I don't want to be that way. But religion is pretty strong too. Because I know it's wrong.

R. G.:   Do you feel it's sinful?

KYLE: Yes.

R. G.:   I'm not sure if I understand whether it's the idea of being gay or the idea that gay people don't live happy lives that's even more—

KYLE: I think it's both.

R. G.:   It's both.

KYLE: Even if I was gay, I might feel happy and everything, but I know, I would know it is wrong. I know it would be.

R. G.:   You also told me that you had crushes on girls. You had sexual intercourse with a female. Do you think it's possible that in that case you would fall in love with a woman and get married and have your children and not be bothered by the homosexual feelings?

KYLE: I might. I think I probably would be. I mean, maybe I wouldn't, but if I loved somebody that much. But I never really loved anybody that much.

R. G.:   But are you worrying that if you met somebody—a woman like that—the homosexual part would get in the way? Is that your fear?

KYLE: It is.

R. G.:   Why do you think it would get in your way?

KYLE: I've read a lot of books and stuff, and it usually does.

R. G.:   What have you read?

KYLE: I don't know—books and stuff—and it seems to happen all the them.

R. G.:   Well, I guess the answer is that it's variable from person to person. There are men who have homosexual feelings who marry and have children and don't get bothered by homosexual feelings during their marriage at all. And there are some who do. And for those who do, I guess the way they try to handle it also varies from person to person.

KYLE: They become bitter?

R. G.:   Some people just suppress the feeling. Some people act on them and have some relationship outside the marriage. In a way, it's not that different, I suppose, from men who are totally heterosexual who in times of their marriage also feel some sexual interest for people other than their wives, and they also have sex outside the marriage.

KYLE: That's the way society accepts things.

R. G.: Well, society doesn't exactly wholeheartedly embrace extramarital sex, even if it's with a heterosexual.

KYLE: I don't think I'd divorce because of the gay feeling. Maybe if I did something with another man and my wife found out about it, maybe she would divorce me. But I've never been really in love with a woman before to want to get married.

R. G.: You are only eighteen, just eighteen. It's not that you have exhausted the potential for finding a woman of your choice. You live in a pretty small town. Are there very many women your age?

KYLE: Most of them that are my age got pregnant or married or something.

R. G.: Or both pregnant *and* married. So it sounds like in terms of the opportunity to meet people, you have to go away from your hometown. And college is an ideal place. On this campus alone there are probaby seven thousand unmarried, unpregnant women, which is probably more than your entire hometown has.

Anticipated Parental Reaction to Kyle's Bisexuality

R. G.: How do you think your mom would feel if she knew that you had some feelings for males as well as for females?

KYLE: I think it would probably hurt her.

R. G.: How do you feel your dad would feel?

KYLE: I think maybe he suspected it, and that's why he treated me the way he did. He'd probably feel guilty.

R. G.: Why would he feel guilty?

KYLE: Because it's partly his fault.

R. G.: Do you think if your dad treated you differently as a kid, that he had been a warmer, more affectionate father with you, that that would have changed the way you feel now about males and females in terms of your sexual and romantic feelings?

KYLE: Probably. Maybe.

R. G.: Why?

KYLE: I never had really close relations. I had closer relations with women than I did with any man.

R. G.: Why should that influence whether you are romantically interested in men now?

KYLE: That would influence why I wanted to be a girl when I was little. Because when you are a child, I think you copy what you see. And I didn't have any strong male influence.

R. G.: Do you think your mother, if she had behaved somewhat differently with you when you were a little boy, that would have affected the way you feel now?

KYLE: She did what she thought was right. She probably loved me too much, but she couldn't have done anything else. I suppose I kind of hate her for taking me to the baby-sitter. I don't know if that was the whole root of the problem.

More Reflections on the UCLA Experience

R. G.: I don't know either. What about the UCLA experience? Let's say you hadn't gone to UCLA at all and hadn't had the treatment with the other doctors. Do you feel that your sexual or romantic feelings now would be different?

KYLE: I'd probably be a total basket case.

R. G.: How?

KYLE: I'd probably think of myself as a girl. They did a lot for me. I think it might have been a little late, I don't know. I guess maybe it's been up to me.

R. G.: Do you think you would have had more gay feelings now?

KYLE: Yes.

R. G.: Some day if you were a father and you had a boy who was four who was, let's say, dressing up in girls' clothes and saying he wished he were a girl and playing with dolls, would you bring him to a place like UCLA?

KYLE: Yes.

R. G.: Why?

KYLE: I would take him where he would be helped.

R. G.: Do you think sometimes though that bringing a boy to a place like the UCLA program with that psychologist can also cause more conflict in a boy rather than help him?

KYLE: I think it might have a little with me because of the way my parents handled it.

R. G.: How do you mean?

KYLE: Well, I felt really ashamed, and I didn't want anybody to know, and when the research guys would come to check on me, I didn't want anybody to see me with them. Maybe that wasn't my parents' fault, it's just—people don't really understand.

Kyle's Expectation of My Reactions to His Sexuality

R. G.: I recognize the difficulty in talking about the things you did. That is the first time you said some of those words out loud, and I guess you weren't really sure of what my reaction was going to be.

KYLE: I thought you would be mad.

R. G.: Why?

KYLE: Well, because the whole purpose of everything you did, I thought, was to keep me from being like that. I thought you would be disappointed in me.

R. G.: What do you think now? Do you think I am disappointed?

KYLE: No.

R. G.: No, I'm not disappointed. I'm not ecstatic; I'm not disappointed. It's not a question of my approving or not approving of who you are. It's finding out who you are, and if you are having a conflict somewhere, to see if I can find a way to handle the conflict. I think the principal concern in terms of the initial evaluation and referral to the psychologist when you were a young boy was not to prevent you from becoming homosexual fifteen years later. It was because you were unhappy being a boy back when you were four, and because kids who are four, five, six, who do a lot of girl-type things get a lot of teasing from other kids. The goal was to reduce the stress you were feeling back then. As to whether you lead a married, family life-style or a gay life-style or both, it's not for me to have a feeling one way or the other about that. My concern is that whatever you do, you be happy doing it.

CONCLUSION

The apparent powerlessness of treatment to interrupt the progression from "feminine" boy to homosexual or bisexual man is revealed further by examination of the full sample of twelve boys who entered a therapy program. Nine emerged as bisexual or homosexual. This proportion is comparable to that of the entire group.

Common sense would suggest that the reason some boys entered therapy was greater concern by their parents over the boys' cross-gender behavior. When we rated the mother's and father's attitudes toward their son's behaviors at the time of initial evaluation, we found that parents of sons who entered therapy were more worried that the cross-gender behavior portended problems with later sexuality. This concern might work in concert with therapy. However, the results, showing no major impact of treatment on sexual orientation, suggest that this greater concern did not operate to influence later sexuality.

Age of the child upon entering therapy might also relate to later sexual orientation. Intervention at an earlier age might be expected to interrupt more effectively the atypical pattern of sexual development. However, the boys who entered therapy averaged about a year *younger* at evaluation than those who did not enter therapy.

Should we be surprised that the treatment intervention did not abort the development of homosexual arousal? For behavior modification treatment to influence sexual orientation, it is necessary to presume direct developmental continuity between childhood cross-gender behavior and adulthood homosexual behavior. Our data show that this is not invariably the case. For psychoanalytic treatment to deter homosexual outcome, there must be resolution of posited unresolved facets of preoedipal and oedipal development that are directly related to a lingering same-sex sexual orientation. Controversy over psychoanalytic theory, and mixed results of psychoanalytic treatment when attempting to reorient homosexuality in adulthood, point to major conceptual problems here. Treatment designed to promote identification with a male therapist, perhaps remedying a deficient father-son relationship, rests on the premise that homosexual arousal reflects feminine (or at least deficiently masculine) identification. While the premise may have some merit (chapter 3), again, this association is not invariable, and the period in which this deficit operates appears to be in the first few years. This early interval may be a critical developmental period beyond which the deficit cannot be remedied.

Sexual orientation aside, are those who were treated better adjusted psychologically? Results on psychological testing offer only modest comfort for treatment advocates. Scores on the Tennessee Self-Concept Scale (chapter 6) do not differ for those who had therapy and those who did not. The only hint of an advantage is on the scale of self-satisfaction. Here the full group of previously "feminine" boys scored significantly lower than the previously "masculine" boys, but the previously "feminine" boys who were treated had scores tending to be closer to the previously "masculine boys." That the difference is not statistically significant may be due in part to the small number of subjects available for comparison.

Nor was anyone obviously *harmed* by treatment. Opponents of therapy have argued that intervention underscores the child's "deviance," renders him ashamed of who he is, and makes him suppress his "true self." Data on psychological tests do not support this contention; nor does the content of clinical interviews. The boys look back favorably on treatment. They would endorse such intervention if they were the father of a "feminine" boy. Their reason is to reduce childhood conflict and social stigma. Therapy with these boys appeared to accomplish this. Reduction of conflict and stigma will remain viable treatment goals until society evolves to the point of accommodating greater latitude in the boyhood expression of currently "sex-typed" behaviors.

8

"Identical" Twin Boys, One Masculine, One Feminine: Revisited as Men

Twins tempt. They lure the researcher to speculate, usually beyond the limits of data. They flirt with relative impunity, because they are ideal research subjects for those who remain hell-bent on distinguishing the impacts of nature and nurture. But the very fact of twinning—by the nature of its rarity—frustrates. The samples are too small. Only one in eighty-seven births is a twin. Of these, only about one-third are monozygotic (genetically "identical"). And the problems do not stop with rarity.

Most twins are reared together in the same household, so that behavioral similarities may be explainable by similar environments as well as by similar genes. Thus, the researcher needs monozygotic twins separated at birth. Two more problems: first, most twins are not reared apart, and second, when they are, their homes may not be sufficiently dissimilar to maximize the impact of a particular environment. Typically, one twin is not dispatched to a poor mountain mining community while the other is placed on a plush suburban estate.

And if these detours on the road to distinguishing nature from nurture are not sufficient to frustrate the researcher, an enormous pothole opens when the study focuses on homosexuality. Again, numbers. If only 4 percent of males are exclusively homosexual and another 6 or 7 percent are primarily homosexual (Kinsey et al., 1948), most monozygotic twins, reared separately, should be heterosexual. About 90 percent of hetero-sexual twins reared apart would be expected to have a heterosexual co-twin, just as would *any* two males who are unrelated and reared separately. Therefore, finding a heterosexual co-twin for a heterosexual twin is not very exciting.

Not surprisingly, researchers have found very few pairs of twins, reared apart, where at least one is homosexual. If every co-twin were also homosexual, even with the small number, it would be tempting to come down on the side of nature. It would be more tempting if the homes in which the boys were raised were strikingly dissimilar, with one home being the type that is often thought to produce male homosexuality (absent father, overbearing mother, etc.) and the other the type that is thought to produce heterosexuality. However, if both homes are of the type believed to yield homosexuality, our excitement should be calmed.

Finally, when the findings are mixed—that is, not *all*, but some, homosexual twins have homosexual co-twins—our enthusiasm yields to frustration. Regrettably, this is the case with the handful of twin pairs who have so far been uncovered in this dream design.

A few earlier reports describe homosexuality in twins. The classic report is that of Franz Kallman (1952), who found high rates of concordance for most psychiatric states in twin pairs. His spectacular finding with homosexuality was that of thirty-nine homosexual twins presumed to be monozygotic, all co-twins were also homosexual. While zygosity might not have been precise, and a sampling bias could have operated, and while sexual orientation ratings were grossly categorized, this concordance rate cannot be easily dismissed. However, since the Kallman paper, there have been reports of a few monozygotic twin pairs in which only one co-twin was homosexual. One report is of special interest in that it reflects on the twin pair in our study.

Four sets of male twins considered monozygotic, and in which one co-twin was homosexual, were described. In all four pairs, the child whose name was most clearly associated with the father evolved the "masculine" role. (This was also the case with our twin pair described below, Paul and Frank, Jr.) "Naming, perhaps, is the clearest indication of later identification patterns and eventual sexual role. In these families naming appeared to be a concrete manifestation of the allocation of the twin to either the mother or father" (Mesinkoff et al., 1963, 734). In one pair, the mother encouraged one twin to play with dolls and learn dancing and discouraged him from sports and play with boys. When the child was six, his father stated, "It was clear that one [twin] was like a boy while the other was like a girl" (735).

Our co-twins, described in 1974 and revisited here, are this study's metaphor. One illustrates the progression from "sissy" boy to homosexual or bisexual man. Both epitomize the nature/nurture dilemma in explaining sexual identity development.*

---

* The probability that the twins are monozygotic is very high. The total ridge count on the digits for both boys is 192. Both boys have identical findings for the following red cell antigens: ABO, Le, Rh, Go, MNSs, Fy, Lu, Kk, Jk, P, and Vel. Additionally, phosphoglucomutase, haptoglobin, 6-phosphogluconate dehydro-

THE PARENTS DESCRIBE THE TWINS AT AGE EIGHT

General Behavior

R. G.:   How different are the two boys in regard to masculinity?

MOTHER: Very. First of all with actions. Frank walks like a clodhopper. Paul, on the other hand, walks femininely. He is on the prissy side. He has a feminine ring to his voice. He is like a female when he gets upset. He thoroughly enjoys playing with dolls. He and his sister can play day upon day upon day. His brother will deliberately go out and get into a football game or anything with the older boys in the neighborhood. Paul will still dress in women's clothes, but he's getting out of the habit because he knows it really aggravates us. He will put hair clips in his hair. When they play house, Frank is always the father and Paul is always the mother or sister.

Early Differences

R. G.:   Did they look different at birth?

FATHER: Paul looked a great deal heavier and rounder, a good-looking baby. The other like a spider monkey.

MOTHER: Frank was very badly mutilated. Oh, he looked like a drowned baby bird. He was a very ugly infant. Paul had big eyes and was a pound heavier, so his face was fuller.

FATHER: He was the best looking of the two.

MOTHER: We always got comments in the double stroller, "Oh, how nice! A boy and a girl." You can guess who they thought was the girl and who they thought was the boy.

R. G.:   Paul was the girl?

MOTHER: It was Paul they thought was the girl. It used to infuriate me. The two of them dressed identical. Never did I put lace or frills on.

R. G.:   What were they responding to? Why did they think Paul was the girl?

MOTHER: Because Frank just took off like a little old man. He never looked like a baby. Never. Paul did. He looked the picture, with the rosy cheeks, round face, blue eyes, blond hair. Paul was always the cuddlier of the two boys. You could hold him. You tried to hold Frank, and he would do everything but bite you.

R. G.:   Was one twin more active?

MOTHER: Up to four months there was nothing you could identify. After that I would say Frank over Paul. When they were still in the playpen, which puts them a little under a year, Frank reached over and bit Paul

---

genase, and adenylate kinase electrophoretic types are identical. These findings essentially preclude the possibility that the twins are dizygotic.

on the ear something fierce, and Paul didn't do anything. He just curled up.

R. G.: Were there as many times that Paul was dominant?

MOTHER: I would say it was almost equal.

Preference for a Boy rather than a Girl

R. G.: Did you have preference when you were pregnant for a boy or a girl?

FATHER: A boy.

MOTHER: Personally, if I were given the choice, I would have rather had a girl. However, he wanted a boy. He's the last Frank Riley. And therefore, because he wanted a boy, I wanted a boy. I had to have a girl too.

One Twin Named for Father

R. G. (to father): You're the last Frank? You named one of the boys after you?

MOTHER AND FATHER: Yeah.

R. G.: How did you decide which twin to name Frank, Jr.?

MOTHER AND FATHER: First born.

FATHER: We found out before they were born they'd be twins, and we decided the first born would be Frank, Jr.

MOTHER: Now I wish we could go back and change their names.

R. G.: Why?

MOTHER: Even though we haven't gone into detail in front of the children as to why Frank was named after his father, it almost looks—I can see, looking through Paul's eyes—that he got Daddy's name because he's the one that Daddy liked.

Onset of Behavioral Differences

R. G.: When did you start noticing a difference?

MOTHER: Four, four-and-a-half. Paul preferred the friendship of the little girls in the neighborhood and enjoyed playing with dolls and took more of an interest in his sister than his brother. His brother was becoming very masculine at the time. Paul didn't want to participate in sports. He'd much rather clean house. I don't know whether it was a preference for me or for what I did—the fun of getting all dressed up or putting on makeup or doing dishes or grocery shopping. These seemed to be the things he preferred to do. I was the one who did them.

At age three, the "prefeminine" boy contracted an infectious disease involving lymph nodes of the axilla and neck. His illness radically modified the roles each parent played with each twin. For two-and-a-half years, the mother repeatedly drove the "prefeminine" boy to a hospital (an hour each way) for extended evaluation and treatment. Meanwhile, the father was at home with the "premasculine" boy.

FATHER: I think the reason I kind of laid off a lot of sports with Paul was because he was down here in the hospital, and I had a chance to be with Frank more and tried to keep him occupied with sports during these periods of time. The reason I didn't push Paul that much was because his little arm was bad at the time, and it was hard to make him do it. I gave up on him until the last couple of years. I was upset because he didn't want to do it.

MOTHER: Paul was always invited to be included with his brother, to participate, whether it was kite-flying or basketball or baseball, but he didn't. All the females in the family said, "You can't do that to him. That isn't his cup of tea."

FATHER: The operation affected his arm, and he wasn't quite as active. Everything has been toward the fact that maybe you can't push him like that because he's that way.

MOTHER: It gave him an excuse for not competing with his brother. This is where his aunt came into the picture: "Well, he can't throw a ball like Frank, because he has a hurt shoulder."

The parents became reluctant to return for reevaluation when the twins were about ten. Intermittent telephone contacts indicated that both had some delinquency problems during their early teenage years and then entered the military. Both were reported to be emerging as heterosexually oriented.

INTERVIEW WITH PAUL AT AGE TWENTY-ONE

Catching Up

R. G.: Let's see, you were about ten when I saw you last, so obviously there's a lot of years to catch up on. Why don't you give me a general synopsis or outline of what's been happening with you?

PAUL: Well, I went as far as going into high school before saying "forget it," and after that went almost a year-and-a-half or so doing absolutely nothing; caused my parents tons of headaches. So one summer I made up my mind I was gonna go to the service, the navy, so I did that for about two years. Now, I'm a sales representative, and I'm doing that and have had a relationship now for about a year-and-a-half.

Homosexual Relationship

R. G.: What kind?

PAUL: With a guy. And it's been a headache, a real headache, miserable,

I've been miserable and yet I've been happy. I don't know if you can relate to that but it's—

R. G.:   Well, you can tell me more about it.

PAUL: When I was in the service I had my first real experience with a male, and it was different. Then I went through that kind of relationship with this guy for three or four months and just decided I really didn't want that, I didn't want to be tied down to any specific person. So I did my own thing, and then I came home and one of my mother's friends, I went out with him as a lover for about four months. And he's not on good terms with my family anymore.

R. G.:   I can't imagine why!

PAUL: It was a real mess, real mess. And then I met this guy. He's—he made me very miserable yet I could not let him go, he could not let me go, and we're so violent, both of us, as far as just our relationship. I'm not a violent person, but he and I are gonna kill each other if something doesn't happen. We're just now kinda trying things again. He and I are not gonna let each other go. I was going out with a girlfriend before I met him, and I had a good time with her, and then he came along and I went head over heels for him, you know, and since we broke up about a month ago and I was seeing this girl again and we're happy, real happy, and she's the type that will let me live my own life. But he puts me through some awful head trips.

R. G.:   What sort of trips?

PAUL: He's just the most jealous thing there ever was. Really, I've never met a girl in my whole life that was jealous or possessive as he is, and I know he loves me. And I don't want to scare my parents about being gay, you know, because I'm afraid that this is the way I am, because I tried it both ways and this is what I want, and he, in a way, scares me about it.

R. G.:   Because you think this is the way gay relationships have to be?

PAUL: Yeah, this is my first real relationship, you know. The others were just different. This is the first real love I've had for a guy in my whole entire life.

R. G.:   You've heard that this is the way they all are?

PAUL: Right. And I've seen friends of my parents go through similar things, and it worries me.

Onset of Sexual Feelings

R. G.:   Looking back, when is the first that you remember any sexual interests in anybody, whether it was a male or female?

PAUL: I would say I was about eleven or twelve when I first had a friend of mine that I went to school with.

R. G.:   How old was he?

PAUL: Same age.

R. G.: What do you remember doing?

PAUL: Just touching and looking, and I always slept over. It was my friend, and I guess I always slept over there, but we never did anything, and I was about eleven years old. Then I hadn't seen him for about two-and-a-half years, and I guess I was about fourteen or fifteen—I didn't have any sex with him, I just did the basics with him.

R. G.: What does the basics mean?

PAUL: Blow-job. Not any sexual intercourse or anything like that. Touching and so forth, but that was pretty much it.

Heterosexual Relationship

PAUL: And actually I was seeing this girl, who I also went to school with and had known her since I was a senior, and I went off and on with her for about two-and-a-half years, and I still at the same time kinda, you know, looked at boys and thought about guys but yet wanting to be with her right along. Well, then I just didn't know what two guys did together.

R. G.: What age?

PAUL: About fifteen to sixteen or seventeen.

R. G.: What were you doing sexually?

PAUL: Intercourse when I was about sixteen for the first time.

Bisexuality

R. G.: Back then in those years—let's say fourteen, fifteen, sixteen—was the sexual drive stronger for a male or for a female or about equal?

PAUL: It was about equal, I would say, but I—I don't know, I was too shy to go out and try it with a guy.

R. G.: How about in fantasy?

PAUL: About even I would say.

R. G.: What about masturbation? I'm trying to get a sense of—at the beginning of adolescence—whether your sexual interests were equally divided between men and women, even before you were actually having experiences.

PAUL: Oh, most of the time when I would masturbate I would be fantasizing more of being with a male than a female.

R. G.: What about wet dreams?

PAUL: Mostly about guys. There happened to be this guy, a friend of my mother's, that for some reason he was always there.

Heterosexual Satisfaction

R. G.: Let's go back to when you were having the sexual relationship with this girl when you were about fifteen.

PAUL: Well sixteen was my first time that I actually had intercourse with a girl.

R. G.:   How was that experience for you?

PAUL: Wonderful, yet I still was thinking about, you know, a male on the side.

R. G.:   When you were having sex with her, did you fantasize about being with a guy?

PAUL: Not until after being with her for about a year.

R. G.:   Were you seeing any guys on the side?

PAUL: No. She kept me content, I was just totally content with her.

R. G.:   When you were seeing her, did you think that all the gay feelings were gone?

PAUL: No, not at all.

More Heterosexuality

PAUL: I was with a girl when I was in Italy, and I hurt her so bad. I was with her for eight months until one time I could not even get turned on to her—it was awful.

R. G.:   Tell me about that relationship.

PAUL: It was an Italian girl, a beautiful girl. More than anything I was just so—she was so beautiful, and she had taken very good care of me, and I was over there, knowing nobody, having nothing, and she was just total security for me. And we carried on for about three months until I finally decided I really liked this girl, you know, and she was sexually attracted to me, and we made love for almost a year, and then just one day we tried it and I could not do it. I don't know what it was. It was the weirdest feeling I've ever had in my life, and I hurt her so bad.

R. G.:   Well, there could be lots of reasons for not turning on—

PAUL: No, I know, but even from there on I could not—I just didn't want to have sex with her anymore. I was going to gay bars and stuff with her too.

Erotic Arousal to Males

R. G.:   Were you fantasizing about other men during the relationship with her?

PAUL: No.

R. G.:   Would you sometimes masturbate to fantasies about guys?

PAUL: Yeah.

R. G.:   But you weren't following through on it?

PAUL: Uh uh. I was not really carrying on any kind of relationship, nothing.

R. G.:   Why?

PAUL: The Italian guys, most of them are all uncut guys, and that probably turned me off a lot of guys.

R. G.:   What do you mean, uncut?

PAUL: Uncircumcised, and every Italian guy is like that. I just don't like that. And they're just sort of weird, they're not into relationships. Just fucking or eating it. I couldn't find a guy that I could settle down with.

R. G.:   You said you had some brief relationship with a guy while you were in the service. When was that?

PAUL: He was an American guy. That was before her. And we were always real good friends during our relationship. He was always with us really, a threesome. And, we were just—we were two different people sexually.

R. G.:   In what way?

PAUL: I could get turned on to his body; he couldn't get turned on to mine.

R. G.:   To what extent are you interested in the leather/chain/jean/key ring type guys?

PAUL: Leather?

R. G.:   Yeah, super macho ones with the motorcycles and nazi jackets.

PAUL: No. I would like to fantasize about that, you know—as an ideal, it does turn me on, but I could never hold a relationship with a guy like that.

R. G.:   Has your lover gotten into bondage?

PAUL: He likes to occasionally tie me up, but never—not to be whipped. One time I was in a gay bar, a leather bar, and he had to work so I went by myself, and I met this guy. He had gotten really drunk and he was gorgeous, had pierced tits—that turns me on. I was in the bar with him, and he had just gotten so drunk that I said I would drive him home, so I drove him home and I went up to his place with him. Never in my life have I been so abused. He was a very strong guy. The first time to be tied up and to be thrown down and just radically abused. He was scaring me, but then again I just wanted to beat him up and fuck him, you know. That's just the way I felt, because he was gonna fuck me and no way. I wasn't gonna mind to lay down with him, I wasn't gonna allow him to fuck me. First of all he was—he had the biggest damn erection in my life. I said "No, no, no," and he was dead set on he was gonna fuck me, but I just turned off, and we got into a real fight. I fucked him and left.

R. G.:   How masculine or feminine do you see yourself?

PAUL: I don't think I'm that masculine. I've never been classified as being somebody that was the leather type or real rough or macho type, just real quiet and wouldn't hurt a person, and that's the way I classified myself as well. But as far as being feminine, I admit I have feminine ways, but I try my hardest not to flaunt it in public. I try to be as discreet as possible.

Brother's Sexuality

R. G.:   Let me ask you a bit about your brother. How is he developing sexually?

PAUL: He will fuck anything. He's really—he's living with a guy now but he's not gay, he's real—you have to see him to believe it, he's real macho-macho, yet he's—he sells himself to older guys in the bars to make money, because he needs that money all the time, and yet I know that he loves a woman, loves to fuck a woman, and I'm sure that he's never been fucked, you know. Guys told me they fucked him, but I don't believe it. I know he doesn't turn on to them, but yet he's totally acceptable to my way of life, and he's gotten involved with gay people and—

R. G.:   Tell me about the extent of his involvement with gays.

PAUL: Well, there's a bar, a particular bar that he goes to that you can hustle or sell yourself when you need money, and he does it. When he needs money, he goes down there.

R. G.:   He always does it for money?

PAUL: Yeah.

R. G.:   Does he ever do it just for pleasure?

PAUL: Oh, no, he'd kick somebody's ass for that if he doesn't get paid, you know. He doesn't hate gays at all, he's totally acceptable to my way.

R. G.:   How does he label himself? Does he think he's bisexual, gay, or—

PAUL: When people ask, "Yeah, he's bisexual," but he doesn't want me to tell 'em that. He just gets pissed off. He thinks he's straight, as far as he's concerned.

R. G.:   That's just trade?

PAUL: Uh huh. And he's been doing it for so long. I've been home almost two years and he even—all the time I really never knew what he was up to, until one night I went with him and he told me about this.

R. G.:   Of all the ways that a guy can make money, okay, why do you suppose that this is a way he's selected?

PAUL: I think a lot of gay older men do have money, and this particular place they do have money, and they'll treat you and buy you this and buy you that. They wine him and dine him all the time. Sometimes I'm led to believe that maybe he does like what he's doing, but yet I can't ever think that he is gay; bisexual, yes, but not gay.

R. G.:   How masculine or feminine is he?

PAUL: I don't know one feminine thing about him.

R. G.:   Is he super macho or does he—

PAUL: He's a super macho. He walks macho, he's—

R. G.:   Exaggeratedly, or is he—

PAUL: No, that's him.

R. G.:   How much sex experience with women has he had?

PAUL: A hell of a lot. I had sex before him, he was just still looking until he was about seventeen, I think he was, when he first really had a relationship with a woman. He said he just fucked some and he thought it was weird. He's really mean to girls. He gets beautiful girlfriends, and sometimes he just fucks 'em and leaves 'em, and I hate this about him because I like his girlfriends. I'll tell a girl before he even gets involved, "You'll be sorry!" You know, "This guy's a jerk, he's not ready for a relationship." He goes through it once every week. If he's got one one week, he's still got six others that he's fucking with.

Erotic Interest between the Brothers

R. G.:   To what extent, if any, have you had sexual interests in your brother?

PAUL: Never have.

R. G.:   How do you explain that?

PAUL: I don't know. Everybody swears up and down I've had sex with my brother, anybody that has known us as brothers. I don't know. I can't do it. I've seen him in the nude and he doesn't turn me on, nothing about him.

R. G.:   Do you think he has any interest in you?

PAUL: No. Although people have offered to take both of us home at one time in bed. I wouldn't do it, not for a thousand dollars. He offered like five hundred bucks to go home with him, and the way my brother was—it's like, "What're you talkin' about?" No way, I couldn't. It would not turn me on.

R. G.:   This guy wanted you two to fuck each other or he wanted to fuck both of you?

PAUL: He wanted my brother to fuck me, and no way, and my brother was there, and he said, "Yeah, I'll do it."

R. G.:   Your brother was willing to do it?

PAUL: Yes. I think he would fuck anything. I would starve and die before I would.

R. G.:   He was up to it?

PAUL: Yeah, he was totally up to it. He was so pissed off at me.

R. G.:   Why?

PAUL: 'Cause he could have made $250. No way.

Theory of Homosexuality

R. G.:   Play psychologist for me now. You described a very different pattern of behavior, at least now, between you and your brother. Why do you suppose that you're so different? I mean, you're genetically the same. What accounts for the—

PAUL: I want beautiful things in life, he will take 'em as they come.

R. G.:   Why do you suppose he's got more macho interests—leave the sex out for a minute, just in terms of macho interests versus yours, looking back at your relationship to your mom and dad and his to your mom and dad—

PAUL: Oh, I can relate to my mother, when he couldn't. I remember all my life I was my mother's—you know, I was always—more with my mother, not my father, and he was totally opposite.

R. G.: How did that evolve?

PAUL: My brother didn't wanna do things I wanted to. I wanted to be with my mother and clean the house, he wanted to go out and play baseball with my dad.

R. G.: How far back do you remember that difference between the two of you?

PAUL: Forever.

R. G.: You described being around your mother. Was that your preference, or do you think your mother sorted you out between the two of you?

PAUL: My mother did it and my dad did the same thing with him. I thought that I was forced to be with my mother by my father, and he was forced to be with my father by my mother.

R. G.: Tell me about that.

PAUL: Just 'cause of the things that he wanted to do, and my father felt I could get more interested in helping her clean the house than he could, you know, and he could be out hammering nails. And my dad felt that he could be more interested than I could. This is what I felt. And I still feel the same way.

R. G.: Was it true, or was their perception wrong?

PAUL: I don't think my brother was ever actually jealous of me and my mother, but I was always—I didn't want to be with my father, but I was jealous of my brother sometimes. It was no big thing, I just never really cared for my father. He wasn't my favorite, I wanted to be with my mother.

INTERVIEW WITH FRANK, JR., AT AGE TWENTY-ONE

Mom's Boy and Dad's Boy

FRANK: We're like night and day, me and my brother, if you haven't already noticed.

R. G.: Tell me how are you different.

FRANK: I guess he's more like Mom's boy, and I'm my dad's type boy.

R. G.: Has that always been the case?

FRANK: Yeah, he's Mommy's boy and I'm Daddy's boy.

R. G.: Why do you think that happened?

FRANK: That's something I have never figured out, and no one else has been able to figure it out. I was with my dad and always played baseball, active and doing things. And my brother was more like cleaning house and doing things with my mom—just like night and day.

Sexual Differences

FRANK: He likes guys and doesn't like girls. I shouldn't say that, but he's got a boyfriend now, you know what I mean? And he likes girls, girls like him, but he doesn't want to have relationships with any girls. I don't know why. I'm just the opposite. I'm kinda embarrassed by that because I'm his twin brother, and I've gone to places and his friends think I'm him, which is kind of an embarrassment.

R. G.: How do you mean, you're the opposite?

FRANK: He's into feminine, steady-type things—I'm more masculine than feminine. It's obvious, everybody knows it. They can look at him and say I'm very opposite—you're masculine and he's the feminine one. You know, I got girlfriends, I always got girlfriends.

Denial of Homosexual Interest

R. G.: To what extent, if any, have you had sexual interest in men as a small or big part of your own interests?

FRANK: Myself?

R. G.: Yeah.

FRANK: I just really never had any interest for it, you know. I got too many girlfriends. I'm having too much fun with the girls.

R. G.: When did you start going after girls?

FRANK: Sixteen, fifteen.

Earliest Crushes

R. G.: Did you have any crushes before then?

FRANK: Yeah.

R. G.: What age?

FRANK: Sixth grade.

R. G.: Did you go out with the person?

FRANK: Yeah, as a matter of fact, I did. I remember her name, too.

R. G.: How long did you go out?

FRANK: I went over her house and played house or whatever, and stuff like that. She was in the sixth grade, I think.

R. G.: When did you have your first sexual experience?

FRANK: Sixteen.

R. G.: And how was that for you?

FRANK: An experience, something new.

R. G.: Was it a disappointment in any way?

FRANK: No.

R. G.: The first time is sometimes very difficult for guys.

FRANK: I don't know what it is, they come natural to me. I'm not embarrassed or shy or anything like that. They just come right and say, "Hey, I'd like to have sex, let's do this and that." I've been like that, and I can remember laying in the girl's bed with her, and it didn't bother me. I'm not shy. I don't beat around the bush.

Sexual Dysfunction

R. G.: Sometimes guys when they first have sex have difficulty in getting an erection or keeping an erection, or other guys have a problem coming quick, and they would like to have it last longer.

FRANK: I wish that was the case for me.

R. G.: What?

FRANK: I mean, I would want to hold back for five minutes instead of five seconds.

R. G.: Do you come quicker than you would like to?

FRANK: Yeah.

R. G.: Always or sometimes.

FRANK: Sometimes. Depends on who I'm with.

Heterosexual Experience

R. G.: How many women do you think you had sexual intercourse with in your life?

FRANK: Oh, jeez, over a hundred—a lot. And the total amount of times that I had sex is uncountable. Since I was about sixteen I've had about forty different steady girlfriends. I don't really—I don't know, for some reason I don't stick to a girl that long because I get tired of 'em. It's been like that for about the last three or four years.

R. G.: What's the longest you've gone with one girl?

FRANK: Six months.

Attitude toward Paul's Homosexuality

R. G.: What do you think about your brother being primarily gay?

FRANK: Well, I don't like it. He's my brother, and I love him, and I'll do anything for him, but it's an embarrassment to me because I'm a twin, you know, and I've heard a couple of remarks from some of his gay friends.

R. G.: What kind of remarks?

FRANK: Like, "Little Frank should be gay instead of butch. You're such a stud, and you're straight, and it's not good for you," that kind of stuff. Every time I'm around my brother, he goes to his gay bars, and I can't take it. I get a headache. It's not my bag right now.

Theory of Homosexuality

R. G.: Why do you think he's developed as gay?

FRANK: I think and believe it's because he's been always growin' up with my mom, you know. He just developed with my mom, and that's the way he is, Mom's boy.

R. G.: Why would growing up mostly with your mom make you gay?

FRANK: I don't know if you know much about him, but me being around him, I know, because I've been around him too, but most gay people are just like girls, like ladies, you know? They're just really flamy and butterfly and stuff, and I think it's from being around mother and following the mother around and going grocery shopping and acting like a lady all the time. It just builds up in you and you become gay. I detest it. He's my brother and I have to go through the embarrassment, you know, twin brother at that. People go, "Well, are you gay or bisexual or anything?" I heard that a few times.

R. G.:   Are you bisexual?

FRANK: Should I be?

R. G.:   Have you had sex experiences with guys as well?

FRANK: No, I haven't really thought about it. It hasn't even crossed my mind.

Confrontation with Paul's Report

R. G.:   According to your brother, there have been times you've gone to gay bars and you've gotten money to have sex with guys. That's what he says.

FRANK: God, that's what *he* does. I've gone to gay bars with him, but I just can't get into that. It's not me. I haven't been to a gay bar since— gee, I can't even remember, it's been a long time. The only time I ever would go was with—if I went with him or something—but I've never gone there myself or something and try to do something like that. That was more his bag, you know.

R. G.:   He claims that you've gotten paid or you get paid sometimes for having sex with guys.

FRANK: I've got a full-time job, I don't need that, you know.

R. G.:   How about when you were younger? Was there a time when you were in your teens that you ever did that?

FRANK: Never.

R. G.:   Why would he say that about you?

FRANK: I don't know. That's a good question. I'm just curious why, you know. I've never done the stuff myself—

R. G.:   To me, it doesn't really matter whether you've had sex affairs with men or not. I don't care if you have.

Acknowledgment of Reluctance to Tell the Truth

FRANK: Even if I did I probably wouldn't tell you I did because I don't like it, you know, I can say I detest it. The stuff to me is—he's my brother, so I'm gonna accept it.

R. G.:   You said, even if you had you wouldn't tell me about it?

FRANK: Okay, well, I guess I did.

R. G.: See, it's important I know—

FRANK: For your study, of course.

R. G.: I need to know for the research. What we are trying to do is to look at as much early-life behavior that we have—we have a lot of talks with your parents, we have psychological tests that you completed as a little boy, psychological tests that your parents completed—and what we're trying to do now is to look at the test results and look at how your personality has evolved, not just sexually, but lots of ways. So it's important that I know what your thoughts are and what your sex experiences have been, because that's really the basis of this study. So if your brother doesn't tell me the truth, or if you don't tell me the truth, that really screws up the whole—

FRANK: Right, well, I don't know why he would say that, that's why I'm curious to know why he would say that, 'cause I never done a thing like that. I've gone to a lot of gay bars with him, but I never had any sexual experience with a male, that's the bottom line.

R. G.: Okay. Let me ask you a related question. There are guys who sometimes have girlfriends and who are straight who go to gay bars and hustle gays. That's a way of making money, it's an easy way of making money. A guy who does that, would you think that that guy was gay, bisexual, or straight?

FRANK: It's hard to say. In between I guess, mixed up—I don't know, it's hard to say. There's an old saying, "You'll make a hole, you'll make a pole." I don't know—straight, bisexual, in between, or something.

R. G.: Do you think that a straight guy would be able to have sex with another male for money because the money was there?

FRANK: There's not enough money for me, not enough money for me there, you know, to go out and do somethin' like that, so I really can't say. If you give me a thousand dollars right now, it's just not my way of living right now. You never know. I realize he is a twin, so you're gonna be like your brother. I doubt it. I got too much going there to score for myself. I don't think it'll ever happen.

R. G.: Would you think that I would disapprove if you told me that you had had experiences like that?

FRANK: No. I would be hesitant to say yes I did, but you know I didn't, so, you know. You know, my dad would bash me up on something like that. I just—you should hear the way I talk about him. I don't—you know, my brother is my brother—like I say, "He's my brother and I love him, but I hate him, you know. Man should be a man, not a flyin' torch going torchin' around, butterflyin' around, you know, *a man's a man!*" I don't know what would make my brother think that. Maybe he's—I don't know. I don't know how to reconcile something like that, because I just never had any desire, only for women.

THE TWINS' MOTHER DESCRIBES THEM AT TWENTY-ONE

Frank's "Homosexuality"

R. G.: I get the sense from the two boys that you've had your hands full.
MOTHER: Frank, Jr., loves easy money.
R. G.: What sort of things has he done for easy money?
MOTHER: Oh, ripped off anything we've ever had and sold it. Selling narcotics, I'm sure turning tricks down in Hollywood, I know that—
R. G.: *That* twin?
MOTHER: Yeah.
R. G.: What do you mean, turning tricks?
MOTHER: Sexual affairs with he's and she's or whoever would pay him. In fact I think he's living with a fellow right now that does who knows what! But I personally feel that he does it for the money and the excitement, rather than any other reason.
R. G.: Why do you think that he's had sex with men?
MOTHER: I just have a feeling he is. Number one, he's living with this guy who apparently is a homosexual, and of course the other twin says so. One of them will fink on the other one. And I just have a suspicion.
R. G.: What makes you think that the guy that he's living with is homosexual?
MOTHER: My other son definitely said he was. I've talked to him, and he appears to be.
R. G.: You've talked to him in person or on the telephone?
MOTHER: On the telephone. I work with gay men twenty-four hours a day [as an interior decorator], and if he's not, I'll bark like a pink fox.
R. G.: What's your source of information that your son's hustling on the Boulevard?

Arrest for Prostitution

MOTHER: Through the guy that he's living with. When he was picked up the last time by the police, he was picked up for prostitution.
R. G.: He was arrested by the police for that?
MOTHER: Uh huh. Probably four, maybe five months ago.
R. G.: And what happened with the charges?
MOTHER: That I don't know. Anyway, he was picked up. I talked to him, because that's where my son was living, and it was male prostitution, that's what he was picked up for.
R. G.: Does his dad know?
MOTHER: I think that I got mad at him not too long ago and told him. And I finally said, "Your perfect son, he really was picked up for it."

R. G.:   Do you have an idea that he's had other male-male experiences besides maybe hustling on the Boulevard?

MOTHER: I would suspect that he does, but I don't know.

R. G.:   Why would you suspect that?

Experiences in Gay Bars

MOTHER: One of my best friends—who is not a good friend now, was for about thirteen, fourteen years—said that he saw him down in gay bars in Hollywood all the time, and he was picking up on guys or they were picking up on him.

R. G.:   What age was this that he was in gay bars?

MOTHER: I'd say about fifteen, fifteen-and-a-half when they first started going down into Hollywood, the two of them.

R. G.:   What's your perception of his sexuality?

MOTHER: I think he's bi, I really do. He's macho in his attitude and relationships with people, but I just do not perceive that he is 100 percent totally a heterosexual. If the price was right, he would do it. If there happens to be a he that he's with or a she, it probably doesn't make a whole lot of difference, and I don't know, but that's what I feel.

Paul's Sexuality

MOTHER: Paul, on the other hand, is homosexual.

R. G.:   Is there any heterosexuality in him, or is he exclusively homosexual?

MOTHER: I think homosexual. I don't know—my experience with homosexual men has been that they always have very close female friends, and of course he does have his close female friends.

R. G.:   When did you become aware of the fact that he was homosexual, or that he's had homosexual relationships?

MOTHER: I would assume that I first suspicioned that that had a great deal to do with him not living at home by the time he first started disappearing. And of course we came to you when he was seven, eight years old—I had a suspicion.

R. G.:   But then you were concerned about feminine behavior, not sexual behavior.

MOTHER: Correct. And I'm still—but I would think in a child that that would be the first clue to possibly he was going to turn out to be a homosexual boy. He still prefers, you know, housework and being around the house—the classic example of the homosexual men that I know. He's classic.

Concerns about Paul's Boyhood Behavior

R. G.:   Were you worried when you first came to see me that Paul was going to become gay, or were you worried primarily by the fact that he was feminine and was being teased, or that he was unhappy being a boy?

MOTHER: I think he was unhappy being a boy, or the confusion in his mind that society says that boys do these kinds of things and he was not doing those kinds of things, which didn't particularly bother me, but I am married to a very dyed-in-the-wool conservative kind of person, and I wanted to know I think how to help him be able to cope. I've had gay friends for years and I work with gay people.

R. G.: Did you think that he was going to become gay when you first came to see me?

MOTHER: Yes.

R. G.: When do you think his behavior changed from being a feminine boy to when you were aware that he was sexually interested in males?

MOTHER: I would say quite possibly fairly recently, for a year, year-and-a-half.

R. G.: Before that there weren't gay experiences?

MOTHER: To my knowledge, he wasn't.

R. G.: Did you think that he was still feminine before he went into the military?

MOTHER: Uh huh, in comparison to his brother or his father or my father, yeah. Not swishy kind of fly-through-the-air boy, but yeah.

R. G.: Was he dating girls then?

MOTHER: Yup.

R. G.: Was he having sex with them, as far as you know?

MOTHER: Well, with this one girl, I know. I'm sure that there was a sexual experience there.

R. G.: Did you like her?

MOTHER: No.

R. G.: Why?

MOTHER: Mainly because she stole our motor home.

Paul's Future Sexuality

R. G.: How do you see him sexually progressing over the next five, six, seven years, in terms of whether it's men, women, both?

MOTHER: I think he as an individual is probably more comfortable now than he was a year ago and at ease, because he was just a time bomb. I really believe that he probably will stay with men. I would like to believe that maybe I'll be a grandma someday, and that won't happen, but that's just my wish. That's not anything that I really am going to be looking forward to, because I don't think it'll happen.

R. G.: If you could have your wish, and let's assume that the other son essentially winds up being heterosexual, married with a bunch of kids, how would you prefer seeing this boy in terms of his sexuality?

MOTHER: Whichever he's the happiest with. I'm not upset by the fact that he has a male partner, if that's what he wants to do, but it's a little bit uncomfortable with the daddy, you know. Christmas, this might be a drag, or Thanksgiving might be a pain in the neck, or something along those lines, but if he's perfectly content, I certainly would not be the one that would shut the door and say, "I never want to talk to you again because you're a homosexual." No way.

INTERVIEW WITH PAUL AND FRANK AT AGE TWENTY-TWO

Current Sexuality

R. G. (to Paul): Do you have any interest in females at the present time?

PAUL: I still see my old girlfriend once in a while.

R. G.: Is there a sexual relationship at all?

PAUL: Yeah. Since the last time I saw you, my girlfriend is pregnant.

R. G.: From you?

PAUL: Yeah.

R. G.: Congratulations!

PAUL: She's having an abortion. The one time we decide we were going to get together, she gets pregnant.

R. G.: How often do you see her?

PAUL: I haven't seen her now for about two months. When she went to have her abortion, I didn't meet her down there and she was very upset.

R. G.: What percentage of your sexual interest now is for females and what percentage for males?

PAUL: Never have a percent for female.

R. G.: But a little bit left over for at least one girl.

PAUL: Oh, yeah.

R. G. (to Frank): How many girlfriends have you had since I talked with you last?

FRANK: I'm still with one. I'm with her. Pretty much engaged. I have been seeing a couple of girls on the side that she knows about. She trusts me.

R. G.: But she's the primary girlfriend?

FRANK: Yes.

R. G.: Are you getting engaged?

FRANK: Well, she's got the ring on. She's wife material.

Differences in Individual Reports of Frank's Sexuality

FRANK: So, what's the reason to have us back again today?

R. G.: I wanted to reconcile that disagreement you guys had last time. You had a disagreement individually, and I wanted to get the two of you together to see if I could figure what the hell is going on.

FRANK (to Paul): Remember, I talked to you about, you had told Dr. Green something about I hustled at one time in my life, or a couple of times, or whenever it was? As far as I knew, I mean that was news to me. I knew nothing. The way I kind of picked it up from you was that somebody just pumped some information into your head that I was doing that, because I had been to a couple of bars with you.

R. G. (to Frank): Let me hear what your side is. I'm just trying to find out what's happening. It's really important for my research—knowing you guys for so many years—to try to understand where you both are right now so I can make comparisons back to when you were kids.

FRANK (to Paul): I mean, I've been to bars, I drank, I been to bars with you. That's the only reason I could think that anyone would want to get down my pants.

PAUL: I have this one particular bar, it's notorious for hustling, and someone was saying, "Your brother was just in here a couple of minutes ago." "Oh, really?" You know, I had brought him there for the first time. And the places were notorious for hustling. I can't figure out what he ever would be doing there when I wasn't in there with him, unless he was with gay men.

FRANK: We were in there together a lot, and he never left me.

R. G. (to Paul): Are you also saying that he had been there at times when you weren't there?

PAUL: Yeah.

R. G. (to Frank): What's your response to that?

FRANK: I don't feel like going places unless I'm with him or somebody else, you know, that I can back out if I have to. I don't know, I've been in the bars a few times, like he says, in the "Numbers" bar, pretty heavy for that type of stuff. Okay? It's been a long time since I've been in there. I guess the only time I really went in there, and even when I went in there, you know when I was doing nothing.

R. G. (to Frank): You've got something of a reputation where you'll do a lot of things for money. You like money.

FRANK: I'm a hustler.

R. G.: You hustle for money, and one of the ways that guys, good-looking guys like you, hustle for money, is to go home with some gay guy and let him pay you good money for getting his rocks off.

FRANK: Me, I've been doing real good. I do bricklaying.

R. G.: Okay, but you haven't been doing bricklaying for your whole life. I'm talking about a couple of years back.

FRANK: I been doing it for a while. I've always had a job and always been employed.

R. G.: You also have always hustled when you needed money.

FRANK: Yeah, I could. Okay, the money's there, I know that.

R. G.: You got a record, for Christ's sake, for hustling. You got a police record for prostitution.

FRANK: No, "suspected."

R. G.: Okay. Suspected, suspected of prostitution.

FRANK: Suspected of hustling.

R. G. (to Paul): What do you make of that episode? Do you think he was really hustling?

PAUL: Either that or dry dealing.

FRANK: You know we got sucked in, all of us. This guy gets in the car, three of us in the car with some old man, this guy must have been sixty years old, and this other guy is all over me, and, God, I just want to take it out and party, light a joint in his car. Little did we know that we were riding around with a cop. "Pull up . . . window down. Put your hands on the dashboard."

R. G.: How far can you go without getting somebody to put a knife in you or beating the shit out of you?

FRANK: Most of the guys buying in a bar that are willing to pay people are too ugly and fat and lame to go out and get a piece by themselves without having to pay for it. I'm not tiny, okay? I can stand up for myself, and if I need the money, I can get it, one way or another. I took money from people a couple of times. "I'll take a shower and then I'll be ready to get it on with you." Then I got out the front door.

R. G.: Took the money and ran? You never had a guy get that close?

FRANK: No.

R. G.: Why not?

FRANK: I don't know. I haven't tried it yet. I'll have to find out one of these days. It doesn't seem to be killing my brother, so I guess it's not too bad.

R. G. (to Paul): Do you believe this guy?

PAUL: Hey. I would love to find out if he has had sex with a guy. I'd shit if I knew that he did it.

R. G.: Why would you like to know that?

PAUL: Because I think everybody should try something like that.

FRANK: God, someone's got to carry on the family name.

R. G.: Well, *he* almost did it last week. He's doing better than you're doing.

FRANK: True. Yeah, he's knocking virgins up. I haven't found any of those yet.

PAUL: I am as fertile as a damn flower bed!

FRANK: I mean, I'm not saying I've never had the cock touched by a guy. I've hitchhiked, and guys put their hands on my leg and try to rub me and stuff like that, and it gets me pretty mad. Okay. I just can't tell you I have when I haven't. Okay? If I did I would.

R. G. (to Paul): Do you think you'll wind up straight someday?

PAUL: I don't want to yet. But I look at too many old gay men that have really nothing, no family. They're paying for it. They are always looking at young boys. I don't want to be like that at all. Yet a lot of them are very successful, but I don't think that's the life I want for the rest of my life. I want kids, I want a family.

R. G.: A few years from now, you'll walk in here with a girlfriend, getting married and having kids.

PAUL: I really strongly believe that'll happen.

R. G.: The same day he walks in here with his boyfriend and says, "Guess what, Dr. Green, I really am gay." Isn't that a wonderful prediction?

PAUL: Yeah, I love it.

FRANK: Never believe that.

Theory of Different Sexualities

R. G.: What do you think right now, why you guys are so different? Genetically, you're the same. You are identical twins, which means that your genes, your chromosomes are the same. How do you explain the fact that you're so different in terms of your sexuality, your lifestyle?

PAUL: He's been around the wrong people.

FRANK: I think I've got another real good reason. My dad told us the reason, 'cause when we grew up, my mom was taking care of both of us at the same time, she said we were splitting things up, my dad kind of kept his eyes on me.

PAUL: I don't think that's why. I really don't.

FRANK: My dad and I get along so well now.

R. G.: More about back then when you were kids. You were very different when I first saw you, when you were eight.

PAUL: I hated my father.

R. G.: Why?

PAUL: I just didn't want to be with him. I was scared of him.

R. G.: How far back do you guys remember being different from each other?

FRANK: When we were playing baseball.

R. G.: He was playing baseball and you weren't?

FRANK: We both were.

PAUL: But then I quit it and you kept on.

R. G.: What about before then? I saw you guys when you were about eight.

FRANK: Can't remember back that far.

PAUL: Barbie dolls...do you remember that? My girlfriends and I used to play with Barbie dolls with the girls on the block.

R. G.: You used to play with Barbie dolls and the girls, but he didn't?

PAUL: A lot of boys do that.

R. G.: But he didn't.

FRANK: No.

R. G.:   I wonder why you weren't into that and you were?

PAUL: I didn't even like getting dirty. He didn't care.

R. G.:   But why would such a difference in interests arise?

FRANK: That's something you have to determine. You're the psychiatrist.

R. G.:   But you lived it.

FRANK: Yeah, we lived it, but it's hard to pinpoint something like that, half of my life ago.

PAUL: I just liked girls and to play with girls. A lot of boys didn't like me.

FRANK: Like when we were younger, he used to have more girlfriends than me. I wasn't too interested in girls. I wasn't even thinking about it at the time—having a girlfriend or anything like that. I can remember back that far when he was getting all the girlfriends.

R. G.:   Were they sexual girlfriends or play companions?

PAUL: Play companions.

R. G. (to Frank):   What your parents say was that your mother sort of looked after him, and your dad looked after you. Do you remember that happening?

FRANK: Yeah, Dad and me used to go out and play catch and baseball.

PAUL: They never asked me, so I never went.

R. G.:   How far back do you remember that?

PAUL: About eleven. I was into planting.

FRANK: My mom was heavy into planting, and he picked up on that.

PAUL: I was with my mom all the time, going to the market.

R. G.:   Now, why would there be that split in your family?

PAUL: Because of my dad.

R. G.:   Why?

PAUL: Because I was too mellow.

R. G.:   You were too mellow?

PAUL: Too much like a girl for him. I didn't want to do anything with him. I didn't like him.

R. G.:   Why would that develop? You can't argue that you were born that way, 'cause you were born the same.

PAUL: Don't ask me. You got me. You can say I was scared when I played baseball, I didn't want to go golfing because I didn't want to be out swinging.

R. G.:   Were you ever hit by a baseball and hurt?

PAUL: No.

FRANK: I was.

R. G.:   You were, but you kept playing? And he wasn't and he didn't. Go figure that out.

FRANK: That's a good reason, you know. I was more of a go getter, stand up and fight.

R. G.:   I always thought that the fact that you had this illness, that that really slowed you down in terms of being out there roughing it up with other boys, and that your father probably found it easier to relate to your brother.

FRANK: Because I was with him, my father.

R. G. (to Frank): He was out there playing sports, and (to Paul) you were sick. You had a major illness, you were on drugs, surgery, and I think your mother used to be primarily responsible for taking you back and forth to the hospital.

PAUL: I don't remember my father once bringing me to the hospital.

R. G.: I think it was your mother who took charge of your medical care. I think he was out there roughhousing with the boys, and then I think when you came home, your brother was more available to his dad to play sports because he was in better shape and had been doing it all day, whereas you were the sick kid and you couldn't use your arm.

PAUL: Yeah, it affected my arm.

FRANK: I seem to believe that would be some of the reason why we were so close. When he was in the hospital, I was home and I was playing sports, and my dad wanted to get into it with me.

INTERVIEW WITH PAUL AT AGE TWENTY-THREE

Heterosexual Marriage

PAUL: I got married. I'd been seeing this girl. We saw each other when I was seeing my male lover. I broke up with him. She and I were going to have a baby. She was pregnant, so we got married.

R. G.: She is the girl you've had intercourse with before?

PAUL: Yeah. I would say over three or four years.

R. G.: If she hadn't gotten pregnant, would you still have gotten married?

PAUL: I honestly do not know. We decided to keep this baby and she miscarried. Oh my God, I was really upset. I was actually looking forward to it and really started feeling like a father, and she felt like a mother already. We've been trying again. I want a kid. I'm still seeing my male lover on occasions. I can't seem to get away from him. It's really strange. She knew him and knew of our relationship. She's trying very hard.

R. G.: She knows you still see him?

PAUL: Yeah. I try lying to her, but she knows. Every time I see him, she knows I see him. There are times I haven't seen him for two or three months.

R. G.: Why did you break up?

PAUL: He broke my nose. All my friends said get away from him, so I just got up and left. This girl and I had always kept in touch, and she knew what was going on.

Aversion to Homosexuality

R. G.: Why do you think it was that after breaking up with him you didn't wind up primarily with another guy?

PAUL: To be honest with you, a relationship with a guy—I'm talking about a lover-type of relationship—is hard. I haven't lost my desire to have a male. Believe me, it's still there. But to have another long-term relationship, I just couldn't do it.

R. G.: Why?

PAUL: I want to say it's too unstable. Although in the straight relationship, she and I have our ups and downs. I have no desire to have another relationship with a guy. I need to have someone, and she has always been there.

R. G.: So you're thinking that in a male relationship you wouldn't have emotional support?

PAUL: No.

R. G.: Is this relationship better because this girl is special, or because she is a woman?

PAUL: I think she's special.

R. G.: Let's say she suddenly vanishes from the earth and you are on your own again. Do you think you would seek out a relationship with a man?

PAUL: No, I wouldn't, I would actually try to find another girl.

R. G.: So the guys would be all right sexually, but not to have a romantic relationship with?

PAUL: Not to have a romantic relationship with, no. I could honestly say I would never do it again. I woke up too many times with bums. I've done so much better.

Heterosexual Activity

R. G.: Tell me what sex is like with you two.

PAUL: We are not a really sexual couple. At first it was like it was so strange, because I hadn't had a girl for so long, and I just found myself getting more and more attracted to her and having sex with her throughout the relationship. I enjoy having sex with him, too, but she and I have very good sex.

R. G.: You said it's not a very sexual relationship.

PAUL: With him and I, we'd probably have sex every single night, and with her we have sex once or twice a week.

R. G.: Why so different?

PAUL: I'm just not as horny as I used to be. I work really weird hours. I work a lot.

R. G.: You don't think it's also the fact that women aren't as erotic to you?

PAUL: No.

R. G.: Were you ever tired when you were with him and worked a lot?

PAUL: I was such a bum then, I was doing nothing. Now I work really hard so we can save money.

Erotic Fantasies

R. G.: When you jerk off, what do you think about?

PAUL: Her and him.

R. G.: What percent of the time when you jerk off do you think about females versus males?

PAUL: I'd say forty females. I do fantasize a lot about having her on top of me, and we are really getting along really good. But I'm also thinking about a guy. It's always when I really want it bad she doesn't want it, and when she really wants it bad I don't want it.

R. G.: So a little bit more than half about males?

PAUL: Yeah, about two-thirds males.

R. G.: What about in the last six months, in terms of actual sexual contact with another person—what percent has been with a female, what percent with a male?

PAUL: Mostly with her.

R. G.: When you are having sex with him, do you still think about her?

PAUL: No.

R. G.: When you are having sex with her, do you think about him?

PAUL: No.

R. G.: You turn off the separate channels. Compare for me, if you can, sex with her and sex with him.

Heterosexuality versus Homosexuality

PAUL: She is very busty, and I love her nipples, but he has a real nice built chest and firm and nice nipples. I'm a nipple person. That's my biggest turn on. She is more loving and tender. He gets on top of me like a man. He's real manly about it. He's stronger, and with her I'm in control. I'm the man. I know what turns her on, whereas I don't know that I really turn him on.

R. G.: And what about the feelings?

PAUL: That's different between the two. When I'm with him, he just sits on me so freely, God, I think he is doing this with everybody, am I going to pick up a disease? She's always real wet, and she can come several times. I like that, because I can come two or three times with her, whereas when I'm with him I can come once and I want him to get off of me, I've had enough. The sensation with her is more stimulating to me. I just know she loves me when we're making love. When I'm with him, we are just fucking, that's all we are doing.

R. G.: Is the sex when you come with one of them more powerful?

PAUL: It used to be more powerful with him even when I was with her, but we are getting into these positions now like her lying on her stomach. I like when I can hold on to her, I feel really strong. I can come more often with her.

Future Sexuality

R. G.: Where do you think your sexuality will be, let's say, in five years?

PAUL: Well, I've been thinking about that. Will I really lose this desire for men? People I've talked to say never. I would really like to lose it. I really would. I don't want to destroy this girl's life. She's such a good girl, and I just don't want to screw her up. This is not something that is going to go away overnight. I hope in the future I can just get away from all this. I hope I can get away to a desolate island.

R. G.: That's not going to take away your attractions.

PAUL: I know. I really just want to lose it. I just want to get rid of it. Like I said, I don't want to screw up her life.

R. G.: Let's say you two, like a lot of other heterosexual couples, had a falling out.

PAUL: Okay, well then it wouldn't bother me. But now I feel real responsible, and I don't want to hurt her.

R. G.: If she wasn't there, then it would be okay to have gay feelings?

PAUL: Yeah.

R. G.: So it's really more her than your not wanting to have gay feelings.

PAUL: Yeah.

R. G.: In terms of people other than your male lover and your wife, do you get turned on more with women or men?

PAUL: I like to see pretty ladies, but I turn on more with guys.

INTERVIEW WITH FRANK AT AGE TWENTY-THREE

Homosexual Relationship

FRANK: I've experienced a lot of new things since the last time I saw you.... I met this actor guy who is a flaming homosexual who has kind of helped me get on my feet. In return he had a favor that he asked for, and that was for me fulfilling his needs. Like, I scratch his back and he scratches mine. It's been kind of nice. He has helped me pull out of my rut, and I got a lot of things out of it so far. He helped me get started with the business. I go on trips. I kind of work for the guy at the same time. He wants me to be his other half, his lover type, which I'm not too hip on because I've got a girlfriend and I got a kid on the way. But actually, things are going real good. I think I picked up a good one.

R. G.: What do you do sexually?

FRANK: A number of things. He acts like he's the lady, so take it from there. He's the lady and I'm the man, just like husband and wife type, is how he acts. It's really weird. I'm kind of having a hard time dealing with it. I mean this guy is strictly tuna.

R. G.: Do you have intercourse with him?

FRANK: Oh, yeah.

R. G.: You screw him in the behind?

FRANK: Oh, yeah. That's all we do. Like, he's the lady and I'm the man.

R. G.: How about oral sex?

FRANK: No. We tried it. He doesn't even expect me to do it.

R. G.: Does he go down on you?

FRANK: Yup, exactly. It's like experiencing sexual relations with another lady, is what it is. This guy is a male, but to me he's a lady more than he is a man. It's his professional career and lifestyle.

R. G.: Does he dress as a woman?

FRANK: On stage, yeah.

R. G.: What made you decide to do this?

FRANK: It's a shocker to me. But like I say, it's kind of helped me in a sense that I wanted to work so hard to get where I wanted to get—it's kind of helped me in that sense. I guess that's the basic reason. I don't like it, it's nothing I don't think I would permanently like to do. For right now, he's helped me get on my feet. He knows that I am basically a straight guy, and that I'm kind of just taking care of him in order for him to take care of me. But I don't mind. It's a little embarrassing sometimes, going out in public with the guy. I just can't relate to that yet.

Sexual Identity

R. G.: If somebody were to say to you, "Are you straight, are you bisexual, are you gay?" what would your answer be?

FRANK: Straight. I wouldn't want anyone to find out ever. I don't think I could handle that.

R. G.: How about in your own mind?

FRANK: I think I'm pretty straight. You can't really think you are straight when you are doing those kind of things, you know. I think in my own head that I'm still straight, just for my own ego.

R. G.: Does seeing this guy interfere with your girlfriend in any way?

FRANK: I got her completely convinced that I am his security guard. She has no idea, no suspicion. She knows he's gay and all that stuff. She has no suspicion about me. That's just the way I carry myself. Not like my brother—he's a dead give-away.

Current Heterosexuality

R. G.: Is sex with your girlfriend different now that you are seeing him?

FRANK: It's not as persistent. I don't have as much with her as I used to.

R. G.:   Why is that?

FRANK: I don't know. It used to be like every night—"Come on, I want to make love to you." Now it's not like that. Whenever she wants to do it, she does it. She can go three weeks without having sex, so I get my urges once in a while and say, "Let's have some sex."

R. G.:   Is it because you are getting it somewhere else?

FRANK: I don't know. No, it's not that because I still prefer the hole better than the pole, as they say. I don't know, it's just weird. Maybe my sex drive is slowing down. I'm running two heads at the same time.

R. G.:   Are you seeing anybody else sexually except your lady friend at home and this guy?

FRANK: Occasionally. It just depends if I go to a bar or something and meet someone and go home with her or whatever.

R. G.:   When you have sex with this guy, is he cross-dressed as a woman?

FRANK: No. He's just like a man and carries on the image of a lady.

Sexual Fantasies

R. G.:   If you walk down the street and you see an attractive person of either sex, male or female, which turns you on more?

FRANK: Female still, definitely. Men don't turn me on. Believe me, I will let go of him when I have to.

R. G.:   But you are able to get a hard-on and you are able to come?

FRANK: Yeah. I just kind of close my eyes and fantasize about something else.

R. G.:   What do you think about?

FRANK: Some girl or whoever, one of my latest.

R. G.:   Do you always do that, or sometimes can you concentrate and think that this is a guy and still get a hard-on?

FRANK: Sometimes I can. I can keep it up thinking of a guy, but basically I fantasize about some girl or something to keep it up. It doesn't really turn me on, but I can do like I said—it's really bad to say—for the money.

The Relationship

R. G.:   Why had you not done this in the past? You must have met rich guys, gay guys, who would have paid you.

FRANK: I smelt gold, I guess.

R. G.:   Do you have any emotional feelings for him at all?

FRANK: I care for the guy.

R. G.:   Anything that resembles a love feeling?

FRANK: No. I care for him. I'd be there if anything ever happened to him. But no love feeling for him.

R. G.: You see him about once a week?

FRANK: Yeah, for about the last five or six months. Oh, when we are out of town, sometimes we are together about a week at a time. I can't handle being gone that long. I was with him for a week and a half, and I was going nuts and couldn't wait to get out of there.

R. G.: Why?

FRANK: 'Cause I can only handle so much. It's like we were in Reno, and I wanted to do my thing, and when I spend all that time with him I get bored. So I say, "I got to get home, my wife is sick and she is going to have a baby," or whatever. Any kind of excuse.

R. G.: When people see you together, do they know you are a couple?

FRANK: He makes it very clear that we are to anybody and everybody. "This is my husband." It's embarrassing. He makes it clear to anybody. Most of the time where he goes, there are a lot of nice pretty girls, and they always go, "Who is this guy" and all that stuff, and he says, "Oh, this is my husband, don't get too happy." He doesn't give me a chance or them a chance to make any kind of move. It's weird.

PSYCHOLOGICAL TEST DIFFERENCES

At age eight, Paul and Frank differed in psychological testing. Two standard tests that separated the full groups of "feminine" and "masculine" boys also separated the twins. The pattern of difference for Paul and Frank was the same as with the larger groups (chapter 6).

On the It-Scale for Children, Paul scored 38, Frank, 72. Paul's score is within the typical female range, Frank's within the typical male range. On the Draw-A-Person test, Paul drew a female first, Frank a male. This difference is also consistent with that for most males and females.

On the Cattell Personality Factor Instruments, a general personality measure, the twins differed by the arbitrary difference of 20 percent or more on four scales (or factors). Paul scored as more easily upset, Frank as more calm and stable. Paul scored as more tender-minded, Frank as more tough-minded. Paul scored as more forthright, Frank as more shrewd. Paul scored as more tense and driven, Frank as more relaxed. The full group of previously "feminine" boys also scored significantly higher for being easily upset and for being more tense and driven (chapter 6).

On the Tennessee Self-Concept Scale, Paul and Frank differed by the arbitrary difference of at least twelve points on six subscales. Paul scored lower on his capacity for self-criticism, his extent of confusion and conflict over his self-perception, his sense of physical self (his view of his body, state of health, skills, and sexuality), and on a measure of personal self (his sense of personal worth). He scored higher on a measure of social self (his sense of adequacy in social interaction), but also higher on general maladjustment. The full group of previously "feminine" boys also scored lower on the measures of physical self and personal self (chapter 6).

On the Adjective Check List, where the person checks off self-descriptive adjectives, the twins differed by a standard score of twelve or more points on three scales. Paul checked more adjectives indicative of succorance (soliciting sympathy, affection, or emotional support from others), and affiliation (seeking and maintaining numerous personal friendships), but fewer indicative of achievement (striving to be outstanding in pursuits of socially recognized significance). The full group of "feminine" boys also scored higher on succorance (chapter 6).

TWO TRACKS OF SEXUAL IDENTITY DEVELOPMENT

In chapter 10, I formulate a developmental synthesis for "feminine" boys and homosexual men. That composite derives from dozens of families. As the twins may be the single case metaphor of the full study, I will do the same here.

First the stage was set. The first-born twin was named for his father. This initial designation affected the quality of the father-son relationship. The effect was on both the father's early identification with that son and the son's later identification with the father. One twin was "attractive" and more receptive to holding; the other resembled "a spider monkey" and was squirmy.

Then the play was enacted. When diverse patterns of sex-typed socialization operated, the twins' receptivity to these influences differed markedly. One was sick. The sick label not only affected self-image, but also modified his relations with parents and peers. The intrafamily schism was such that the sick twin became the mother's charge. The healthy twin interacted primarily with father. While the healthy twin's social skills, learned with his father, were conventionally "masculine," a younger sister provided alternate recreational activities for the sick twin, whose physical handicap deterred male peer group participation. Two developmental tracks ran through the family. One carried the mother, Paul, and the sister. One carried the father and Frank, Jr.

Nature/Nurture

The twins provide a model for understanding the interaction of genetics and socialization with sexual identity.

Divergent socialization experiences during boyhood shaped gender-role behavior as "feminine" in one twin and as "masculine" in the other. However, the twins' later sexual orientations do not differ as much as with most of our other previously "feminine" and "masculine" boys. This is explainable by the constraining influence of their common genetics.

Their similar genetic contributions to sexual orientation define the limits within which their childhood experiences can modify later erotic behavior.

That genetics does not account entirely for gender-role behavior is demonstrated by the twins' different activities in childhood. That genetics does not account entirely for sexual partner preference is demonstrated by the twins' different patterns of adolescent and adult erotic behavior. And the greater degree of homosexual orientation in the previously "feminine" twin demonstrates the influence of early gender-role behavior on later sexual orientation.

The twins are this study's metaphor.

9

Theories of Boyhood "Femininity" and Manhood Homosexuality: Parents and Sons Speculate

Supply far outstrips demand with theories of homosexuality. So why offer more? Most theories of homosexuality are written by heterosexual clinicians, attempting to construct coherence from the loose associations of patients. Others emanate from armchair theoreticians whose hands remain unsullied by patient contact.

I remain condemned to silence at social occasions when asked, "What causes homosexuality? Is it inborn or learned?" My silence derives partly from ignorance, my inability to supply the definitive answer, and partly from wisdom, my knowing the complexity of any responsible answer.

We abound in professional theories of homosexual development and of "masculine" and "feminine" behavior. It is time for the amateurs, those unfettered by dogma, whose only handicap is being stationed so close to the players that they may not clearly see the play.

The following examples were selected to illustrate a diversity of theories.

THE DEVELOPMENT OF "FEMININITY"

Example 1 (Bobby, Chapter 5)

A negative male image

MOTHER: Possibly he saw things while I was still married that just turned him against men in general, and he just doesn't want to be one.

R. G.: What sorts of things?

MOTHER: My husband wasn't any good. He never worked. I was always

353

the one that was working. He was always loaded on something. Anything he could get his hands on, he was loaded on. That's why he is where he is today—in prison.

R. G.:   What sorts of things?

MOTHER: Well, he was going overboard with bennies. He was dropping a hundred a day, which is enough to kill anybody. He'd stay up four or five days in a row, then come back and shake for a couple of hours after taking a handful of reds to go to sleep—and sleep for a couple of days while I was getting up, going to work, and taking care of the baby. Cleaning, cooking, and everything else, and his father was asleep or gone. Then he started with acid and methedrine and was just going hog-wild on everything that he could find, and there were many times that he would get mad at me, and he'd take it out on me. He hit me many times. And I remember one night in particular, and this may have had some traumatic effect on the boy. We were in the process of splitting up, and he was supposed to be sleeping in the living room. He came home one night—two or three in the morning—dragged me out of bed. He dragged me out of there into the living room and he actually raped me because I was fighting him off and screaming and crying, and right in the middle the baby woke up, and he came into the living room and saw what was going on, and I cooled it immediately, and I said, "Can you stop long enough for me to put him back to bed?" And he did, but, you know, it could have had some kind of meaning to him.

R. G.:   How old was he?

MOTHER: He was almost three. He does remember a lot of things. For a long time he would say, "Mummy, you must have been a bad girl because Daddy used to spank you," and so on. He does remember him hitting me, and my crying all the time, and he may just think that daddies are no good, though he has said things to me like, "Why don't I have a daddy?" or "Where's my daddy?" or "Are you going to get me a new daddy?"

Example 2

A mother implicates her husband and the birth of the boy's sister

MOTHER: I guess the very obvious thing was that he had a father who was not a very nurturing person, not physically affectionate, not verbally affectionate. And I had just had a girl baby, and I spent all that time with this girl baby. This was a really sick baby who I was breast-feeding, who was vomiting all the time. When she wasn't vomiting, she was having diarrhea at the other end. He saw that she was with me all the time and that I wasn't giving him the affection, because prior to that I was the one that was really the primary nurturer. I spent all of my time with my son, talking to him and reading and singing with him and going places with him. I never went anywhere that I didn't take him with me. And then all of a sudden I was just changed, a hundred and eighty degrees.

R. G.:   How old was he when your daughter was born?

MOTHER: Three exactly. It sounds very simplistic, but I really can't think of anything else that happened in his life that was different, because I'm a very emotive person, and although I still was affectionate with him, I can remember being very, very tired and probably pushing him away at times and expecting that his father would take up the slack. Only he never did.

Example 3

A son blames the absence of a father figure and a mother who wanted a daughter

SON: Well, for one, because I was never raised around a man, and I never had my father there, you know. My brothers were there off and on, very more off than on. And like, when I was away, I was with my grandmother and my auntie. When I came out here to L.A., I was with my mother and grandmother. I never really had a male image to enforce in me this and that, you know, so I guess that might have had a strong influence on the future.

R. G.:   Your brothers were older?

SON: Much older. They were into their thing. They really didn't have time for a little brother, except for my brother which is the second— he's the one that spent most of the time with me, more time than anyone.

R. G.:   How much time?

SON: When I came out here, we spent quite a bit of time together, but I was very young then. It was during the time I was crawling and he was changing my diapers, and then I had started walking and talking, that period of time. And then when I came out here to live, he was moving away, so really not that much time.

R. G.:   Do you think your mother influenced you in some way to be more feminine?

SON: Yes, I do. She already had two boys before I was born, and she wanted a girl so badly. She even told me she prayed about it, and she wanted a girl so she could dress it up pretty.

R. G.:   How old were you when she told you that?

SON: I was about six or seven, I think. She would bring me baby dolls and things. She had to work, and I was with my grandmother and auntie. She would bring me—instead of trucks—baby dolls and dolls with long hair.

R. G.:   Do you remember that?

SON: Oh, yes, I remember that quite well. Recently, I asked her whether she ever thought that I would become a hairdresser. And she said, "Yeah, I sort of had an idea that you would," and I said, "Why did you bring me baby dolls—purposely, or what?" And she said, "No, but I knew that's what you liked, and I thought that by doing it quite naturally, you would have some type of interest in hair by playing with dolls and things like that." And we laughed about it.

R. G.: Did your mom have any males, any boyfriends around when you were a kid?

SON: No. Mother? Mommy dearest? No. She's a workaholic, for one thing, and she finds peace by herself. I remember a statement she made. A friend of hers was asking her, "Why don't you have any boyfriends?" and she said, "Honey, don't no man have any golden balls. I'm doing fine just like I am."

His mother indicts his father but also considers her wish for a daughter

MOTHER: My two other sons weren't feminine. They liked basketball, sports. They didn't have more contact with their father. They were around women all their lives. All three stayed with their grandmother, my sister. But this boy was left there at age two. He never forgot it. The others were fourteen to sixteen. His father never lived with him. But when the boy was young, he was around his dad a lot.

His father had those tendencies, too. He never was normal with sex. He didn't naturally get hard. He wasn't a man—he wore men's clothes. He never reacted like a man—he had no sexual desire. This boy has a different father from my other sons.

R. G.: Anything else?

MOTHER: I think the whole thing in a nutshell is the fact that he might have heard me mention that I wanted a girl, and I think he's been trying to be one from the time he heard it. I don't know when or how he heard it, but he's been trying to be what he thought I wanted him to be.

Example 4

Love from a man is seen as a substitute for affection from father

R. G.: Was there a time when you were a little kid that you remember wanting to be a girl?

SON: Yes. In grammar school. I guess around eight or nine.

R. G.: What was the appeal?

SON: I guess partially to get love from a man.

R. G.: Why do you think so?

SON: Sexually, he'd take care of you.

R. G.: Why would that have been an important thing to you back then?

SON: I guess because my dad wasn't home a lot because he was working. My dad had more things in common with my brothers, like sports, watching sports on TV. My dad would play catch outside with my brother.

R. G.: Did he make up that time with you in some other way, or were you left out?

SON: I don't think he ever made it up.

Example 5

A mother sees herself as her son's role model

MOTHER: He's just with me too much, I think. Just wants to be like me. When we're in the store, when we go shopping and he sees a dress, he says, "Gee, I wish I was Mom. If I was, I'd get that." He'll ask me if I like it, and if I say, "Yes, it's nice," he'll say, "Don't you wish you had it?" I'll say, "Oh, I don't know," and try to change the subject.

R. G.: Do you think he spends more time with you than most boys his age spend with their mothers?

MOTHER: He shadows me. If I sit down to read, or if I'm mending— sewing something—he's always standing there looking over my shoulder, watching what I'm doing. I'll say, "Go play or something," and he'll say, "I don't want to." He's always watching everything I do.

R. G.: And does he look at your husband in the same way?

MOTHER: No. It got to the point where he wouldn't do anything with his father. Last year he wouldn't even go to the store with him. If my husband was going to the store and he'd tell the kids, "Come on, let's go—let's get the car," the first thing my son would ask was, "Is Mama going?" If I wasn't going he would say, "I don't want to go. I'll stay home with her."

Example 6

Positive women and negative men

SON: When I was a baby or from when I was zero to five, I was just raised in an atmosphere where there were two very dominant women. My grandmother's a very dominant woman and a very strong-willed person, and my mother is also. And then, I guess, I didn't have any male figure around. I think that my contacts with men were very bad through my mom's divorces. They were always fighting, and I remember every time I would come home from a visit with my father, my mother would go into this whole thing about what a fuckhead he was. If you said, "Oh gosh, I had so much fun over at Dad's, Dad's such a great guy," she'd say, "Oh no he's not." I think it just gave me a negative attitude. I think basically it was that, you know, having just the female figure around.

R. G.:   Do you remember wanting to be a girl?

SON: When I was real little I can remember wanting to, and then it just sort of—I didn't have that desire. It was just like putting on the clothes. I never preoccupied myself with that thought.

R. G.:   Why do you think you wanted to be a girl?

SON: Maybe I wanted to be like my mother. You know how children role-model after their parents. I think that was the only parent figure around, so I just probably chose that outlet. And because she wasn't a very passive person, I think it made me more tempted to pick up her behavior traits.

THE DEVELOPMENT OF HOMOSEXUALITY

Example 1

A son speculates about a remote relationship with his father and an early homosexual "seduction"

R. G.:   Why do you think you evolved sexual interests primarily for males? You know more about you than anybody else in the world.

SON: All right. My biological father—I really didn't have that close—I've really been close with him the last year, we've been getting along really well. He never really paid that much attention to me. I never felt him really wanting—I mean, when he tried to teach me how to play baseball, he threw the ball at me because he was so pissed at me that I couldn't do anything. He had no patience with me whatsoever. I guess I've been mothered very much, so maybe that's it.

R. G.:   Why would that make you turn on sexually to males?

SON: I have no idea whatsoever. You could answer that better than I could. You're studying me.

R. G.:   I'm trying to get my clues from people who have actually lived through it.

SON: Okay. When I first had any sexual anything with anybody, it was with my uncle. And that still haunts me because that was really freaky, and I really question how I would be if he had not done the things he did to me when I was twelve. And then there was my mother's nephew. Has she spoken about him at all? He moved back here recently. Before he went away, he had made little advances to me, and I accepted. That was one time. When he came back, I was scared to be in the house with him, and he approached me and he said, "I remember what we had and what we did, and I want to know if you're gay or what you consider yourself." I said, "I'm bi," and he said, "Well, I want to find out what will happen if I'm making advances towards you," and he's kinda lurching toward me, and he's really slimy. I said, "I'm having an affair with someone right now. I would really feel awful if I did anything with you."

R. G.:   How old were you when you had that experience?

SON: Twelve or thirteen, or maybe eleven or twelve, it's really shaky.

R. G.:   How often did you have sex with him?

SON: I had sex with him three times, but that made enough of an impression on me, and he was awful.

R. G.:   Did you enjoy the sex?

SON: I didn't—at least not then.

R. G.:   But why did you say it made such an impression on you?

SON: Okay, I contradict myself. I did, I had to enjoy it, but then when I discovered greener pastures and that this is not really the way people can have this. I found it more exciting for me when I got older.

R. G.:   So you are thinking if that initiation hadn't taken place—

SON: I don't know where I'd be right now, I really don't, so that maybe was it. Maybe that made such an impression on me and I was shell-shocked.

R. G.:   Why did he approach you?

SON: He was looking at a dirty magazine, and he turned the page, and he said, "Look at that guy, he has a big hard-on." And he looked at me, and I had a hard-on because I was looking at the magazine, and he just jerked me with his hand, and that's what happened.

R. G.:   It happened three times, you said.

SON: And the other times—I don't even remember how those came about. I think one time he caught me playing with myself, and another time he just came over, and he came into my room, and he decided, "Okay, here, we're gonna do this." I guess I like to look at it as if he raped me, because then I'm not at fault.

His parents cite a theory of heredity

MOTHER: I would base it on genes. His father has a brother that's homosexual. I have a brother who's homosexual. Back further than that I can't go, because I don't know. I don't think that I would put it on environmental, but he made a statement the other day, we were discussing this, and he said, "Well, I didn't really grow up in the most masculine environment." He said, "Dad wasn't playing sports with me. I wasn't involved in sports." And I said, "I have to remind you that we bought all of these different games, all of these different sports, and you never would participate. We wanted to involve you in this, but you wouldn't participate, you didn't like it. And you had every opportunity at school to participate, and you wouldn't do it." So I really wouldn't know what to base it on except our genes.

R. G. (to father):   How about yourself? If you had to construct a theory, what would you say?

FATHER: I kinda think the same way. Because in my family we have a similar situation which came about recently. My sisters' kids are gay.

R. G.: Your sisters' kids are gay?

MOTHER: He has two sisters. One has two daughters, both of them are gay. One has two sons, and one of the sons is gay.

R. G.: Okay, but you are not his biological father.

MOTHER: But I have one son that's gay, and a brother that's gay. And his *real* father has a brother that's gay.

FATHER: But then there's the environmental. I remember the incident of a woman whom we left him with when we were courting who did very feminine things with him.

MOTHER: She would cross-dress him. She'd buy him ballet slippers and put things in his hair and play dolls with him, this type of thing. She treated him like a little girl. She had contact with him when he first came home from the hospital, for the first three years of his life.

R. G.: She was there every day?

MOTHER: She was there practically every day of his life. She was like a surrogate mother.

R. G.: When did you find out that she was doing this?

MOTHER: We knew it all along. We were aware of it to a certain extent, but we thought, "This is just something that he'll go through," and I remember it happening with my mother. My brother would get these things and put it on his head and do all these things, so I thought, well, you know, so what. You know, little boys, it's all right if they play with dolls, it's all right if they do this. What harm can it do?

Example 2 (Larry, Chapter 5)

A son implicates his brother and looks to a strong bond with his mother

SON: My God, you know, I don't believe that it comes from birth. I do not believe that there were too many female hormones or too many male hormones. It's really how the child is developed. I think it's a psychological situation where it can be broken, because if it's hormonal, which I really doubt, I don't think you can do anything to control that; I don't think you can control that unless you have a bunch of injections. But there's no person to blame. I cannot blame my father. It was started so early in my life because of my brother who was four years older, so I was getting exposed to it sooner.

R. G.: What was happening with your brother?

SON: He's the one that introduced me to the homosexuality, you know, recognizing my parts of my body, and recognizing that I have sexual tendencies. Then I was growing older and it was freaking me out. So that was presented to me, you know, and then I had both sides, and then it just grew into this whole thing. If I had had no brother, I don't think I would have even gone down that road. And I'm not blaming my brother; this is just my own weaknesses. Later on I started thinking, "Well, my brother did whatever."

R. G.: Looking at your mother and father and your relationship with your parents, do you feel there is anything there at all that would have influenced your developing toward homosexuality?

SON: Just liking my mother more, and I think when you're young and you really like someone you want to be like them. You want to get their other good attributes, you want to get their personality, you want to handle the situation the way they would, and I think by envying my mother I wanted to be like her, and I think that kind of brought on being the other person with the guy, you know, and just putting myself in a different place. It's just that and being so close to her and doing this and doing that, and she says, "Go get me my shoes" or something. There's always the curiosity of a kid to try on a bigger shoe, so I—you know, it just falls into the curiosity stage.

R. G.: Was she different with you than she was with your brother?

SON: Yeah, I was the baby, after four years of my brother. He had to grow, you know, 'cause it was the baby this, the baby that. I was very close, and then she became very attached to me. I think my parents had a lot of problems and they still do. I mean, they're like borderline divorce as it is now. Then when my father rejected my mother and that made her feel that, okay, if he takes anything, she's got her baby, me, to talk to who doesn't say he wants to go to the potty, he just sleeps there, and I think there was a certain thing that grew between us, a certain kind of bond even when I was younger, you know. I think this is a lot of the things that really brings us close together, and I think that's where it developed because I wanted to be like her. I loved her. She did everything so nice; I wanted to be as nice as she was, just the whole thing.

Example 3 (Joseph, Chapter 5)

A son looks to the escapes of childhood and the later fear of sexual competition with his father

SON: I have a very strong theory. I've been doing a lot of thinking about that. First of all, I was the only son. My parents were very cherishing, nurturing with me and they let me get away with a lot of stuff. I was a really good child, but they made it a real sort of flowery, nice little cushiony world around me, and I was always just like nice and sweet and helpful. And because of the leg problem I would like hardly ever participate in sports, and I would do stuff like be creative, learning music. I would escape with dance, the arts, the dreamworld stuff. I really liked special effects and I really liked magic, and I remember when I was like four or five I thought when I saw a Disney film or

Cinderella, and I thought it was the coolest thing I ever saw, and I wanted to be the fairy godmother so I could disappear and make magic. I remember my mom making a little magic wand, and I wore a nightgown, and I was the fairy godmother doing all this magic stuff. Then when I was older, because of early puberty, I retreated a lot into the background, especially when, I don't know, around preadolescence, like twelve. I was so scared because I'm so much older looking, and so I drew back into that corner.

And then when the actual opportunity—when I was fourteen or fifteen I started talking to my dad about it, and I learned something about him. He was extremely, extremely sexual because he was a bachelor for forty-three years before he married my mother. When he was in the army, that really intimidated me, extremely. When I talked to my dad it just seemed like—well, he wasn't even on my level. Even now when I talk to him, it's like, "You know, when you're in the army we used to come in every weekend and get laid as many times as we can." I'm just going, "I don't know, I can't relate to this." So it was hard for me to get started sexually with a woman, it was like this mental block. When my dad lost his virginity at sixteen or something, and I wanted to around fifteen-and-a-half, almost sixteen, and I couldn't— it was almost like I had to compete. I've always been competing with my father all my life, and that was like another thing I had to beat him at, like get it done early before him, and I couldn't, and that like really crushed me. I was really nervous about it for a long time.

And then I found that I started getting attracted to men around sixteen, seventeen, and around when I was seventeen I had my first experience. I found it to be a lot easier because I found that I was a lot more familiar from my own needs with what the other person wanted than opposed to what a woman wanted.

R. G.: But then when you did have experiences with women and you realized that you could be sexually comfortable with females, why didn't that come forward as a preference?

SON: It didn't take precedence then because I think I liked men too much by that time. So it was like this sort of pull between the two things. The more I talk about it, the easier it is for me to just like get it out in the open, but you know, my whole family is so heterosexual.

R. G.: Most families *are*.

Example 4 (Bobby, Chapter 5)

A son denies the importance of not having a father figure and looks to the role-modeling influence of mother

R. G.: What do you think, now with the advantage of hindsight, looking back over many years, about why you're gay?

SON: I think I was born that way. I don't think there was any point in my life where somebody came by and went zap, you know. Or the lack of my having a father, those years and when I did, my mother's second husband, I was abused so that—

R. G.:   What do you mean, abused?

SON: Well, he was addicted to heroin, and my mother didn't know it at the time she got married, and so there was—I saw him shoot up a couple of times, and he knocked me around once in a while. Then I went to junior high, which was very painful because I was the school scapegoat for two-and-a-half years. If there was somebody to pick on, it was me. And the easiest thing to do if you're going to pick on someone is to attack their sexuality. Well, in eighth grade nobody is sure of himself, and I don't care what anybody says. You're patterned towards heterosexuality by society and parents. I've seen a lot of people that I went to junior high school with who were just as mean and nasty to me that are now gay. Right around that time I had my first real relationship with another boy. I had fooled around, but I was coming to terms with myself.

R. G.:   Are you saying that the fact that you didn't have much contact with a father early in life did not contribute to your being gay?

SON: No, it didn't. I don't think it had anything to do with it.

R. G.:   Why not?

SON: I don't think that my not having a father role to pattern after made that much of a difference, because I was patterning myself after the head of the household which at the time was my mother—made me act feminine in a lot of ways because that was my only role model, but I didn't know of her sexuality per se. So I don't think that really had anything to do with it.

R. G.:   What do you mean, you didn't know of her sexuality?

SON: I mean I knew she was a woman, but I didn't know that—I didn't really know what people did in bed. So I didn't say, "Well, this is what she does, so this is what I'm going to do," or anything like that.

R. G.:   But you knew that she was attracted to men because she had men in her life. So why couldn't that have served as the model for you to be attracted to men?

SON: Being a single woman, she was always keeping ahead of her femininity because she had to be attractive to the opposite sex, and I guess that was the only model that I had. Also, in that time the man that she married, that she was married to for those four years, was not the picture of masculinity. We didn't get along anyway, and he never—I never saw him as trying to straighten out my actions because I was very effeminate.

R. G.:   What do you mean, he wasn't the picture of masculinity?

SON: He was a very small man, very—he was loud when he wanted to be but he never really seemed like a big man, not size-wise, but big in himself, and so in a sense even when they were married my mother was the one who was wearing the pants.

R. G.:   Why should it carry through then, why you developed as a feminine boy and are later turned on by male bodies?

SON: In my experiences, or using myself as an example, I have a very small body, I'm not muscular, and I seem attracted to the more muscular, more butch type. Maybe it's because of something that I don't have. For a very short while I went to a gym. I saw results quickly, and I got scared and I stopped going. I still haven't realized why, but I saw myself with a chest and I felt, "Wait a minute, that's not gonna fit in with—it's something new, a new look." Not that there's any one set answer, but maybe it's the fact that females socially and in society are attracted to males. So along with the actions that are passed to a boy from his mother or in that sense some of the thought patterns— my mother used to always—we used to sit down and talk, and she would tell me about her dates, what they looked like and everything, and I used to seem very interested in that. That could have something to do with it.

Example 5

A heterosexual man describes his homosexual brother

SON: You know about my gay brother, right?

R. G.:   Yeah.

SON: It kinda strikes me funny, you know, that we both grew up in the same environment situation. I wonder, how did we differentiate so much? I mean, we differ on every point, but this seems so extreme that I'm often curious of how he decided to go one way, and I guess— I never "chose" to go the normal route because I didn't feel that I had the choice, you know. I haven't ever had any desire to have sex with a guy, but I often wonder about my brother in that respect.

R. G.:   Looking at your own earliest years—let's say your relationship to your parents and your brother's relationship to the same people—do you see any distinctions?

SON: Sure. He was always the aesthetic person, I was the science person; he was the English person, I was the one who went for sports; he went for walks on the beach. People described him as—when—just by looking at him as someone who's a fashion designer or something like that. He's got that artistic kind of look to him, and it shows in his personality.

R. G.:   How about back then, when you were a little kid?

SON: He was never accepted socially with his friends or generally with the people in his classes, and I guess I grew up in a clique ever since kindergarten through ninth grade, but he always had troubles relating to his friends or his peers his own age. People always used to make

fun of him because he could never play sports as well as the other
guys and because of his name, Bernard. It was just a funny name, you
know how kids are?

R. G.: Was he a feminine boy? Nonathletic doesn't really—

SON: Feminine? How would you describe feminine?

R. G.: Liking to dress in girls' clothes?

SON: No, no.

R. G.: Playing with dolls?

SON: No.

R. G.: Making believe he was a girl?

SON: No. He liked to cook.

R. G.: But he wasn't feminine, just nonathletic?

SON: Right, and uncoordinated.

R. G.: Do you think there was a difference in your mother's relationship
to the two of you?

SON: I guess I am my father's son. Therefore, my mother tried to comfort
my brother more, but I think I am as close to her as he is. It's just
that I get more affection from my father.

R. G.: But as far back as you can remember, there was that difference in
how he related to the two of you?

SON: Sure.

R. G.: And you think your mother sort of filled the void? You don't think
that she was inherently closer to your brother initially?

SON: No, I don't think, I really don't. I think that I was more influenced
by my father.

R. G.: Were you influenced more by your father because he took a different level of interest in you, or because innately your interests were
closer to your dad's?

SON: I think just innately we were closer. It just happened that the
interests coincided. I would not do something because he told me to
do it or because it would please him. I would say that it just coincided.

Example 6

The sexual need for males is seen as a substitute for
nonsexual attention from males

R. G.: A couple of years ago, you told me that you had some sexual
feelings about males. To what extent did that evolve over the last
couple of years?

SON: It's disappeared. Almost completely. In fact, I think my relationship
with guys has become much more sure. For example, I don't feel self-
conscious hugging a very good friend if he's male, but I wouldn't want
to sleep with another guy or have any kind of sex with another guy.
That's just not something I do right now.

R. G.: How strong were your feelings a couple of years ago?

SON: Sometimes they were very strong.

R. G.: Why do you think they decreased?

SON: Because I think I have found the attention I need from guys through my friends, and I have discovered how much fun girls can be, so the sexual or romantic interest has declined.

R. G.: How did that displace the sexual and romantic needs with guys you had earlier?

SON: Probably through a very complicated process. That is a feeling I have. As I came to be friends with people with whom I can discuss very personal feelings, then the need to perhaps have sex with them, or think about having sex with them, disappeared. Because I think often sex and romantic feelings are simply an extension of very deep personal feelings.

R. G.: It's not like you're saying they are substitutes?

SON: Not necessarily substitutes, but an extension, and if you can deal with—perhaps a substitute is a better word, now that I think about it—but if you can deal with the emotions themselves, then you don't need to extend.

R. G.: It sounds like if one went up, the other went down.

SON: Yes.

R. G.: You found yourself more able to relate comfortably to males, and sexual feelings to males decreased?

SON: Right.

R. G.: Were you feeling a deprivation of being able to relate comfortably to males?

SON: Not a deprivation. Well, deprivation is a very strong word. But say that I knew that I did not share many common interests with other guys my age, and I had a sense that that was wrong. Now, I have common interests with my friends. I no longer have a sense of the way I was, not being interested in sports or things like that, as bad, as negative.

THE RELATIONSHIP BETWEEN "FEMININITY" AND HOMOSEXUALITY

Example 1

A mother sees the relationship as inevitable

R. G.: One of the things that has emerged in our research is that there is this association between being a feminine boy and later being a gay man. And that's a mystery why that association should be there.

MOTHER: That's a mystery? Did I *mishear* you?

R. G.: Okay, then why do you think there *is* this association?

MOTHER: Well, the little boy identifies with his mother, with the feminine aspects of being a human being rather than the male aspects. He sees mother as something to be emulated, and, "I want to be like her, I want to wear her dresses and shoes, and boys are too rough and loud and noisy, and their games, you can get hurt in them, and it's safe to play with dolls, and it's safe to play with little girls." It's just assuming the identity of the person that you feel closest to, feel most comfortable with.

R. G.:   Why should the son then be gay?

MOTHER: I'm trying to get into my son's shoes. Okay, so I look up to women, and I think they're wonderful, and I want to be just like them. And then slowly as he grows up to his teenage years, he's feeling like a woman, and he's looking at other men as a woman would look at a man. He's looking from a female aspect of the beauty of a man's body. He said to me, "Women's bodies are ugly," and on TV, with these porno flicks that come on late at night, and he says, "Ugh, how gross" when they show women, "those gaping holes." And he's so brutal, and I say, "Will you stop it." And he says, "Ugh, that's disgusting." "It's beautiful," I tell him, and he says, "It's gross to me and disgusting and ugly." I say, "You're so weird."

We do have a good rapport as far as this goes. Maybe it's a little bizarre mother-son relationship, but it's there, and we do laugh a lot, and we're honest. I don't know if it's too good and close for mother and son. It frightens me—the overbearing mother causes a homosexual child. It's probably true [laughs]. Now that I've done the damage. Jesus [laughs].

Her son sees himself as always having been homosexual but initially thinking only women had sex with men

R. G.:   Why do you think there is this association between having some feminine, girl-type interests when you were young, as you did, and now as a grown man, being sexually turned on by men?

SON: I just thought that was the way I was, that I was born having a little bit more feminine qualities than most boys.

R. G.:   Well, that might explain why you might have had some early feminine interests, but why should that later be associated with being turned on by men?

SON: Maybe it was because I had always been homosexual, and I thought in order to have a sexual relationship with men, back then, I'd have to be a woman. I couldn't be a man and have a sexual relationship with a man. Maybe then, you know, I never thought about men making love to men. I always thought I had to be a woman to have a relationship with a man.

R. G.:   Are you saying that your sexual attractions to men came before you started the dressing up and playing with Barbie dolls?

SON: I think it was during that time, but you know—I think I've always had an attraction towards men. I can remember when I was thirteen or fourteen, I always thought it would be better to be a woman and to have sex with men, you know, have sexual relationships with men than to be a man. Because it's more accepted.

R. G.: But you had thoughts of wanting to be a girl when you were, like, five. Do you think that you had sexual feelings for men then?

SON: I think I must have. I just didn't know what the feelings were or anything. I probably did.

R. G.: That's an interesting theory.

SON: Well, I always thought about that. I don't think that now—I'm happy the way I am—but before, when I was less aware of myself and had less confidence in myself, I thought it would be a lot better to be a woman to have a relationship with a man, because that would be more accepted.

Example 2

A self-fulfilling prophecy

SON: I have an older sister, and so I was basically around female people. I know they tend to label people if a little boy grew up without a father, and they have a mother figure, they tend to grow up to be homosexual, or they tend to have feminine ways. Maybe that's why I had some of these actions or gestures, being around a female and not having a male figure for a while. But yet there is another aspect of my life— that's having homosexual feelings, and then you think, well, you know— a little boy plays with dolls and dresses up like a little girl, and he's going to grow up being a homosexual.

R. G.: Tell me why you think there might be that association.

SON: Well, if you think the guy really wants to be a girl, and if he is playing with dolls and dressing up as a girl, he is fantasizing about being a girl as he grows older. And girls fantasize about men. But I'm happy being a male.

R. G.: When you are having sex with a male, do you ever fantasize that you are a female?

SON: No, but I fantasize that I would like them to be dominating. I don't fantasize about being female.

R. G.: So, why should there be that link? If the wish to be a woman is gone—

SON: It's just, I guess, a stereotype. You grow up playing with dolls and dressing up as a girl, and you are going to grow up being gay.

R. G.: Let's say the stereotype is true. Let's assume that every single boy that plays with dolls, dresses up, plays as a female, and is called sissy,— everyone turns out gay. Why would that be?

SON: Maybe because they have been told, "Ah, he's a sissy." And you are called a sissy and your parents say it's wrong, you shouldn't be a sissy. I guess they more or less pound it into your head time after time, and then maybe you start perceiving yourself as being a sissy and you start believing, "I am, maybe I am."

R. G.: Why should the sissy part become gay?

SON: Because they say homosexuals act real sissified, which a lot of them do. They act very feminine.

Example 3

Desire to be attractive to males

SON: I played with my femininity at an early age, and even though I was told that it was bad and wrong, and my mother freaked out, I still managed to hang on to it somehow. I think that's affected my sexuality. It's allowed me to see it from a different perspective. I don't know if I'm what you'd call a classic homosexual. I see myself as being very different from a lot of people, straight and gay.

R. G.: Why should there be the association?

SON: For me, I think—I dressed up as a girl or woman to attract a male, at least in my teen ages. I think I was just in love with this pretty, soft friend who was much more colorful and feminine.

R. G.: Why should that be associated with a later sexual interest in males?

SON: Well, I don't see myself now as necessarily desiring to be a woman, but that seems to have been what I was striving for when I was a child and dressing up. Perhaps I was too young to really think about what I was doing—I mean, I can't recall dressing up and thinking, "Now some man will like me." I mainly remember just the sensation of it—the sensation of it was like a very strong feeling, and maybe that was a presexual feeling, and maybe that's what carried over into becoming a homosexual.

For some men, boyhood "femininity" and sexual interest in males are seen as age-dependent expressions of the same, continuing developmental process. It is the female identity expressing itself in the language first of boyhood, then of manhood.

For some men, boyhood "femininity" is viewed as a means of receiving love from males. During adulthood, this "femininity" is no longer necessary: the need for love and affection is met by the established pattern of sexual exchange.

10

Sum, Substance, and Speculation: My Turn

Previous chapters provided the rationale, methodology, and findings for this fifteen-year study of male sexual identity development. They recounted the autobiographies of males evolving from divergent boyhoods to diverse manhoods. They focused on relationships with parents. They examined attempts to divert some males from experiencing sexual identity conflict. Here, I offer some speculations, in an effort to complete this psychosexual odyssey.

"SISSY" BOYS TO GAY MEN

As reported in chapter 4, follow-up interviews with two-thirds of the original group of "feminine" boys reveal that three-fourths of them are homosexually or bisexually oriented. By contrast, only one of the two-thirds of the previously "masculine" boys on whom we have follow-up data is homosexually or bisexually oriented. This linkage between boyhood "femininity" and manhood homosexuality has long been suspected. Not only do the retrospective data summarized in chapter 1 suggest it, but a few prospective studies document it.

In the late 1950s and early 1960s, while a medical student at Johns Hopkins, I studied a pilot sample of "feminine" boys under the direction of John Money. An early follow-up of five of these boys, reported in my 1974 *Sexual Identity Conflict in Children and Adults*, found that three were exclusively homosexual and two bisexual. Three of the original five were later reported in another follow-up of nine previously "feminine" boys. Here, at least eight were predominantly homosexual (Money and Russo, 1979).

Another thirteen "feminine" boys were studied decades ago by Harry Bakwin. Two became homosexual. Another, initially seen at nine, was described as "normal" by his mother at seventeen, and another, also first seen at nine, was described as a "quite normal boy" by his mother at fourteen. A boy seen at eleven was "unchanged" at thirteen, except that he had stopped cross-dressing, and another, first seen at five, later "expressed disgust" at the idea of homosexuality when he was thirteen. Others were lost to follow-up (Bakwin, 1968).

Sixteen boys described in medical records made during childhood as showing "feminine" behaviors were later interviewed during adulthood at the University of Minnesota. Two had become homosexual, three transsexual, and one a transvestite (Lebovitz, 1972).

Finally, Bernard Zuger (1984) has reported follow-up findings on his sample of fifty-five males seen for early "feminine" behaviors. Thirty-nine were preadolescent when first evaluated. About two-thirds of the full sample are reported to be homosexual, although it is not clear how many of these were in the group seen prior to teenage, and the number of men rated "homosexual" or "probable homosexual" who are actually bisexual (2–4 on the Kinsey scale) is not reported.

Explanations for this association between boyhood "femininity" and manhood homosexuality can embrace physiological or psychosocial theory. The physiological explanation posits a neural organization, perhaps gene-activated, that affects prenatal hormonal output. Hormonal levels modify the central nervous system to mediate boyhood nonerotic and manhood erotic behaviors more commonly found in persons with the other major pattern of this system—females. From the physiological perspective, cross-gender behavior in childhood and homosexual behavior in adulthood are age-dependent expressions of the same underlying, evolving pattern of female sexual identity.

Psychosocially, the link between "femininity" in boyhood and homosexuality in manhood is explainable within either a psychoanalytic or a social learning context. Within a psychoanalytic framework, incomplete psychological separation of the male child from its mother results in excessive feminine identification by the male. This interferes with progression through the oedipal phase with its normal psychosexual outcome, identification with the father and the later pursuit of other females as sexual partners (chapter 3). Within a social learning model, the boy's interests, skills, and attitudes are shaped by his social milieu, composed of girls and women. As he matures along this female-type developmental track, his romantic needs and erotic patterns are those of his social network. He, too, seeks males.

INTERPRETING OUR DATA

The "recipe" approach to preparing a developmental model of homosexual orientation is a tempting tradition. A cup of father absence, a dash of maternal dominance, a sprig of peer rejection, and a pinch of early homosexual seduction combine to yield the homosexual man. But this approach is problematic. The same ingredients do not always yield the same product. One wonders—as with the ingredients that constitute living protoplasm—whether, if we combine the *necessary* early life ingredients for homosexuality, they are *sufficient* to yield homosexual life.

When statistical science moved beyond the chi square and the t-test, which merely addressed the question of whether groups differed on some variable, it contemplated the *extent* to which one variable is related to or, more ambitiously, *predicts* the properties of another variable. This is a thorn in the side of the researcher in behavioral science. How much of a behavioral outcome can be "explained" by an earlier factor?

For example, while more homosexual men may have been father-absent, *to what degree* does early father absence predict later homosexuality? Suppose that father absence and later homosexuality in a sample are highly correlated—the correlation coefficient (r) being .7, only .3 away from the exact fit, perfect correlation of 1.0. The p level may be less than .001, signifying that the likelihood of the association between the two variables being one of chance is less than one in a thousand. But this high correlation of .7 explains less than *half* the story—or the *variance*—comprising the development of homosexuality, because the amount of variance explained is the product of multiplying the correlation coefficient by itself. After multiplying .7 by .7, 51 percent of the development of homosexuality is *not* explained by father absence. So in the recipe approach, we add another "precursor" element, such as a domineering mother. Perhaps r now climbs to .8, and we now "explain" 64 percent of the development of homosexuality. But, no matter how many ingredients are added, we invariably fall short of a complete recipe.

What of the elusive fraction? Is it the vital force that eludes laboratory chemists attempting to create life, the vital force that seizes the necessary ingredients and makes them live? Is it that unmeasurable individual biological receptivity that interfaces with experiential events and forges them into the elusive object of research testing? Or do we actually have it all but remain tricked by our too modest instruments? Do our instruments delude us into thinking that they are not measuring all that is there when in fact they *are*?

Another problem is that some research findings are conceptually puzzling. For example, variables may differ for families at the time of their entry into the "feminine boy" or "masculine boy" group. But some of these variables may not differ within the "feminine boy" group in relation to the extent of the boys' "femininity." And a variable associated with entry into the "feminine boy" group may not be related to whether a "feminine" boy exits as a homosexual or heterosexual man, even though in our study only "feminine" boys emerge as homosexual.

Furthermore, researchers hoping to link earlier life experiences with later behaviors must be sobered by the knowledge that two persons interacting with identical events may experience them differently, while two persons interacting with discrepant events may experience them similarly. Finally, the nonspecificity of our shorthand codes, such as "father absence," poses another problem. "Father absence" affects two boys differently as it translates into direct impact on the boy and into impact on others who remain with the boy. "Father absence" for the son is "husband absence" for the mother.

DEVELOPING "FEMININITY"

Some "popular" or "commonsense" theories of the development of cross-gender behavior in boys or homosexuality in men received only partial support in our study. One was that the mother and/or father had wanted a girl during the pregnancy with this son. However, the absence of a major difference between the groups may be the result of biased reporting. The popularity of this theory of parents feminizing sons may inhibit parents of "feminine" boys from stating that they had wanted girls. Parents are not inclined to blame themselves for the development of what they see as problematic behavior.

But this not-so-subtle pattern of cross-sex child rearing may not be the pattern to look for. Research on behavioral conditioning demonstrates that certain types of subtle conditioning are the most difficult to extinguish. In the nonsubtle strategy, provide a reward every time for performance of a specific act, and soon the act is regularly performed in anticipation of the reward. Learning is rapid, but so is forgetting. Stop rewarding, and the new behavior will fade and disappear. An extrapolation of this conditioning model to the development of boyhood cross-gender behavior requires that the parent *invariably* reward the boy's "feminine" behavior, be it cross-dressing, doll-play, or female role-taking. Once the reward ceases, the behavior should soon recede, unless there is a critical developmental period during which this reward pattern consolidates a behavioral pattern that becomes locked in.

But consider the commonly found pattern of parental response to early boyhood cross-gender behavior in our study. Often, the "feminine" behavior was ignored. Occasionally, it was positively received and considered cute or funny. Photos of cross-dressed children, retrieved from family albums, visually document this response, as seen in about 15 percent of our group. (It is the unusual parent who memorializes a child's offensive behavior on film and mounts it in the family archive.) This irregular pattern of positive reinforcement, without punishment, is essentially that of "intermittent positive reinforcement." It is this pattern of conditioning that is found in laboratory experiments to be the most difficult to eliminate. It endures well beyond the time of any obvious pattern of reward (Carlson, 1984).

Reinforcement Theory

Considerable support was found in our study for the thesis that a parent's responses to a son's early expression of gender-role behavior will influence the extent to which these behaviors are continued. Clinically, it was apparent that most parents of the "feminine boy" group, especially mothers, either reacted positively to their son's early cross-gender behaviors, or reacted neutrally to it, for a period of two to four years. Statistically, there was a high correlation between ratings of parental positive responses to a son's early cross-gender behaviors and the extent to which these behaviors were shown at the initial evaluation. These findings are consistent with the social learning theory of the development of sex differences as described in chapter 2.

It should not be construed, however, that there was a duet of support or discouragement of "feminine" or "masculine" behaviors by the mother and father within an individual family. Most fathers supported "masculine" behavior, although fathers who had wanted a girl during the pregnancy with this son were more supportive of the son's early cross-gender behaviors. In about one-third of the families of "feminine" boys, the boys were rated as receiving positive reactions to early cross-gender behavior from their mothers, but not from their fathers. However, the overriding influence on gender-role behavior appears to have been the mother's reinforcement, perhaps due to the considerably greater amount of time shared by most mothers and sons than by most fathers and sons.

The question remains whether parental reinforcement of cross-gender behaviors will have a similar effect on the behavior of all boys, or whether cross-gender behaviors will emerge more readily in some. Parental reinforcement may operate within predispositional limits of the child. However, the behavioral differences between our two groups of boys do not appear to be entirely a function of innate features of the children. If the presence or absence of pictures of a boy cross-dressed, taken by parents and placed in the family photo album, are an indication of early parental support of cross-dressing, then some contribution appears to derive from parents. When parents in the contrast group were asked whether their sons ever cross-dressed, and the answer was yes, they were asked whether they had any pictures illustrating it. They all said no.

Alternatively, boys in the contrast group may not have spontaneously shown as much early cross-gender behavior. Perhaps, for extensive cross-gender behavior to develop, there must be an interaction between a sufficient degree of such behavior appearing spontaneously, an initial positive reaction to the behavior by parents, and a receptivity by the boy to parental reinforcement.

"Beautiful" Infants

Descriptions of infant sons in terms rated as more "beautiful" were more often given by parents of the "feminine" boys. And these "beautiful" descriptions were associated with more positive parental reactions to sons' early "feminine" behaviors.

The perception of "beauty" may well be in the eyes of the beholder. How biased those eyes may be is suggested by a study of parents and their newborn male and female infants in a maternity ward within twenty-four hours of the child's birth. By then, mothers had held the infants, and fathers had viewed them through a window. Parents then described their infant. Mothers saw sons as cuddlier, fathers saw daughters as cuddlier. Sons were seen as "big" more frequently than daughters, although they did not actually differ in length or weight. Relevant to our finding that parents of "feminine" boys described their infant sons as more "beautiful" was the finding that "the feminine cluster [of descriptive words]—beautiful, pretty, and cute—was used significantly more often to describe daughters than sons" (Rubin et al., 1974, 517).

Whatever the objectivity of our parents' descriptions of their infant's appearance, the impression generated in the parents may be the important factor. Parents who see their infant as beautiful and feminine, and then are more supportive of his "feminine" behavior, may be enacting a self-fulfilling prophecy. Parents expecting such behavior as natural may not discourage it. Lack of discouragement may enhance it.

Alternatively, parents with behaviorally "feminine" boys may retrospectively distort their impressions of the infant's appearance in the reflected light of his current appearance. However, statements from those outside the family supporting parents' impressions should be less biased. On the other hand, it could be that such comments were not actually *made* more frequently, only *remembered* more frequently.

Parent/Young Child Shared Time

Considerable research energy went into determining the extent of parent-child time spent together during the son's first years. While this dimension for mothers ran contrary to prediction—based on social learning theories and "common sense"—findings with fathers underscored their salience as family members.

In our assessment of Stoller's thesis that mothers of "pre-feminine boy" infants hold their son for excessively prolonged periods—an interaction that can present obstacles to the son psychologically separating from mother—we found that no differences were reported by the mothers in our two groups. However, the quality of the mother-son exchange must be appraised as well as the quantity. Stoller has also noted that there are cultures in which mothers hold children abundantly during the first years, but where there is not an abundance of transsexual males (Stoller, 1969, 168).

The finding of less mother-"feminine son" shared time during the son's early years could be interpreted as inconsistent with a social learning basis for a son developing a "feminine" identification. However, even within a group of families where mothers spend less time with their sons than in a contrast group of families, mothers still spend more time with sons than fathers do. And when these mothers react positively to the sons' early cross-gender behaviors (as they tended to do in our study), and when these sons' fathers spend relatively less time with them (as was also true in our study), the requirements of social learning theory are met.

Parents may bias reports about how much time they or their spouses spent with their sons. Mothers of "feminine" boys are well aware of the popular theory that "too much" mothering can produce a "sissy." Thus, these mothers might underreport contact with sons. They might also tend to scapegoat or blame their husbands for not having spent enough time with the "feminine" boy. Reciprocally, these fathers might overreport the extent of mother-son contact as well as their own.

To assess such bias, mothers and fathers were independently questioned about parent-son contact during the earliest years and rates of agreement were computed.* We found only minimal support for a differential bias between the two groups when reporting mother-son interaction in the first two years. Further, an analysis of the direction in which mothers and fathers differed in their report of mother-son time revealed no systematic bias; that is, mothers were not consistently underrating their time with sons compared to that reported by fathers.

With fathers of "feminine" boys, there is even greater security regarding their reports of time shared with sons.† We found no strong evidence

*For daytime mother-son contact in year one, the reports of "feminine boy" parents did not correlate as well as those of "masculine boy" parents ($r = .34$ versus .64), but for nighttime mother-son contact, "feminine boy" parental reports correlated better ($r = .53$ versus .39). For mother-son daytime contact in year two, the correlation was essentially nil between the parents of "feminine" boys, whereas parents of "masculine" boys agreed moderately well ($r = .46$). For reports of nighttime mother-son contact in year two, parents of "feminine" boys agreed moderately well, but not as well as parents of "masculine" boys ($r = .47$ versus .63).

†For the number of waking hours spent together per week in the first year, parents of "feminine" and "masculine" boys have comparable rates of agreement ($r = .44$ and .36), and for the second year there is considerably more agreement between parents of "feminine" boys than between parents of "masculine" boys ($r = .58$ versus .02). Regarding father-son contact at the time of initial evaluation,

that mothers of "feminine" boys were scapegoating their husbands, or that these fathers were inflating the extent of their involvement with sons.

As reported in chapter 3, father-son shared time in the boy's first years appeared as a critical variable for the development of sexual identity. Since less father-son shared time was associated in our study with a son being "feminine," and being a "feminine" boy was associated with being a homosexual or bisexual man, we attempted to assess the relative influence of these two variables on sexual orientation. Using a multiple regression analysis, we find that being a "feminine" boy has a stronger relationship with later homosexual arousal than does early father-son shared time. It appears that the association for father-son time and later homosexual orientation operates through the variable of being a "feminine" boy.

Our "feminine" boys were generally alienated from their fathers. One interpretation of this distance is that the early "femininity" of the boy repels the father. However, another possible sequence is that boys who are not yet "feminine" but already alienated from their father identify with their mother because it is she who is successful in obtaining love and affection from the father. Regrettably, for the son, this identification with the mother does not serve the boy's "purpose," as his "femininity" drives the father further away. The boy is caught between a rock and a hard place. Our "feminine" boys were also alienated from their male peers. Thus, throughout childhood, their relations to other males were wanting.

Male-affect starvation is what I see as a continuing force operating from early childhood in males who had a poor relationship both with their father *and* with male peers. This hunger may motivate the later search for love and affection from males. It may be fed in a homosexual liaison. A striking illustration is example 1 in the father-son section of chapter 3.

Sex-Role Dichotomies

On their way to "masculinity" and "femininity," infants and young children utilize cues and clues to categorize themselves as belonging to one of two major categories of persons: like mommy or like daddy, like brother or like sister, male or female. There are several sources of learning.

Anatomies teach. An earliest possible signal directing a child to correct self-placement is witnessing the "anatomic distinction between the sexes" (as Freud elegantly put it), and to compare its own genitalia with a male and with a female. Thus, a parent's level of comfort with household nudity, the opportunity for a child to see a parent disrobe occasionally, or the opportunity to bathe or shower with a parent or sibling can be an important early cue in establishing this first component of sexual identity. In a two-parent family, the child may witness genital configurations and

---

parents of "feminine" boys are again in better agreement than are "masculine boy" parents ($r = .61$ versus $.07$).

categorize its own genitalia as more like one or the other. With an absent parent (usually father), an older brother may provide a basis for comparison with mother. But without any other males, the boy, seeing mother nude, may judge the anatomic distinctions as signs of *maturation*, not *gender*.

Parents teach. A child may be clothed more like one parent than the other and define its sex in this way. A child may be told by parents that it will grow up to be like mommy or daddy.

Media teach. Television and books categorize gender on cultural, but usually not on genital characteristics.

Peers teach. In peer play there is not only the opportunity for observing cultural artifacts, but also the opportunity for genital comparison. Children play in the time-honored exchange, "You show me yours, I'll show you mine."

INTEGRATING THE FINDINGS

Attempts to weave our findings into a coherent pattern can engage several strategies of data analysis. I can provide detailed verbatim interviews as in chapter 5, spanning decades, the autobiographical product of a research *inquisition*. Or I can provide a path analysis, derived from multiple regression techniques, that leads (or follows) life through a maze of statistical coefficients. Or I can offer an inferential biographical exercise in which the clinical researcher translates interviews and statistics into a free-floating personalized interpretation of another's life.

The verbatim interview is the type of analysis I pressed in the 1974 volume—these were the data that constituted to me the valid underpinning of this psychiatric research. They could be examined and interpreted by the individual reader. They were full reports, not interpretations or condensations of data. That pleased some readers and frustrated others. Some wanted me to go out on a limb and play with the material—that I should risk the fall rather than they.

In that book, I worried that drawing together a developmental synthesis might be *synthetic:* "The disparate descriptions presented ... make it clear that no consistent etiologic pattern exists for extensive boyhood femininity. From details frequently reported in these cases, however, something of an etiologic pattern can be sketched. The sketch is not an exact likeness of the history of any one boy or his family. It is composed primarily for those who experience a compelling need for law and order in their theoretic universe" (Green, 1974, 239).

My current reluctance to perform this type of exercise is no less. The risk is greater now, with adult sexuality yet another step along this precarious limb. On the other hand, I am not congenial to reducing all behavioral processes to the ebb and flow of neurotransmitters. There is something to be said for building a model, partly out of clinical impressions (chapter 5), partly out of statistical correlations (chapter 3), and partly out of what people say about the reasons for their being the way they are (chapter 9). So I will update the 1974 developmental model.

Developmental Synthesis: Clinical

All children are not created equal. They bring with them a range of temperamental attributes and predispositions, some of which may be related to sexual identity development. The best candidates for this contribution are those early behaviors that appear to be, in part, hormone dependent, based on studies up the evolutionary hierarchy from mouse to monkey to Man. Male-female differences exist in the levels of these hormones before birth, as well in the behaviors related to these hormones after birth. Further, within the population of both males and females, there is variability in both the level of hormone and the extent of behavior.

Specifically, we have evidence pointing to prenatal androgen (male hormone) levels influencing behaviors such as timidity, aggressivity, participation in rough-and-tumble play, and interest in newborns (and perhaps in their surrogates, baby dolls) (Maccoby and Jacklin, 1980; Ehrhardt and Baker, 1974; Jacklin, Maccoby and Doering, 1983). These behaviors are traditionally sex-typed. Newborns with differing predispositions toward these behaviors will have differing early socialization experiences. Earliest experiences with peers, with mother, and with father will all be tempered by this temperamental distinction.

During a pregnancy, prospective parents are not always neutral as regards the sex of their fetus. Some couples destined to have a boy wish for a girl. In some families, this strong wish (or wishful thinking) may contribute to an impression that a male infant possesses features more frequently reported for girls. This impression may affect the manner in which parents expect certain behaviors from the infant or promote others in the infant. When these children are objectively "feminine" in appearance and elicit comments from others outside the family, such as, "Oh, what a beautiful girl," not only may the parents' perceptions of the child be influenced, but the child's self-image may also be modified.

Yet another influence on the parents' perceptions and the child's self-image may be the child's medical history—significant illnesses and injuries, hospitalizations, and special care. This may evoke an image of being frail and less available for robust male-male activity, and may promote increased parental protection.

The accoutrements of females appeal to most children. For many infants the soft-textured, sparkling, colorful artifacts of females provide considerable interest. Their relative attractiveness may be substantially greater to those children in whom the appeal of other activities, such as rough-and-tumble play, is diminished.

Parents generally do not see a child's sex-typed behaviors during the first two or three years as portending anything about future sexual development. Mothers may initially find cross-gender behavior "cute" or "funny." They may reward it and rarely, if ever, discourage it. Some boys experience additional positive reinforcement for cross-gender behavior from relatives, baby-sitters, or other adults. With the father traditionally serving as the principal enforcer of sex-role codes (chapter 2), his absence, absolute or relative, at the initiation or continuation of a boy's cross-gender behavior, may result in a lack of direction toward traditional activities.

Initial interaction with male peers is problematic. A boy's nondisposition to rough-and-tumble play, and perhaps his predisposition for doll-play, set him apart from most male peers. "Boys play too rough" is the *team cry* of "feminine" boys. The boy finds the domestic activities of his mother more comfortable than the recreational interests of his father. In families with more than one male child, he may become "mama's boy," while his brother becomes "daddy's boy." The social skills and mannerisms the boy is learning are "feminine." These behaviors set him further apart from the male peer group.

With a universe boldly illustrated in only two "colors," black and white, a child who feels it cannot keep up with activity black or does not want to do activity black (which defines maleness), logically concludes it is, or needs to be, white (female). Before gender constancy (chapter 2) is achieved, change of dress, change of play, or change of role provides the solution.

Early grade school brings social distress. Without "masculine" skills, without the capacity for full participation in the rough-and-tumble play of early boyhood, with "feminine" mannerisms, and with minimal input from the father, it is difficult for the boy to move off the "feminine" developmental track. He is labeled "sissy." There is increased isolation from males.

Concurrently, if the father is present, he rejects the son because of the child's "feminine" behaviors. Perhaps, by default, the mother becomes increasingly the favored parent and a source for increased female identification. There is an *identification gap* between boy and father.

The boy sees mother obtaining the attention from father or other males for which he hungers. An apparent solution to this deficit is to be like mother. But, as described above, this backfires. Throughout the childhood years, there is male-affect starvation: male peers reject, the father rejects.

As a teenager, the boy's manneristic "femininity" and sensitivity set him apart from many same-age males. These are signals to some other males of a young man's potential erotic availability. Early sexual experiences with males provide the longed-for affection. This affective component renders such experiences distinctive from those of other young males who engage in early male-male sexual contact. On the other hand, early heterosexual arousal receives little positive reinforcement. The "feminine" adolescent boy is less attractive to teenage girls.

This developmental track leads from "feminine" boy, to bisexual early adolescent, to homosexual late adolescent and young adult man. This synthesis has the advantage of integrating innate contributions of the child, psychological features of the parents, and sociological patterns of the environment. This exercise may be more "artistic" than "scientific." But recall the caveat at the book's outset.

Developmental Synthesis: Statistical

An alternate method of constructing a developmental synthesis utilizes t-tests, correlation coefficients, and regression analyses. We identify differences between the groups, such as time spent between son and father in year two. We look for the relationship between variables, such as the time the father spends with his son in year two and the father's wish for a girl during the pregnancy. We look at the son's later sexual orientation in relation, separately, to the father's wish for a girl and the time he spent with his son. We may try to forge a developmental chain utilizing these statistical procedures.

Path analyses are often used in long-term research. In such an analysis, causality is presumed when an earlier variable is associated with a later one, and in the direction of a prior prediction. However, in our study, a path analysis is problematic due to the exploratory nature of the study and the relatively small number of families studied. On the other hand, schematically linking the variables may be useful in attempting to structure the findings. We may place variables as they would have occurred sequentially. From this we obtain a developmental synthesis.

Mothers of "Feminine" Boys

A mother with a distant relationship with her mother had less premarital sociosexual experience and more desire for a girl during the pregnancy with this boy. This mother reacted positively to her son's early cross-gender behavior. A mother who saw her infant as "beautiful," or a mother whose son was hospitalized in his early years, also reacted positively to her son's early cross-gender behavior. These reactions occurred in the context of relatively less mother-son shared time. By mid-childhood, the boy was very "feminine." Then, during pre- and early adolescence, the mother did not discourage the son's conventionally feminine behavior.

Fathers of "Feminine" Boys

A father who was less conventionally masculine in boyhood did not discourage the boy's early cross-gender behavior. A father who saw his infant son as "beautiful" also did not discourage his son's early cross-gender behavior. A father who wanted a daughter during the pregnancy with his son spent less time with the son. By mid-childhood, the boy was

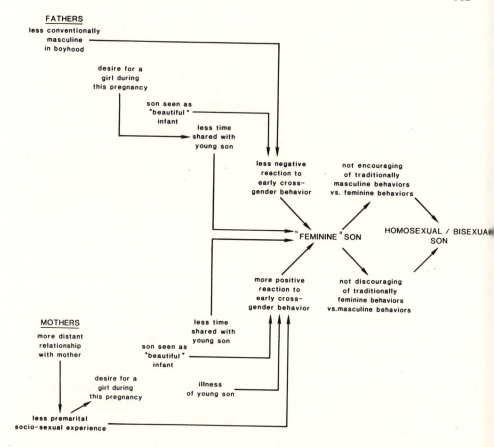

FIGURE 10.1 Schematic representation of statistically related mother and father variables for the "feminine boy" group, placed sequentially in time.

very "feminine." Then, during pre- and early adolescence, the father did not encourage the boy's conventionally masculine behavior.

Figure 10.1 is a schematic representation of this synthesis. While the variables are placed sequentially as they would have occurred in time, the lines connecting them should not be interpreted to mean causality, only a sequential correlation. These data have been described more formally in chapter 3. (See also Green, Williams, and Goodman, 1985).

The clinical developmental synthesis noted earlier does not form a perfect fit with this statistical developmental synthesis. The clinical synthesis is a composite impression from speaking with dozens of families over fifteen years. As such, it is subject to the vagaries of clinical observations. The statistical data result from analyses of ratings of interview segments by research colleagues, plus responses by parents to questionnaires. Some of the data are composite variables derived from these two sources. As such, they are subject to the vagaries of that technique. These two formulations may sometimes tap the same dimensions and yield the same impression, other times not. Biases of the reader may suggest which developmental synthesis is less "synthetic."

The power of these developmental syntheses can be tested by the study of another group of "feminine" and "masculine" boys and an analysis of the same variables. As Stoller's earlier findings were elaborated and explored in this study, so may the next researcher elaborate and test these new findings. In American baseball, about half a century ago, there was a sequence of three players who, when throwing the ball to each other in succession, had a major impact. It was Tinker to Evers to Chance. Similarly, I toss these findings to the next researcher in line, at the risk of leaving them to chance.

The extent to which we demonstrated specific influences of parents in initiating and perpetuating their sons' "femininity" is less than some readers (or we) might have wanted. Perhaps our measuring instruments are too crude. Perhaps we didn't listen carefully enough to the right answers. Or perhaps our sample was skewed against our uncovering many "findings." If parents, by their attitudes and behaviors, initiated or facilitated their son's cross-gender activity, they might be less likely to seek consultation about the boy's behaviors. Thus, the probability of finding parent-initiating or perpetuating factors in families who do present themselves for evaluation and study is reduced.

OTHER FINDINGS

One "Feminine" Boy per Family

Several times I implied or stated explicitly that there was only one "feminine" boy (by the study criteria) in our families with more than one son. In the developmental synthesis derived from clinical impressions, different developmental tracks within a given family were described that could account for this finding. More specifically, the formulation of why our "identical" twins (chapter 8) diverged on sexual identity underscored where different early life experiences of brothers may correlate with divergent patterns of gender role and sexual orientation. Further, the narratives given by our families in chapters 3, 5, and 9 are descriptive of different patterns of parenting within families that may be associated with different patterns of sexual identity.

Rarity of Homosexual or Bisexual Men in the Comparison Group

I should also speculate about why there is apparently only one bisexual man and no homosexual man in the group of previously "masculine" boys. As described in chapter 1, these boys were not selected on the basis of their masculine behavior. They were selected on the basis of whether features of their family constellation—such as race, number of older brothers, marital status of the parents—matched a "feminine boy" family. This comparison group might be expected to yield some bisexual or homosexual men at follow-up, in that the classic Kinsey group's study (1948) suggested that about 4 percent of adult males are exclusively homosexual, and another 6 percent predominantly homosexual. If these figures are valid, we could expect one exclusively homosexual man in the comparison group and two bisexual or predominantly homosexual men.

One explanation for our finding is that with such a small number of expected homosexual men their absence is merely due to chance. Another possibility is that if about two-thirds of homosexual men were "feminine" boys (chapter 1), that pool of prehomosexual boys was not represented in the comparison group who, by "chance," were all conventionally "masculine." Thus, the probability of any bisexual or homosexual men emerging from the comparison group would be diminished to nil. Or perhaps, as these men continue to mature, one or two will evolve as bisexual or homosexual. Or perhaps one or two bisexuals or homosexuals are in the subsample lost to follow-up. Or perhaps one or two concealed their sexual orientation from me.

NATURE/NURTURE

The statistical correlations reported above suggest the importance of socialization factors influencing the development of sexual identity. But there is too much variability, too much nonspecificity in the findings. So, "back to nature."

Biological factors may differentiate the two groups of boys in our study, perhaps to the degree that they partially account for the development of different behavioral patterns. However, the patterns of socialization reported here would not be altered. This book is a description of the experiential variables of two groups of boys with markedly different patterns of sexual identity.

I doubt that a biological factor can completely explain the development of these boys' different patterns of sexual identity. Nor do I believe that a biologic factor can completely explain the emergence into homosexuality of some of the previously "feminine" boys. This simplistic etiological basis is at odds with what we found for our "identical" twins in chapter 8. Reciprocally, I doubt that socialization influences fully explain the development of "femininity" and/or homosexuality. There are too many exceptions for every rule. Consider father-son interaction:

Father Present: "Feminine" Boys, Homosexual Men

EXAMPLE 1

MOTHER: I want to tell you something. He's had a too-devoted father. This is my impression, because he spent more time with him than any man will spend with a child.

EXAMPLE 2

R. G.:   To what extent were you able to spend time with him in his first year?

FATHER: A lot. During the day we used to wrestle a lot.

R. G.:   Compared with most fathers, how would you rate the time [with your son]?

FATHER: I had a lot of time—I would hold him a lot.

R. G.:   How about the second year?

FATHER: Quite a lot.

R. G.:   What kinds of things would you do together?

FATHER: We wrestled a lot, kid games, hide-and-seek, walks.

R. G.:   How much time did you have compared with the average father?

FATHER: More.

Father Absent: "Masculine" Boy, Heterosexual Man

R. G.:   To what extent did your son have contact with males during his first two years?

MOTHER: Not very much at all.

R. G.:   Did your son have any contact with his father?

MOTHER: No. We were separated since he was six months old, and he hasn't seen him since.

R. G.:   During his first two to three years, were you dating at all?

MOTHER: Yes.

R. G.:   Would these men come into the house and be visible to your son?

MOTHER: No.

While there may be constitutional differences between the sexes at birth and during the first years, it is baffling to comprehend how they could explain the full range of sex-typed behavioral differences. Innate programming may account for the greater expression of rough-and-tumble play and aggressive behavior by males across species and cultures (Young et al., 1964; Whiting and Whiting, 1975), but is there really an area within the brain that makes a dress more attractive than a pair of pants, a truck more attractive than a tea set?

If we understood the development of "fetishistic" arousal, (the sexual arousal to nonliving or unusual objects), we might better understand the development of heterosexual and homosexual arousal. It remains a grand mystery why the penises of some men swell, heat, and pulsate to inanimate objects. True, through a string of logical associations, we could fabricate a connection between a woman's dress and the female body, but what of the esoteric fetish? What string of fanciful sexualities promotes erotic arousal to the handlebars of a ten-speed English racing bicycle (as with a patient of my colleague, Joe LoPiccolo)?

While I write of male peer group and father alienation (male-affect starvation), what links this to erotic arousal at puberty? Why not merely a linkage to idolizing the high school gym teacher or to apprenticing in business to an older male? Why do not *all* male-affect-starved boys eroticize males? What vital force forges the link?

Robert Stoller finds elements of revenge and hostility to be driving dynamisms that link historical insults to patterns of current genital arousal (Stoller, 1979). Is retribution being served when a seventeen-year-old boy is penetrated by a twenty-seven-year-old man? Freud suggested in *On Narcissism* (1914) that he, the boy, may become him, the father. If so, the boy, as the father, is not merely obtaining the formerly deprived love; he *is* the lover, the father, now loving the son. Having lost the object of love, he becomes the object, and in so doing gains control by choosing objects for love.

I do not find this line of thinking all that alien to my phenomenologically framed "mental apparatus." While I do not believe it explains why *all* male-affect-starved men may adopt this defensive solution, it may be an explanation for some.

Or is the direction of sexual arousal "mindless"? Is eroticism principally an "innate releasing mechanism"—ethologist Konrad Lorenz's term for the awakening of a prenatally programmed behavioral response—at the developmentally appropriate time, when triggered by a preordained cue? A classic example is the duckling following the mother duck. Here again, our theoretical struggle is with the *nature* of the stimulus that triggers the innate releasing mechanism. The *mechanics* of arousal are not our quandary. The male *fetus* has erections. But physiologic arousal remains to be linked to an external stimulus.

As we cascade down the evolutionary hierarchy, the relentless pursuit of heterosexual reproductive behavior emerges with increasing vigor. (I remember, as a boy, raising guppies and having all but one member of a brood devoured by their voracious mother. This little survivor was nourished by me in isolation until it was nearly full grown, with its beautiful fin and tail colors. I then introduced him into the larger tank with adult male and female guppies. Like a horse out of the starting gate, he made for the closest female guppy and "penetrated" her. The young mind of this researcher was not unimpressed with that single-mindedness of heterosexual purpose.)

I find it hard to believe that sexual orientation is a developmental end point for a series of *chance* early-life events that position one on the heterosexual-homosexual continuum, a "sexual orientation lottery." What an inefficient way for a species to survive the hazards of evolution, requiring of each generation that it learn again how to be reproductive! If there were not some "mindless" driving force behind heterosexual arousal and the curiously congenial fit of the penis into the vagina, with vaginal lubrication promoting entry and ejaculation, survival of homo sapiens would have been an even more colossal long shot.

However, if heterosexuality is "programmed," it does not necessarily follow that homosexuality is also programmed. And if homosexuality is "learned," it does not necessarily follow that it is a pathological derailment from the heterosexual track. I argued against these illogical conclusions over a decade ago during the successful fight to remove homosexuality from the American Psychiatric Association's catalogue of mental disorders (Green, 1972).

Finally, arriving at the conclusion of major biological influences behind sexual orientation must not be by default. To reach for the biological ring on the sexual identity merry-go-round because social science research fails to uncover the critical life events is not science. The conclusion may be right, but the reasoning wrong.

Eighty years ago (1905), the young Freud noted:

> The nature of inversion [homosexuality] is explained neither by the hypothesis that it is innate nor by the alternative hypothesis that it is acquired. In the former case we must ask in what respect it is innate. ... In the latter case it may be questioned whether the various accidental influences would be sufficient to explain the acquisition of inversion without the cooperation of something in the subject himself. ... The existence of this last factor is not to be denied. (Freud, 1953, 140–41).

EFFECTS OF CLINICAL EVALUATION

Biological forces aside, the parents' decision to enter our study may have had a profound impact on the son's sexual identity development. Prior to evaluation, usually for a period of about two to four years, parents were at least neutral to the boy's cross-gender behaviors and sometimes responded favorably. However, at the time of initial evaluation, most parents were concerned. The emergence of this concern may be the most marked "intervention" into the boy's emerging sexual identity. It may explain why only one boy evolved as transsexual and none as transvestic.

As noted in chapter 1, the recalled childhood behaviors of adult transsexuals closely resemble the behaviors of these boys. Further, about half of adult transvestites report commencing cross-dressing prior to adolescence (Prince and Bentler, 1972). Aside from the relatively low rates of transsexualism and transvestism in the general population, there are other considerations that may explain why these two outcomes are nearly absent from our study.

First, transsexualism. Most adult transsexuals were not evaluated or treated for their cross-gender behaviors during childhood (Green, 1974). If this lack of professional attention is a reflection of a lack of parental concern for the emerging cross-sex identity, and if absence of parental concern permits the continued evolution of this identity, then such boys might be expected to evolve the most atypical pattern of identity. As described in chapter 1, this pattern is transsexualism.

Second, transvestism. Cross-dressing was the cross-gender behavior of most concern to the parents when they consulted me. Parents made a concerted effort to interrupt their sons' cross-dressing. Perhaps when such interruption occurs prior to puberty there is no opportunity for cross-dressing to become linked with sexual arousal and masturbation. It is this behavioral triad that is the hallmark of transvestism.

But consider homosexuality. If early cross-gender behavior is so tightly linked with later homosexual arousal, why doesn't the interruption of cross-gender behavior result in heterosexuality (chapter 7)? One possibility is that early cross-gender behavior, at a critical developmental phase, establishes an "incubation period" for later expression of homosexual arousal. As long as the boy's behavior is cross-gendered during this period, homosexual arousal will emerge years later, irrespective of the pattern of gender-role behaviors during the intervening years. If so, then therapy, be it formal (delivered by paid professionals) or informal (delivered by the peer group and the larger society via teasing and sex-role standards), though changing gender-role behavior, will not affect sexual orientation. Alternatively, the atypical boys may not have changed internally but were merely conveying a *veneer* of "masculinity." Perhaps they modify behaviors to the point of reducing stigma. Furthermore, some of the earlier behaviors of concern were age-dependent, such as Barbie doll play. (Even few twelve-year-old *girls* play with Barbie.) But the change is not all deception. The boys, as young men, rarely retain a conscious wish to be female and rarely cross-dress (chapter 5).

DANGER OF THE DATA

By reporting the findings of this study, I could frighten some parents of young boys. The findings are easily misinterpreted. They should *not* be interpreted to mean that a boy's occasional dressing in girls' or women's clothes, playing with dolls, making believe he is a mommy, playing games with girls, or having no interest in rough-and-tumble play and sports are behavioral problems of childhood and/or harbingers of later atypical sexuality. The behaviors shown by these boys were well beyond the range of cross-gender behaviors shown by many boys, boys who are *not unhappy being male*. Indeed, if the "feminine" boys had been girls, they would have been traditionally feminine girls. Furthermore, the cross-gender behaviors were not found in isolation but together formed a consistent portrait of a cross-sex identity, a syndrome. And even then, with the pervasive nature of the boys' cross-sex identity, not every one became homosexual or bisexual. For a given "feminine" boy, the answer to the question, "Will this boy become gay?" must be, "We don't know."

There is temptation and danger in translating these and other researchers' findings into advice on how to raise traditionally sex-typed children, and, in turn, how to maximize the prospects of a heterosexual adulthood. The data do not tell us that. There is far too much variability. Even if they did, I would not argue to teach the "lessons" learned. There is far too much variability in the lives of men who *also* happen to be heterosexual or homosexual.

Others do not agree. Two "how-to" books have already been spawned. First was Peter and Barbara Wyden's 1968 work, titled *Growing Up Straight: What Every Thoughtful Parent Should Know about Homosexuality*. Then there was George Rekers's 1982 work, uniquely titled *Growing Up Straight: What Every Family Should Know about Homosexuality*.

LAST THOUGHTS

A Personal Note

The fifteen years of this study were very gratifying. I learned a lot from these families. I hope that in the process I also helped some. I hope, at least, that I did not harm any.

At the close of each interview with the boys, I gave them my card so that they could telephone or write to ask questions or discuss problems. That invitation remains open.

A Quip

I will suggest one more result of this study: it will displease many professionals. Psychoanalysts will flail in rage against their couches because of the "superficiality" of the material. Other clinical psychiatrists and psychologists will clutch their Blue Crosses in frustration over the lack of "interpretation" of the material. Sociologists will pound their demographic tables in anger over the neglect of "social influences" on the material. Developmental psychologists will crunch away at their Apples, hungry for more "reliability measures" of the material. And thirsty biologists will find the material "dry," due to its neglect of hormones and neurotransmitters.

And, A Prophecy

My "co-travelers" in this study will continue to move on, their sexual itineraries far from completed. For some, sexual fantasies will emerge as behaviors; for others, behaviors will recede to fantasy.

Nick may continue to grapple with homosexual arousal. Whether he will be able to find comfortable expression of his sexual, romantic, and general life needs remains problematic. Larry may again oscillate between the poles of anatomy for sexual gratification. Joseph may be able to integrate a primary homosexual arousal with his needs for a wife and children. Todd may become his "ideal woman."

These men paused, but were not arrested at a point in time. I did not write what I did, when I did, as if these descriptions of their lives were to end with a period. Not even with a semicolon. With a comma, perhaps....

Children and Parents
Look Back
at Our Study

EXAMPLE A

Mother (speaking of an eleven-year-old son, two years after entering our study)

MOTHER: I've been doing a lot of thinking about this issue. I've gotten involved in the women's movement, and of course they're taking a long hard look at roles. I've been going through a lot of turmoil about it because I don't know what I would do now, given a three-year-old boy again, how I would react if he wanted to play with the doll. The whole thing is looking very murky to me now. Women historically have been damaged a lot by the kinds of things that role-playing has done, but that also makes me take a look at boys' roles and what they are. I think I remember saying I didn't care if my son wasn't overtly a football type, but I felt strongly that I didn't want him to develop feminine characteristics. On the one hand, I'm grateful for my stand.

R. G.: Do you feel that by taking the stand, you've done some damage to him? Or are you looking at it in a way that's not related to your son's issue, just that roles shouldn't be like that?

MOTHER: I think both. I think the way that kids are raised now is pretty fucked. I think it's starting to change. I feel now in retrospect that I had very rigid ideas about what masculine and feminine were, and I'm a little bit afraid of it because I know if you take my premise to its end conclusion, it looks chaotic. It looks bisexual. It scares me.

Note: Examples are the same families as those in Prospect.

R. G.: What about the kinds of reactions that your son was getting from the other kids when he was showing the feminine behavior?

MOTHER: Well that's what makes a strong part of me glad that I took a stand. Because, you know, socially, whether the values were right or wrong, he was being ostracized, and I appreciate what I did for that reason.

R. G.: To my view, that is the key issue. I think it still is true today, with the new pediatric population, that kids who are grossly very feminine do get ostracized and stigmatized by the peer group. I respect the general issue that there shouldn't be rigid sex-role stereotyping. But I'm not sure we're doing a five-year-old or seven-year-old very feminine boy a favor by saying to him, "Well, the world is really all screwed up, it's not you. Just go out there and wear a dress."

MOTHER: Yeah, I know. I'm very sensitive to that, and I feel relieved that I wasn't confused at that time—that I was sure what I believed in. I think I said once that it wouldn't bother me so much if my son did turn out to be bisexual. I have had sexual feelings for women from time to time. It seems almost healthy for me in a way. But a feminine man still really turns me off. I just can't help it. I'm thinking that from the very first time he picked up a doll I was horrified.

The same mother (when son is eighteen)

MOTHER: For many years I was rejecting of him in a lot of ways. I was very rejecting of his cross-dressing—I hated it. It was just causing me so much pain. His accusation is that I handled that real wrong. He said I became so outraged, and I should have just accepted his cross-dressing and his effeminacy and let him be who he was and not set such a moral tone to it.

R. G.: Was it a moral tone, or were you concerned about the ostracism?

MOTHER: I don't know if a kid at that age can distinguish. When I say moral, I think he thought he was a bad person for doing that. God, I hated it, and he knew it.

R. G.: He was also getting teased.

MOTHER: I know, and he felt it.

R. G.: And so you weigh the possible trauma of a parent moving in a bit heavy-handed, perhaps, versus letting a kid go his merry way and having thirty-five kids move in heavy-handed.

MOTHER: Yeah. I agree with you.

R. G.: It's not much of a choice.

MOTHER: It's a bad choice, either way, and I've been able to stand up for myself. He has gotten angry with me in different conversations— "You shouldn't have done that to me"—and my position has always been, "I could not help it." If I had it to do all over again, I don't know if I would have done it differently.

Son (age eighteen)

SON: I remember the day that my mother first took me here. She, like, drove up and took me in a car and said, "We're going somewhere," and we never went anywhere, so I knew something was up. She goes, "I'm going to take you to see a psychiatrist," and I knew instantly that that meant something was wrong with me. I go, "What's wrong with me?" and she goes, "You're not supposed to dress up," and I said, "Well, Flip Wilson does on TV." She goes, "That's different," but she couldn't tell me *how* it was different.

R. G.:   Looking back now, many years later, what's your feeling about your mother having brought you here?

SON: I think it was good. I'm glad that she did. For a long time I thought that it wasn't good, but it was good—I feel good about having gone through it. Your research, I think it's basically good.

R. G.:   Why?

SON: Because I think it's a crucial issue. I think it's important, very important. It's something that's not being looked into very much.

EXAMPLE B

Son (age eighteen)

R. G.:   Looking back, how do you feel about your parents bringing you here when you were a kid?

SON: I'm glad they did, because I knew once a year this topic was going to be discussed. I was thinking, "Okay, great, I have given this guy whatever he needed to know, so okay, I've helped somebody by it. At least one person. Something's been done with it constructively."

R. G.:   Over the years that you were coming here, did you feel that I was taking any position about you in terms of what I wanted you to become, gay or straight?

SON: No. No, and I hated that. I always told my mom I hated you so much, because that man is the most *neutral* person in this entire world. He is like, "Yes, you can do this, but on the *other hand*, you know, and on *this hand*," and I'm going like, "That guy is gonna drive me nuts," which was good, because then I—I did it myself.

R. G.:   So back then you wanted me to take a position one way or the other?

SON: Yeah, because I needed some strength, I needed somebody to say, "You should do this," somebody other than my mother and my father. You were an outsider who I would see once a year, and I would say whatever I had to say, and you would go, "Okay, well thanks," turn off the tape recorder, and I'm gone. But I kept coming back. I said, "I'm gonna break that little motherfucker and tell him what I think and let him crack—I'm gonna let him hear—I'm gonna make him say, 'You should do *this*.' " There were a lot of times I remember coming in here and I'd be so hostile, I'd say, "No, I don't wanna go there, Mother, I'm going against my will," and I'd come in here and I'd sit down and say, "I'm gonna attack this little son of a bitch." It was just somebody who I would speak to and I would never hear from him for another year. I would not hear anything back.

R. G.: Why didn't you ask me some question about what I felt?

SON: Because I didn't want to know. There was that other thing over here saying, "Don't ask, you don't wanna hear."

R. G.: Before you go today, do you want feedback from me? Do you want an opinion, or do you want to leave it again that I've heard you?

SON: I want a very generalized opinion about my career, and my past homosexuality, and my desire to be heterosexual. I don't want to hear any details of why I think you should do this and I don't think you should do that, just a very general synopsis is what I want to hear. I don't want to hear any objective hints or suggestions or anything like that, 'cause I made it this far and I might as well keep going.

R. G.: Well, I think you've got a very realistic set of vocational goals in mind, and my guess is that, as motivated as you are and as intelligent as you are, you will succeed in most of the things that you want to do.

SON: I know that, and I'm not being conceited.

R. G.: As far as the sexuality part, I think you are realistic when you say that it's easier to make it in this world as a heterosexual, all other things being equal, than as a homosexual. It's also easier to make it if you're handsome, rich, gentile, white—

SON: I've got 'em all except for rich.

R. G.: But going back to my old posture, *on the other hand,* there are blacks who make it, Jews who make it, poor people who are happy—

SON: That's right.

R. G.: —and there are gays who make it.

SON: That's right.

EXAMPLE C

Mother (speaking of her nineteen-year-old son)

R. G.: If you could look back now, when you first brought your son here when he was five, do you feel that it was a good decision you made to bring him here, or do you feel, in retrospect, it was a mistake?

MOTHER: Oh, no, it wasn't a mistake. I'm grateful. It made me more in touch with what was going on. Just filling out these reams of papers that you gave me each time—they got to be ridiculous after a point. It would keep me abreast of just how far a gay child could go in his behavior, when you have to circle "Does your child still continue to . . ."

And I would look at some of these things and go, "Oh, gee, I guess some kids might still be doing this." It was a point of reference. And I felt like I had someone on my side—someone I could talk to once a year.

R. G.: But how about back then, at the beginning? In terms of coming here for evaluation, the group therapy—

MOTHER: Well, I didn't last very long, if you recall. I was here with the group of ladies and their children—and I didn't give it a chance, I really didn't, because of my own emotional problems at the time. I remember walking out of here angry at you because you wouldn't prescribe Valium for me, which another doctor had done, and calling you some tacky names.

R. G.: You had a bit of a tantrum.

MOTHER: I did. I had a real—

R. G.: I remember that.

MOTHER: I bet you do. And I apologize now for what I did years ago.

R. G.: It's an occupational hazard. Do you feel the experience, in retrospect, was helpful for your son, neutral, harmful?

MOTHER: Well, his recollection of his meeting with you was that he threw a stuffed monkey through the air and it hit you on the head, and you picked up the stuffed monkey and you threw it back, and you hit him. That stands out in his mind.

R. G.: It sounds like something I would have done.

MOTHER: He was a fearsome-type child, afraid to play ball and afraid of outward signs of violence, and/or aggression, and I guess he interpreted this as a sign of aggressiveness by his doctor. When he came out of your office that day, you know, going to the car, he said, "I don't like that doctor." And maybe that's what I wanted to hear, too, and I said, "Tell my why." And he said, " 'Cause he hit me in the head." "Oh, he hit you in the head, did he?" And he still to this day remembers, and he laughs and I laugh about it.

Her Son

SON: Well, I don't think coming here was a mistake. Basically, I think my mother wanted to educate herself as to why I was acting that way, because she was just as puzzled as I was or anybody else about it. I don't think it was a bad idea at all. It helped her, I think.

R. G.: How about *you*?

SON: I really didn't learn a lot—because I don't remember a whole lot about it, things we talked about or anything, because I wasn't in it for that long. I think my mother learned more from it than I did.

R. G.: Do you feel coming here was damaging to you in some way?

SON: No, not at all. If it was damaging, I think there would be something outstanding—I'd know it and I'd blame it on that.

R. G.:   How do you remember feeling about coming here when you were a kid?

SON: I really never asked why she brought me, but I never objected to coming, because it was something to do and it was interesting, going to UCLA for the day—I never objected to coming at all.

R. G.:   You don't feel that she was focusing on something about your behavior and by the focusing on it was causing you more concern?

SON: I thought, back in my mind, that she did bring me here because I was behaving that way, and I just went along with it. I figured it could only help, not hurt.

EXAMPLE D

Son (age twenty-one)

R. G.:   How do you feel about having come here all these years and periodically talking to me, fifteen years now, and having it tape-recorded all during these years? How has it been for you?

SON: That was a part of my life. I'm very angry at my parents because when they took me here they were censuring my behavior.

R. G.:   They were censuring it?

SON: Yes, or they were just saying what I was doing was wrong, and my current therapist thinks I have a lot of difficulties in expressing myself, individuality, because I think that what I'll do, if it's different, it's wrong. She thinks it was silly that my parents brought me here.

R. G.:   How do you feel?

SON: Well, if I had a child and he was doing that and if I were of my parents' background or mentality, if I lived in their society, I would be concerned, probably. Even being who I am, if I had a child—a boy who liked to cross-dress—I would—if he could have someone to talk to, or get some help.

R. G.:   What's your feeling about whether the therapy that we had over those years was helpful to you, harmful, neither?

SON: I don't know, I can't— [long pause]

R. G.:   You're not going to hurt my feelings if you say it was terrible.

SON: No.

R. G.:   I just want some feedback about how you look back at it now.

SON: Oh, I don't know what I—I don't know if I gained anything from it, or what I accomplished. I remember being in this room, and you asked me a lot of questions about my behavior, and I tried discussing— I don't know what that did. I don't know if that taught me to solve problems—because I have a lot of problems now—or if it has taught me ways of dealing with them. It could have perhaps forced me to grow, I mean, just having those troubles, perhaps forcing me at an early age to do some exercise in looking inside of myself. Perhaps that was good about coming here, if it did that.

R. G.: You've known for many years now that I'm writing up some of this stuff. I tape-record it, and some of it's going into journal articles and books. Let's say some day you pick up a book by me, and you read some pages there, and you get a pretty good idea that those words are probably you. You're going to say, "I'm pretty sure that's me, those are my words." How do you feel about that?

SON: I feel, "Good, he used something."

R. G.: He used something?

SON: Yes—all that work, it was worth something.

References

Abelin, E. L. 1978. The role of the father in the preoedipal years. In S. Kramer, moderator, *Journal of the American Psychoanalytic Association* 26:143–61.

Achenbach, T. M., and C. S. Edelbrock. 1981. Behavioral problems and competencies reported by parents of normal and disturbed children aged four through sixteen. *Monographs of the Society for Research in Child Development* #188, 46:1–82.

Albert, A. A., and J. R. Porter. 1983. Age patterns in the development of children's gender-role stereotypes. *Sex Roles* 9:59–67.

Allport, G. W. 1954. *The nature of prejudice*. Cambridge, Mass.: Addison-Wesley.

American Psychiatric Association. 1980. *Diagnostic and statistical manual of mental disorders III*. Washington, D.C.

Bakwin, H. 1968. Deviant gender-role behavior in children: Reaction to homosexuality. *Pediatrics* 41:620–29.

Ban, P. L., and M. Lewis. 1974. Mothers and fathers, girls and boys: Attachment behavior in the one-year-old. *Merrill-Palmer Quarterly* 20:195–204.

Bancroft, J. 1983. *Human sexuality and its problems*. New York: Churchill Livingston.

Bandura, A. 1962. Social learning through imitation. In M. R. Jones, editor, *Nebraska symposium on motivation*. Lincoln: University of Nebraska Press.

Bates, J. E., and P. M. Bentler. 1973. Play activities of normal and effeminate boys. *Developmental Psychology* 9:20–27.

Bates, J. E., W. M. Skilbeck, K. V. R. Smith, and P. M. Bentler. 1974. Gender role abnormalities in boys: An analysis of clinical ratings. *Journal of Abnormal Child Psychology* 2:1–16.

Beitel, A. 1985. The spectrum of gender identity disturbances: An intrapsychic model. In B. Steiner, editor, *Gender dysphoria: Development, research, management*. New York: Plenum.

399

Bell, A. P., M. S. Weinberg, and S. K. Hammersmith. 1981. *Sexual preference: Its development in men and women.* Bloomington: Indiana University Press.

Bell, N. J., and W. A. Carver. 1980. Gender label effects: Expectant mothers' responses to infants. *Child Development* 51:925–27.

Bem, S. L. 1974. The measurement of psychological androgyny. *Journal of Consulting and Clinical Psychology* 42:155–62.

Bene, E. 1965. On the genesis of male homosexuality: An attempt at clarifying the role of the parents. *British Journal of Psychiatry* 111:803–13.

Benjamin, H. 1966. *The transsexual phenomenon.* New York: Julian Press.

Bieber, I., H. Dain, P. Dince, M. Drellich, H. Grand, R. Gundlach, M. Dremer, A. Rifkin, C. Wilbur, and T. Bieber. 1962. *Homosexuality: A psychoanalytic study.* New York: Basic.

Biller, H. B. 1969. Father absence, maternal encouragement, and sex role development in kindergarten-age boys. *Child Development* 40:539–46.

———. 1981. The father and sex-role development. In M. E. Lamb, editor, *The role of the father in childhood development.* 2d ed. New York: John Wiley.

Biller, H. B., and R. M. Bahn. 1971. Father absence, perceived maternal behavior, and masculinity of self-concept among junior high school boys. *Developmental Psychology* 4:178–81.

Bongiovanni, A. M., and A. W. Root. 1963. The adrenogenital syndrome. *New England Journal of Medicine* 268:1391–99.

Bower, T. G. R. 1982. *Development in infancy.* 2d ed. San Francisco: W. H. Freemen.

Brooks-Gunn, J., and M. Lewis. 1979. Why mamma and pappa? The development of social labels. *Child Development* 50:1203–06.

Brown, D. 1956. Sex role preference in young children. *Psychological Monographs* 70, no. 14 (whole no. 421).

Burlingham, D. 1973. The pre-oedipal infant-father relationship. *Psychoanalytic Study of the Child* 28:23–47.

Burton, R. V., and J. Whiting. 1961. The absent father and cross-sex identity. *Merrill-Palmer Quarterly* 7:85–95.

Cahill, S. 1983. Reexamining the acquisition of sex roles: A social interactionist approach. *Sex Roles* 9:1–15.

Campbell, D. T., and J. D. Stanley. 1963. *Experimental and quasi-experimental designs for research.* Chicago: Rand McNally.

Carlson, N. 1984. *Psychology: The science of behavior.* Boston: Allyn and Bacon.

Cattell, R. B., D. R. Saunders, and G. G. Stice. 1957. *Handbook to the sixteen personality factor questionnaire.* 3d ed. Illinois: Institute of Personality and Ability Testing.

Chamove, A., H. Harlow, and G. Mitchell. 1967. Sex difference in the infant-directed behavior of preadolescent rhesus monkeys. *Child Development* 38:329–35.

Clarke-Stewart, K. A. 1978. And daddy makes three: The father's impact on mother and child. *Child Development* 49:466–78.

Clower, V. 1970. The development of the child's sense of his sexual identity. *Journal of the American Psychoanalytic Association* 18:165–76.

Cole, H. J., K. J. Zucker, and S. J. Bradley. 1982. Patterns of gender-role behavior in children attending traditional and non-traditional day-care centers. *Canadian Journal of Psychiatry* 27:410–14.

Conn, J. H., and L. Kanner. 1947. Children's awareness of sex differences. *Journal of Child Psychiatry* 1:3–57.

Constantinople, A. 1979. Sex-role acquisition: In search of the elephant. *Sex Roles* 2:121–33.

Culp, R. E., A. S. Cook, and P. C. Housley. 1983. A comparison of observed and reported adult-infant interactions: Effects of perceived sex. *Sex Roles* 9:475–79.

Diamond, M. 1965. A critical evaluation of the ontogeny of human sexual behavior. *Quarterly Review of Biology* 40:147–75.

———. 1982. Sexual identity, monozygotic twins reared in discordant sex roles and a BBC follow-up. *Archives of Sexual Behavior* 11:181–86.

Doering, R. W. 1981. Parental reinforcement of gender-typed behaviours in boys with atypical gender identity. Ph.D. diss., University of Toronto.

Doll, P. A., H. J. Fagot, and J. D. Himbert. 1971. Experimenter effect on sex-role preference among black and white low-class male children. *Psychological Reports* 29:1295–1301.

Douns, A. C. 1983. Letters to Santa Claus: Elementary school-age children's sex-typed toy preferences in a natural setting. *Sex Roles* 9:159–63.

Eaton, W. O., and D. Von Bargen. 1981. Asynchronous development of gender understanding in preschool children. *Child Development* 52:1020–27.

Ehrhardt, A., and S. Baker. 1974. Fetal androgens, human central nervous system differentiation, and behavior sex differences. In R. Friedman, R. Richart, R. Vande Wiele, editors, *Sex differences in behavior*. New York: John Wiley.

Ellis, A. 1945. The sexual psychology of human hermaphrodites. *Psychosomatic Medicine* 7:108–25.

Epstein, R., and S. Leverant. 1963. Verbal conditioning and sex-role identification in children. *Child Development* 34:99–106.

Evans, R. B. 1969. Childhood parental relationships of homosexual men. *Journal of Consulting and Clinical Psychology* 33:129–35.

Fagot, B. 1974. Sex differences in toddlers' behavior and parental reaction. *Developmental Psychology* 10:554–58.

———. 1977. Consequences of moderate cross-gender behavior in preschool children. *Child Development* 48:902–07.

———. 1978. The influence of sex of child on parental reactions to toddler children. *Child Development* 49:459–65.

Fenichel, O. 1945. *The psychoanalytic theory of neurosis*. New York: W. W. Norton.

Festinger, L. 1957. *A theory of cognitive dissonance*. Stanford: Stanford University Press.

Fitts, W. 1975. *Manual for the Tennessee department of mental health self-concept scale*. Nashville: Counselor Recordings and Tests.

Flerx, V. C., D. S. Fidler, and R. W. Rogers. 1976. Sex role stereotypes: Developmental aspects and early intervention. *Child Development* 47:998–1007.

Frasher, R. S., J. R. Nurss, and D. R. Brogan. 1980. Children's toy preferences revisited: Implications for early childhood development. *Child Care Quarterly* 9:26–31.

Freud, A., and D. Burlingham. 1944. *Infants without families: Reports on the Hamp-*

stead nurseries. Vol. 3, *The writings of Anna Freud.* New York: International Universities Press.

Freud, S. 1953. *A case of hysteria, three essays on sexuality, and other works.* Vol. 7, *Standard edition of the complete psychological works of Sigmund Freud.* London: Hogarth Press.

———. 1955. *Beyond the pleasure principle, group psychology, and other works.* Vol. 18, *Standard edition of the complete psychological works of Sigmund Freud.* London: Hogarth Press.

———. 1957. *Five lectures on psycho-analysis, Leonardo DaVinci, and other works.* Vol. 11, *Standard edition of the complete psychological works of Sigmund Freud.* London: Hogarth Press.

———. 1957. *On narcissism: An introduction.* Vol. 14, *Standard edition of the complete psychological works of Sigmund Freud.* London: Hogarth Press.

———. 1961. Fetishism. In *The future of an illusion, civilization and its discontents, and other works.* Vol. 21, *Standard edition of the complete psychological works of Sigmund Freud.* London: Hogarth Press.

———. 1963. *Introductory lectures on psycho-analysis III.* Vol. 16, *Standard edition of the complete psychological works of Sigmund Freud.* London: Hogarth Press.

Friedman, R. C. 1983. Male homosexuality: Or the need for a multiaxial developmental model. Paper presented at the annual meeting of the American Psychoanalytic Association, New York, December 18.

Goldberg, S., and M. Lewis. 1969. Play behavior in the year old infant: Early sex differences. *Child Development* 40:21–31.

Gorski, R. A., J. H. Gordon, J. E. Shryne, and A. M. Southam. 1978. Evidence for a morphological sex difference within the medial preoptic area of the rat brain. *Brain Research* 148:333–46.

Gough, H. G. 1952. *The adjective check list.* Palo Alto, Cal.: Consulting Psychologists Press.

Gough, H. G., and A. B. Heilbrun. 1965. *The adjective check list manual.* Palo Alto, Cal.: Consulting Psychologists Press.

Green, R. 1972. Homosexuality as a mental illness. *International Journal of Psychiatry* 10:77–98.

———. 1974. The behaviorally feminine boy: Pre-transsexual? Pre-transvestite? Pre-homosexual? Pre-heterosexual? In R. Friedman, R. Richart, and R. Vande Wiele, editors, *Sex differences in behavior.* New York: John Wiley.

———. 1974. *Sexual identity conflict in children and adults.* New York: Basic; London: Gerald Duckworth. Reprint, New York: Penguin, 1975.

———. 1976. One hundred ten feminine and masculine boys: Behavioral contrasts and demographic similarities. *Archives of Sexual Behavior* 5:425–46.

———. 1985. Gender identity in childhood and later sexual orientation: Follow-up of seventy-eight males. *The American Journal of Psychiatry* 142:339–41.

Green, R., and M. Fuller. 1973(a). Family doll play and female identity in preadolescent males. *American Journal of Orthopsychiatry* 43:123–27.

———. 1973(b). Group therapy with feminine boys and their parents. *International Journal of Group Psychotherapy* 23:54–68.

Green, R., M. Fuller, and B. Rutley. 1972. It-Scale for children and draw-a-person test: Thirty feminine versus twenty-five masculine boys. *Journal of Personality Assessment* 36:349–52.

Green, R., and J. Money. 1960. Incongruous gender role: Nongenital manifestations in prepubertal boys. *Journal of Nervous and Mental Disease* 131:160–68.
———. 1961. Effeminacy in prepubertal boys: Summary of eleven cases and recommendations for case management. *Pediatrics* 27:286–91.
———. 1966. Stage-acting, role-taking and effeminate impersonation during boyhood. *Archives of General Psychiatry* 15:535–38.
———, editors. 1969. *Transsexualism and sex reassignment.* Baltimore: The Johns Hopkins Press.
Green, R., D. Neuberg, and S. Finch. 1983. Sex-typed motor behaviors of "feminine" boys, conventionally masculine boys, and conventionally feminine girls. *Sex Roles* 9:571–79.
Green, R., L. Newman, and R. Stoller. 1972. Treatment of boyhood "transsexualism": An interim report of four years' experience. *Archives of General Psychiatry* 26:213–17.
Green, R., C. Roberts, K. Williams, and A. Mixon. 1986. Specific cross-gender behaviours in boyhood and later homosexual orientation. *British Journal of Psychiatry.* In press.
Green, R., K. Williams, and M. Goodman. 1985. Masculine or feminine gender identity in boys: Developmental differences between two diverse family groups. *Sex Roles* 12:1155–62.
Green, R., K. Williams, and A. Mixon. 1987. Feminine and masculine boys who evolve as homosexual or heterosexual men: Six psychological tests. Forthcoming.
Greenson, R. R. 1968. Dis-identifying from mother. *International Journal of Psycho-Analysis* 49:370–74.
Grellert, E. A., M. D. Newcomb, and P. M. Bentler. 1982. Childhood play activities of male and female homosexuals and heterosexuals. *Archives of Sexual Behavior* 11:451–78.

Haggard, E. A., A. Brekstad, and A. G. Skard. 1960. On the reliability of the anamestic interview. *Journal of Abnormal and Social Psychology* 61:311–18.
Hampson, J. L., and J. G. Hampson. 1961. The ontogenesis of sexual behavior in man. In W. C. Young, editor, *Sex and internal secretions II.* 3d ed. Baltimore: Williams and Wilkins.
Harrison, T. R., R. D. Adams, I. L. Bennett, W. H. Resnik, G. W. Thorn, and M. M. Wintrobe, editors. 1958. *Principles of internal medicine.* 3d ed. New York: McGraw-Hill.
Harry, J. 1982. *Gay children grown up: Gender culture and gender deviance.* New York: Praeger.
———. 1984. Defeminization and social class. *Archives of Sexual Behavior* 14:1–12.
Hatterer, L. J. 1970. *Changing homosexuality in the male.* New York: McGraw-Hill.
Haugh, S. S., C. D. Hoffman, and G. Cowan. 1980. The eye of the very young beholder: Sex typing of infants by younger children. *Child Development* 51:598–600.
Heilbrun, A. 1976. Measurement of masculine and feminine role identities as independent dimensions. *Journal of Consulting and Clinical Psychology* 44:183–90.
Hemmer, J. D., and D. A. Kleiber. 1981. Tomboys and sissies: Androgynous children? *Sex roles* 7:1205–12.
Herzog, J. M. 1982. On father hunger: The father's role in the modulation of

aggressive drive and fantasy. In S. H. Cath, A. R. Gurwitt, and J. M. Ross, editors, *Father and child.* Boston: Little, Brown.

Hetherington, E. M. 1966. Effects of paternal absence on sex-typed behavior in negro and white preadolescent males. *Journal of Personality and Social Psychology* 4:87–91.

Hetherington, E. M., and J. Duer. 1971. Effects of father absence on child development. *Young Children* 26:233–48.

Hetherington, E. M., and G. Frankie. 1967. Effects of parental dominance, warmth, and comfort on imitation in children. *Journal of Personality and Social Psychology* 6:119–25.

Imperato-McGinely, J., R. E. Peterson, T. Gautier, and E. Sturia. 1979. Androgen and the evolution of male-gender identity among male pseudohermaphrodites with 5α-reductase deficiency. *New England Journal of Medicine* 300:1233–37.

Jacklin, C. N., and E. E. Maccoby. 1978. Social behavior at thirty-three months in same-sex and mixed-sex dyads. *Child Development* 49:557–69.

Jacklin, C. N., E. E. Maccoby, and A. E. Dick. 1973. Barrier behavior and toy preference: sex differences (and their absence) in the year-old child. *Child Development* 44:196–200.

Jacklin, C. N., E. E. Maccoby, and C. H. Doering. 1983. Neonatal sex-steroid hormones and timidity in 6–18 month-old boys and girls. *Developmental Psychobiology* 16:163–68.

Jolles, I. 1952. A study of validity of some hypotheses for the qualitative interpretation of the H-T-P for children of elementary school age. *Journal of Clinical Psychology* 8:113–18.

Kagan, J. 1958. The concept of identification. *Psychological Review* 65:296–305.

Kagan, J., and H. A. Moss. 1983. *Birth to maturity.* 2d ed. New Haven: Yale University Press.

Kallman, F. J. 1952. Comparative twin study on the genetic aspects of male homosexuality. *Journal of Nervous and Mental Disease* 115:283–98.

Katcher, A. 1955. The discrimination of sex differences by young children. *Journal of Genetic Psychology* 87:131–43.

Kinsey, A. C., W. B. Pomeroy, and C. E. Martin. 1948. *Sexual behavior in the human male.* Philadelphia: W. B. Saunders.

Kinsey, A. C., W. B. Pomeroy, C. E. Martin, and P. H. Gebhard. 1953. *Sexual behavior in the human female.* Philadelphia: W. B. Saunders.

Koch, H. L. 1956. Sissiness and tomboyishness in relation to sibling characteristics. *The Journal of Genetic Psychology* 88:231–44.

Kohlberg, L. 1966. A cognitive-developmental analysis of children's sex-role concepts and attitudes. In E. Maccoby, editor, *The development of sex differences.* Stanford: Stanford University Press.

Kohut, H. 1971. *The analysis of the self.* New York: International Universities Press.

Koppitz, E. M. 1968. *Psychological evaluation of children's human figure drawings.* New York: Grune and Stratton.

Krug, S. 1981. *Interpreting 16PF profile patterns.* Champaign, Ill.: Institute for Personality and Ability Testing.

Kuhn, D., S. C. Nash, and L. Bruckern. 1978. Sex role concept of two- and three-year-olds. *Child Development* 49:445–51.

Lamb, M. E., editor. 1976. *The role of the father in child development.* New York: John Wiley.
———. 1977. Father-infant and mother-infant interaction in the first year of life. *Child Development* 48:167–81.
———, editor. 1981. *The role of the father in child development.* 2d ed. New York: John Wiley.
Lancaster, J. B. 1971. Play mothering: The relations between juvenile females and young infants among free-ranging vervet monkeys. *Folia Primatologica* 15:161–82.
Langlois, J. H., and A. C. Downs. 1980. Mothers, fathers, and peers as socialization agents of sex-typed play behaviors in young children. *Child Development* 51:1217–47.
LaTorre, R. A. 1979. *Sexual identity.* Chicago: Nelson-Hall.
Lebovitz, P. 1972. Feminine behavior in boys: Aspects of its outcome. *American Journal of Psychiatry* 128:1283–89.
Levin, S. M., J. Balistrier, and M. Schukit. 1972. The development of sexual discrimination in children. *Journal of Child Psychology and Psychiatry* 13:47–53.
Lewis, M. 1975. Early sex differences in the human: Studies of socioemotional development. *Archives of Sexual Behavior* 4:329–35.
Lewis, M., and M. Weinraub. 1974. Sex of parent × sex of child: Socioemotional development. In R. Friedman, R. Richart, and R. Vande Wiele, editors, *Sex differences in behavior.* New York: John Wiley.
Lynn, D. B., and A. Cross. 1974. Parent preference of preschool children. *Journal of Marriage and the Family* 36:555–59.
Lynn, D. B., and W. L. Sawrey. 1959. The effects of father-absence on Norwegian boys and girls. *Journal of Abnormal and Social Psychology* 59:258–62.

Maccoby, E. E. 1980. *Social development: Psychological growth and the parent-child relationship.* New York: Harcourt Brace Jovanovich.
Maccoby, E. E., and C. N. Jacklin. 1974. *The psychology of sex differences.* Stanford: Stanford University Press.
———. 1979. Waiting room behavior of fathers and twelve-month old infants. Working paper, Stanford Longitudinal Study, Stanford, Cal.
———. 1980. Sex differences in aggression: A rejoinder and reprise. *Child Development* 51:964–80.
McConaghy, M. J. 1979. Gender permanence and the genital basis of gender: Stages in the development of constancy of gender identity. *Child Development* 50:1223–26.
Machover, K. 1953. Human figure drawings of children. *Journal of Projective Techniques* 17:85–91.
Marcus, D. E., and W. F. Overton. 1978. The development of cognitive gender constancy and sex role preference. *Child Development* 49:434–44.
Mesinkoff, A. M., J. D. Rainer, L. C. Kolb, and A. C. Carr. 1963. Intrafamilial determinants of divergent sexual behavior in twins. *American Journal of Psychiatry* 119:732–42.
Messer, H. D. 1979. The homosexual as physician. In R. Green, editor, *Human*

sexuality: A health practitioner's text. 2d ed. Baltimore: Williams and Wilkins, pp. 116–23.

Michalson, L., J. Brooks, and M. Lewis. 1974. Peers, parents, people: Social relationships in infancy. Study cited in Lewis (1975).

Mischel, W. 1966. A social-learning view of sex differences in behavior. In E. E. Maccoby, editor, *The development of sex differences.* Stanford: Stanford University Press.

————. 1970. Sex-typing and socialization. In P. H. Mussen, editor, *Carmichael's manual of child psychology II.* 3d ed. New York: John Wiley.

Money, J. 1952. *Hermaphroditism: An inquiry into the nature of a human paradox.* Ann Arbor, Mich.: University Microfilms, 1967.

Money, J., and A. Ehrhardt. 1972. *Man and Woman, Boy and Girl.* Baltimore: The Johns Hopkins University Press.

Money, J., J. G. Hampson, and J. L. Hampson. 1955. An examination of some basic sexual concepts: The evidence of human hermaphroditism. *Bulletin of The Johns Hopkins Hospital* 97:301–19.

Money, J., and A. Russo. 1979. Homosexual outcome of discordant gender identity/role: Longitudinal follow-up. *Journal of Pediatric Psychology* 4:29–41.

Morin, S. F., and S. F. Schultz. 1978. The gay movement and the rights of children. *Journal of Social Issues* 34:137–48.

Moss, H. A. 1974. Early sex differences and mother-infant interaction. In R. Friedman, R. Richart, and R. Vande Wiele, editors, *Sex differences in behavior.* New York: John Wiley.

Mowrer, O. H. 1950. *Learning theory and personality dynamics.* New York: Ronald Press.

Mussen, P., and L. Distler. 1959. Masculinity, identification, and father-son relationships. *Journal of Abnormal and Social Psychology* 59:350–56.

Nash, J. 1965. The father in contemporary culture and current psychological literature. *Child Development* 36:261–97.

Norris, A. S., and W. C. Keetel. 1962. Change of sex role during adolescence: A case study. *American Journal of Obstetrics and Gynecology* 84:719–21.

Parsons, T. 1955. Family structure and the socialization of the child. In T. Parsons and R. F. Bayles, editors, *Family socialization and interaction process.* Glencoe, Ill.: Free Press.

Parsons, T., and R. F. Bayles, editors. 1955. *Family socialization and interaction process.* Glencoe, Ill.: Free Press.

Pedersen, F. A., and R. Q. Bell. 1970. Sex differences in preschool children without histories of complications of pregnancy and delivery. *Developmental Psychology* 3:10–15.

Pedersen, F. A., and K. S. Robson. 1969. Father participation in infancy. *American Journal of Orthopsychiatry* 39:466–72.

Perry, D. G., and K. Bussey. 1979. The social learning theory of sex differences: Imitation is alive and well. *Journal of Personality and Social Psychology* 37:1699–1712.

Person, E. S., and L. Ovesey. 1984. Homosexual cross-dressers. *Journal of the American Academy of Psychoanalysis* 12:167–86.

Prince, C. V., and P. Bentler. 1972. Survey of 504 cases of transvestism. *Psychological Reports* 31:903–17.

Pyles, M. I., H. R. Stolz, and J. W. MacFarlane. 1935. The accuracy of mothers' reports on birth and developmental data. *Child Development* 6:165–76.

Rabban, M. 1950. Sex-role identification in young children in two diverse social groups. *Genetic Psychology Monographs* 42:81–158.

Reis, H. T., and S. Wright. 1981. Knowledge of sex-role stereotypes in children aged three to five. *Sex Roles* 8:1049–56.

Rekers, G. A. 1982(a). *Shaping your child's sexual identity*. Grand Rapids: Baker Book House.

———. 1982(b). *Growing up straight: What every family should know about homosexuality*. Chicago: Moody Press.

Rekers, G. A., P. M. Bentler, A. C. Rosen, and O. I. Lovaas. 1977. Child gender disturbances: A clinical rationale for intervention. *Psychotherapy: Theory, Research and Practice* 14:2–11.

Rekers, G. A., and O. I. Lovaas. 1974. Behavioral treatment of deviant sex-role behaviors in a male child. *Journal of Applied Behavior Analysis* 7:173–90.

Rekers, G. A., O. I. Lovaas, and B. Low. 1977. The behavioral treatment of a "transsexual" boy. *Journal of Abnormal Child Psychology* 2:99–116.

Rekers, G. A., S. L. Mead, A. C. Rosen, and S. L. Brigham. 1983. Family correlates of male childhood gender disturbance. *Journal of Genetic Psychology* 142:31–42.

Roberts, C., R. Green, K. Williams, and M. Goodman. Forthcoming. Boyhood gender identity development: A comparison of two family groups.

Roiphe, H., and E. Galenson. 1981. *Infantile origins of sexual identity*. New York: International Universities Press.

Rosen, A. C., G. A. Rekers, and P. M. Bentler. 1978. Ethical issues in the treatment of children. *Journal of Social Issues* 34:122–36.

Rosen, A. C., G. A. Rekers, and L. R. Friar. 1977. Theoretical and diagnostic issues in child gender disturbances. *The Journal of Sex Research* 13:89–103.

Rosler, A., and G. Kohn, 1983. Male pseudohermaphrodism due to 17–hydroxysteroid dehydrogenase deficiency: Studies on the natural history of the defect and the effect of androgens on gender role. *Journal of Steroid Biochemistry* 19:663–74.

Ross, M. 1980. Retrospective distortion in homosexual research. *Archives of Sexual Behavior* 9:523–31.

Rothbart, M. K., and E. E. Maccoby. 1966. Parents' differential reactions to sons and daughters. *Journal of Personality and Social Psychology* 4:237–43.

Rubin, J. Z., F. J. Provenzo, and Z. Luria. 1974. The eye of the beholder: Parents' views on sex of newborns. *American Journal of Orthopsychiatry* 44:512–19.

Rutter, M. 1977. Prospective studies to investigate behavioral change. In J. S. Strauss, H. M. Babigan, and M. Roff, editors, *Origins and course of psychopathology*. New York: Plenum Press.

Saghir, M., and E. Robins. 1973. *Male and female homosexuality*. Baltimore: Williams and Wilkins.

Santrock, J. W. 1970. Paternal absence, sex-typing and identification. *Developmental Psychology* 2:264–72.

Sears, P. S. 1951. Doll play aggression in normal young children: Influence of sex, age, sibling status, father's absence. *Psychological Monographs* 65, whole no. 323.

Sears, R.R., E. E. Maccoby, and H. Levin. 1957. *Patterns of child rearing.* Evanston, Ill.: Row Peterson.

Sears, R. R., L. Rau, and R. Alpert. 1965. *Identification and child rearing.* Stanford: Stanford University Press.

Seavey, C., P. Katz, and S. Zalk. 1975. Baby X: The effect of gender labels on adult responses to infants. *Sex Roles* 1:103–09.

Shields, R. H. 1964. The too-good mother. *International Journal of Psycho-Analysis* 45:85–88.

Sidorowicz, L. S., and G. S. Lunney. 1980. Baby X revisited. *Sex Roles* 6:67–73.

Slaby, R. G., and K. S. Frey. 1975. Development of gender constancy and selective attention to same-sex models. *Child Development* 46:849–56.

Smith, C., and B. Lloyd. 1978. Maternal behavior and perceived sex of infant: Revisited. *Child Development* 49:1263–65.

Smith, P. K., and K. Connolly. 1972. Patterns of play and social interaction in preschool children. In N. B. Jones, editor, *Ethological studies of child behaviour.* Cambridge: Cambridge University Press.

Snortum, J. R., J. F. Gillespie, J. E. Marchall, J. P. McLaughlin, and L. Mosberg. 1969. Family dynamics and homosexuality. *Psychological Reports* 24:763–70.

Snow, M. E., C. N. Jacklin, and E. E. Maccoby. 1983. Sex-of-child differences in father-child interaction at one year of age. *Child Development* 54:227–32.

Socarides, C. 1968. *The overt homosexual.* New York: Grune and Stratton.

———. 1978. *Homosexuality.* New York: Jason Aronson.

Stephan, W. G. 1973. Parental relationship and early social experiences of activist male homosexuals and male heterosexuals. *Journal of Abnormal Psychology* 82:506–13.

Stoller, R. J. 1968. *Sex and gender: On the development of masculinity and femininity.* New York: Science House.

———. 1969. Parental influences in male transsexualism. In R. Green and J. Money, editors, *Transsexualism and sex reassignment.* Baltimore: The Johns Hopkins Press.

———. 1976. *The transsexual experiment.* Vol. 2, *Sex and gender.* New York: Jason Aronson.

———. 1979. *Sexual excitement: The dynamics of erotic life.* New York: Pantheon.

Strayer, F. F. 1977. Peer attachment and affiliative subgroups. In F. F. Strayer, editor, *Ethological perspectives on preschool social organization.* Memo de Recherche #5. Montreal: Université de Quebec, Département de Psychologie, April.

Thompson, N. L., D. M. Schwartz, B. R. McCandless, and D. A. Edwards. 1977. Parent-child relationships and sexual identity in male and female homosexuals and heterosexuals. *Journal of Consulting and Clinical Psychology* 41:120–27.

Thompson, S. K., and P. Bentler. 1971. The priority of cues in sex discrimination by children and adults. *Developmental Psychology* 5:181–85.

Time. 1966. The homosexual in America. 87:40–41, January 21.

Ungar, S. B. 1982. The sex-typing of adult and child behavior in toy sales. *Sex Roles* 8:251–60.

Vroegh, K. 1971. The relationship of birth order and sex of siblings to gender role identity. *Developmental Psychology* 4:407–11.

Weinraub, M., and J. Frankel. 1977. Sex differences in parent-infant interaction during free play, departure, and separation. *Child Development* 48:1240–49.

Whitam, F. L. 1983. Culturally invariable properties of male homosexuality: Tentative conclusions from cross-cultural research. *Archives of Sexual Behavior* 12:207–26.

Whiting, B., and J. Whiting. 1975. *Children of six cultures.* Cambridge: Harvard University Press.

Whiting, J., R. Kluckhohn, and E. Anthony. 1958. The function of male initiation ceremonies at puberty. In E. E. Maccoby, T. Newcomb, and E. Hartley, editors, *Readings in social psychology.* New York: Holt, Rinehart, and Winston.

Williams, P., and M. Smith. 1980. *Open secret: The first question.* Science Series, BBC television production.

Winnicott, D. W. 1953. Transitional objects and transitional phenomena. *International Journal of Psycho-Analysis* 34:89–97.

———. 1958. *Collected papers: Through paediatrics to psycho-analysis.* New York: Basic.

Wohl, R., and H. Trosman. 1955. A retrospect of Freud's Leonardo: An assessment of a psychoanalytic classic. *Psychiatry* 18:27–39.

Wolfe, B. E. 1979. Behavioral treatment of childhood gender disorders. *Behavior Modification* 3:550–75.

Wyden, P., and B. Wyden. 1968. *Growing up straight: What every thoughtful parent should know about homosexuality.* New York: Stein and Day.

Young, W. C., R. W. Goy, and C. H. Phoenix. 1964. Hormones and sexual behavior. *Science* 143:212–18.

Zucker, K. J. 1985. Cross-gender identified children. In B. W. Steiner, editor, *Gender dysphoria: Development, research, management.* New York: Plenum.

Zucker, K. J., P. J. Bradley, C. M. Corter, R. W. Doering, and J. K. Finegan. 1980. Cross-gender behaviour in very young boys: A normative study. In J. Samson, editor, *Childhood and Sexuality.* Montreal: Editions Etudes Vivantes.

Zuger, B. 1970. Gender role determination: A critical review of the evidence from hermaphroditism. *Psychosomatic Medicine* 32:449–63.

———. 1984. Early effeminate behaviors in boys: Outcome and significance for homosexuality. *Journal of Nervous and Mental Disease* 172:90–97.

Zuger, B., and P. Taylor. 1969. Effeminate behavior present in boys from early childhood. II. Comparison with similar symptoms in non-effeminate boys. *Pediatrics* 44:375–80.

Index